## ...HONEN JUMP?

...rising anime stars like Kid Muscle, Kenshin ...e *SHAMAN KING*, *YU-GI-OH!* and *DRAGON* ...ssue of the Japanese Weekly Shonen Jump ...magazine carries the decades-long tradition of Japanese comics propelled by vibrant art and intriguing storylines. Now that VIZ has brought the *SHONEN JUMP* magazine to the U.S., American readers can discover what millions of manga fans already know: no other comic packs more action and adventure between its covers.

**Capture it first in THE SHONEN JUMP MAGAZINE!**
Subscribe now for $29.95 (12 issues) at www.shonenjump.com

## WHAT IS THE SHONEN JUMP GRAPHIC NOVEL LINE?

*THE SHONEN JUMP GRAPHIC NOVEL LINE* is the future of manga—it's the voice of the most exciting titles making the leap from Japan to the U.S.

Each manga title has the unique style and voice of its artist/creator. From *KNIGHTS OF THE ZODIAC*, a never-before-translated classic just now hitting American TV, to 21st-century hits like *THE PRINCE OF TENNIS* and *HIKARU NO GO*, *SHONEN JUMP* has the world's most popular manga. *SHONEN JUMP GRAPHIC NOVELS* bring you Japan's best new talent and new titles, every month.

So brace yourself for an amazing experience as you read through the second *SHONEN JUMP GRAPHIC NOVEL COMPILATION EDITION*. Here's a sample of the intense action, thrilling cliffhangers and coolest characters around. You're about to JUMP head first into the future of manga. Enjoy!

**THE WORLD'S MOST POPULAR MANGA**

# SHONEN JUMP™

## GRAPHIC NOVELS

**www.shonenjump.com**

**EDITOR-IN-CHIEF** Hyoe Narita
**MANAGING EDITORS** Annette Roman, Drew Williams
**ASSOCIATE MANAGING EDITOR** Albert Totten
**COMPILATION EDITION EDITOR** Jason Thompson
**GRAPHIC DESIGN** Judi Roubideaux, Daniel Ziegler
**GRAPHIC NOVEL COVER DESIGN** Sean Lee

**PUBLISHER** Seiji Horibuchi
**VICE CHAIRMAN/CFO** Hidemi Fukuhara
**VP OF MARKETING** Liza Coppola
**VP OF STRATEGIC DEVELOPMENT** Yumi Hoashi
**SENIOR DIRECTOR OF LICENSING AND ACQUISITIONS** Rika Inouye
**STRATEGIC DEVELOPMENT COORDINATOR** Brandon Niven

***HIKARU NO GO***
**EDITOR** Livia Ching
**TRANSLATOR/ENGLISH ADAPTATION** Andy Nakatani
**TOUCH-UP ART & LETTERING** Adam Symons
**SUPERVISED BY** Janice Kim

***ULTIMATE MUSCLE***
**EDITOR** Shaenon K. Garrity
**SUPERVISING EDITOR** Urian Brown
**TRANSLATOR** Joe Yamazaki
**ENGLISH ADAPTATION** James Teal
**TOUCH-UP ART & LETTERING** James Hudnall

***THE PRINCE OF TENNIS***
**EDITOR** Urian Brown
**COMPILATION EDITION EDITOR** Jason Thompson
**COMPILATION EDITION TRANSLATOR** Koji Goto
**COMPILATION EDITION ENGLISH ADAPTATION** Peter Makepeace
**TOUCH-UP ART & LETTERING** Andy Ristaino

***RUROUNI KENSHIN***
**EDITOR** Avery Gotoh
**SUPERVISING EDITOR** Kit Fox
**TRANSLATOR** Kenichiro Yagi
**ENGLISH ADAPTATION** Gerard Jones
**TOUCH-UP ART & LETTERING** Steve Dutro

***KNIGHTS OF THE ZODIAC (SAINT SEIYA)***
**EDITOR** Urian Brown
**TRANSLATOR** Mari Morimoto
**ENGLISH ADAPTATION** Lance Caselman
**TOUCH-UP ART & LETTERING** Dan Nakrosis



**www.shonenjump.com**

**EXPLANATION OF AGE RATINGS**

RATED A FOR ALL AGES — ***ALL AGES*** Suitable for all ages. May contain some violence. Examples: *Hikaru no Go, The Prince of Tennis*

RATED T FOR TEEN — ***TEEN*** May contain violence, language, suggestive situations and alcohol or tobacco usage. Recommended for ages 13 and up. Examples: *Knights of the Zodiac, Ultimate Muscle*

RATED T+ FOR OLDER TEENS — ***OLDER TEENS*** May contain graphic violence, language, suggestive situations, brief nudity and alcohol or tobacco usage. Recommended for ages 16 and up. Example: *Rurouni Kenshin*

# CONTENTS

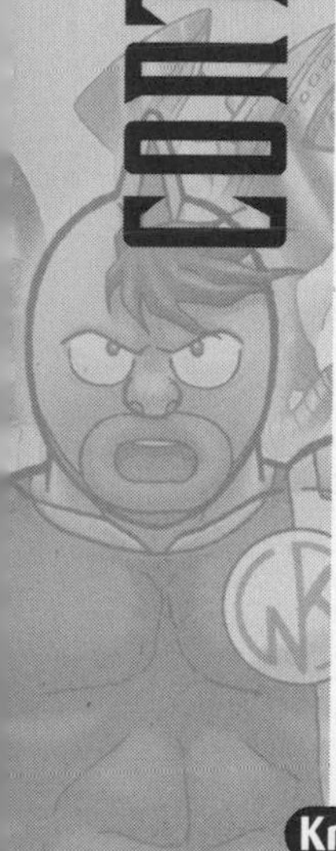



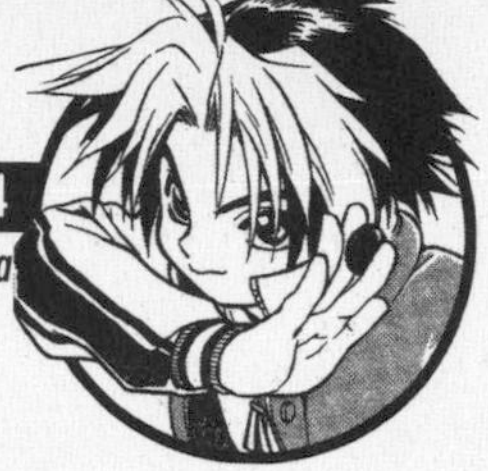



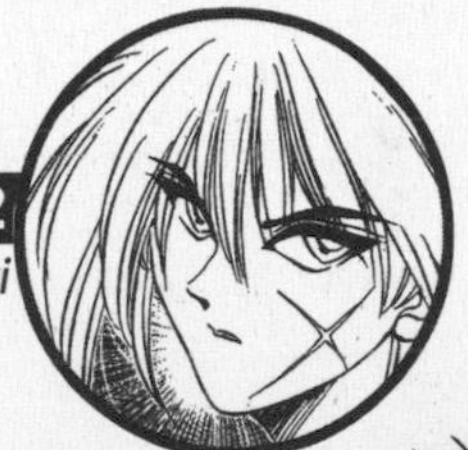



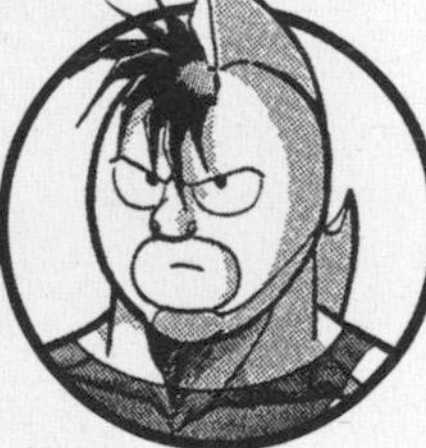



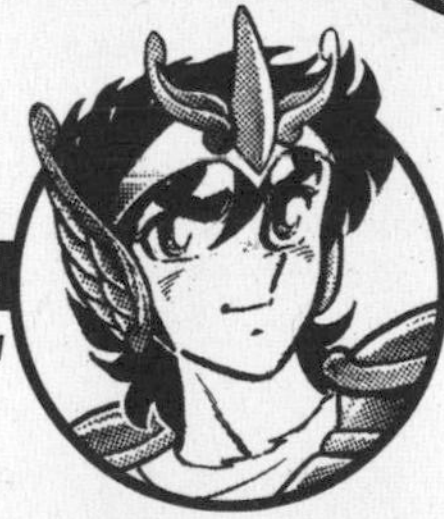



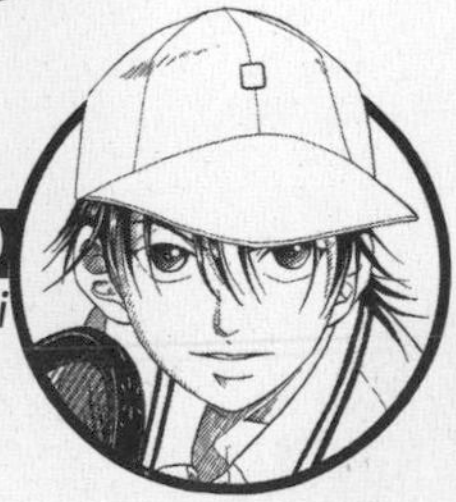

READ THIS WAY

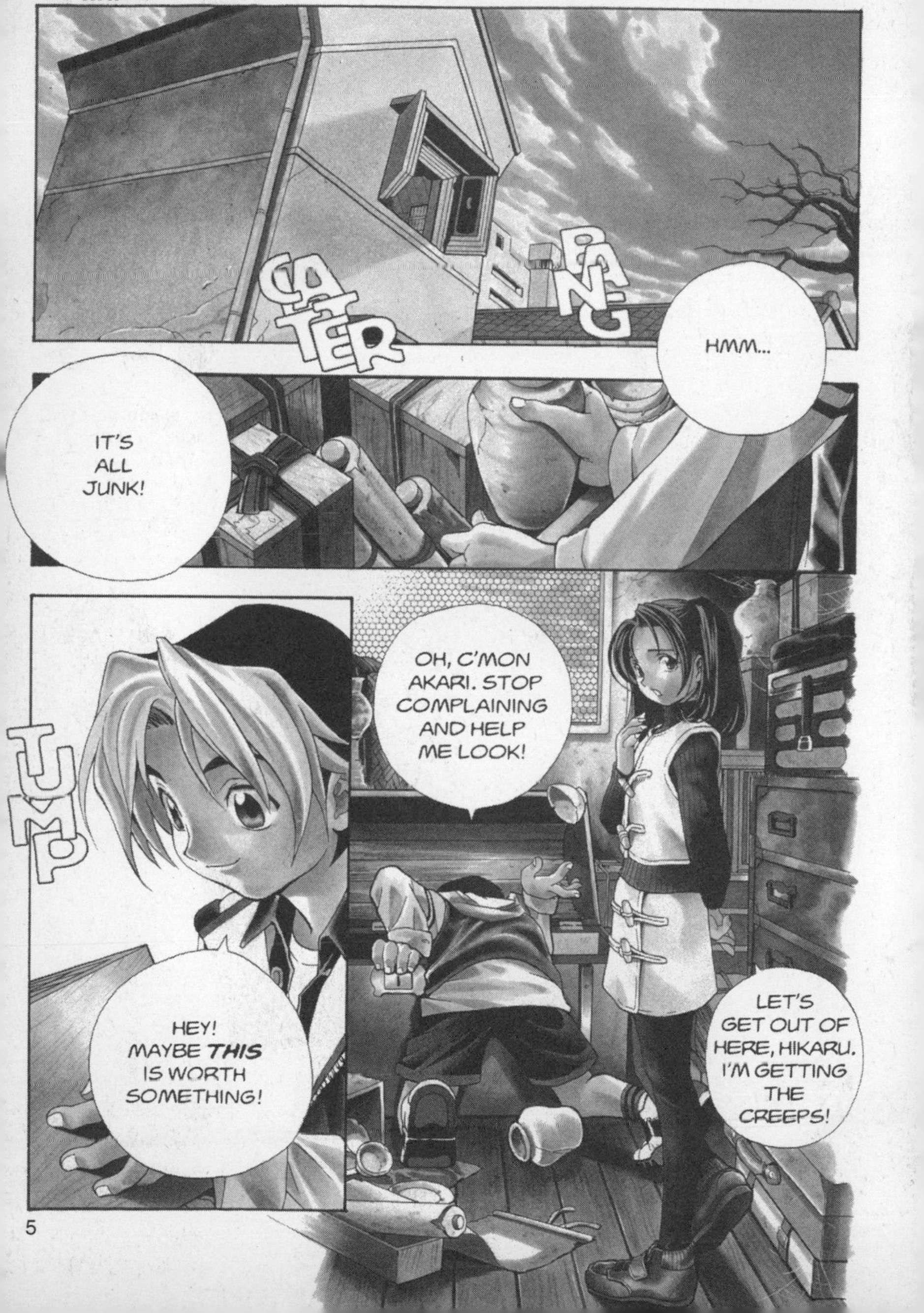
CATTER
BANG
HMM...
IT'S ALL JUNK!
LET'S GET OUT OF HERE, HIKARU. I'M GETTING THE CREEPS!
OH, C'MON AKARI. STOP COMPLAINING AND HELP ME LOOK!
TUMP
HEY! MAYBE ***THIS*** IS WORTH SOMETHING!

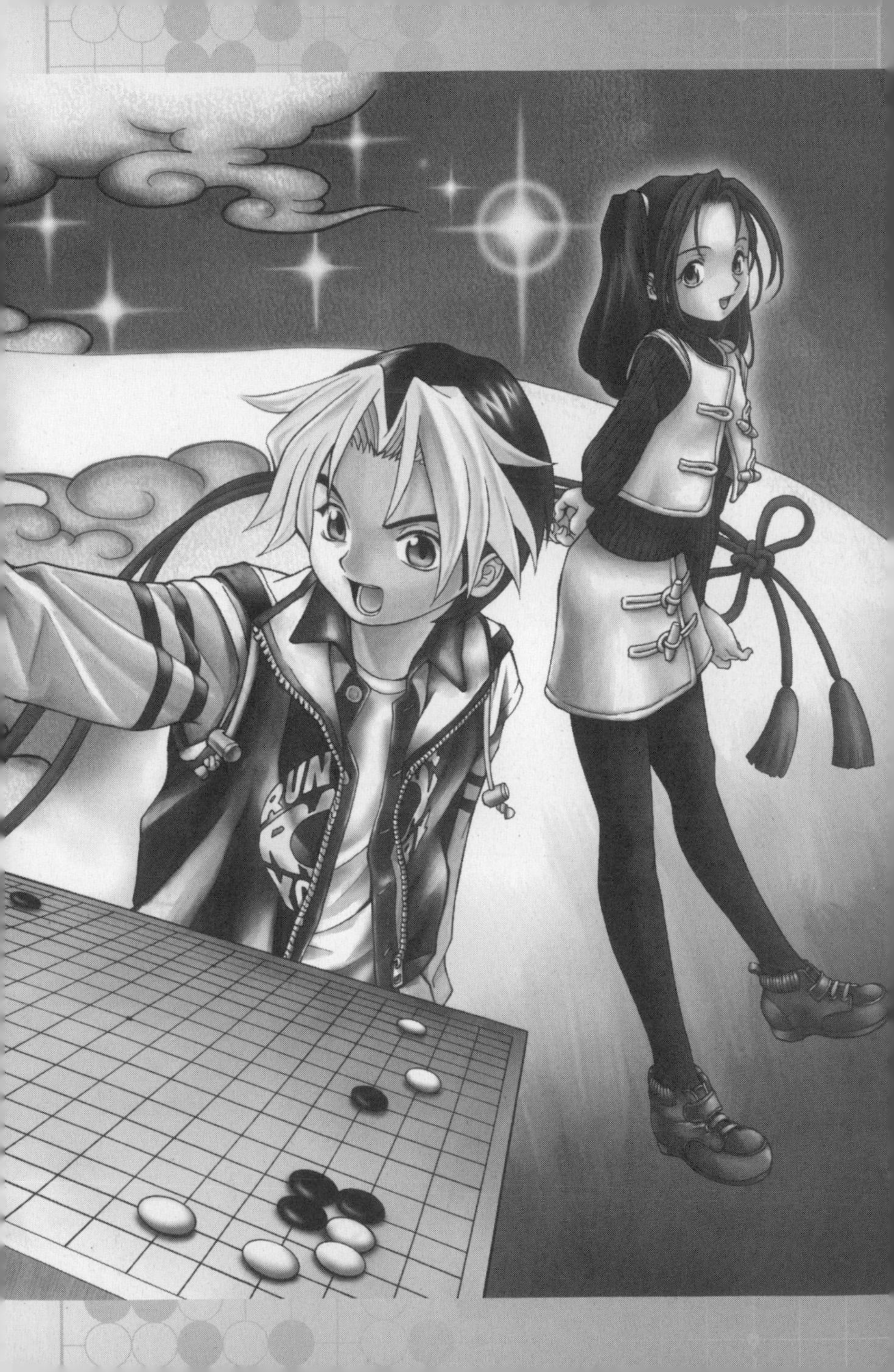

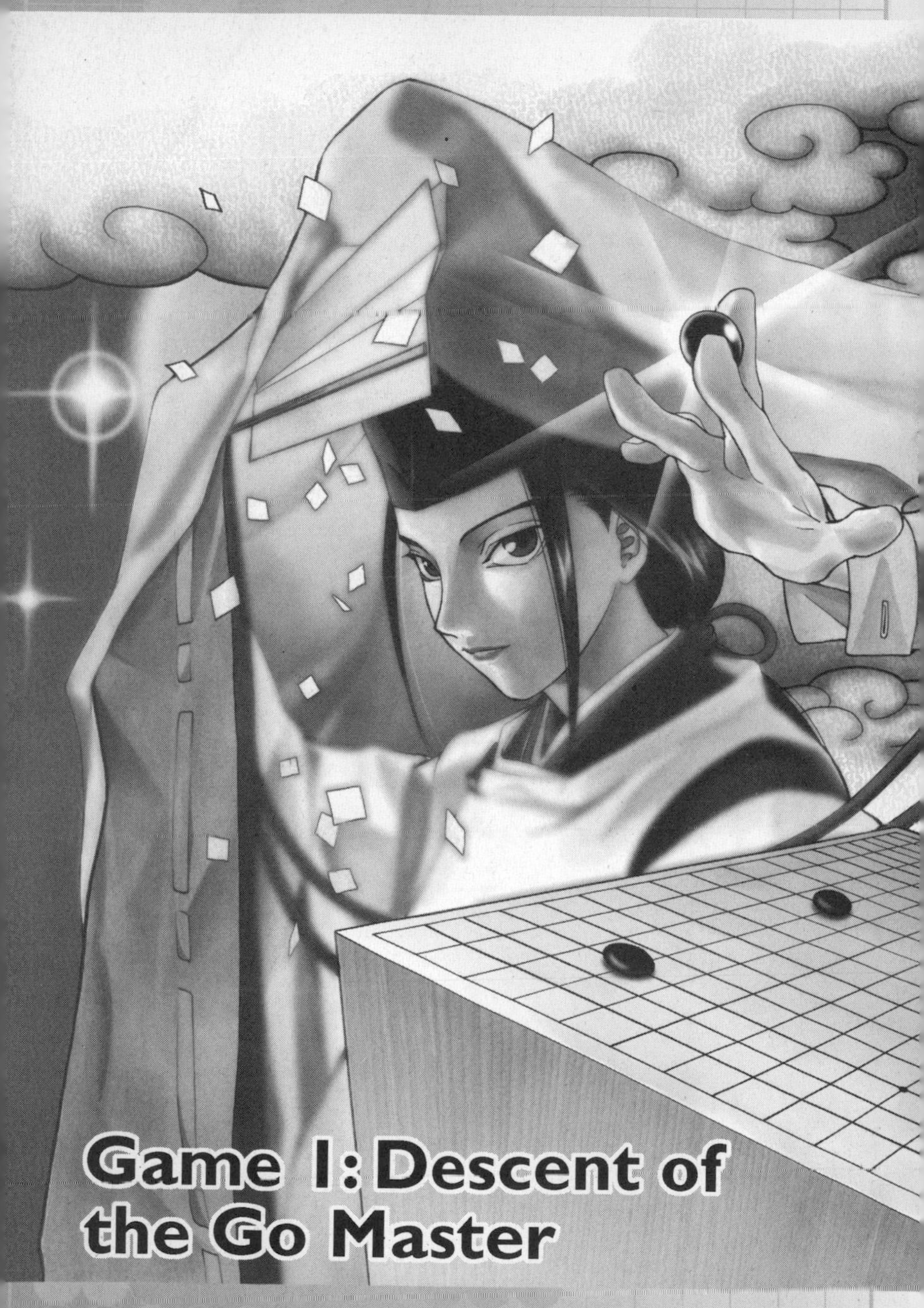

# Game 1: Descent of the Go Master

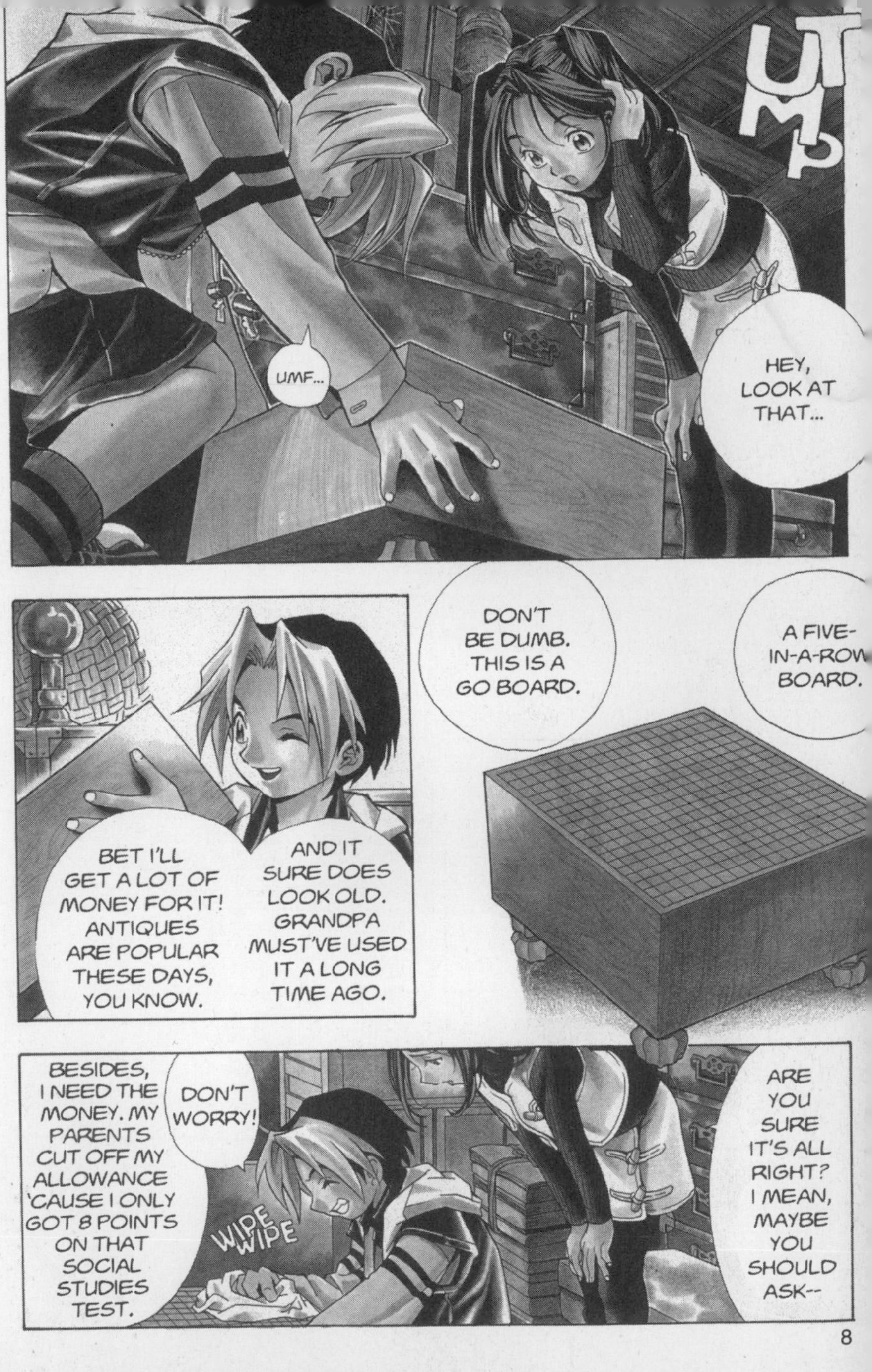
HEY, LOOK AT THAT...
UMF...
A FIVE-IN-A-ROW BOARD.
DON'T BE DUMB. THIS IS A GO BOARD.
AND IT SURE DOES LOOK OLD. GRANDPA MUST'VE USED IT A LONG TIME AGO.
BET I'LL GET A LOT OF MONEY FOR IT! ANTIQUES ARE POPULAR THESE DAYS, YOU KNOW.
ARE YOU SURE IT'S ALL RIGHT? I MEAN, MAYBE YOU SHOULD ASK--
DON'T WORRY!
BESIDES, I NEED THE MONEY. MY PARENTS CUT OFF MY ALLOWANCE 'CAUSE I ONLY GOT 8 POINTS ON THAT SOCIAL STUDIES TEST.
WIPE WIPE

READ THIS WAY

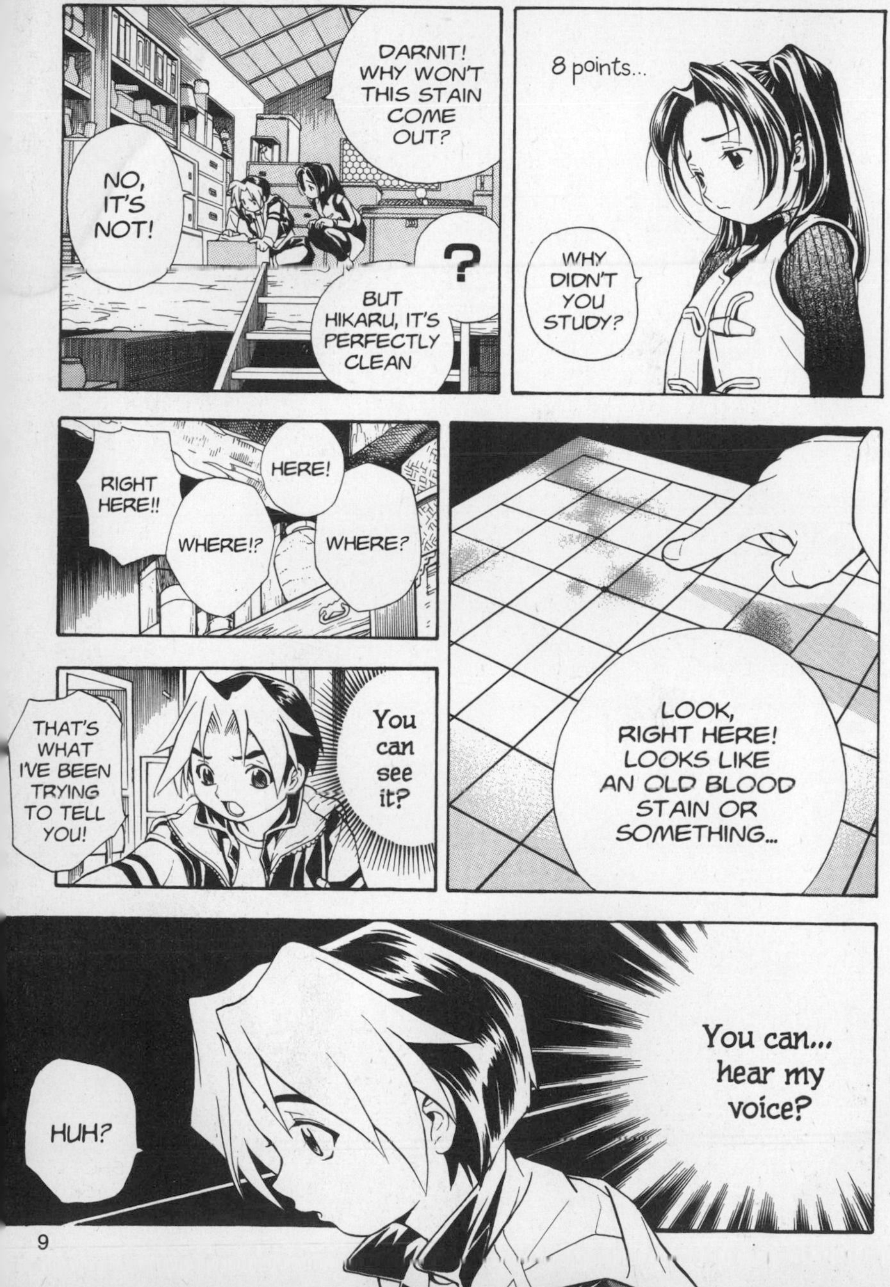
8 points...
WHY DIDN'T YOU STUDY?
DARNIT! WHY WON'T THIS STAIN COME OUT?
?
BUT HIKARU, IT'S PERFECTLY CLEAN
NO, IT'S NOT!
LOOK, RIGHT HERE! LOOKS LIKE AN OLD BLOOD STAIN OR SOMETHING...
HERE!
WHERE?
WHERE!?
RIGHT HERE!!
You can see it?
THAT'S WHAT I'VE BEEN TRYING TO TELL YOU!
You can... hear my voice?
HUH?

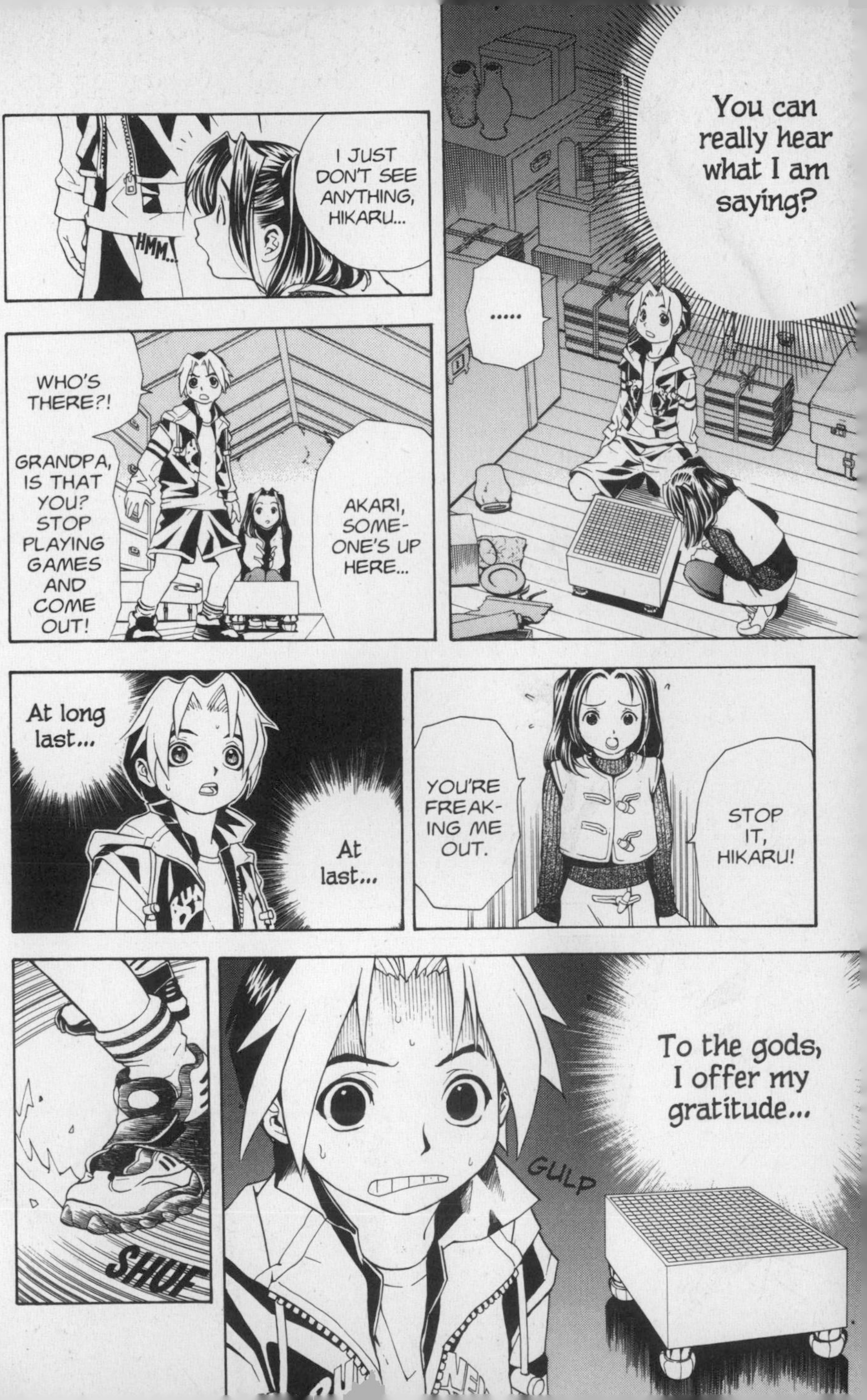
You can really hear what I am saying?
.....
I JUST DON'T SEE ANYTHING, HIKARU...
HMM...
AKARI, SOMEONE'S UP HERE...
WHO'S THERE?!
GRANDPA, IS THAT YOU? STOP PLAYING GAMES AND COME OUT!
STOP IT, HIKARU!
YOU'RE FREAKING ME OUT.
At last...
At long last...
To the gods, I offer my gratitude...
GULP
SHUF

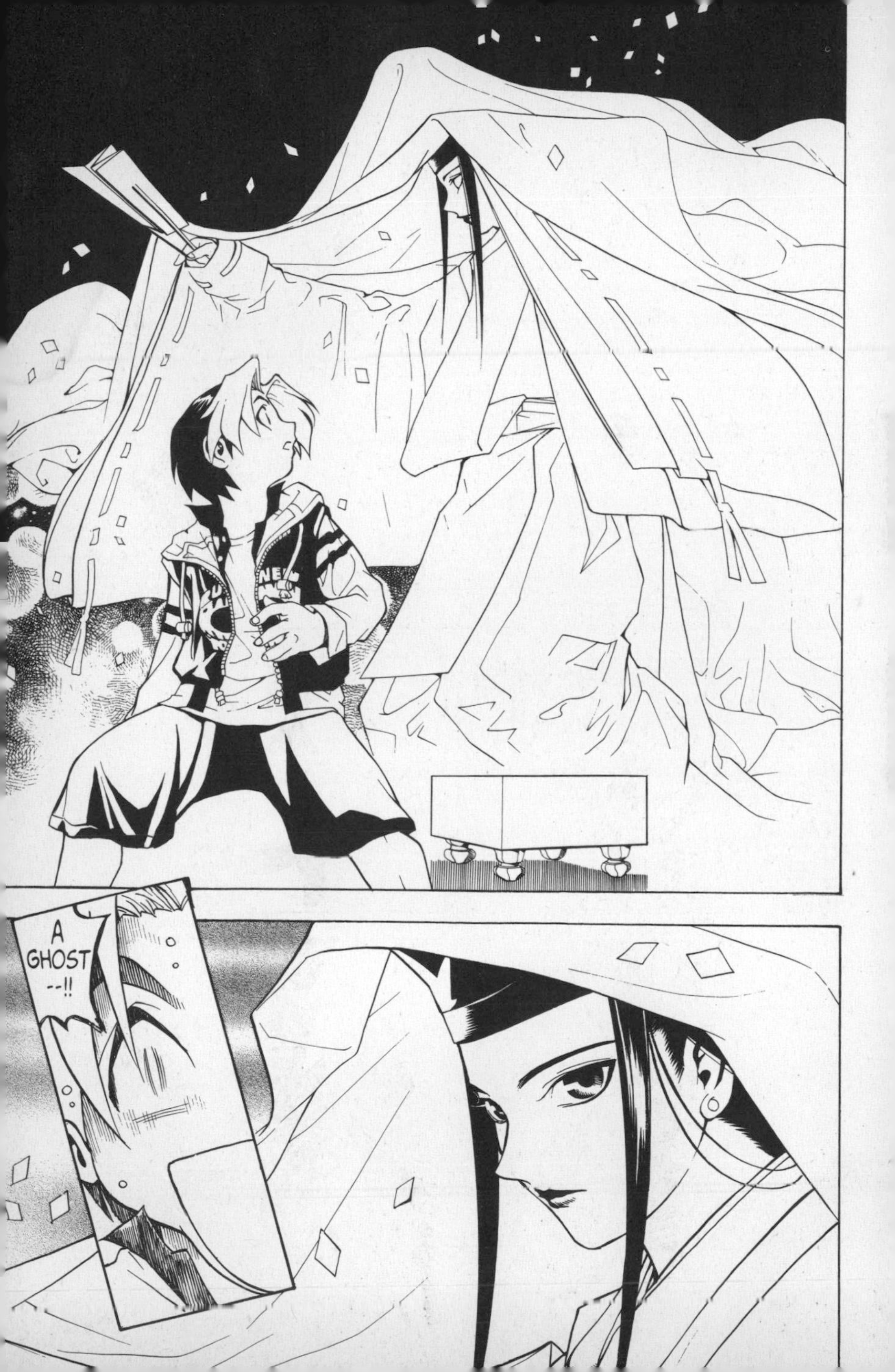
A GHOST --!!

READ THIS WAY

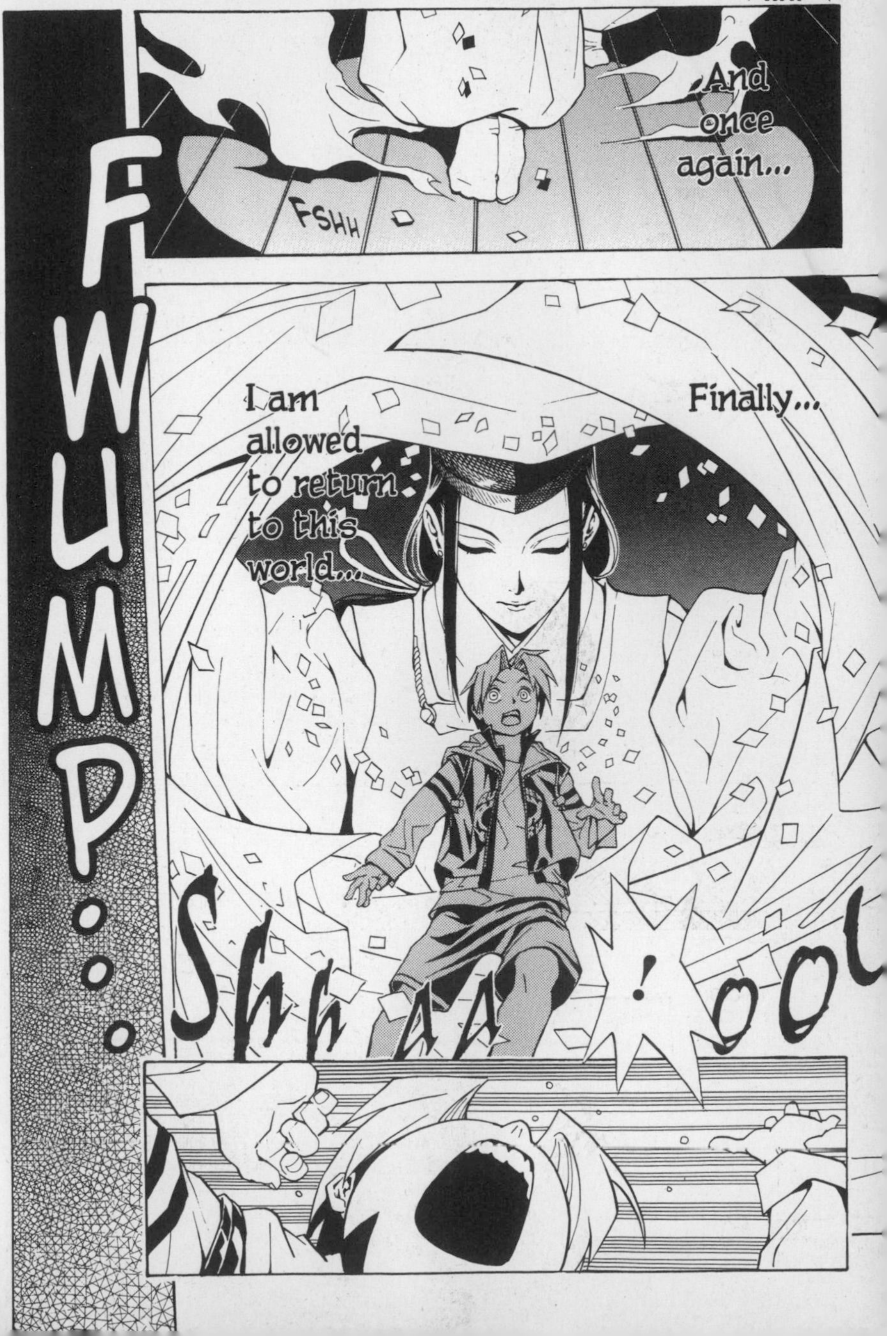
And once again...
FSHH
Finally...
I am allowed to return to this world...
Shhaa
!
ooo
FWUMP...

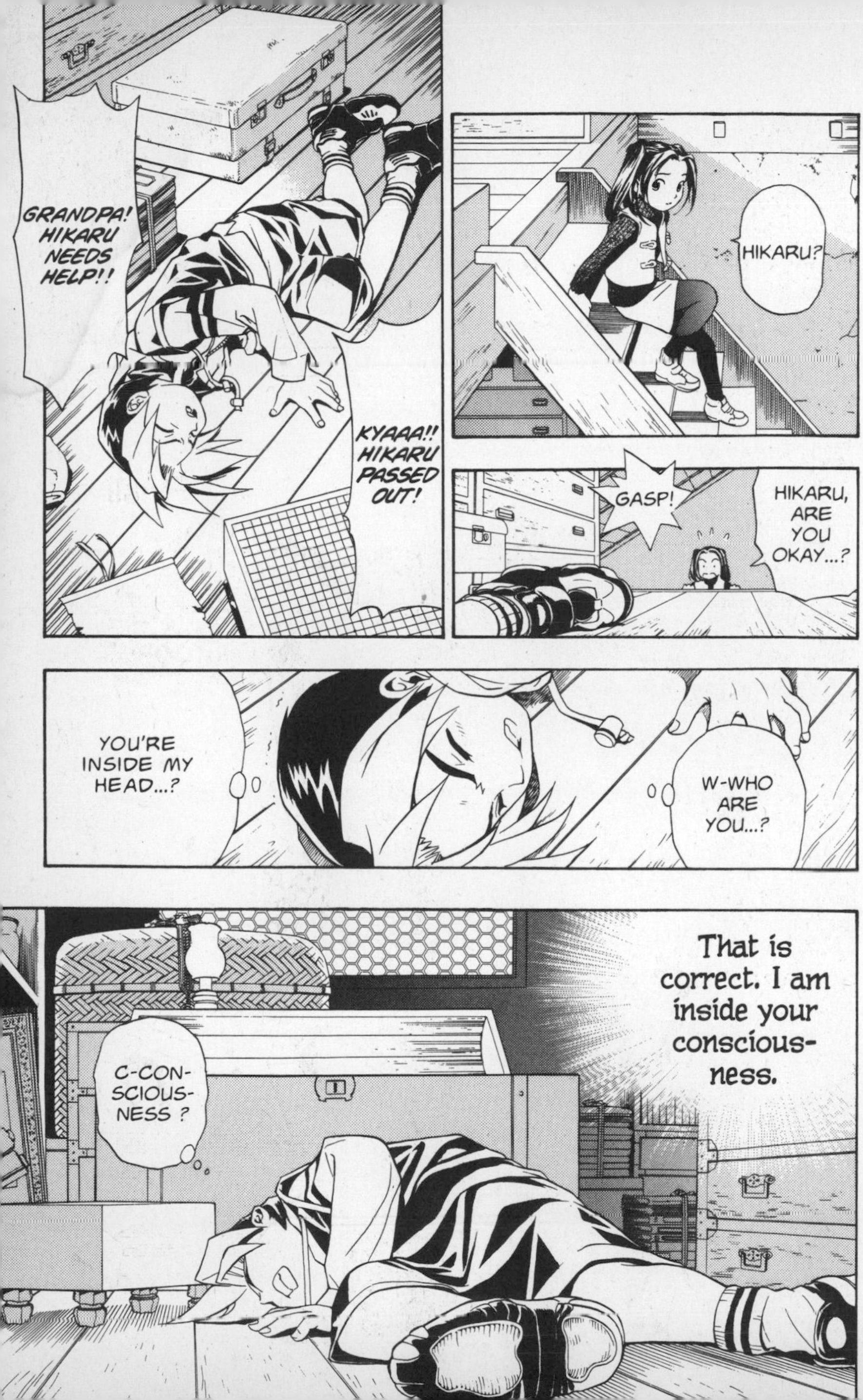

HIKARU?
HIKARU, ARE YOU OKAY...?
GASP!
KYAAA!! HIKARU PASSED OUT!
GRANDPA! HIKARU NEEDS HELP!!
W-WHO ARE YOU...?
YOU'RE INSIDE MY HEAD...?
That is correct. I am inside your conscious-ness.
C-CON-SCIOUS-NESS ?

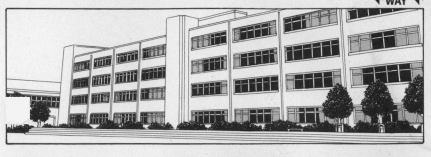

6 — 1

YOUR SCORES ON THE SOCIAL STUDIES TEST LAST WEEK WERE ABSOLUTELY ABYSMAL...

*THAT'S* WHY YOU'RE GETTING ANOTHER ONE, TODAY!

No Fair!

GRMBL

WHAT?!

ARRGH!

NO WAY!!

MMBL

OKAY EVERYONE, PUT YOUR BOOKS AWAY.

ARGH, MY HEAD.

RUSTLE

This sucks!

Darn

RUSTLE

......

SOCIAL STUDIES

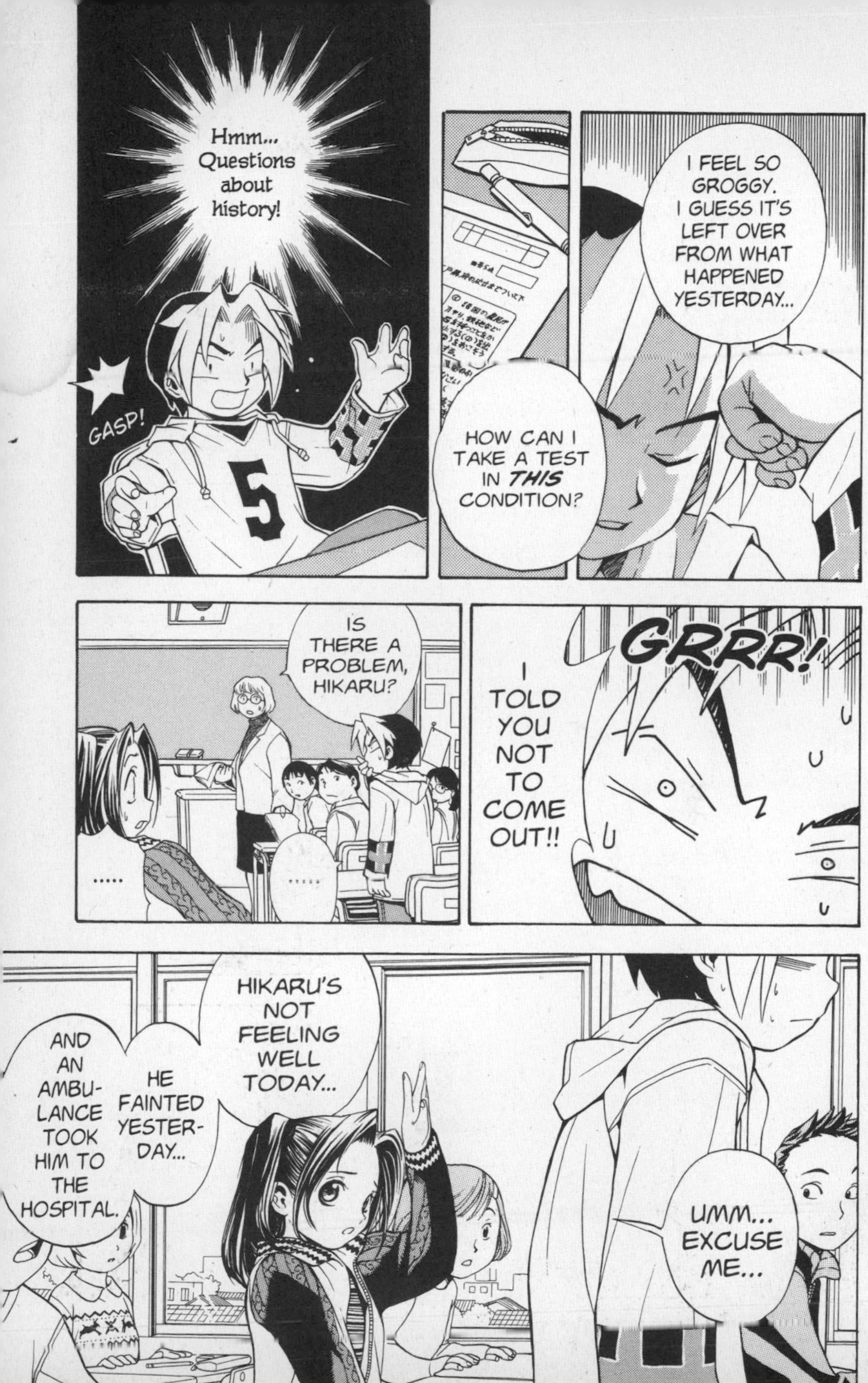
I FEEL SO GROGGY. I GUESS IT'S LEFT OVER FROM WHAT HAPPENED YESTERDAY...
HOW CAN I TAKE A TEST IN *THIS* CONDITION?
Hmm... Questions about history!
GASP!
GRRRR!
I TOLD YOU NOT TO COME OUT!!
IS THERE A PROBLEM, HIKARU?
.....
.....
UMM... EXCUSE ME...
HIKARU'S NOT FEELING WELL TODAY...
HE FAINTED YESTER-DAY...
AND AN AMBU-LANCE TOOK HIM TO THE HOSPITAL.

READ THIS WAY

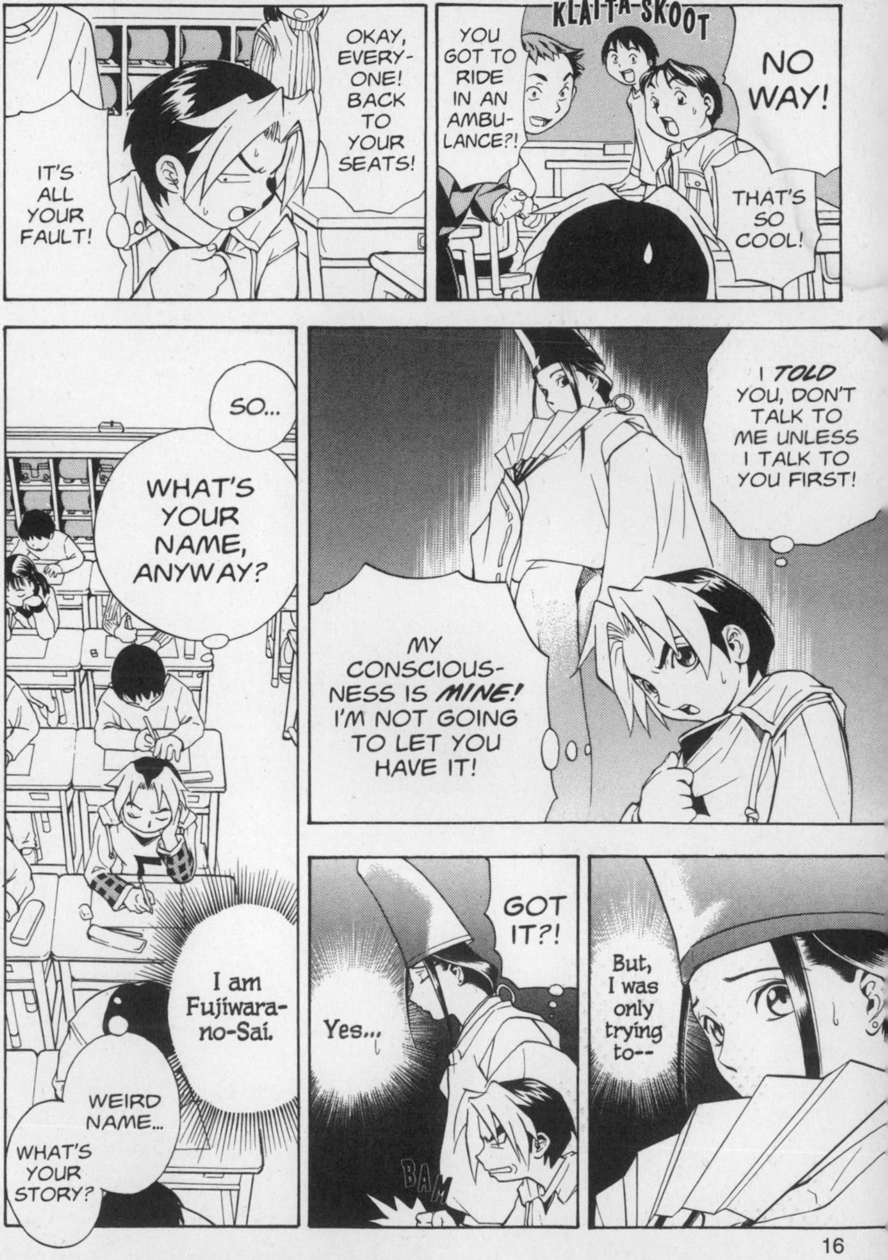
NO WAY!
KLATTA-SKOOT
YOU GOT TO RIDE IN AN AMBULANCE?!
THAT'S SO COOL!
OKAY, EVERYONE! BACK TO YOUR SEATS!
IT'S ALL YOUR FAULT!
I *TOLD* YOU, DON'T TALK TO ME UNLESS I TALK TO YOU FIRST!
MY CONSCIOUSNESS IS *MINE!* I'M NOT GOING TO LET YOU HAVE IT!
But, I was only trying to--
GOT IT?!
Yes...
BAM
SO...
WHAT'S YOUR NAME, ANYWAY?
I am Fujiwara-no-Sai.
WEIRD NAME... WHAT'S YOUR STORY?

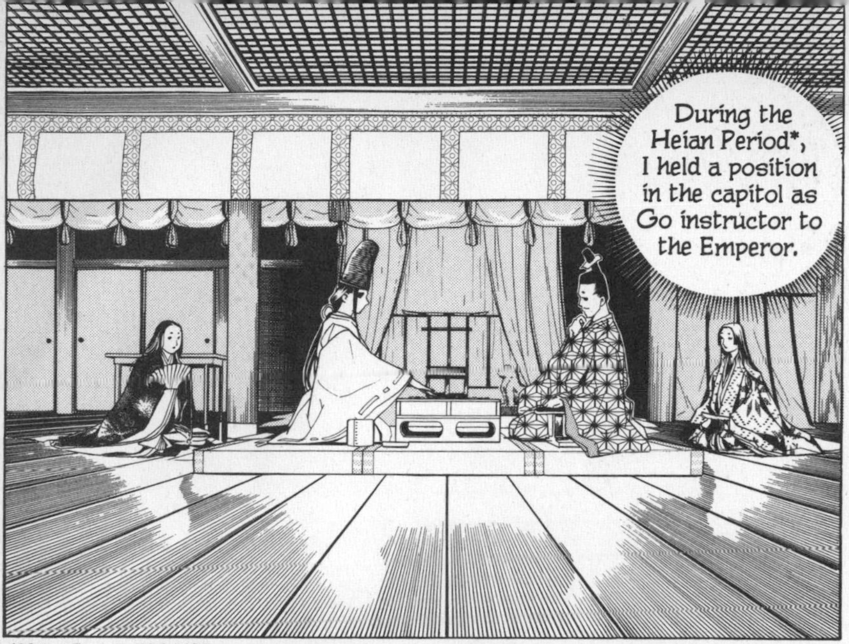
During the Heian Period*, I held a position in the capitol as Go instructor to the Emperor.

*Heian Period: 794-1185

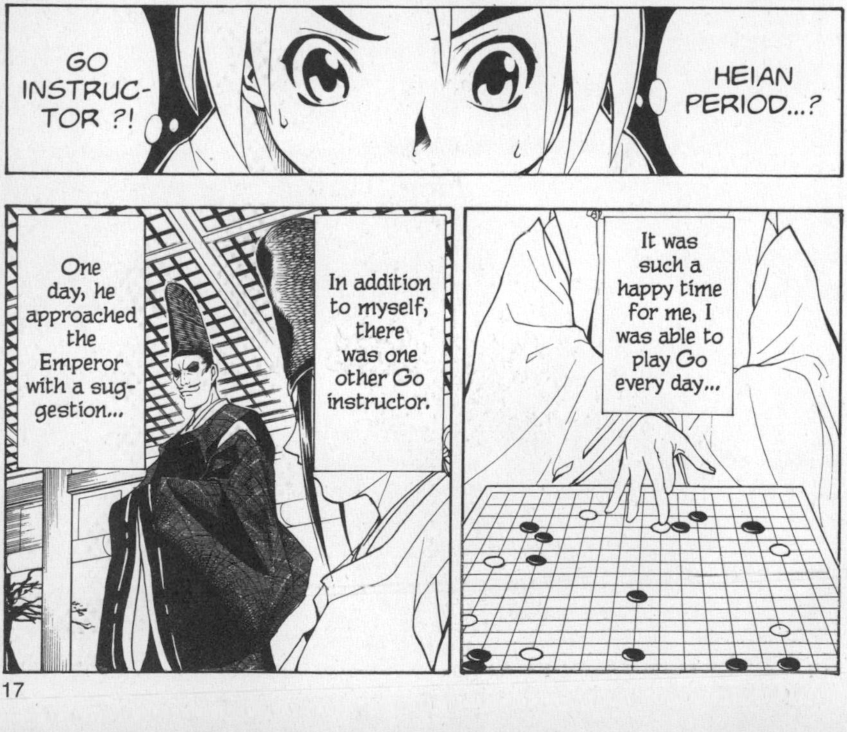
HEIAN PERIOD...?
GO INSTRUC-TOR ?!
It was such a happy time for me, I was able to play Go every day...
In addition to myself, there was one other Go instructor.
One day, he approached the Emperor with a sug-gestion...

READ THIS WAY

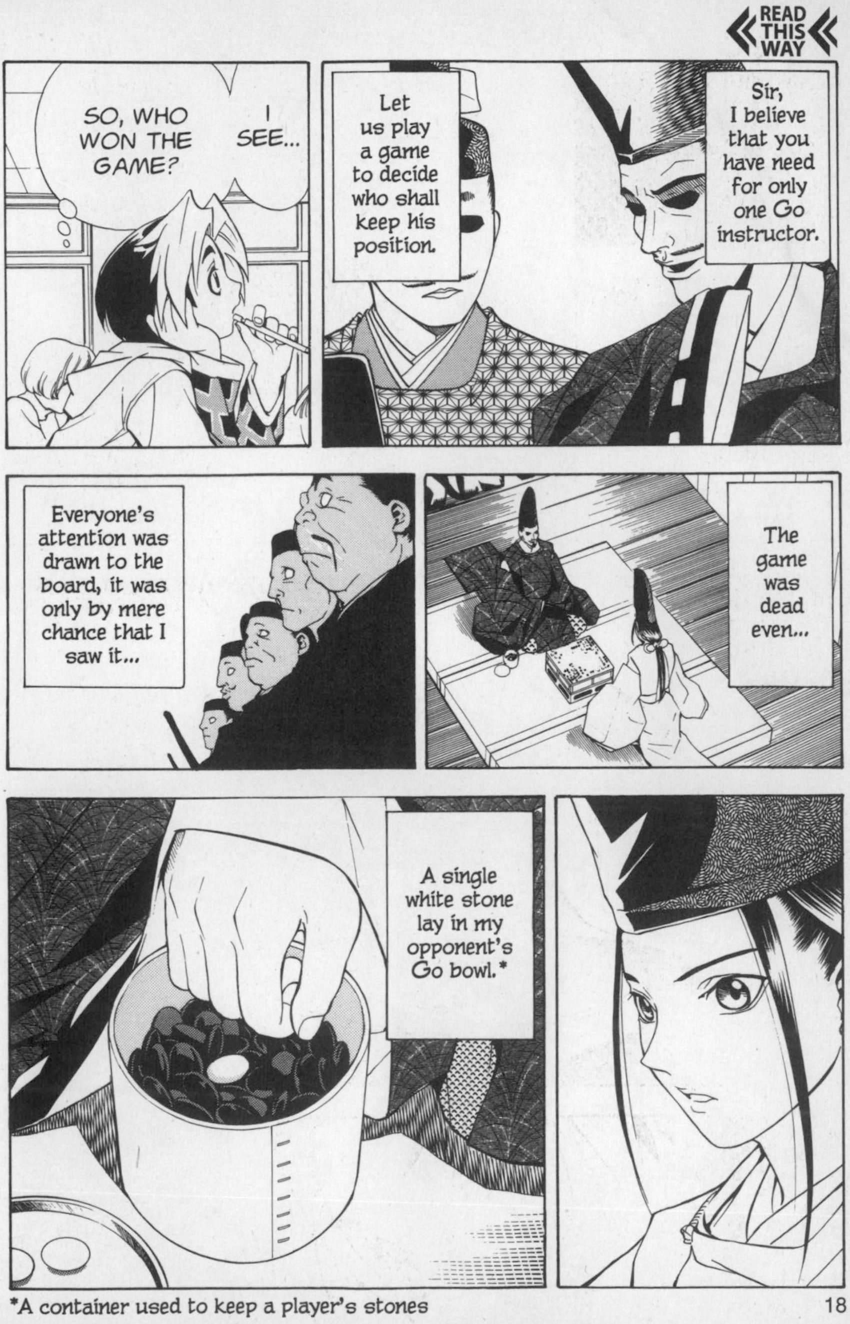

Sir, I believe that you have need for only one Go instructor.
Let us play a game to decide who shall keep his position.
I SEE...
SO, WHO WON THE GAME?
The game was dead even...
Everyone's attention was drawn to the board, it was only by mere chance that I saw it...
A single white stone lay in my opponent's Go bowl.*


*A container used to keep a player's stones

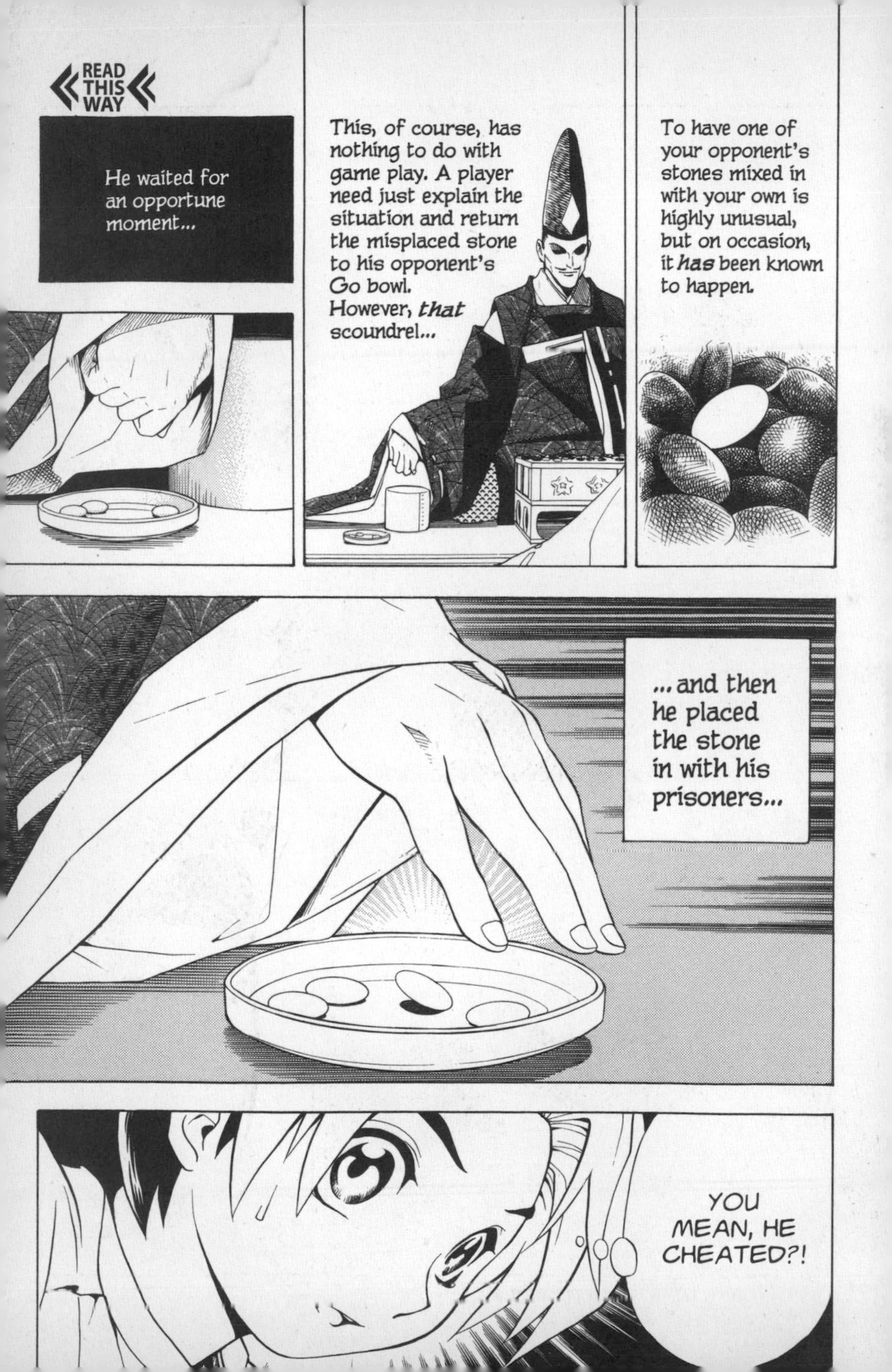
READ THIS WAY
To have one of your opponent's stones mixed in with your own is highly unusual, but on occasion, it *has* been known to happen.
This, of course, has nothing to do with game play. A player need just explain the situation and return the misplaced stone to his opponent's Go bowl. However, *that* scoundrel...
He waited for an opportune moment...
...and then he placed the stone in with his prisoners...
YOU MEAN, HE CHEATED?!

READ THIS WAY

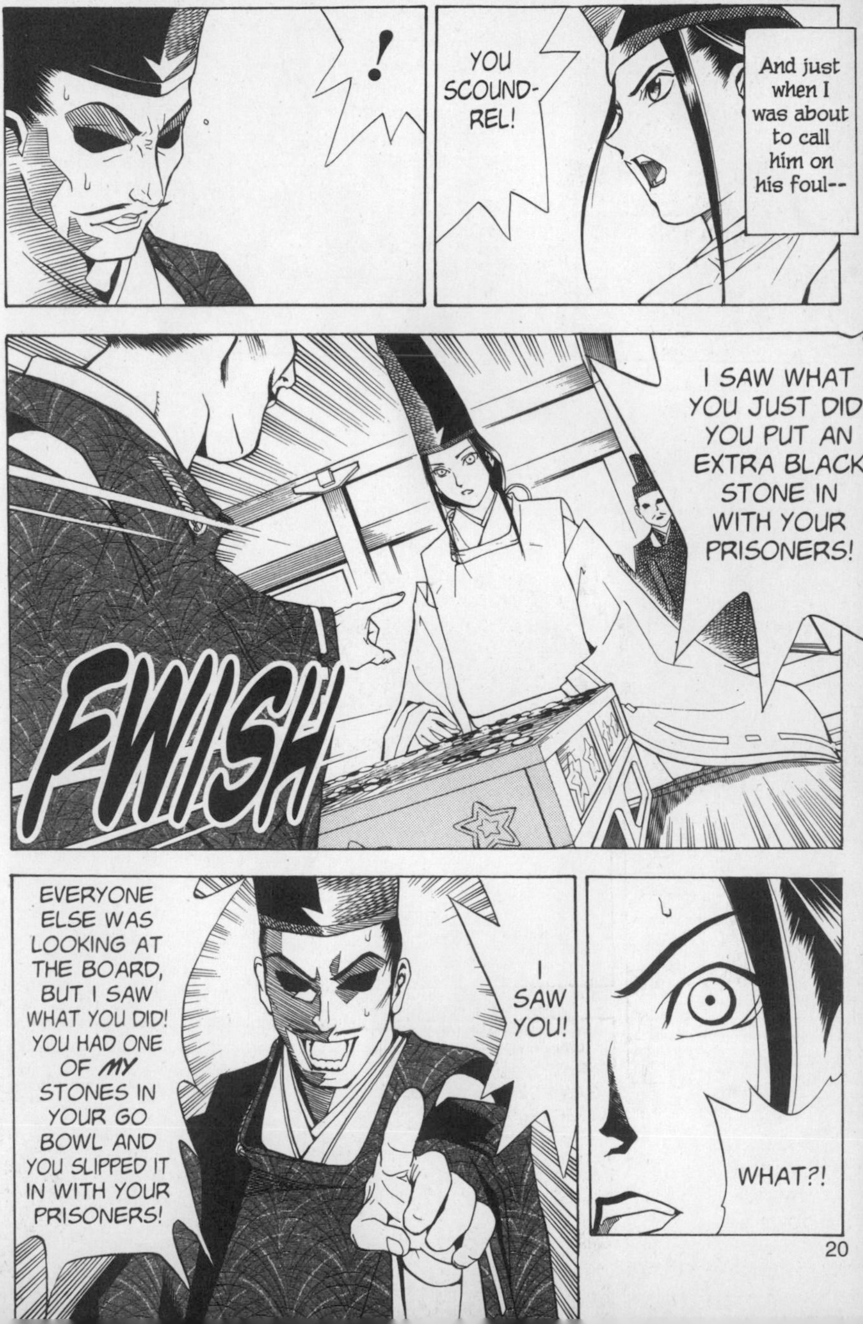

And just when I was about to call him on his foul--
YOU SCOUND-REL!
!
I SAW WHAT YOU JUST DID! YOU PUT AN EXTRA BLACK STONE IN WITH YOUR PRISONERS!
FWISH
WHAT?!
I SAW YOU!
EVERYONE ELSE WAS LOOKING AT THE BOARD, BUT I SAW WHAT YOU DID! YOU HAD ONE OF MY STONES IN YOUR GO BOWL AND YOU SLIPPED IT IN WITH YOUR PRISONERS!

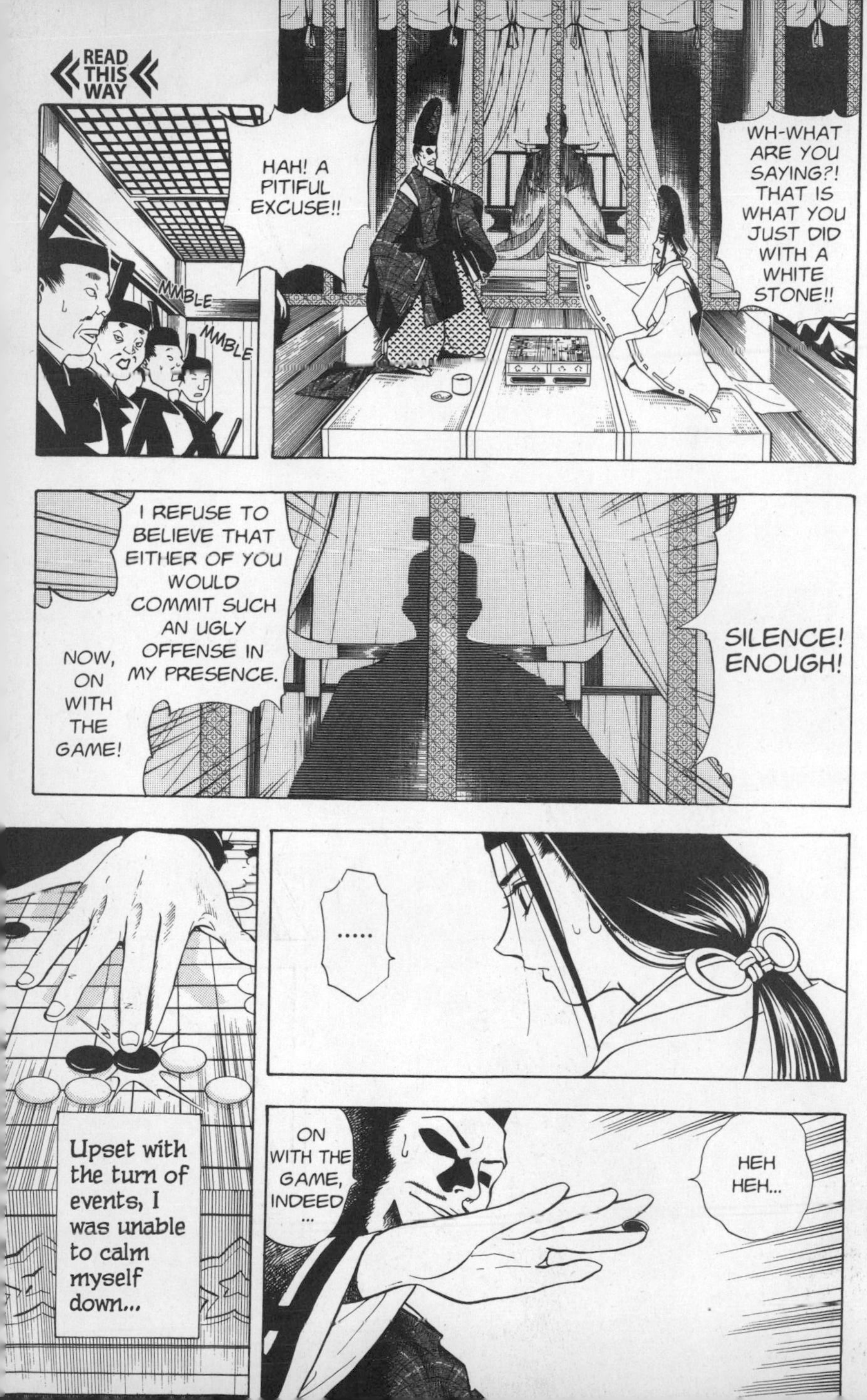
READ THIS WAY
WH-WHAT ARE YOU SAYING?! THAT IS WHAT YOU JUST DID WITH A WHITE STONE!!
HAH! A PITIFUL EXCUSE!!
MMBLE
MMBLE
SILENCE! ENOUGH!
I REFUSE TO BELIEVE THAT EITHER OF YOU WOULD COMMIT SUCH AN UGLY OFFENSE IN MY PRESENCE.
NOW, ON WITH THE GAME!
.....
HEH HEH...
ON WITH THE GAME, INDEED...
Upset with the turn of events, I was unable to calm myself down...

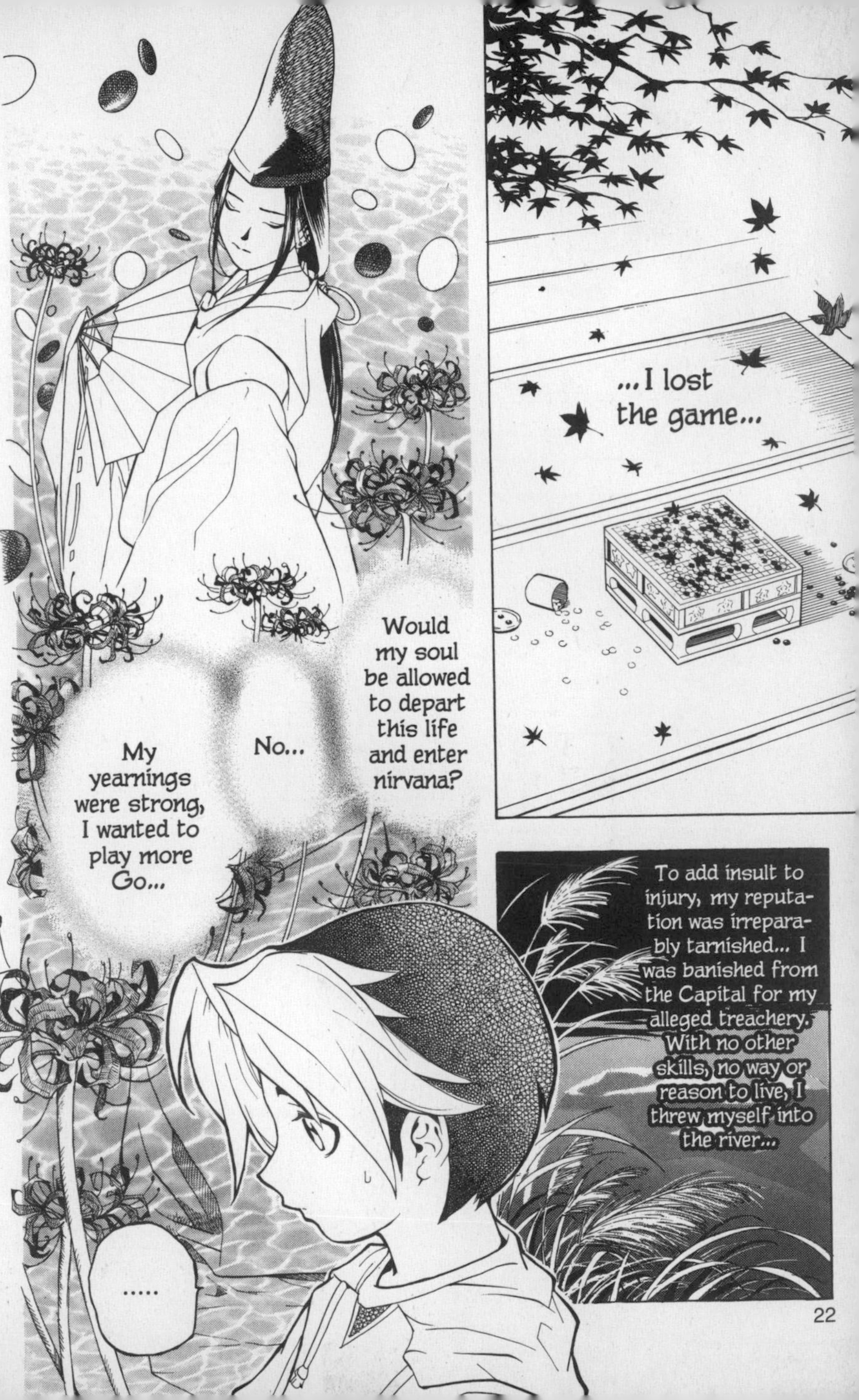
...I lost the game...
To add insult to injury, my reputation was irreparably tarnished... I was banished from the Capital for my alleged treachery. With no other skills, no way or reason to live, I threw myself into the river...
Would my soul be allowed to depart this life and enter nirvana?
No...
My yearnings were strong, I wanted to play more Go...
.....

READ THIS WAY

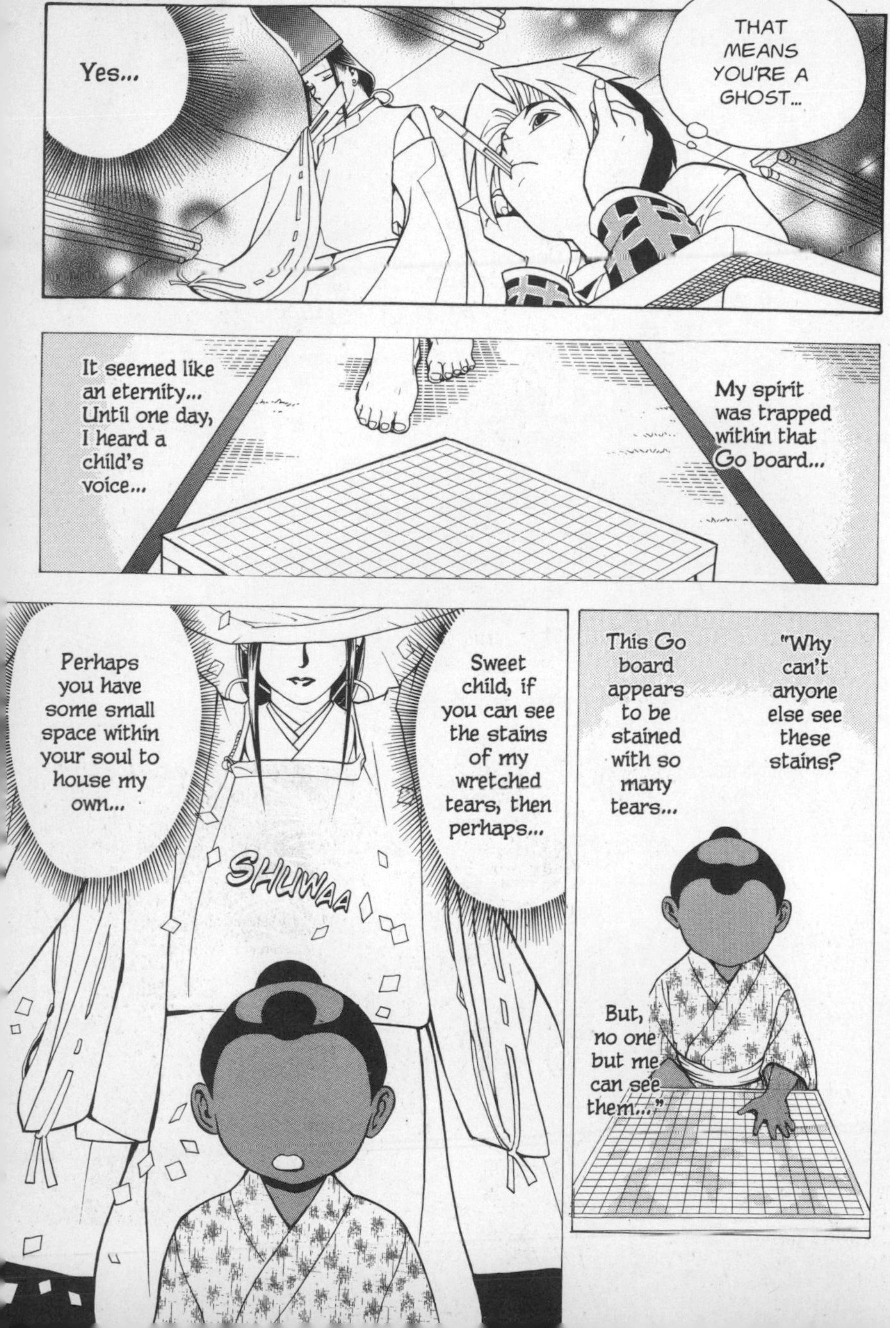
THAT MEANS YOU'RE A GHOST...
Yes...
My spirit was trapped within that Go board...
It seemed like an eternity... Until one day, I heard a child's voice...
"Why can't anyone else see these stains?
This Go board appears to be stained with so many tears...
But, no one but me can see them..."
Sweet child, if you can see the stains of my wretched tears, then perhaps...
Perhaps you have some small space within your soul to house my own...
SHUWAA

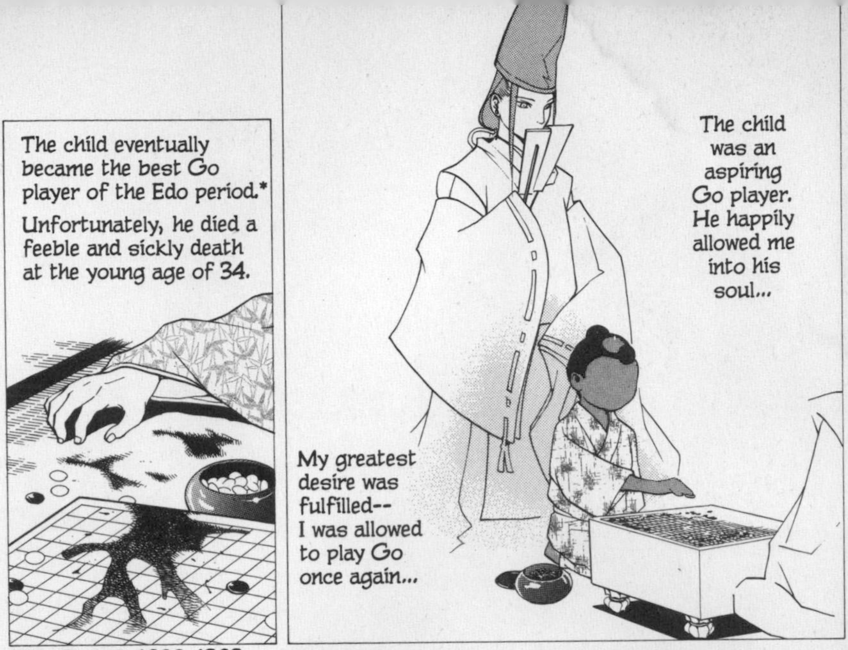
The child was an aspiring Go player. He happily allowed me into his soul...
My greatest desire was fulfilled-- I was allowed to play Go once again...
The child eventually became the best Go player of the Edo period.*
Unfortunately, he died a feeble and sickly death at the young age of 34.

*Edo Period: 1600-1868

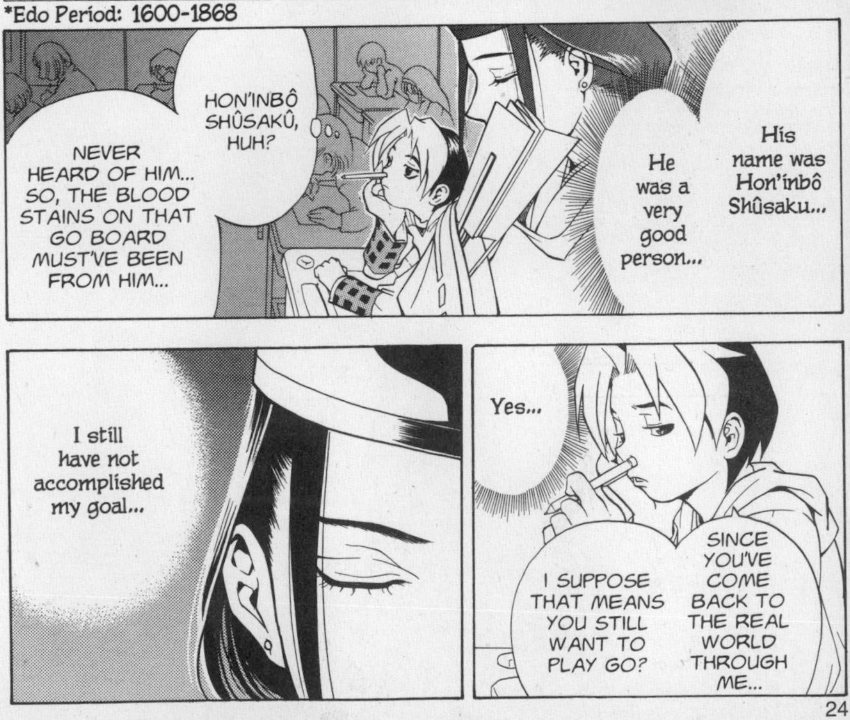
His name was Hon'inbô Shûsaku...
He was a very good person...
HON'INBÔ SHÛSAKU, HUH?
NEVER HEARD OF HIM... SO, THE BLOOD STAINS ON THAT GO BOARD MUST'VE BEEN FROM HIM...
SINCE YOU'VE COME BACK TO THE REAL WORLD THROUGH ME...
I SUPPOSE THAT MEANS YOU STILL WANT TO PLAY GO?
Yes...
I still have not accomplished my goal...

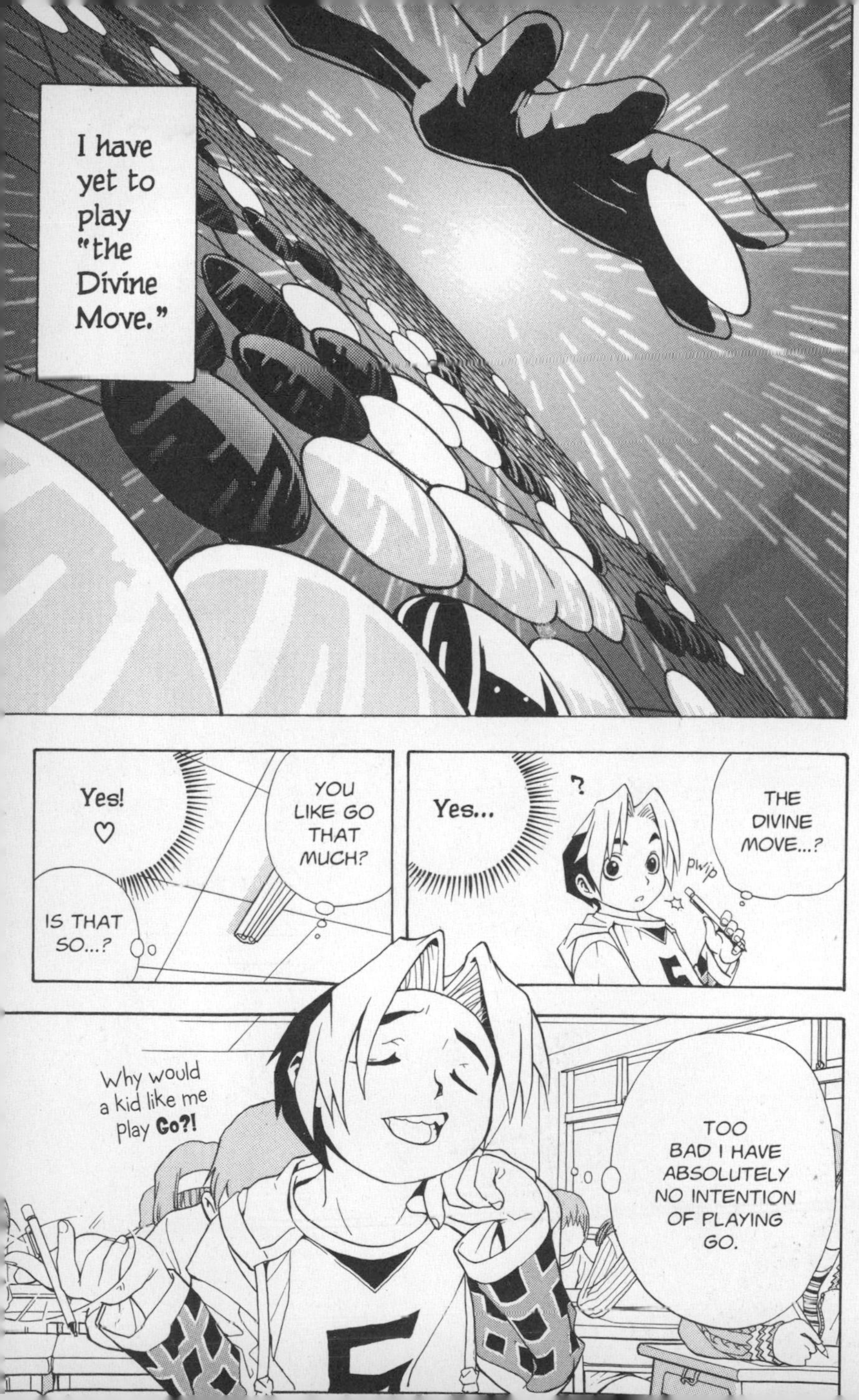
I have yet to play "the Divine Move."
THE DIVINE MOVE...?
?
Yes...
pwip
YOU LIKE GO THAT MUCH?
Yes! ♡
IS THAT SO...?
TOO BAD I HAVE ABSOLUTELY NO INTENTION OF PLAYING GO.
Why would a kid like me play **Go?!**

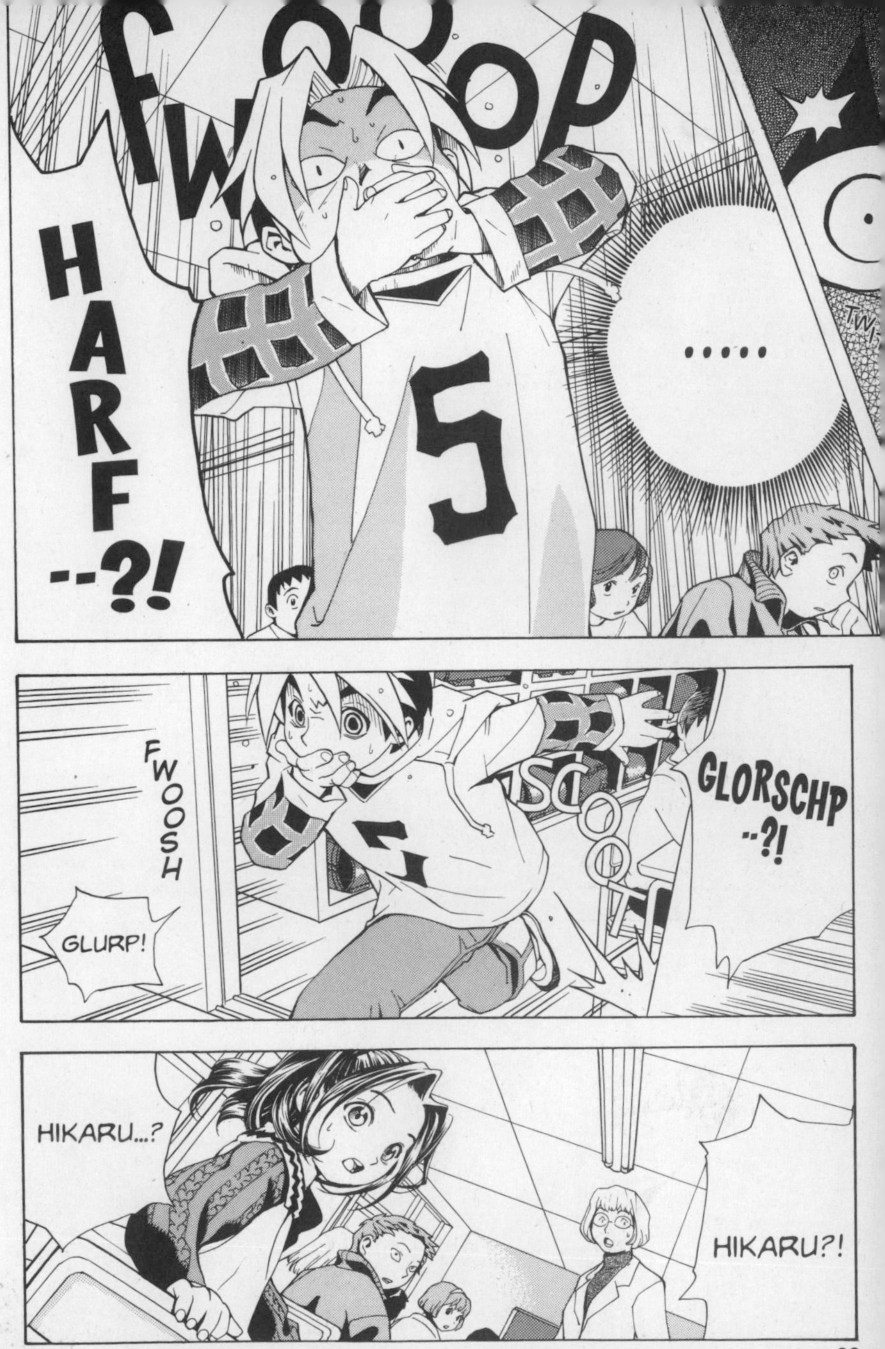
TWI-
.....
FWOOOP
HARF--?!
GLORSCHP--?!
SCOOT
FWOOSH
GLURP!
HIKARU?!
HIKARU...?

READ THIS WAY

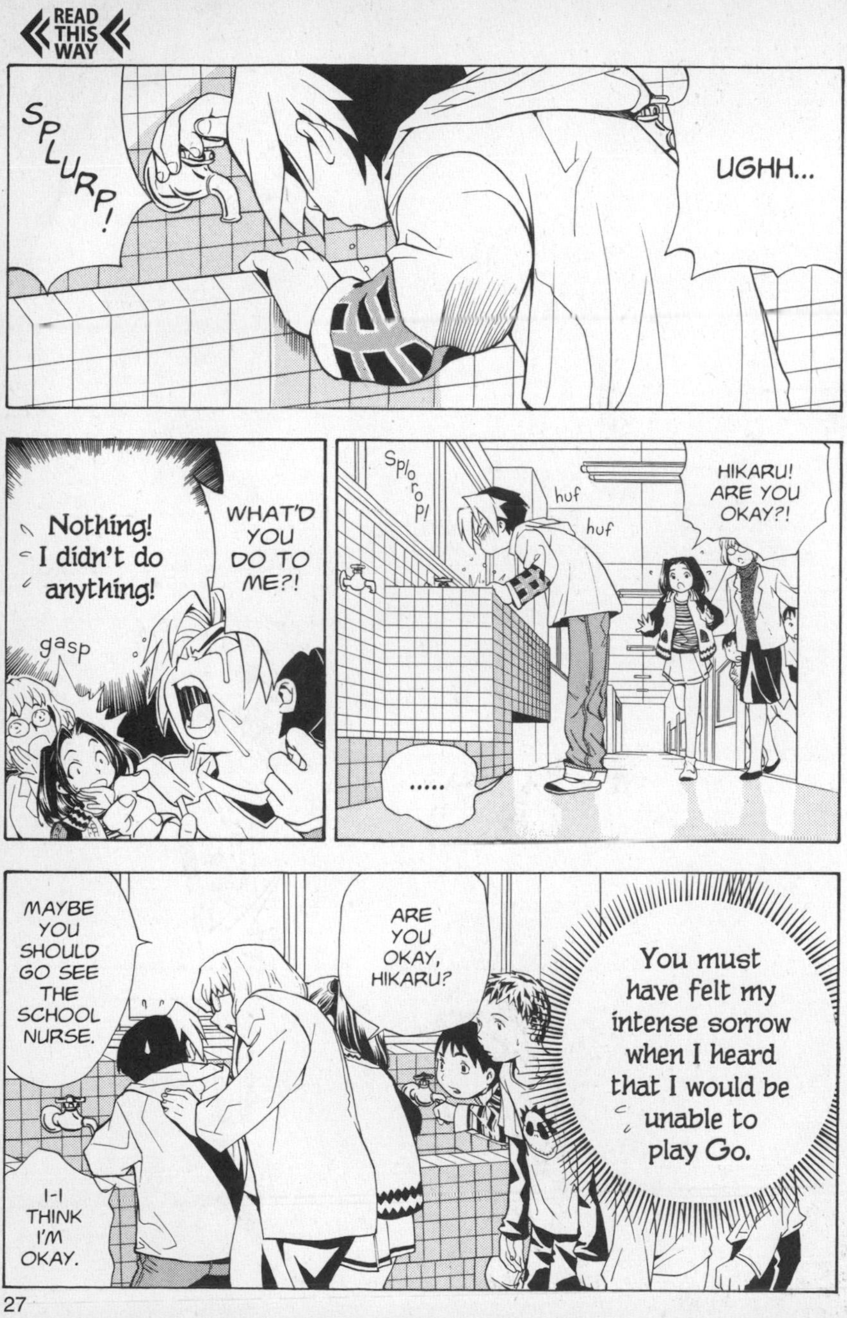
UGHH...
SPLURP!
HIKARU! ARE YOU OKAY?!
huf
huf
Splorop!
.....
WHAT'D YOU DO TO ME?!
Nothing! I didn't do anything!
gasp
You must have felt my intense sorrow when I heard that I would be unable to play Go.
ARE YOU OKAY, HIKARU?
MAYBE YOU SHOULD GO SEE THE SCHOOL NURSE.
I-I THINK I'M OKAY.

READ THIS WAY

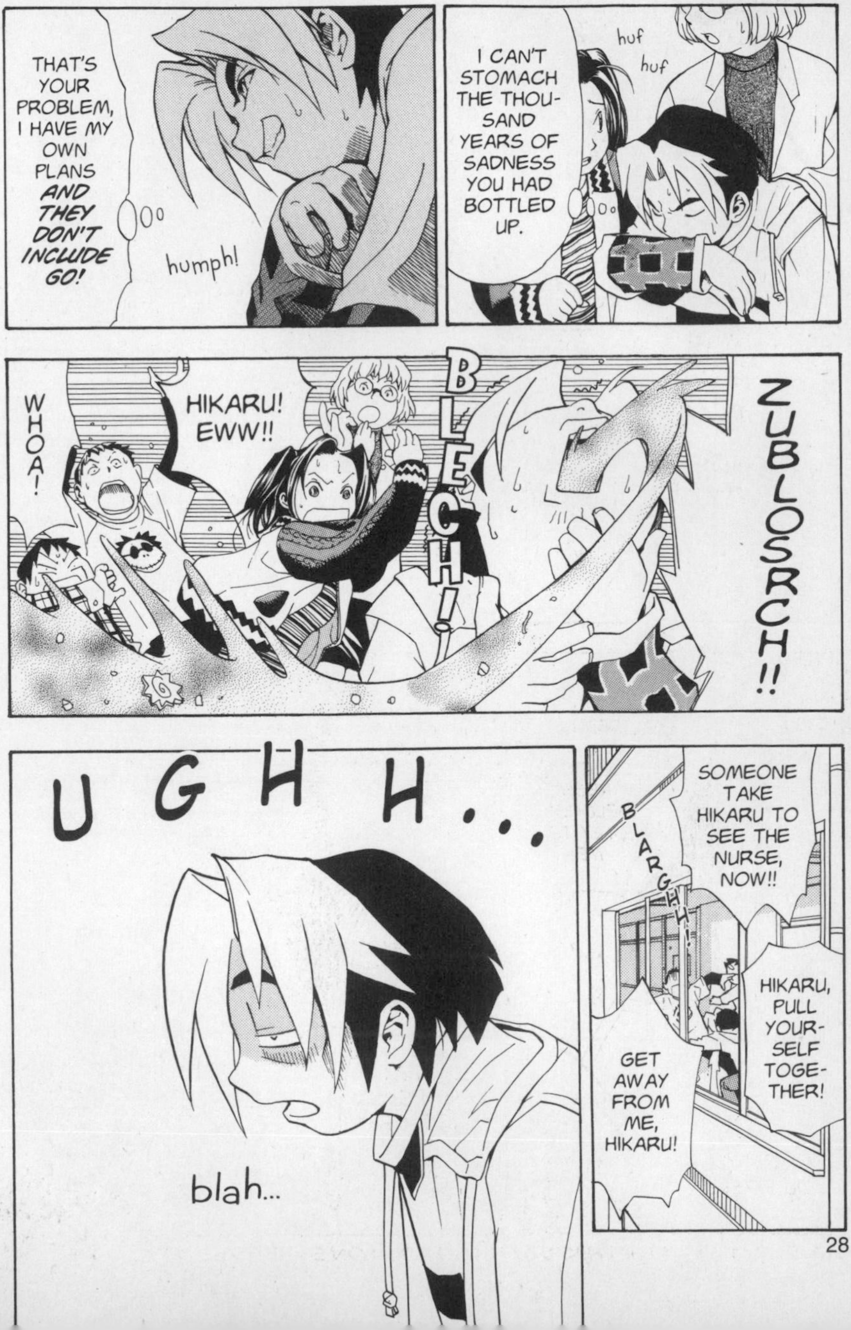

I CAN'T STOMACH THE THOUSAND YEARS OF SADNESS YOU HAD BOTTLED UP.
huf
huf
THAT'S YOUR PROBLEM, I HAVE MY OWN PLANS AND THEY DON'T INCLUDE GO!
humph!
ZUBLOSRCH!!
BLECH!
HIKARU! EWW!!
WHOA!
SOMEONE TAKE HIKARU TO SEE THE NURSE, NOW!!
BLARGHH!
HIKARU, PULL YOURSELF TOGETHER!
GET AWAY FROM ME, HIKARU!
UGHH...
blah...

READ THIS WAY

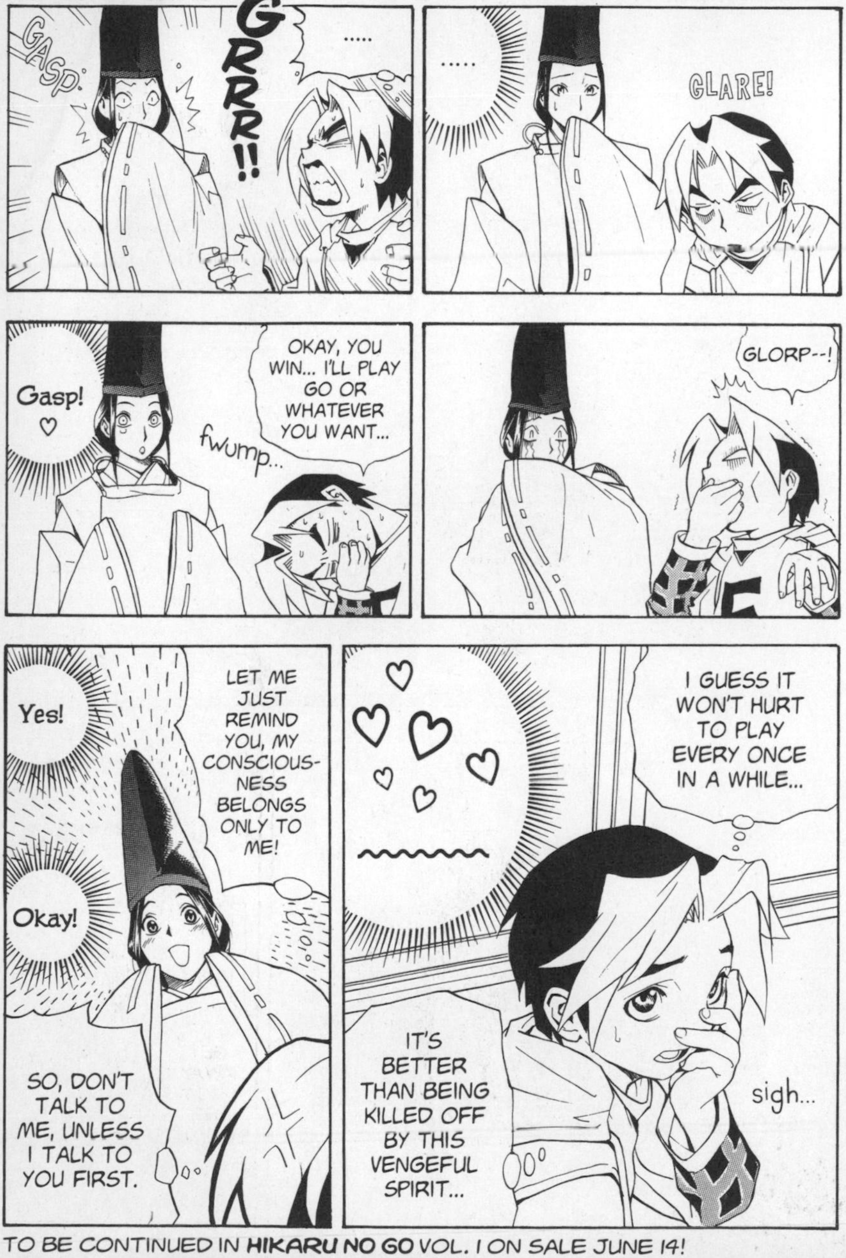
.....
GLARE!
.....
GASp
GRRR!!
OKAY, YOU WIN... I'LL PLAY GO OR WHATEVER YOU WANT...
GLORP--!
Gasp! ♡
fwump...
I GUESS IT WON'T HURT TO PLAY EVERY ONCE IN A WHILE...
IT'S BETTER THAN BEING KILLED OFF BY THIS VENGEFUL SPIRIT...
sigh...
LET ME JUST REMIND YOU, MY CONSCIOUSNESS BELONGS ONLY TO ME!
Yes!
Okay!
SO, DON'T TALK TO ME, UNLESS I TALK TO YOU FIRST.

TO BE CONTINUED IN **HIKARU NO GO** VOL. 1 ON SALE JUNE 14!

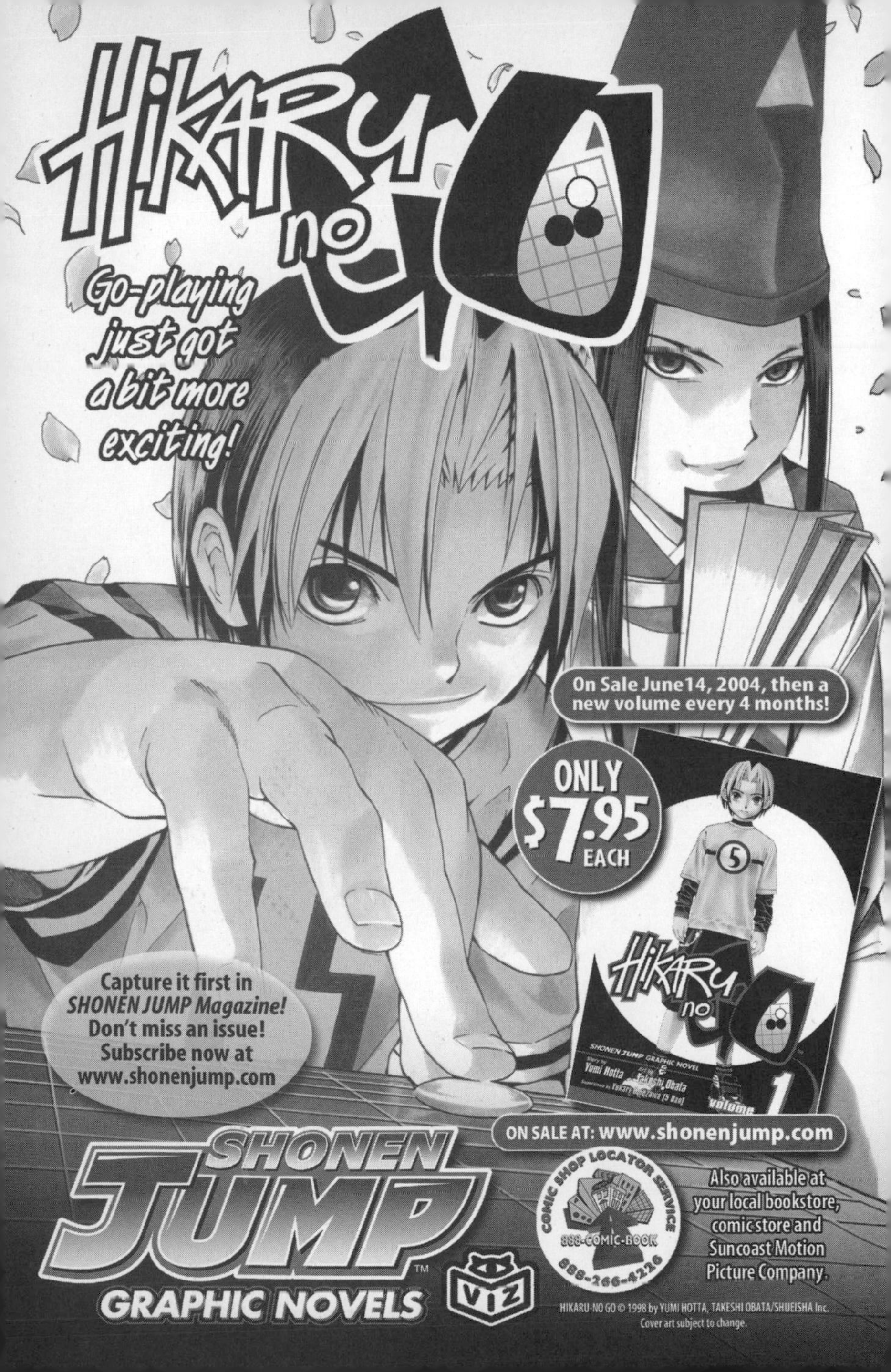
HIKARU no GO
Go-playing just got a bit more exciting!
On Sale June14, 2004, then a new volume every 4 months!
ONLY $7.95 EACH
HIKARU no GO
SHONEN JUMP GRAPHIC NOVEL
5
volume 1
Capture it first in SHONEN JUMP Magazine! Don't miss an issue! Subscribe now at www.shonenjump.com
ON SALE AT: www.shonenjump.com
SHONEN JUMP™
GRAPHIC NOVELS
VIZ
COMIC SHOP LOCATOR SERVICE
888-COMIC-BOOK
888-266-4226
Also available at your local bookstore, comic store and Suncoast Motion Picture Company.
HIKARU-NO GO © 1998 by YUMI HOTTA, TAKESHI OBATA/SHUEISHA Inc.
Cover art subject to change.

# Act 1 — Kenshin • Himura Battōsai

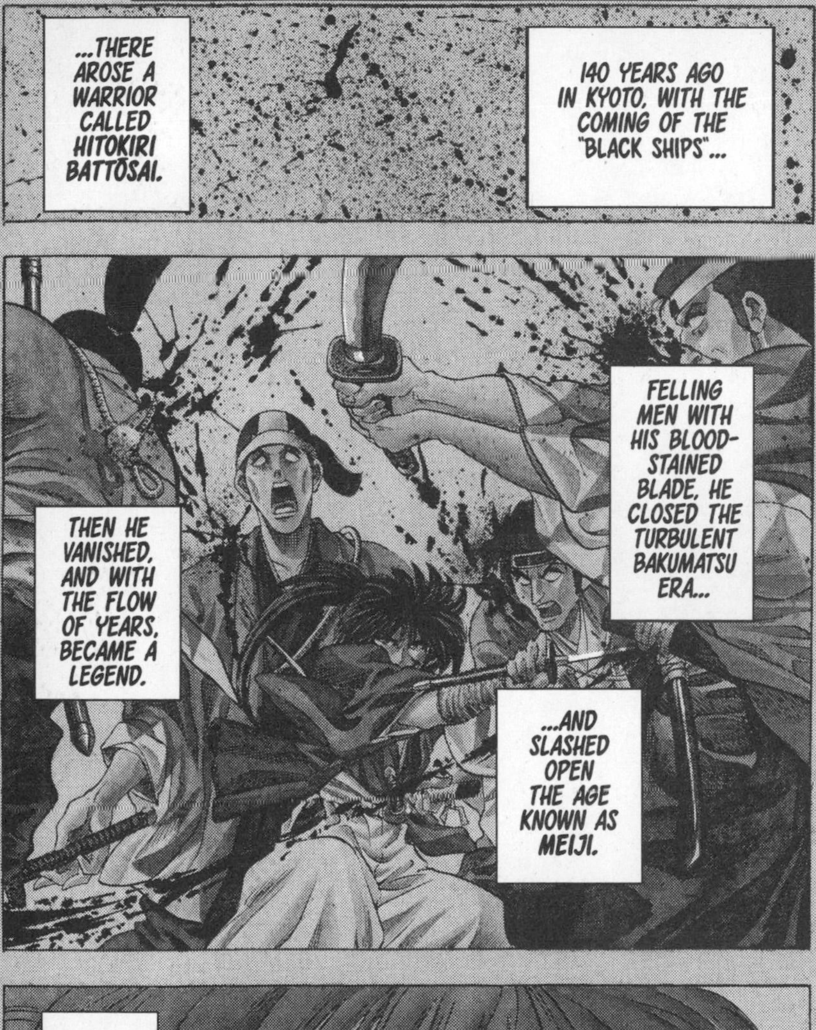
140 YEARS AGO IN KYOTO, WITH THE COMING OF THE "BLACK SHIPS"...
...THERE AROSE A WARRIOR CALLED HITOKIRI BATTŌSAI.
FELLING MEN WITH HIS BLOOD-STAINED BLADE, HE CLOSED THE TURBULENT BAKUMATSU ERA...
...AND SLASHED OPEN THE AGE KNOWN AS MEIJI.
THEN HE VANISHED, AND WITH THE FLOW OF YEARS, BECAME A LEGEND.
IN THE 11TH YEAR OF MEIJI, IN THE MIDDLE OF TOKYO...
...THIS TALE BEGINS...

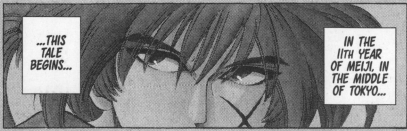

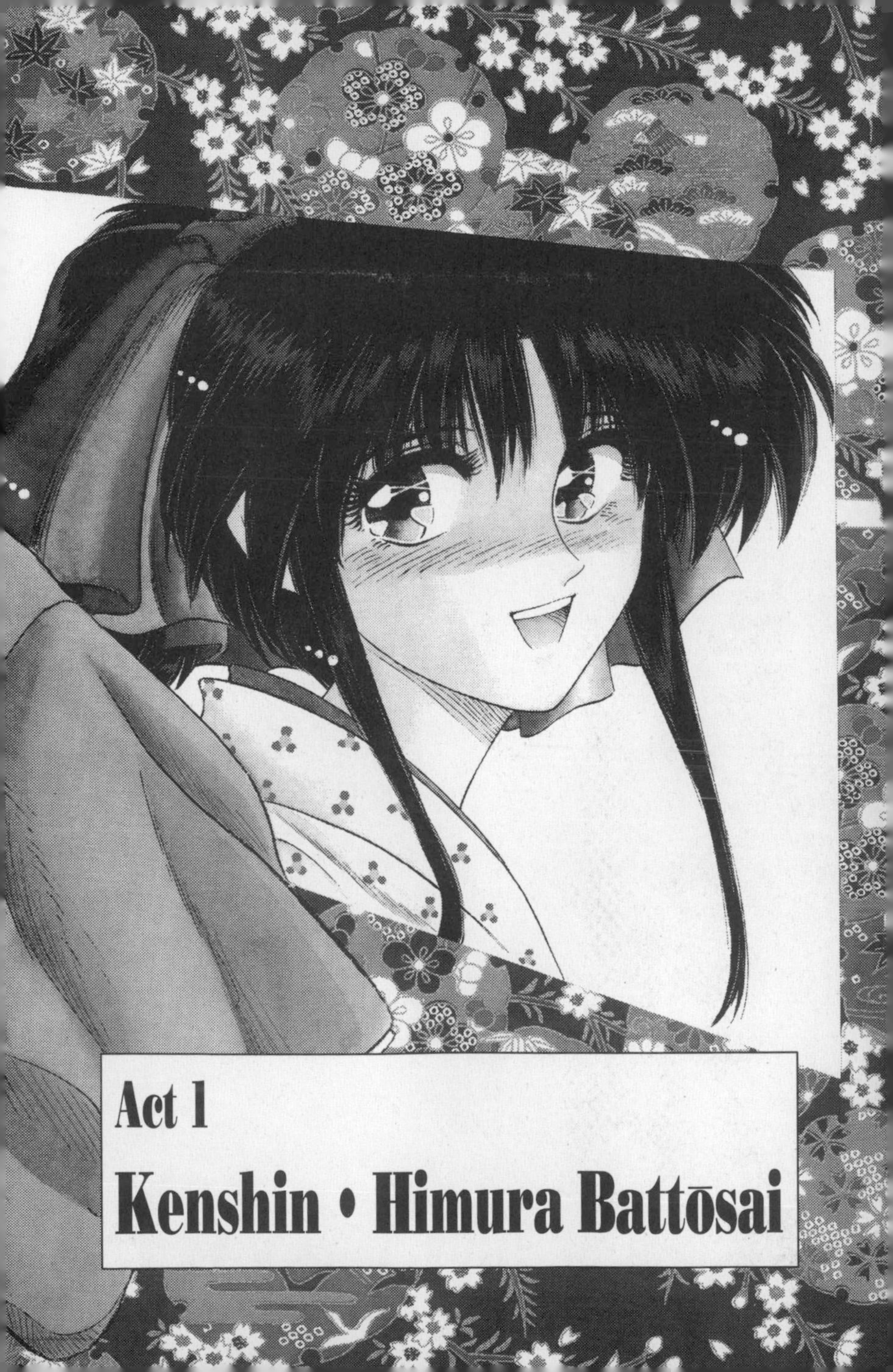

# Act 1
# Kenshin • Himura Battōsai

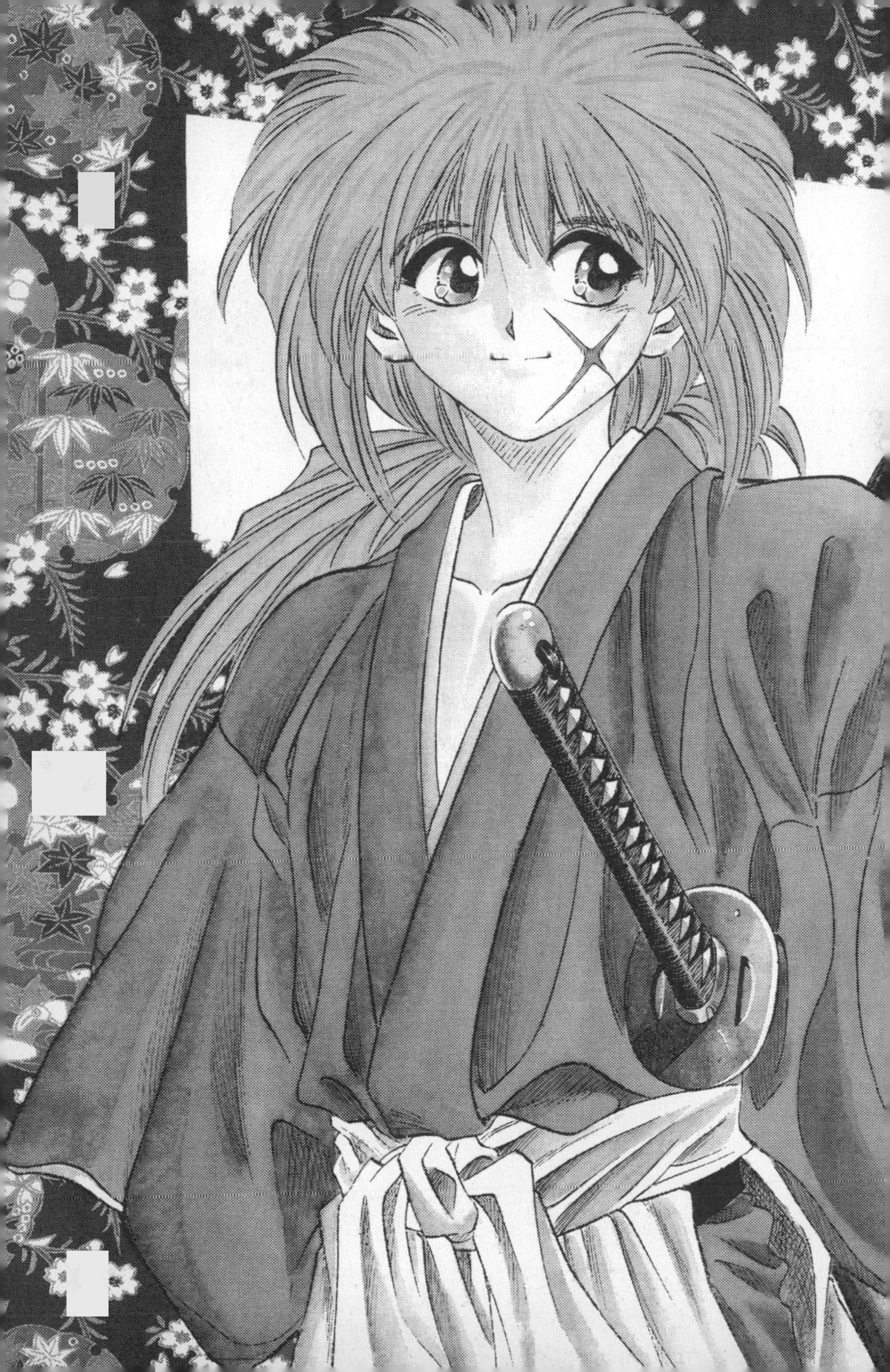

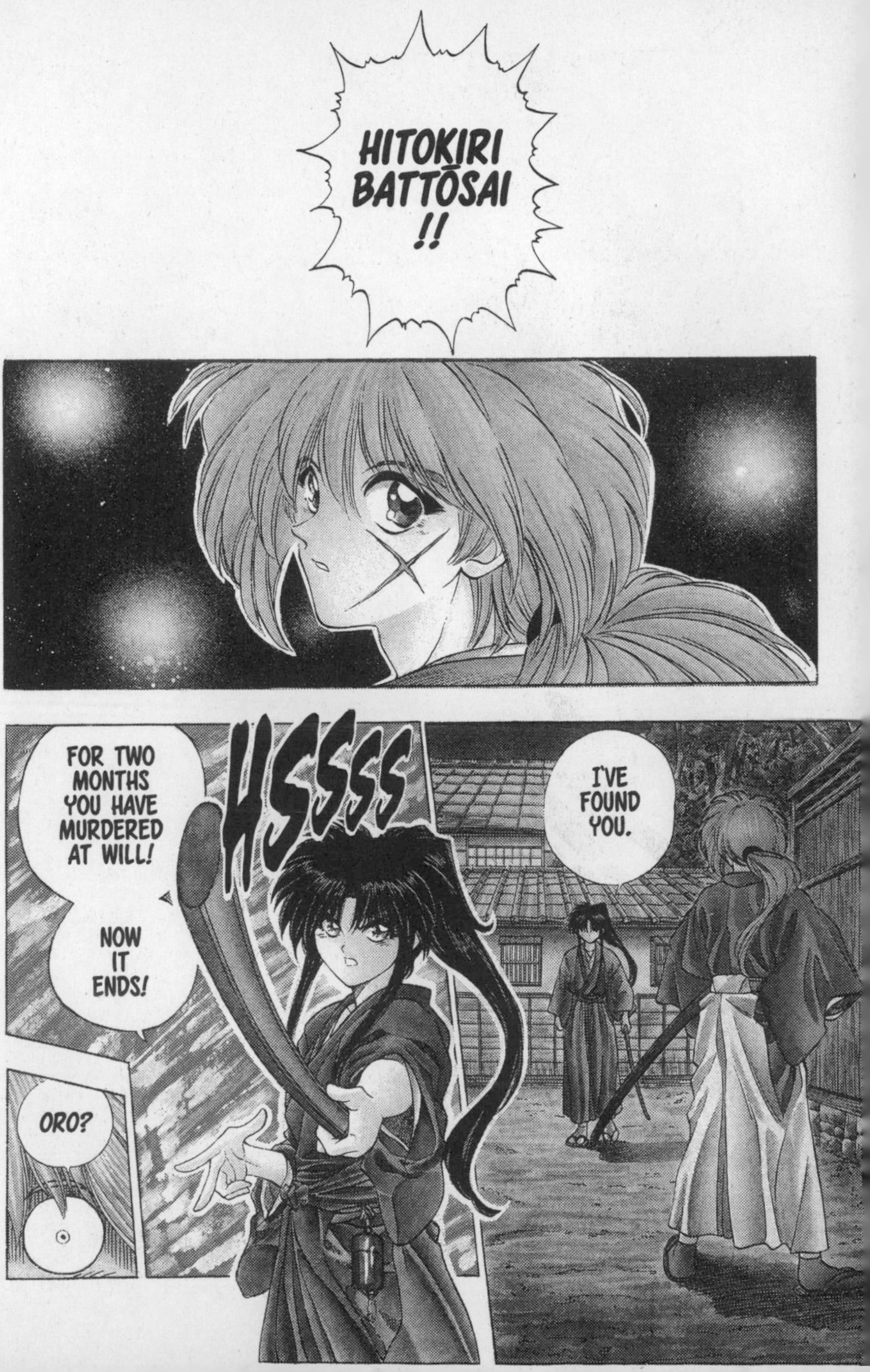
HITOKIRI BATTŌSAI !!
I'VE FOUND YOU.
HSSSS
FOR TWO MONTHS YOU HAVE MURDERED AT WILL!
NOW IT ENDS!
ORO?

READ THIS WAY

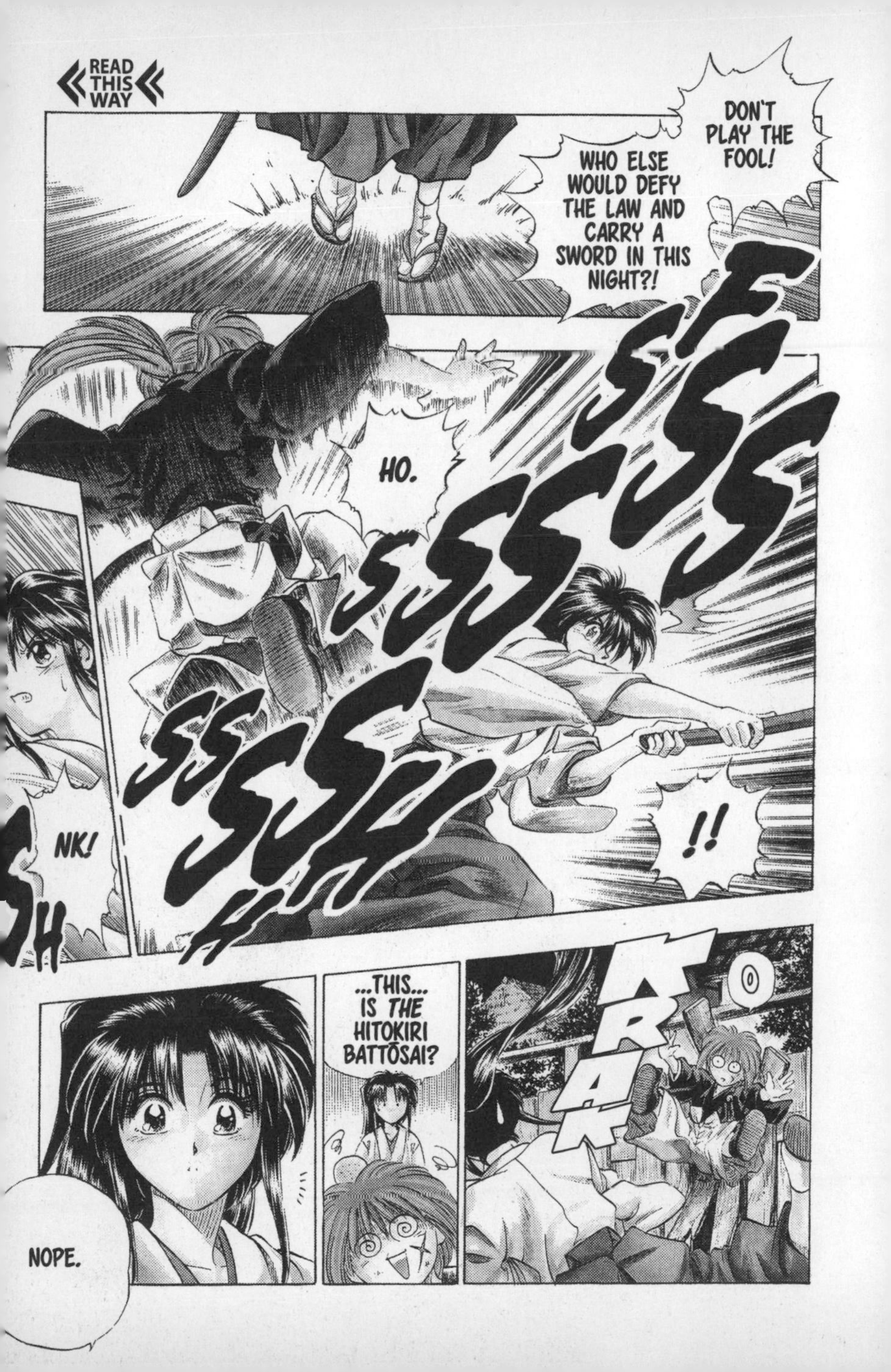

DON'T PLAY THE FOOL!
WHO ELSE WOULD DEFY THE LAW AND CARRY A SWORD IN THIS NIGHT?!
SSSSSSSSSSH
!!
HO.
NK!
SH
O
KRAK
...THIS... IS THE HITOKIRI BATTŌSAI?
NOPE.

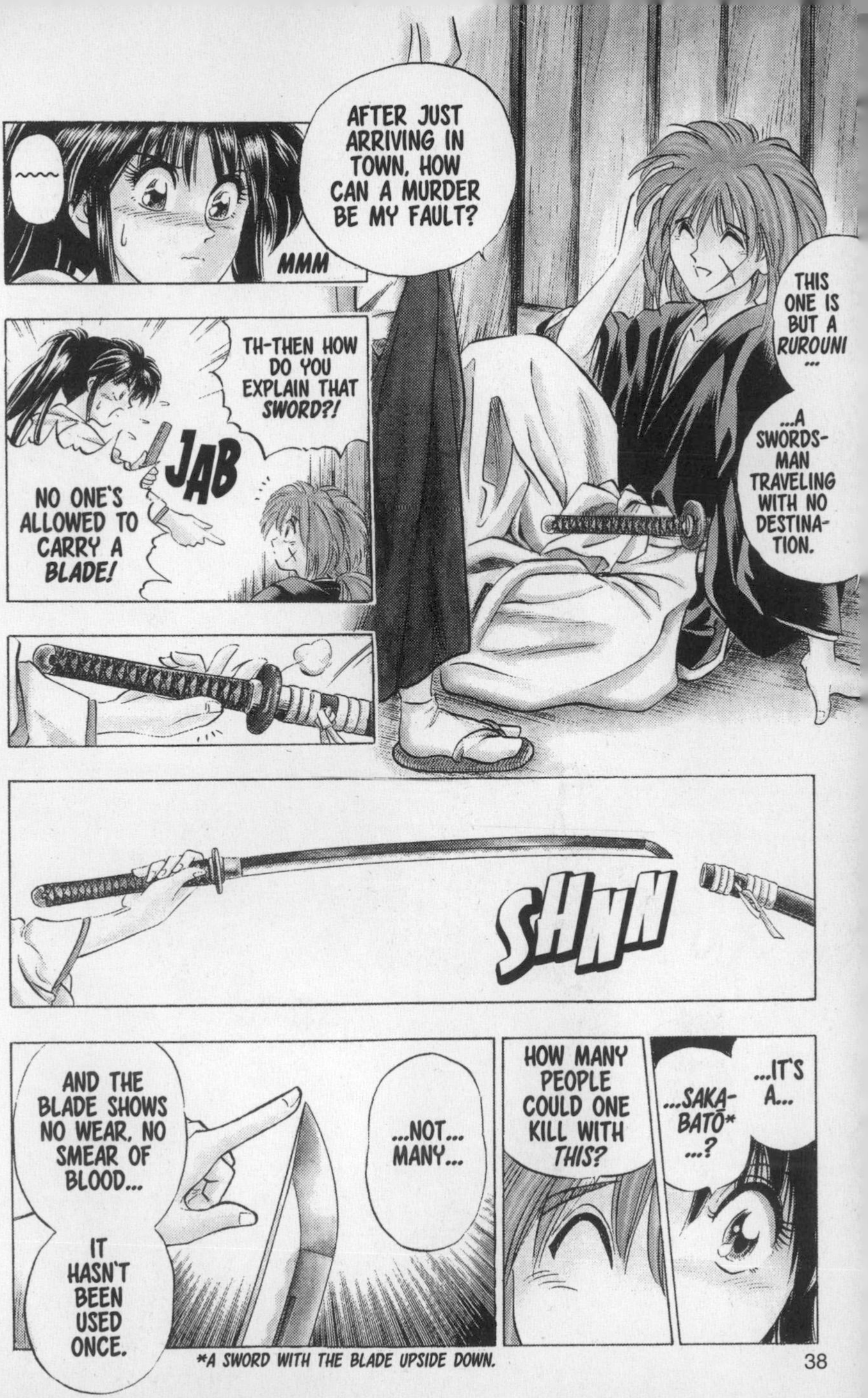
AFTER JUST ARRIVING IN TOWN, HOW CAN A MURDER BE MY FAULT?
THIS ONE IS BUT A RUROUNI ...
...A SWORDSMAN TRAVELING WITH NO DESTINATION.
~~~
MMM
TH-THEN HOW DO YOU EXPLAIN THAT SWORD?!
JAB
NO ONE'S ALLOWED TO CARRY A BLADE!
SHNN
...IT'S A...
...SAKABATŌ* ...?
HOW MANY PEOPLE COULD ONE KILL WITH THIS?
...NOT... MANY...
AND THE BLADE SHOWS NO WEAR, NO SMEAR OF BLOOD...
IT HASN'T BEEN USED ONCE.

*A SWORD WITH THE BLADE UPSIDE DOWN.
~~~

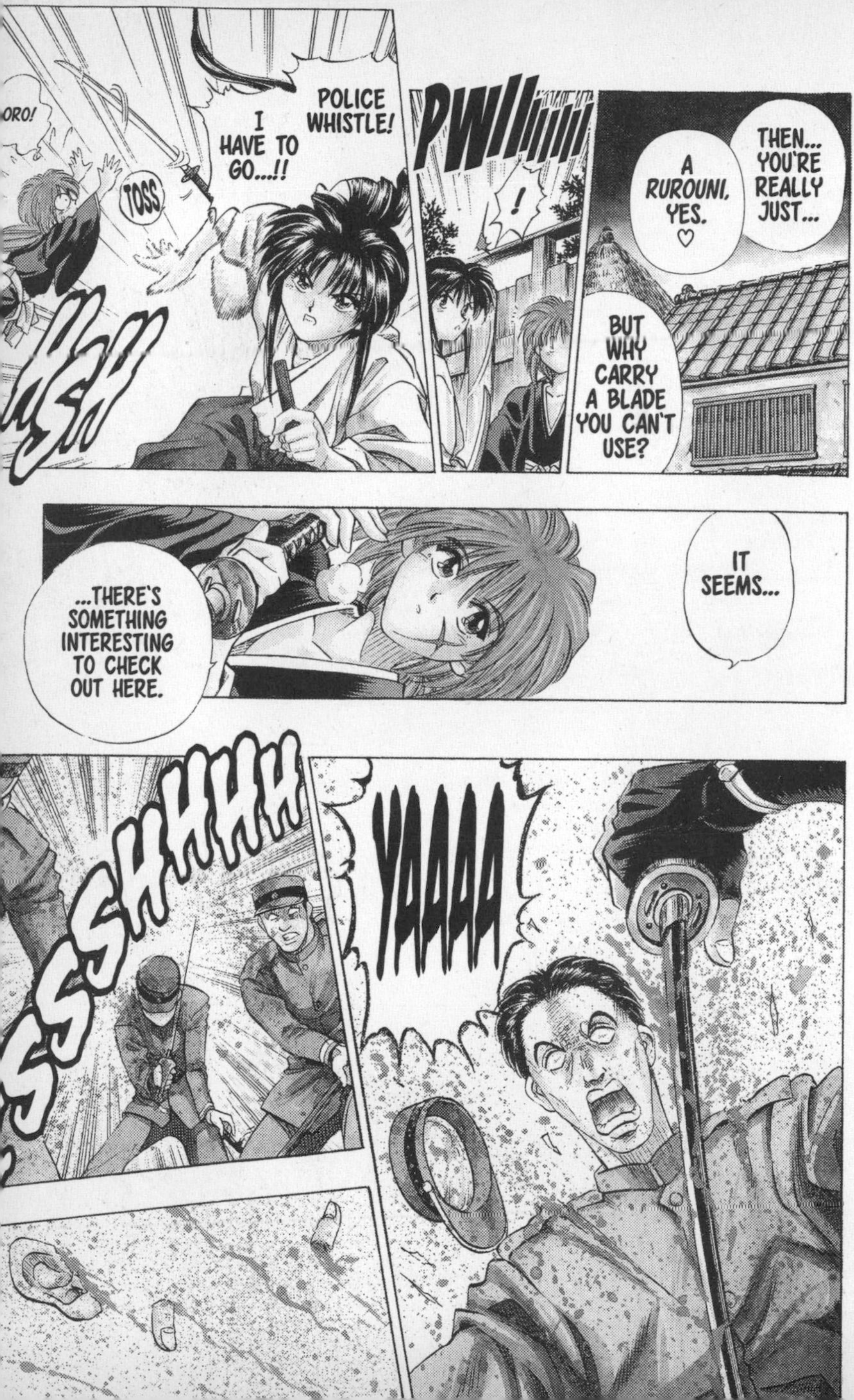
THEN... YOU'RE REALLY JUST...
A RUROUNI, YES. ♡
BUT WHY CARRY A BLADE YOU CAN'T USE?
PWIIiiiiii
!
POLICE WHISTLE!
I HAVE TO GO...!!
TOSS
ORO!
IT SEEMS...
...THERE'S SOMETHING INTERESTING TO CHECK OUT HERE.
YAAAA
SSSHHHH

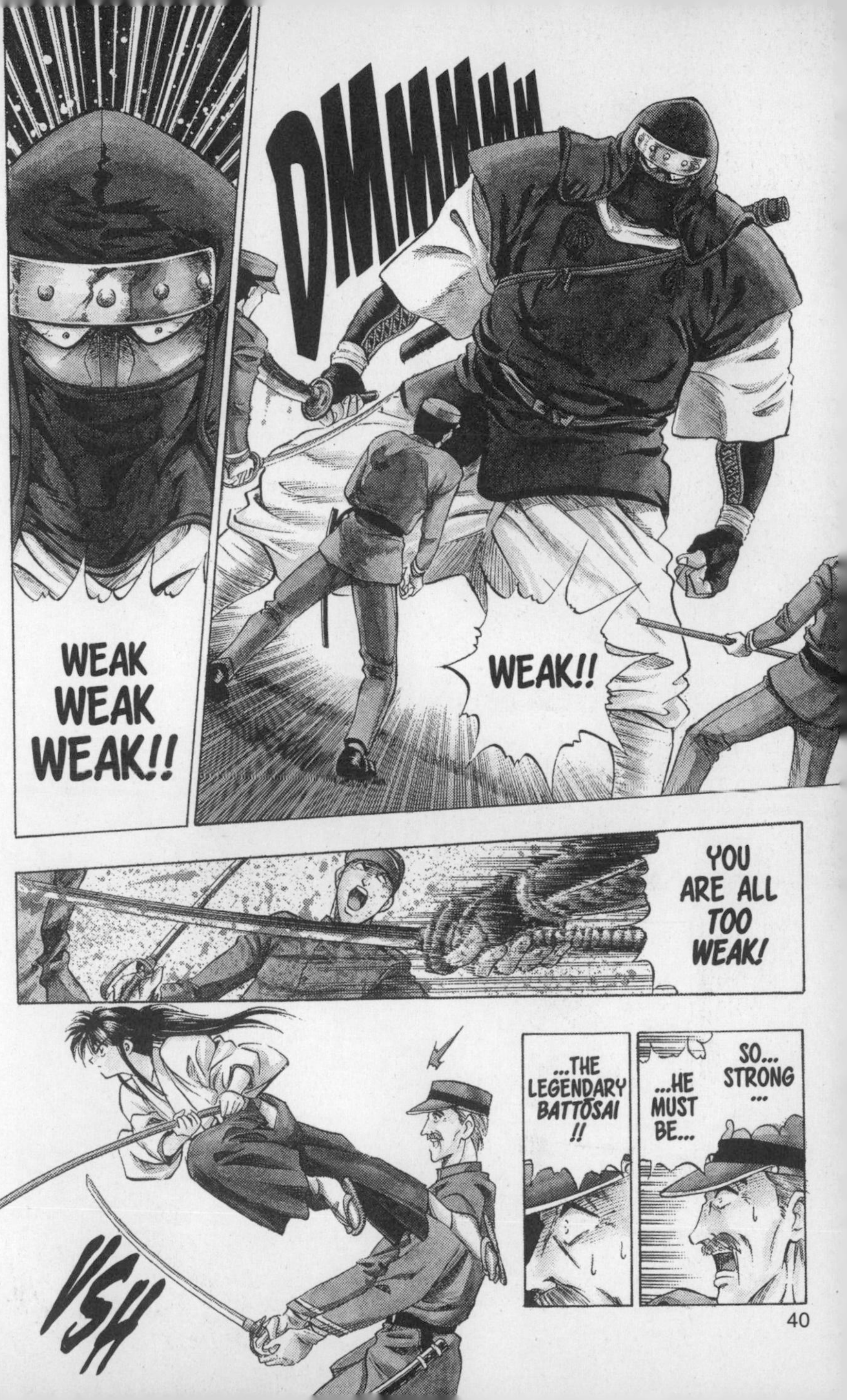
DMMMMM
WEAK!!
WEAK WEAK WEAK!!
YOU ARE ALL TOO WEAK!
SO... STRONG ...
...HE MUST BE...
...THE LEGENDARY BATTŌSAI !!
VSH

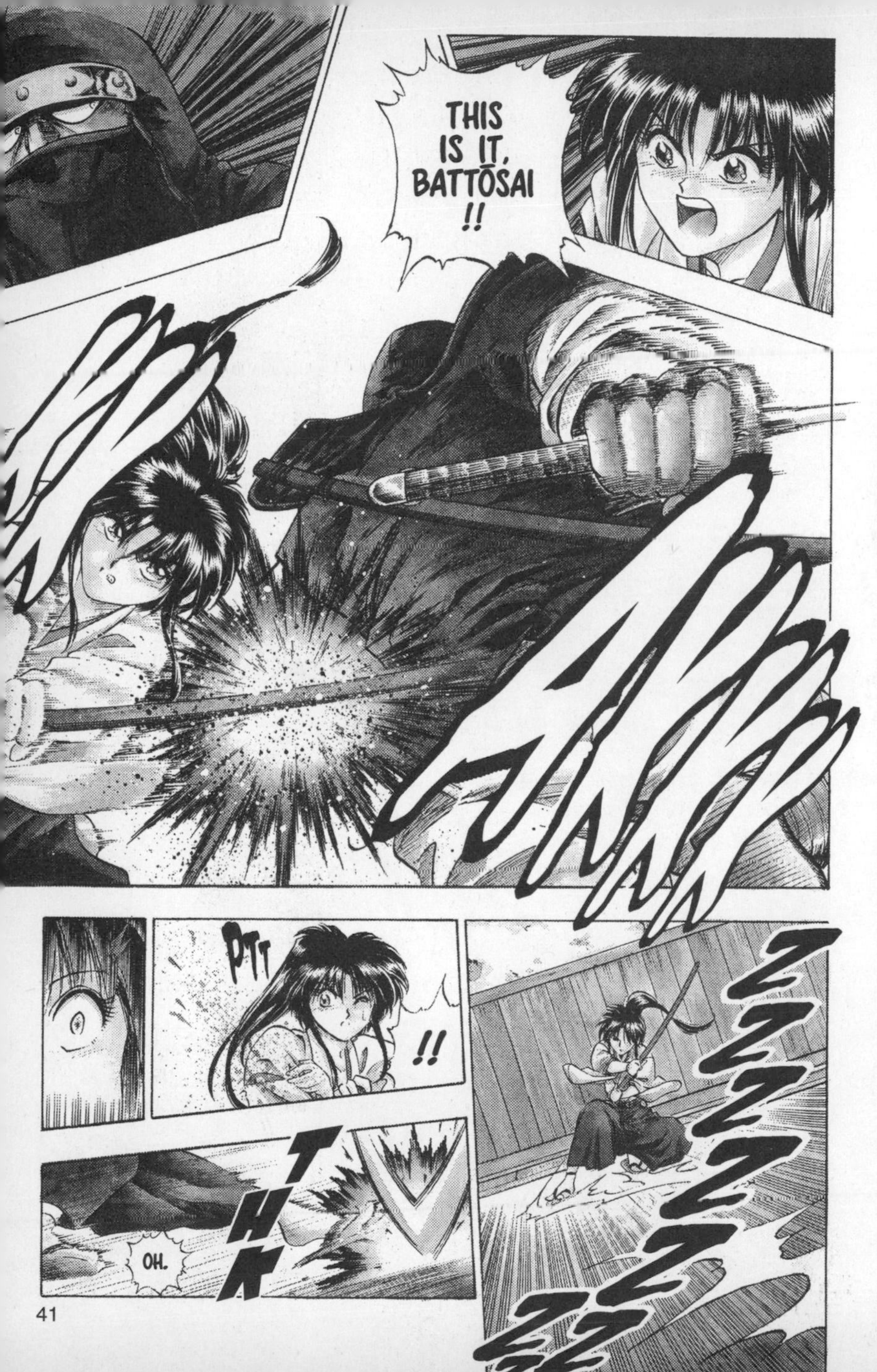
THIS IS IT, BATTŌSAI!!
PTT
!!
THK
OH.

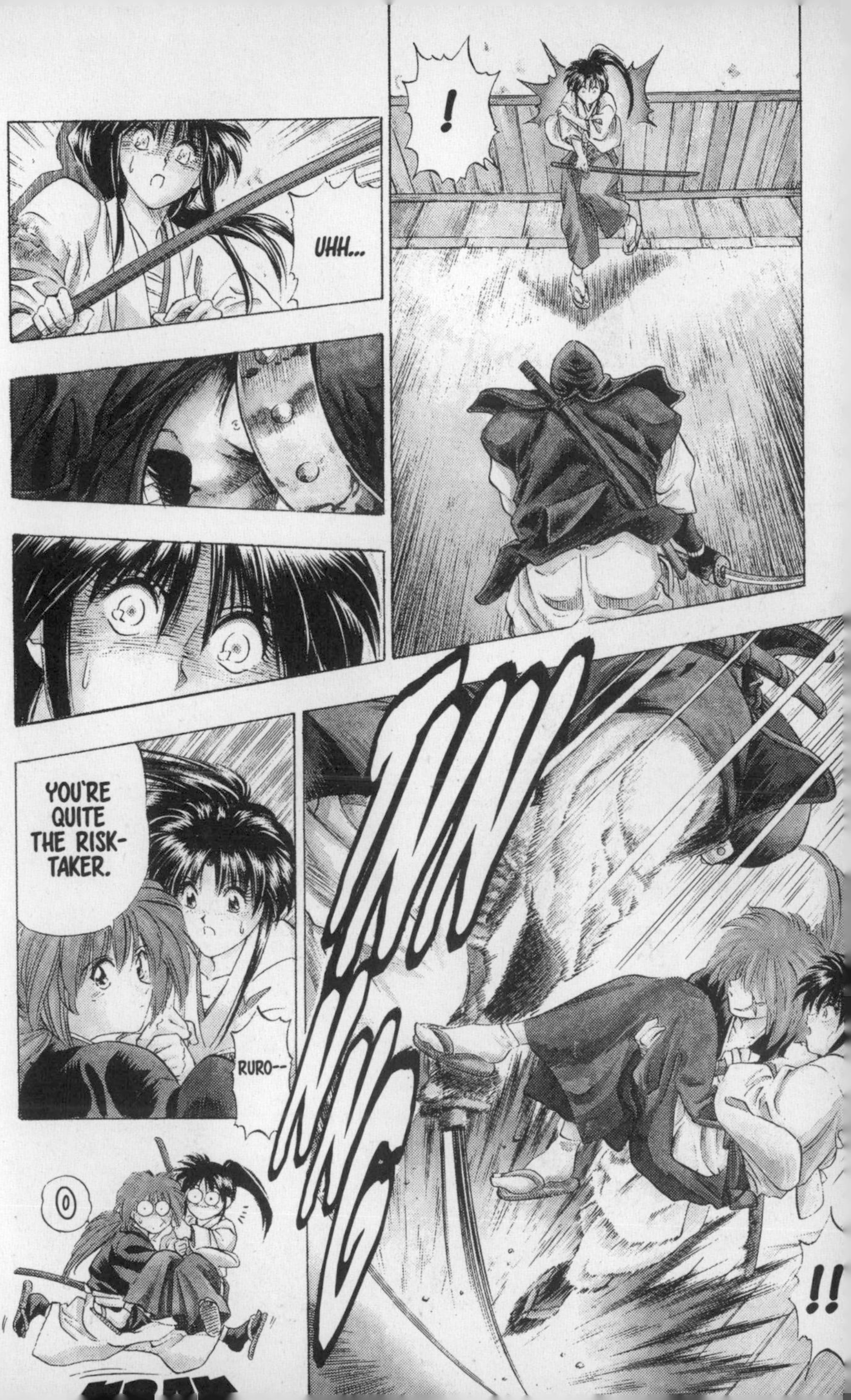
!
UHH...
!!
YOU'RE QUITE THE RISK-TAKER.
RURO--

READ THIS WAY

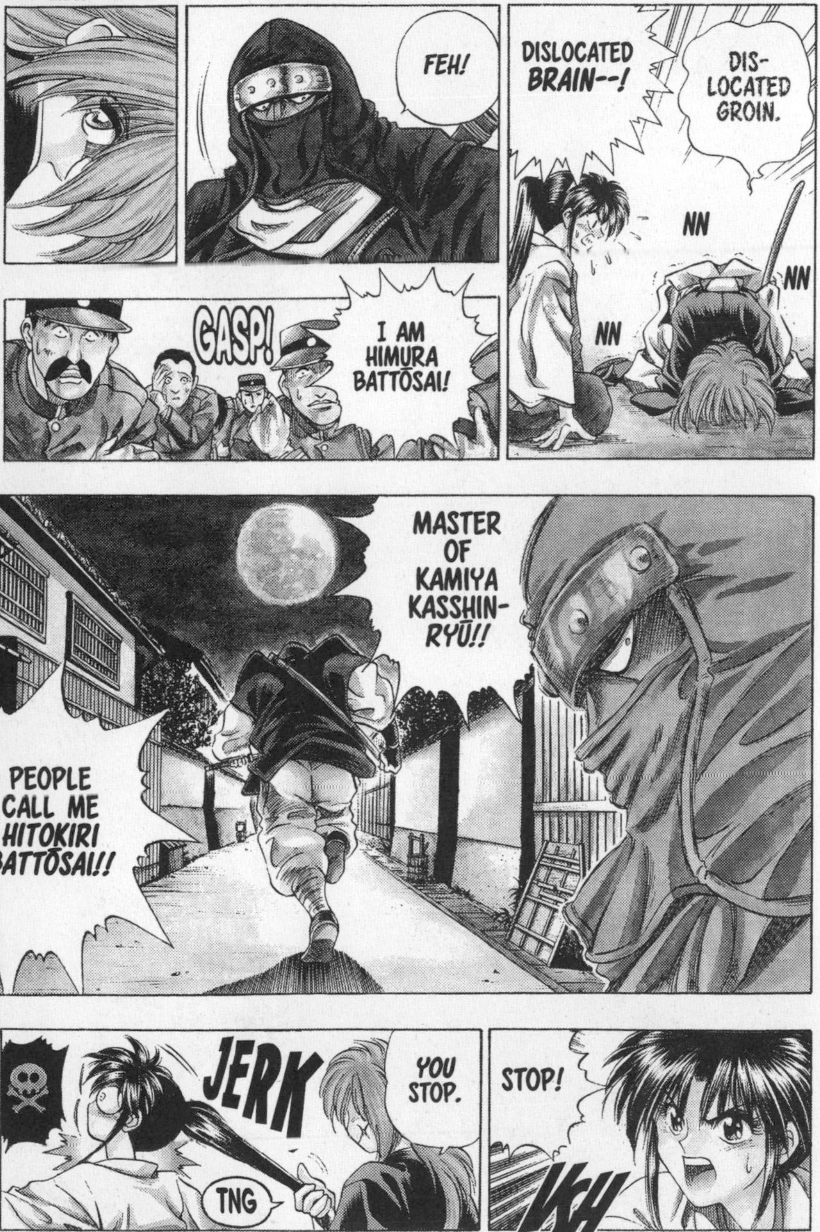
DIS-
LOCATED
GROIN.
DISLOCATED
BRAIN--!
NN
NN
NN
FEH!
I AM
HIMURA
BATTŌSAI!
GASP!
MASTER
OF
KAMIYA
KASSHIN-
RYŪ!!
PEOPLE
CALL ME
HITOKIRI
BATTŌSAI!!
STOP!
VSH
YOU
STOP.
JERK
TNG

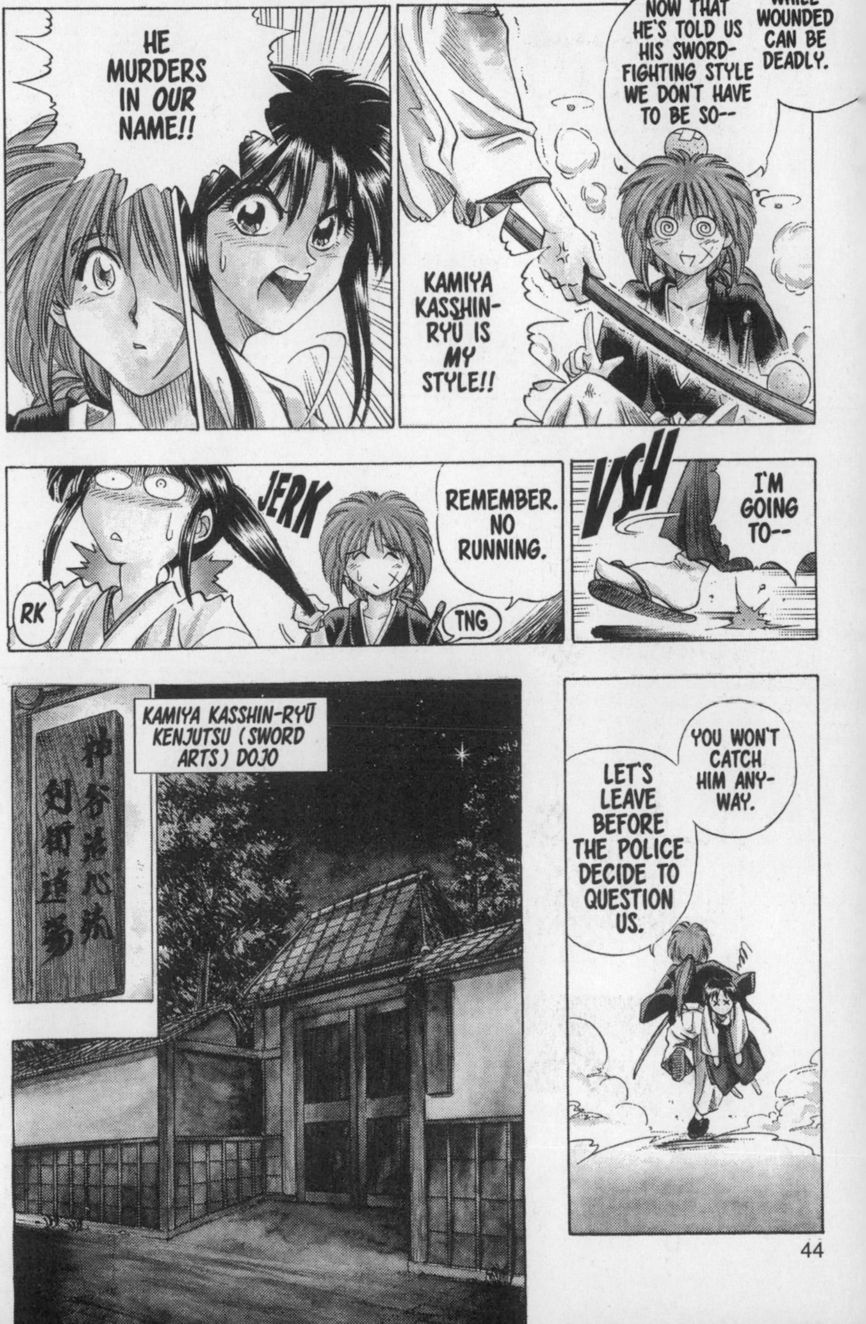
RUNNING WHILE WOUNDED CAN BE DEADLY.
NOW THAT HE'S TOLD US HIS SWORD-FIGHTING STYLE WE DON'T HAVE TO BE SO--
KAMIYA KASSHIN-RYŪ IS MY STYLE!!
HE MURDERS IN OUR NAME!!
VSH
I'M GOING TO--
JERK
REMEMBER. NO RUNNING.
TNG
RK
YOU WON'T CATCH HIM ANYWAY.
LET'S LEAVE BEFORE THE POLICE DECIDE TO QUESTION US.
KAMIYA KASSHIN-RYŪ KENJUTSU (SWORD ARTS) DOJO
神谷活心流
剣術道場

READ THIS WAY

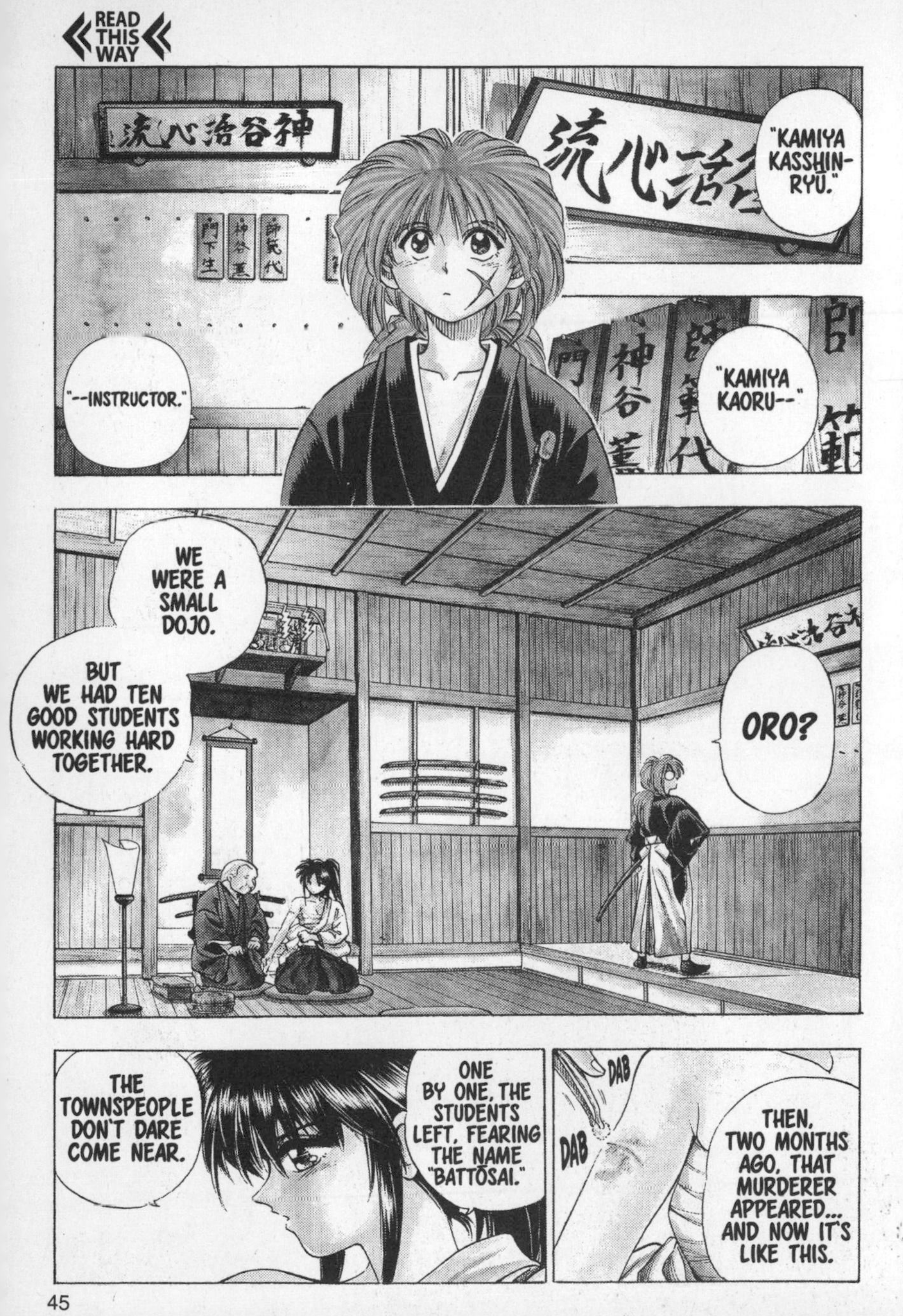

"KAMIYA KASSHIN-RYU."
"KAMIYA KAORU--"
"--INSTRUCTOR."
ORO?
WE WERE A SMALL DOJO.
BUT WE HAD TEN GOOD STUDENTS WORKING HARD TOGETHER.
DAB
DAB
THEN, TWO MONTHS AGO, THAT MURDERER APPEARED... AND NOW IT'S LIKE THIS.
ONE BY ONE, THE STUDENTS LEFT, FEARING THE NAME "BATTŌSAI."
THE TOWNSPEOPLE DON'T DARE COME NEAR.

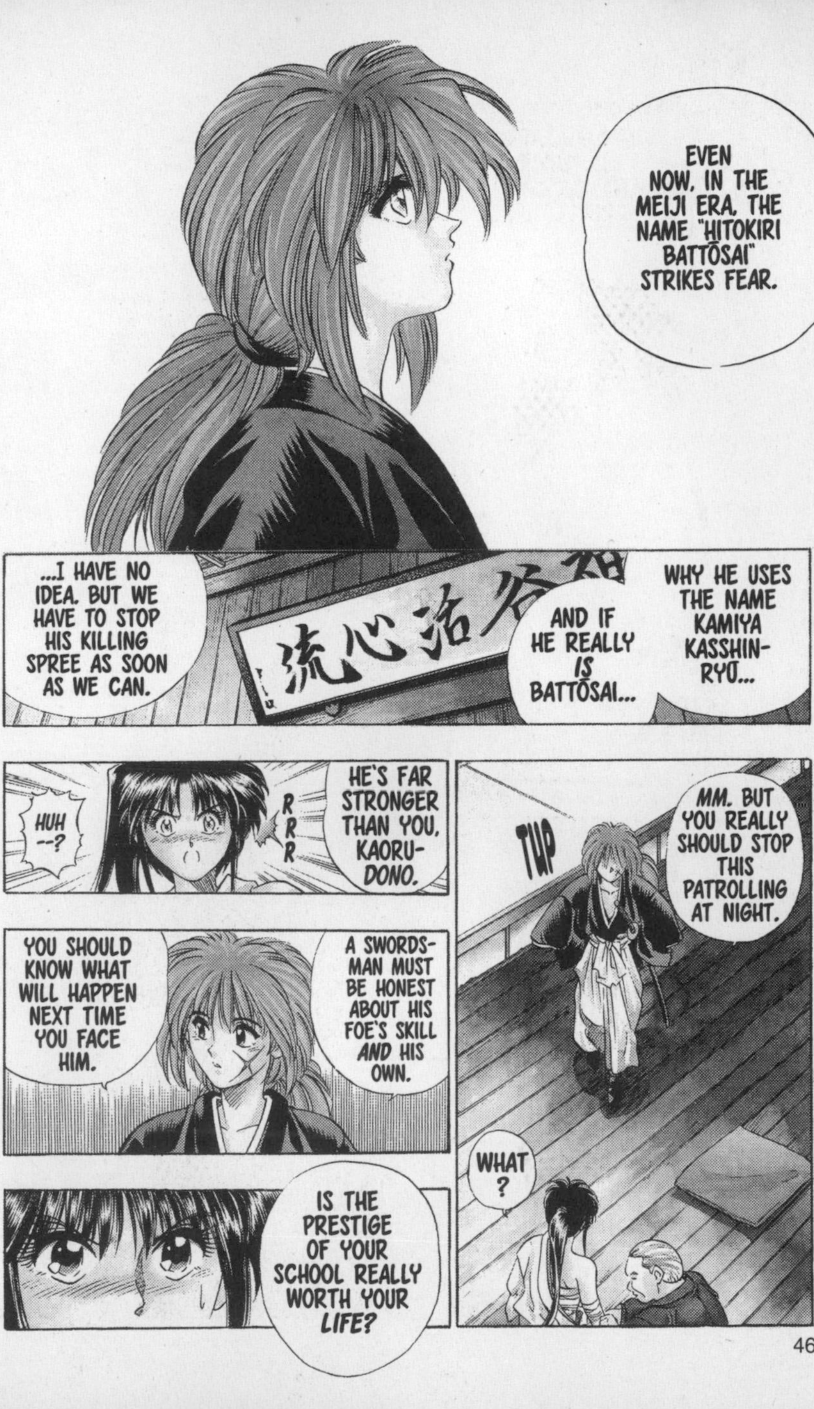
EVEN NOW, IN THE MEIJI ERA, THE NAME "HITOKIRI BATTŌSAI" STRIKES FEAR.
WHY HE USES THE NAME KAMIYA KASSHIN-RYŪ...
AND IF HE REALLY *IS* BATTŌSAI...
...I HAVE NO IDEA. BUT WE HAVE TO STOP HIS KILLING SPREE AS SOON AS WE CAN.
*MM.* BUT YOU REALLY SHOULD STOP THIS PATROLLING AT NIGHT.
TUP
WHAT?
HE'S FAR STRONGER THAN YOU, KAORU-DONO.
RRR
HUH --?
A SWORDS-MAN MUST BE HONEST ABOUT HIS FOE'S SKILL *AND* HIS OWN.
YOU SHOULD KNOW WHAT WILL HAPPEN NEXT TIME YOU FACE HIM.
IS THE PRESTIGE OF YOUR SCHOOL REALLY WORTH YOUR *LIFE?*

READ THIS WAY

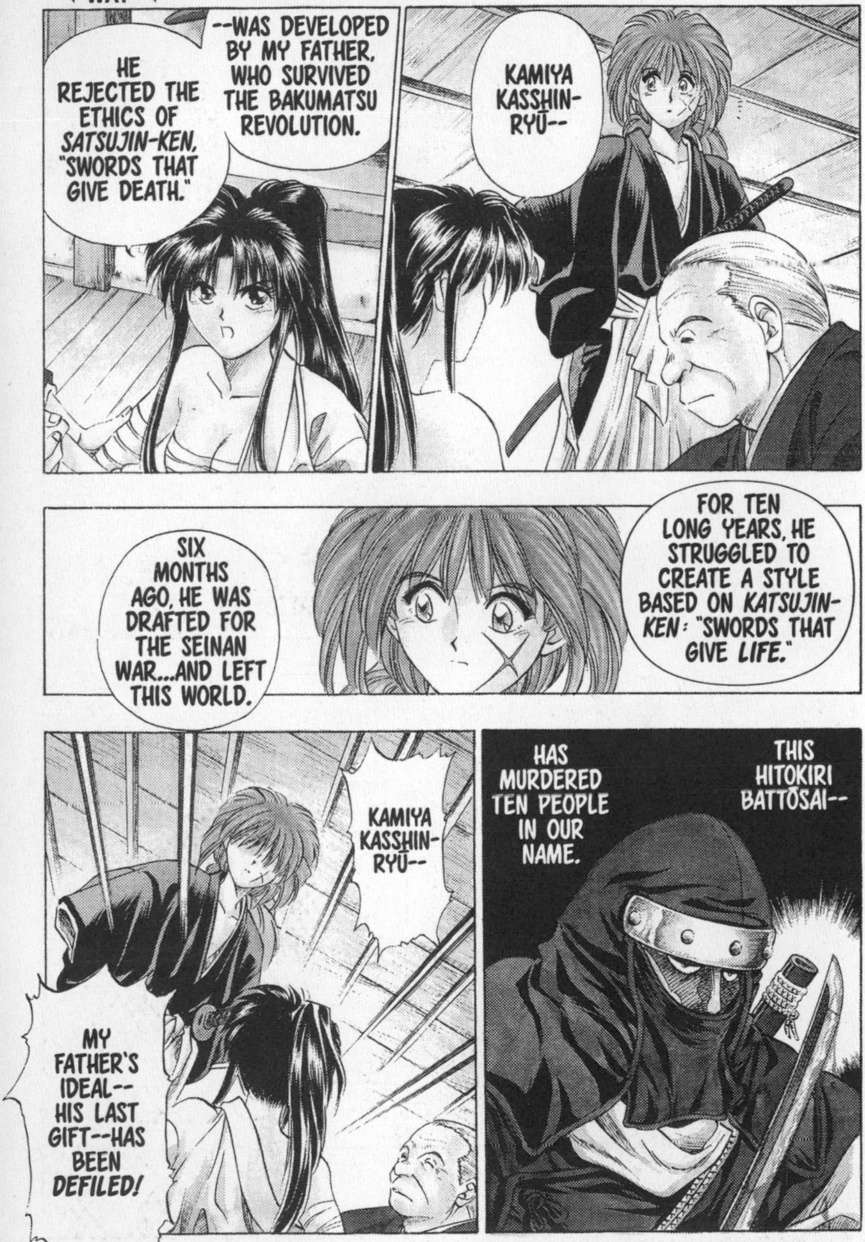

KAMIYA KASSHIN-RYŪ--
--WAS DEVELOPED BY MY FATHER, WHO SURVIVED THE BAKUMATSU REVOLUTION.
HE REJECTED THE ETHICS OF *SATSUJIN-KEN*, "SWORDS THAT GIVE DEATH."
FOR TEN LONG YEARS, HE STRUGGLED TO CREATE A STYLE BASED ON *KATSUJIN-KEN*: "SWORDS THAT GIVE *LIFE*."
SIX MONTHS AGO, HE WAS DRAFTED FOR THE SEINAN WAR...AND LEFT THIS WORLD.
THIS HITOKIRI BATTŌSAI--
HAS MURDERED TEN PEOPLE IN OUR NAME.
KAMIYA KASSHIN-RYŪ--
MY FATHER'S IDEAL--HIS LAST GIFT--HAS BEEN **DEFILED!**

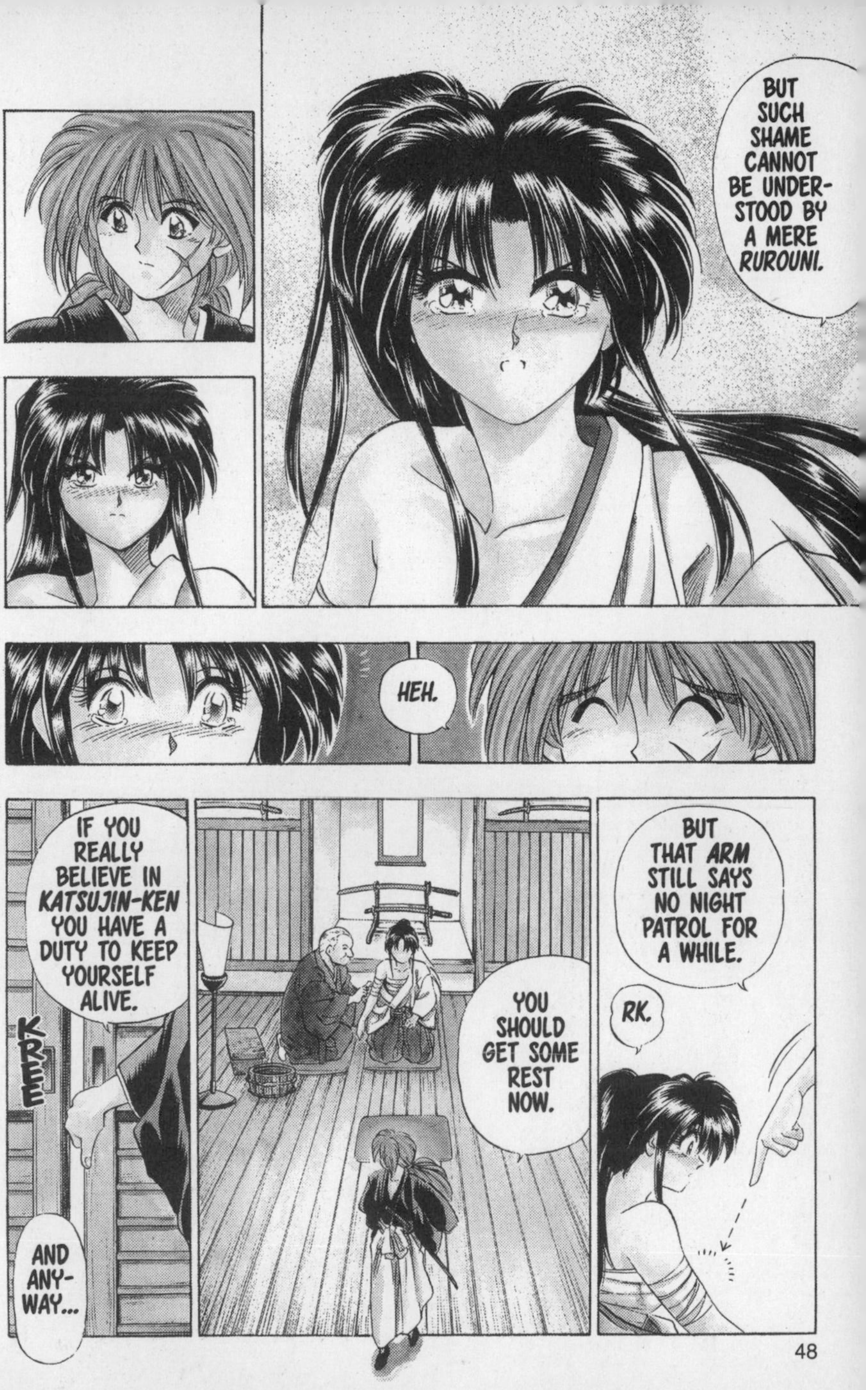
BUT SUCH SHAME CANNOT BE UNDER-STOOD BY A MERE *RUROUNI.*
HEH.
BUT THAT *ARM* STILL SAYS NO NIGHT PATROL FOR A WHILE.
RK.
YOU SHOULD GET SOME REST NOW.
IF YOU REALLY BELIEVE IN *KATSUJIN-KEN* YOU HAVE A DUTY TO KEEP YOURSELF ALIVE.
KREE
AND ANY-WAY...

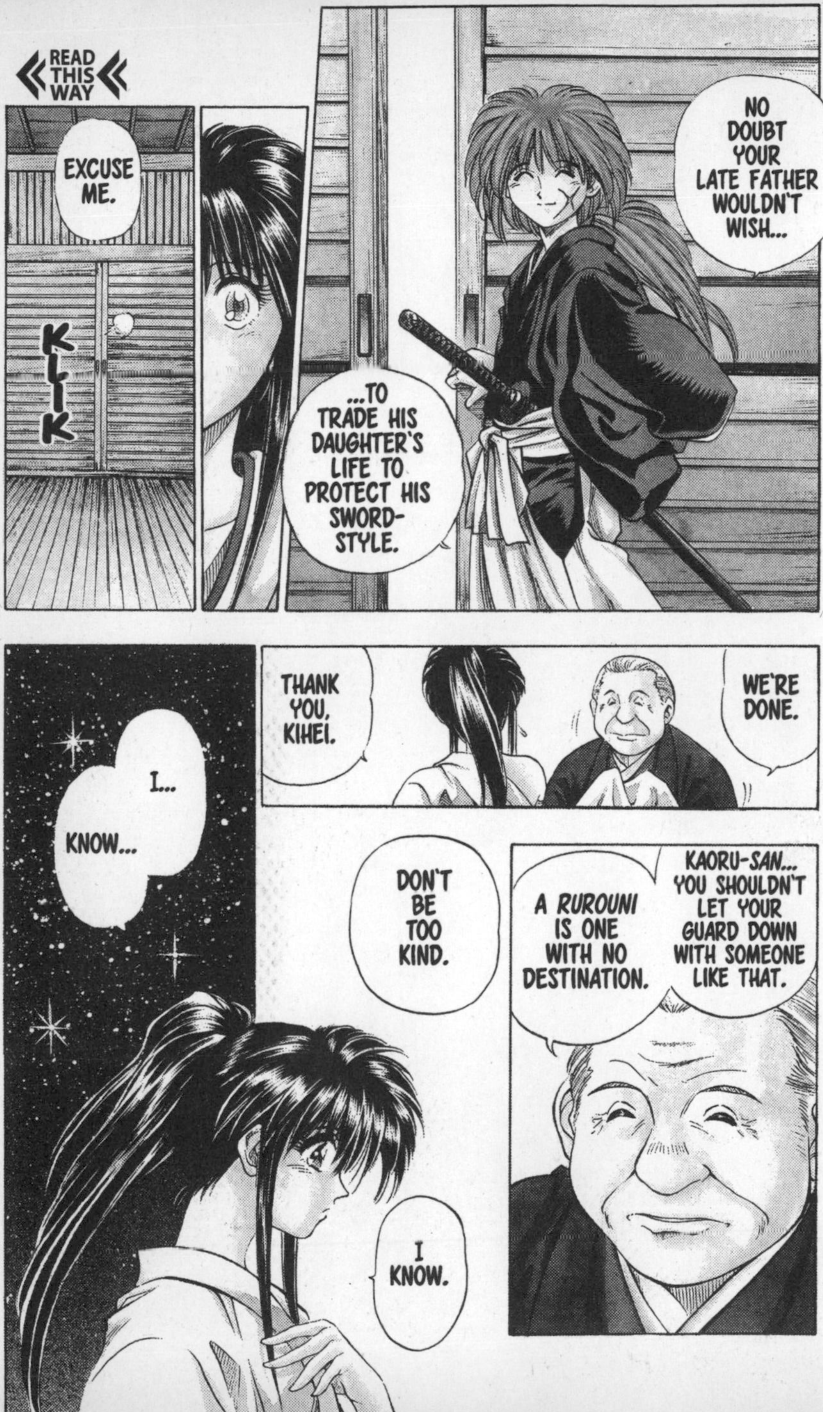
READ THIS WAY
NO DOUBT YOUR LATE FATHER WOULDN'T WISH...
...TO TRADE HIS DAUGHTER'S LIFE TO PROTECT HIS SWORD-STYLE.
EXCUSE ME.
KLIK
WE'RE DONE.
THANK YOU, KIHEI.
KAORU-SAN... YOU SHOULDN'T LET YOUR GUARD DOWN WITH SOMEONE LIKE THAT.
A *RUROUNI* IS ONE WITH NO DESTINATION.
DON'T BE TOO KIND.
I KNOW.
I... KNOW...

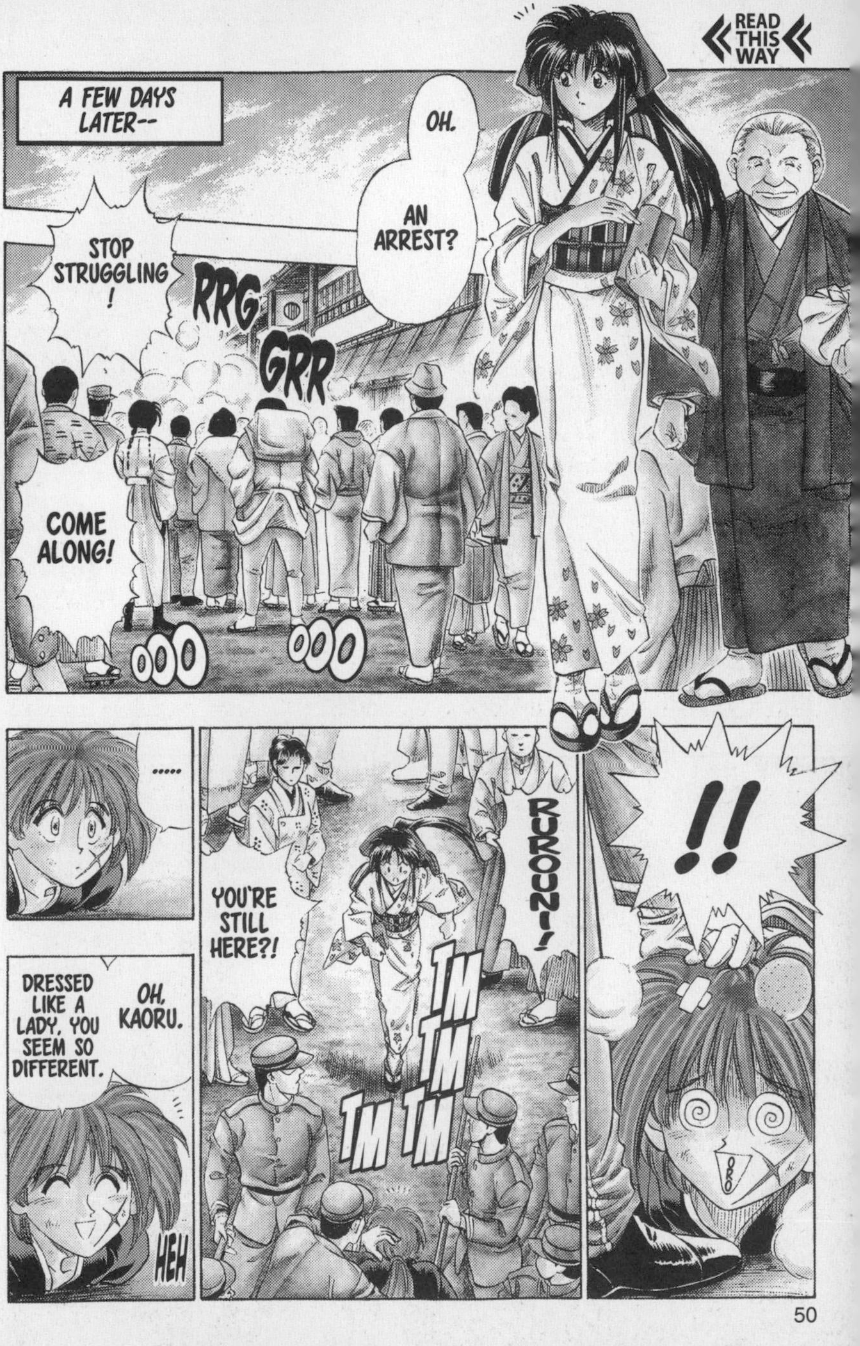
READ THIS WAY
A FEW DAYS LATER--
OH.
AN ARREST?
STOP STRUGGLING!
RRG
GRR
COME ALONG!
!!
ORO
RUROUNI!
YOU'RE STILL HERE?!
TM TM TM TM
.....
OH, KAORU.
DRESSED LIKE A LADY, YOU SEEM SO DIFFERENT.
HEH

READ THIS WAY

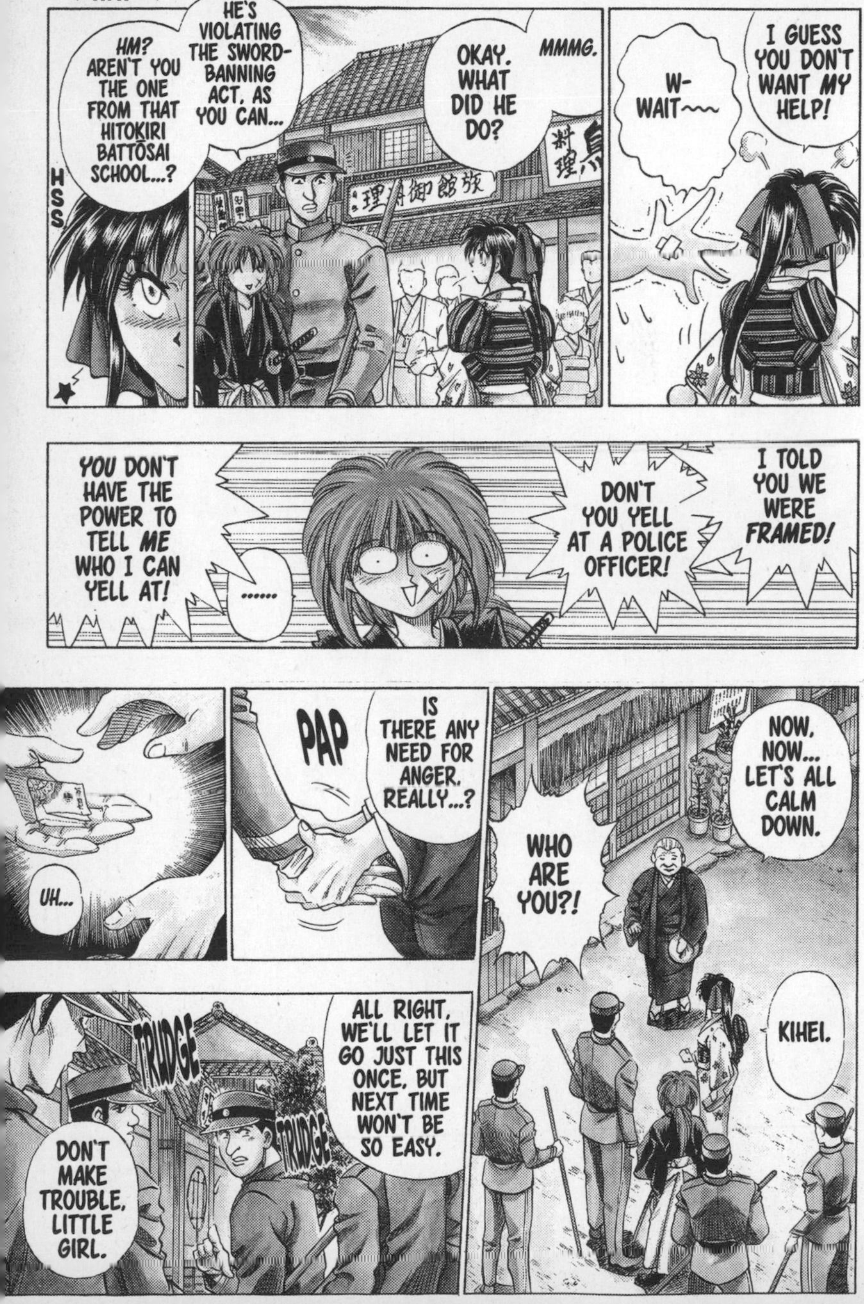
I GUESS YOU DON'T WANT *MY* HELP!
W- WAIT~~~
MMMG.
OKAY. WHAT DID HE DO?
HE'S VIOLATING THE SWORD-BANNING ACT, AS YOU CAN...
HM? AREN'T YOU THE ONE FROM THAT HITOKIRI BATTŌSAI SCHOOL...?
HSS
I TOLD YOU WE WERE *FRAMED!*
DON'T YOU YELL AT A POLICE OFFICER!
......
*YOU* DON'T HAVE THE POWER TO TELL *ME* WHO I CAN YELL AT!
NOW, NOW... LET'S ALL CALM DOWN.
WHO ARE YOU?!
KIHEI.
PAP
IS THERE ANY NEED FOR ANGER, REALLY...?
UH...
ALL RIGHT, WE'LL LET IT GO JUST THIS ONCE, BUT NEXT TIME WON'T BE SO EASY.
TRUDGE
TRUDGE
DON'T MAKE TROUBLE, LITTLE GIRL.

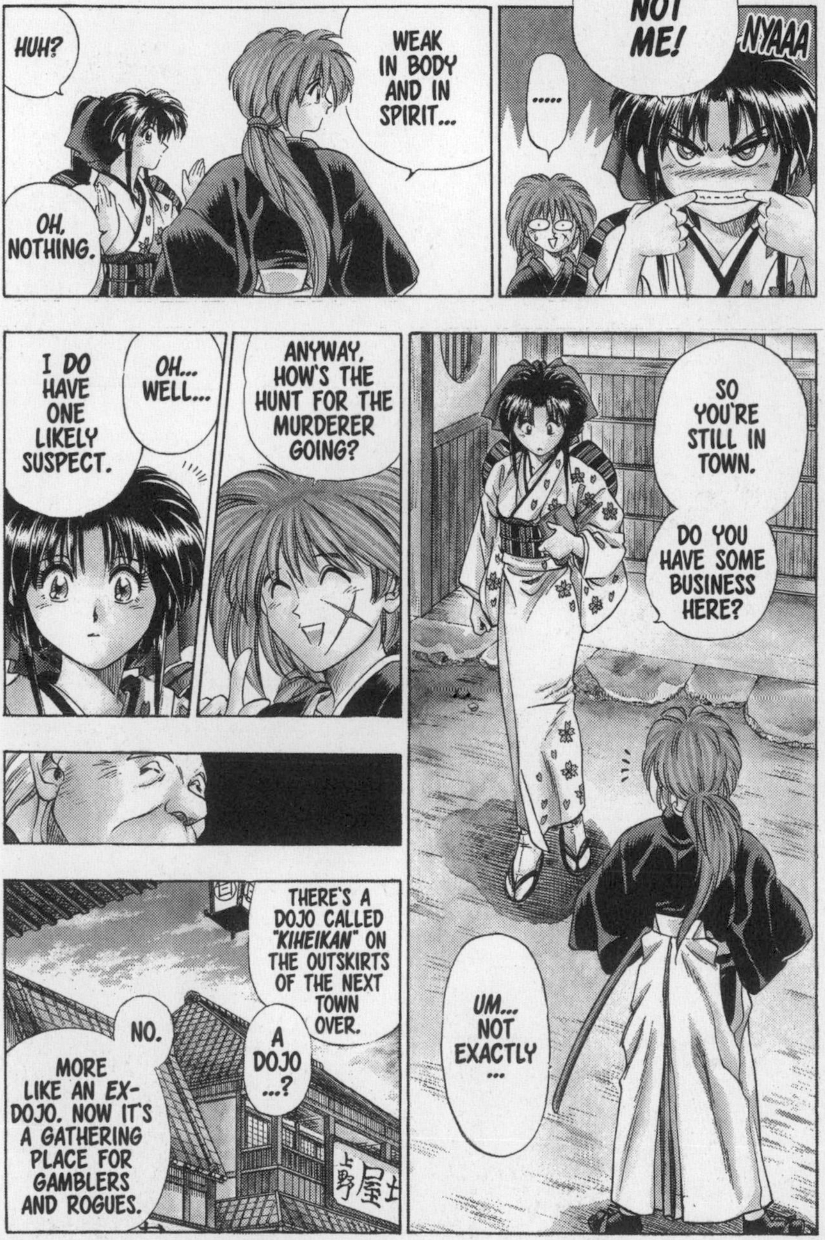
NYAAA
OH, NOT ME!
.....
WEAK IN BODY AND IN SPIRIT...
HUH?
OH, NOTHING.
SO YOU'RE STILL IN TOWN.
DO YOU HAVE SOME BUSINESS HERE?
UM... NOT EXACTLY ...
ANYWAY, HOW'S THE HUNT FOR THE MURDERER GOING?
OH... WELL...
I DO HAVE ONE LIKELY SUSPECT.
THERE'S A DOJO CALLED "KIHEIKAN" ON THE OUTSKIRTS OF THE NEXT TOWN OVER.
A DOJO ...?
NO.
MORE LIKE AN EX-DOJO. NOW IT'S A GATHERING PLACE FOR GAMBLERS AND ROGUES.

READ THIS WAY

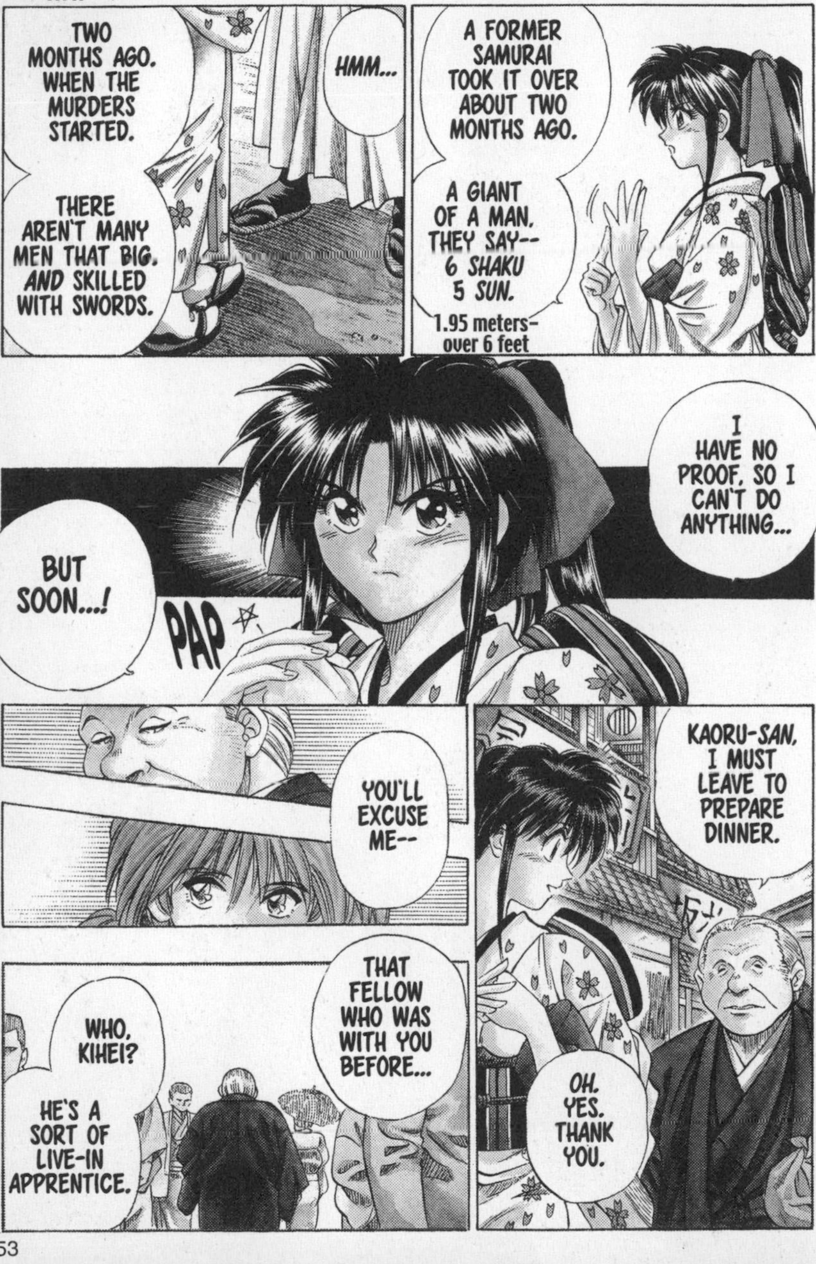
A FORMER SAMURAI TOOK IT OVER ABOUT TWO MONTHS AGO.
A GIANT OF A MAN, THEY SAY-- 6 *SHAKU* 5 *SUN*.
1.95 meters- over 6 feet
HMM...
TWO MONTHS AGO. WHEN THE MURDERS STARTED.
THERE AREN'T MANY MEN THAT BIG. *AND* SKILLED WITH SWORDS.
I HAVE NO PROOF, SO I CAN'T DO ANYTHING...
PAP
BUT SOON...!
KAORU-SAN, I MUST LEAVE TO PREPARE DINNER.
OH. YES. THANK YOU.
YOU'LL EXCUSE ME--
THAT FELLOW WHO WAS WITH YOU BEFORE...
WHO, KIHEI?
HE'S A SORT OF LIVE-IN APPRENTICE.

READ THIS WAY

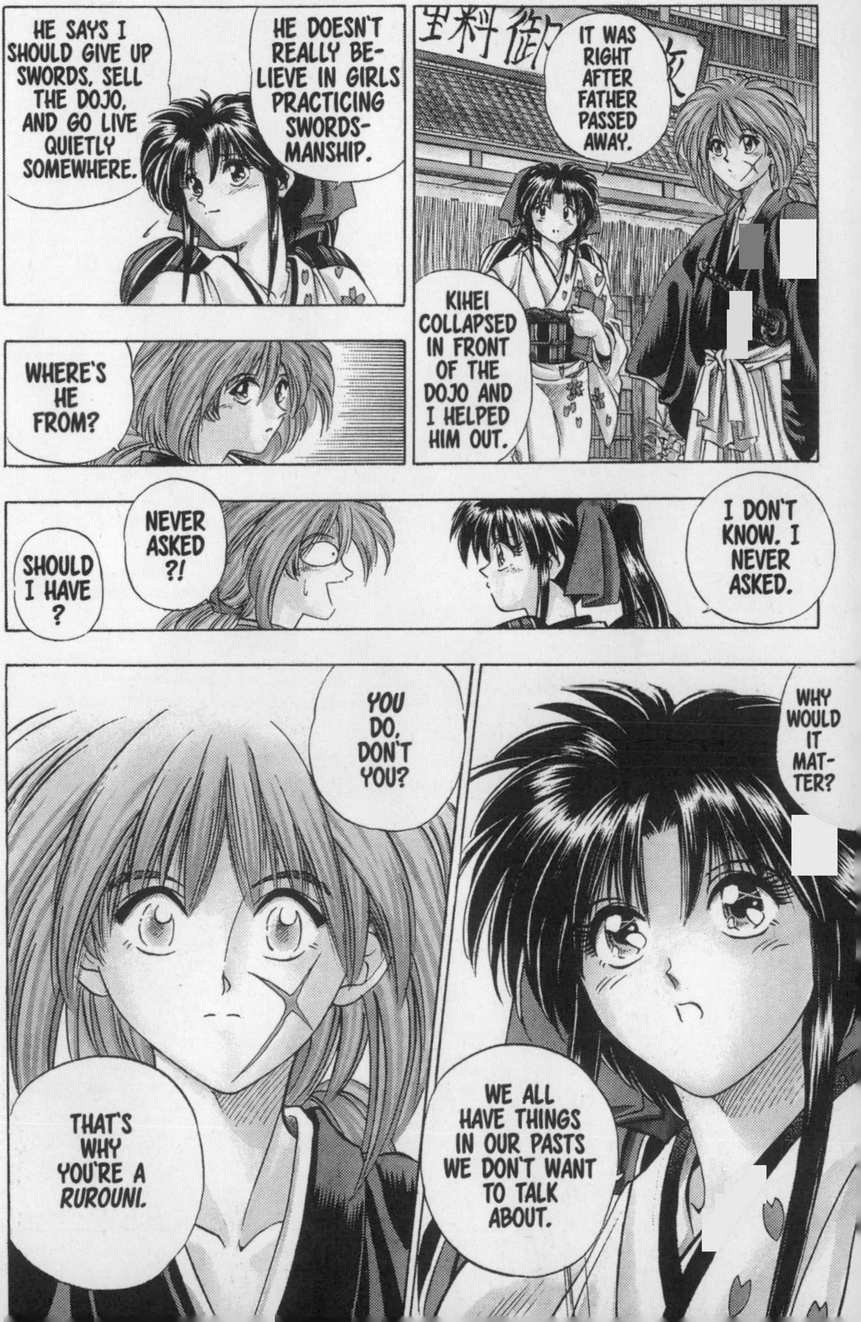
IT WAS RIGHT AFTER FATHER PASSED AWAY.
KIHEI COLLAPSED IN FRONT OF THE DOJO AND I HELPED HIM OUT.
HE DOESN'T REALLY BE-LIEVE IN GIRLS PRACTICING SWORDS-MANSHIP.
HE SAYS I SHOULD GIVE UP SWORDS, SELL THE DOJO, AND GO LIVE QUIETLY SOMEWHERE.
WHERE'S HE FROM?
I DON'T KNOW. I NEVER ASKED.
NEVER ASKED ?!
SHOULD I HAVE ?
WHY WOULD IT MAT-TER?
WE ALL HAVE THINGS IN OUR PASTS WE DON'T WANT TO TALK ABOUT.
YOU DO, DON'T YOU?
THAT'S WHY YOU'RE A RUROUNI.

READ THIS WAY

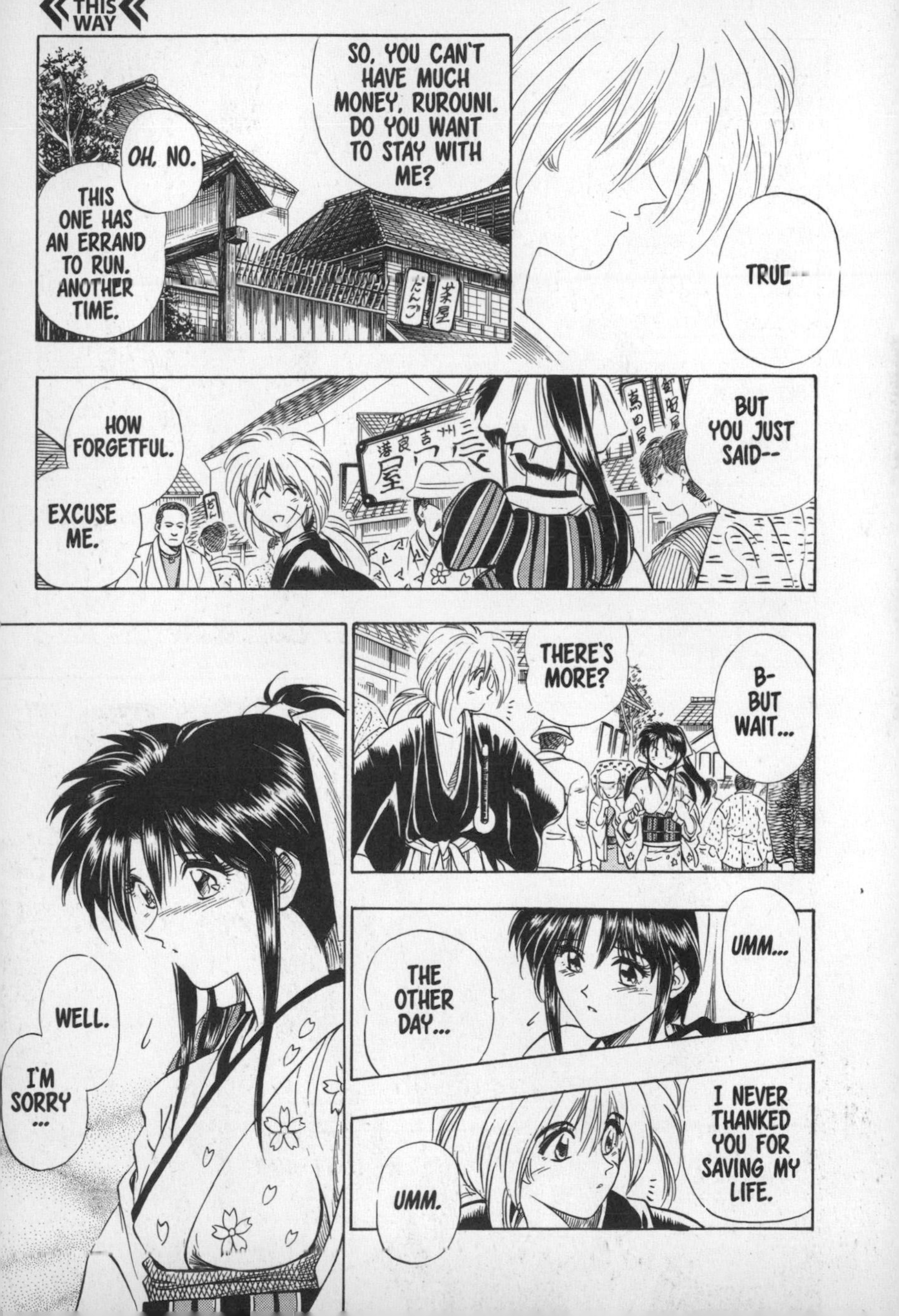
TRUE--
SO, YOU CAN'T HAVE MUCH MONEY, RUROUNI. DO YOU WANT TO STAY WITH ME?
OH, NO.
THIS ONE HAS AN ERRAND TO RUN. ANOTHER TIME.
BUT YOU JUST SAID--
HOW FORGETFUL.
EXCUSE ME.
B- BUT WAIT...
THERE'S MORE?
UMM...
THE OTHER DAY...
I NEVER THANKED YOU FOR SAVING MY LIFE.
UMM.
WELL.
I'M SORRY ...

READ THIS WAY

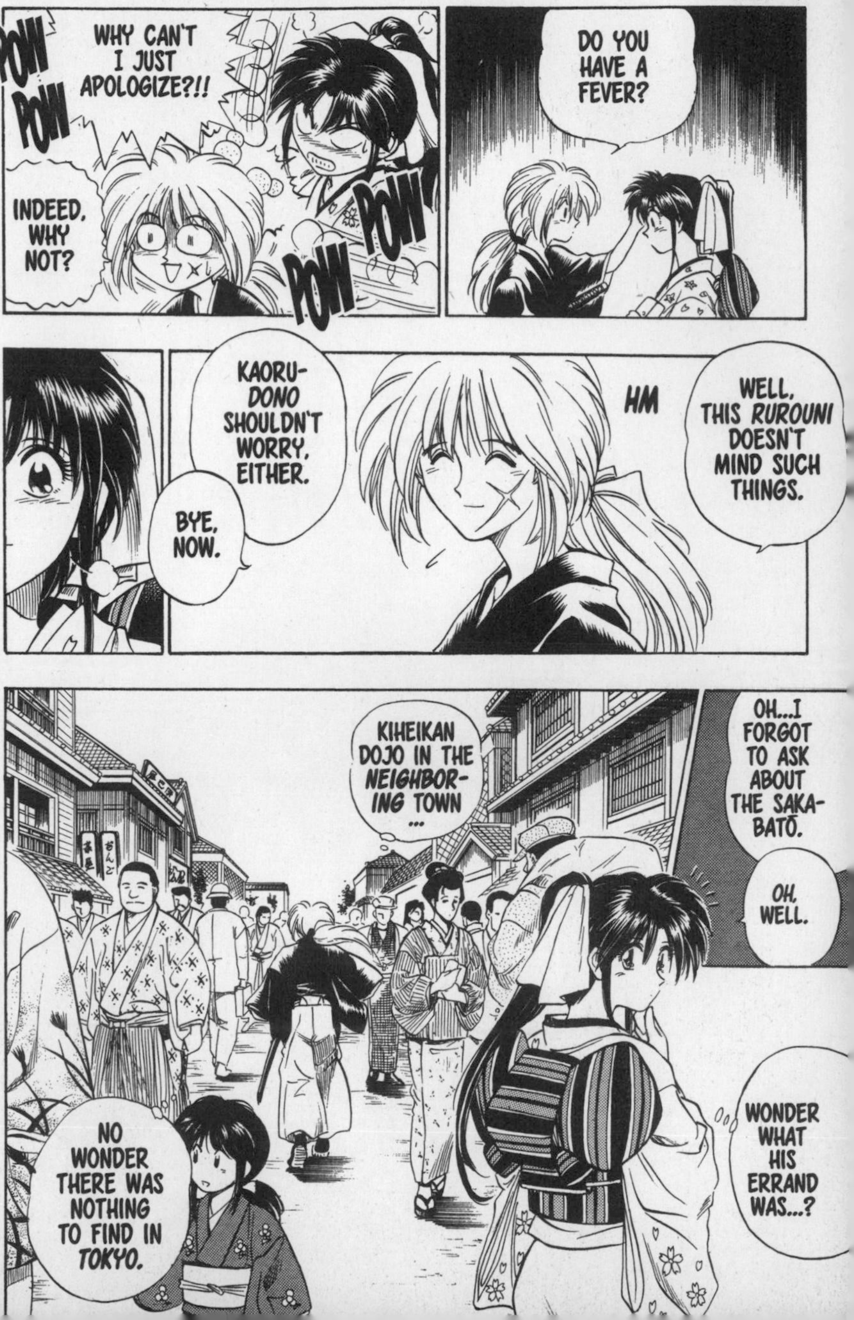
DO YOU HAVE A FEVER?
WHY CAN'T I JUST APOLOGIZE?!!
POW POW
INDEED. WHY NOT?
POW POW
WELL, THIS *RUROUNI* DOESN'T MIND SUCH THINGS.
HM
KAORU-*DONO* SHOULDN'T WORRY, EITHER.
BYE, NOW.
OH...I FORGOT TO ASK ABOUT THE SAKA-BATŌ.
OH, WELL.
WONDER WHAT HIS ERRAND WAS...?
KIHEIKAN DOJO IN THE *NEIGHBOR-ING* TOWN ...
NO WONDER THERE WAS NOTHING TO FIND IN *TOKYO*.

TO BE CONTINUED IN **RUROUNI KENSHIN** VOL. 1 ON SALE NOW!

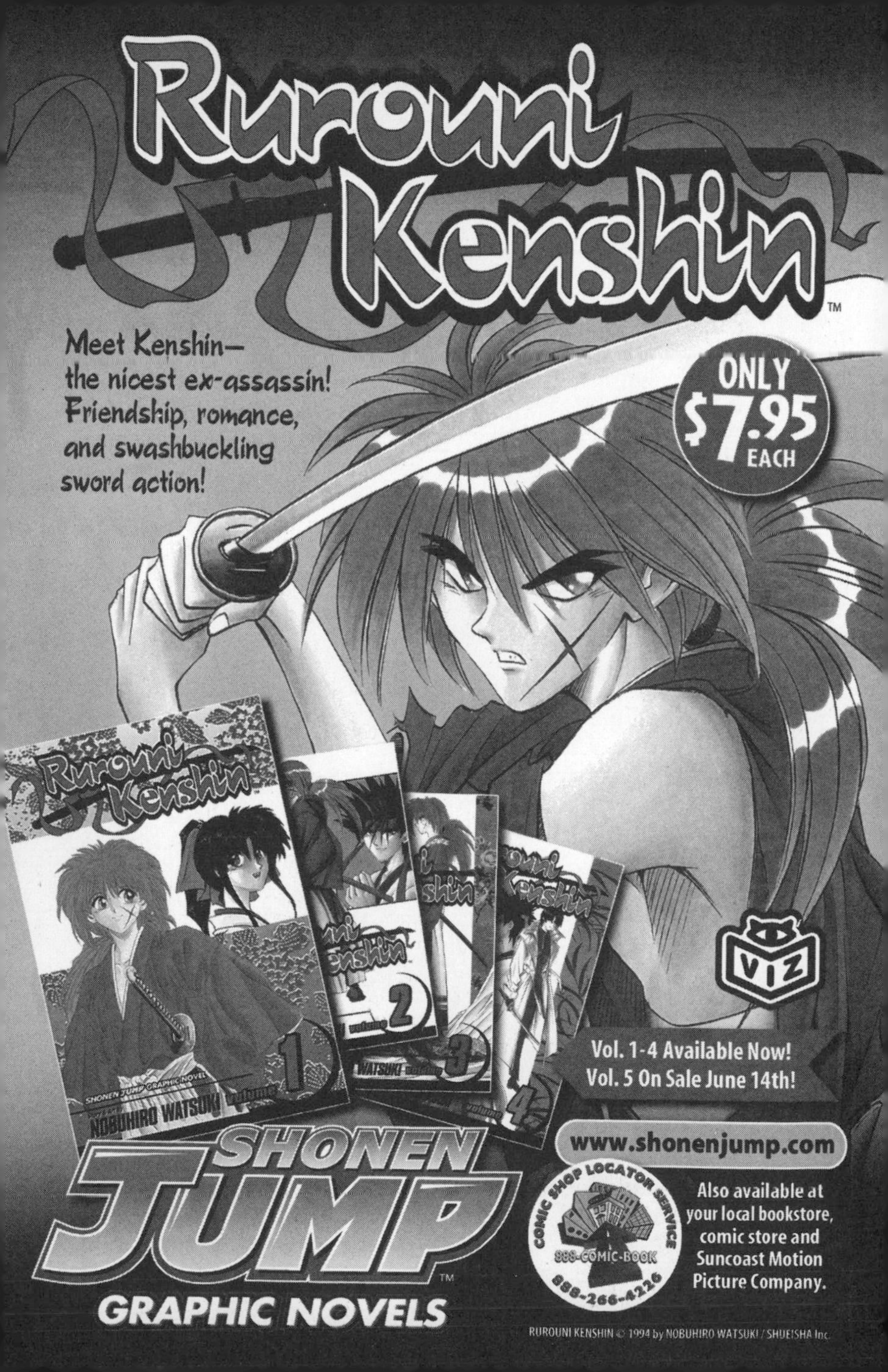
Rurouni Kenshin™
Meet Kenshin— the nicest ex-assassin! Friendship, romance, and swashbuckling sword action!
ONLY $7.95 EACH
Vol. 1-4 Available Now!
Vol. 5 On Sale June 14th!
www.shonenjump.com
COMIC SHOP LOCATOR SERVICE 888-COMIC-BOOK 888-266-4226
Also available at your local bookstore, comic store and Suncoast Motion Picture Company.
SHONEN JUMP™ GRAPHIC NOVELS
VIZ
RUROUNI KENSHIN © 1994 by NOBUHIRO WATSUKI / SHUEISHA Inc.

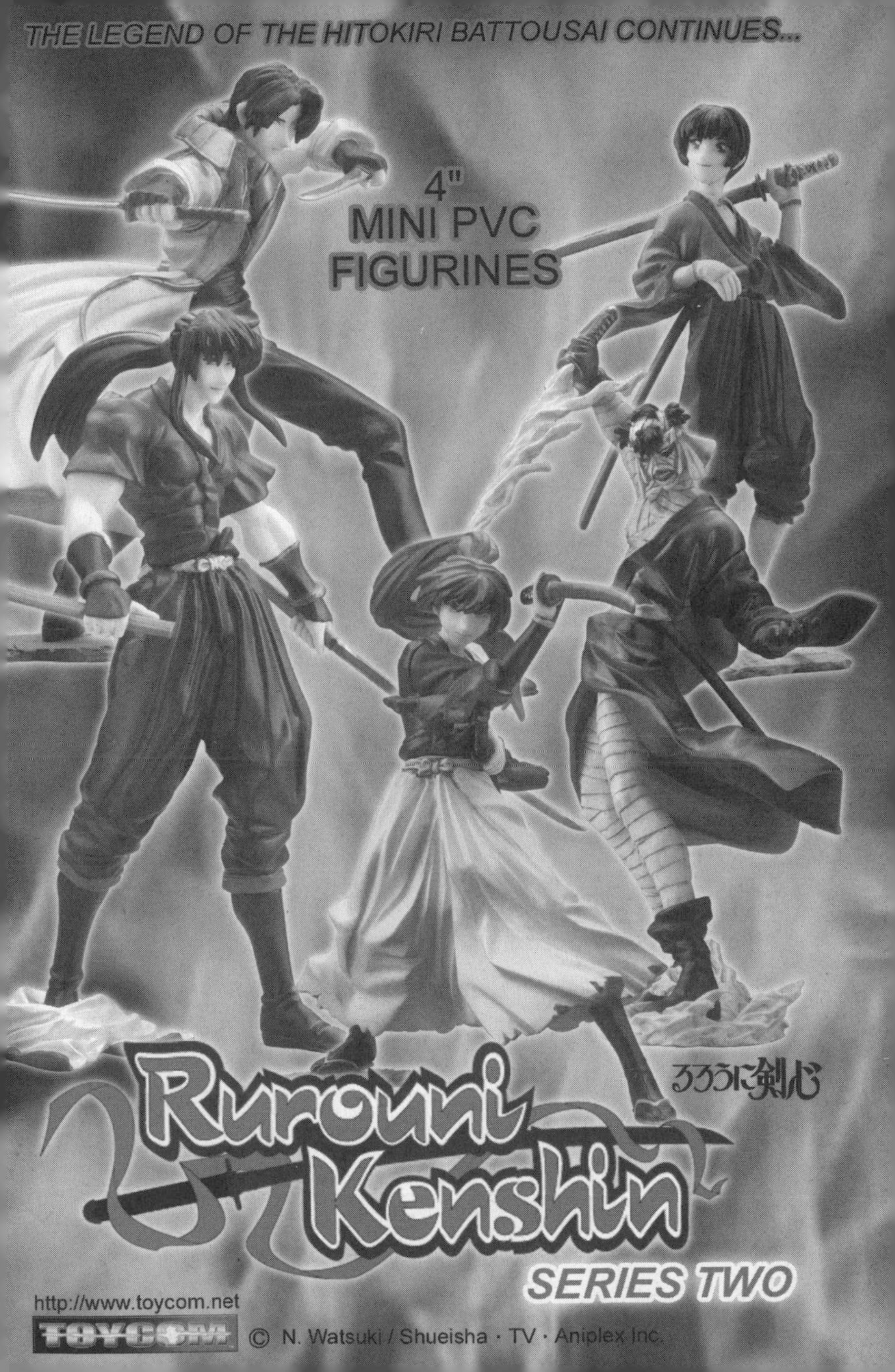
THE LEGEND OF THE HITOKIRI BATTOUSAI CONTINUES...
4" MINI PVC FIGURINES
るろうに剣心
Rurouni Kenshin
SERIES TWO
http://www.toycom.net
TOYCOM
© N. Watsuki / Shueisha · TV · Aniplex Inc.

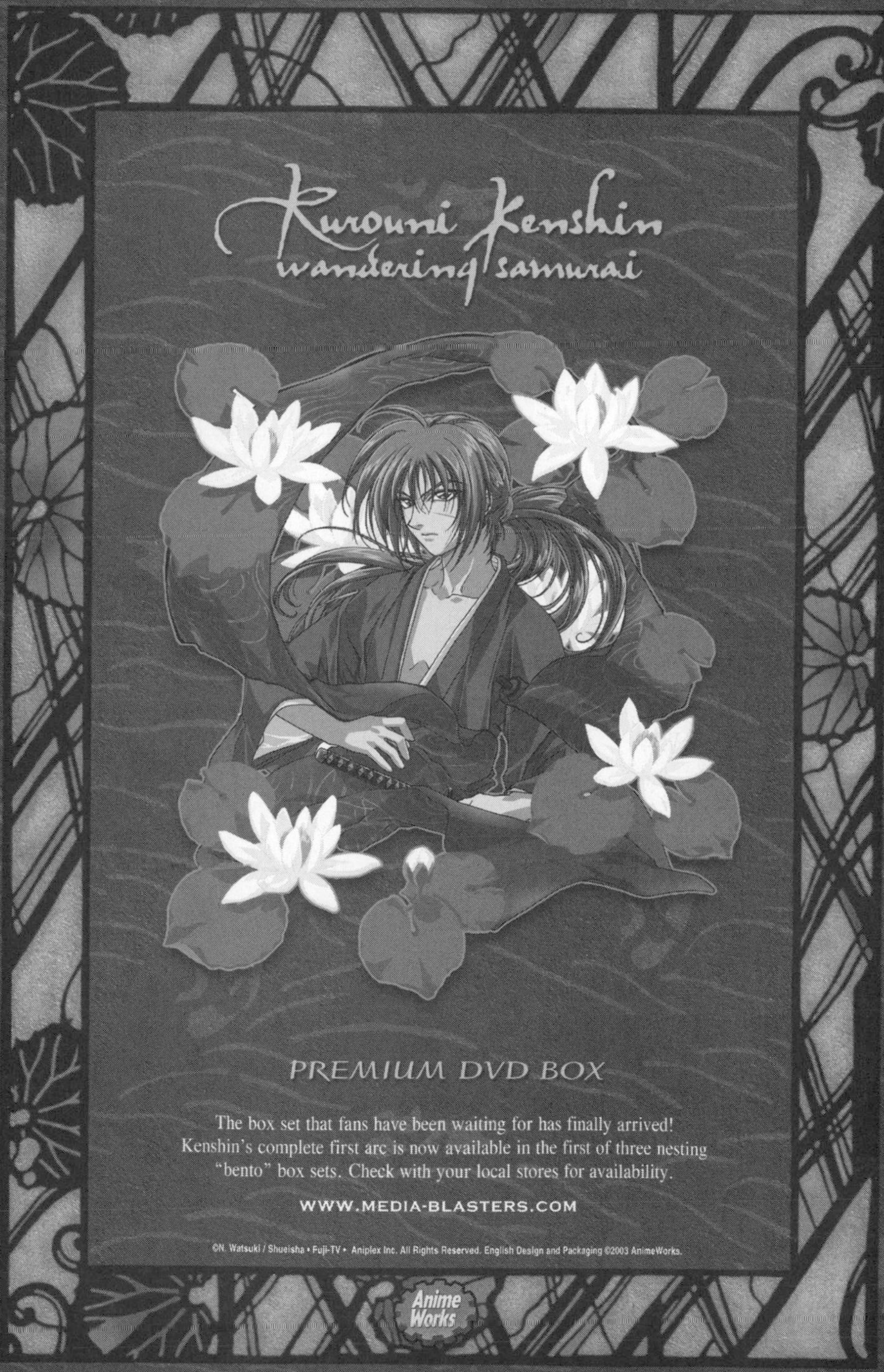
Kurouni Kenshin
wandering samurai
PREMIUM DVD BOX
The box set that fans have been waiting for has finally arrived!
Kenshin's complete first arc is now available in the first of three nesting
"bento" box sets. Check with your local stores for availability.
WWW.MEDIA-BLASTERS.COM
©N. Watsuki / Shueisha • Fuji-TV • Aniplex Inc. All Rights Reserved. English Design and Packaging ©2003 AnimeWorks.
Anime Works

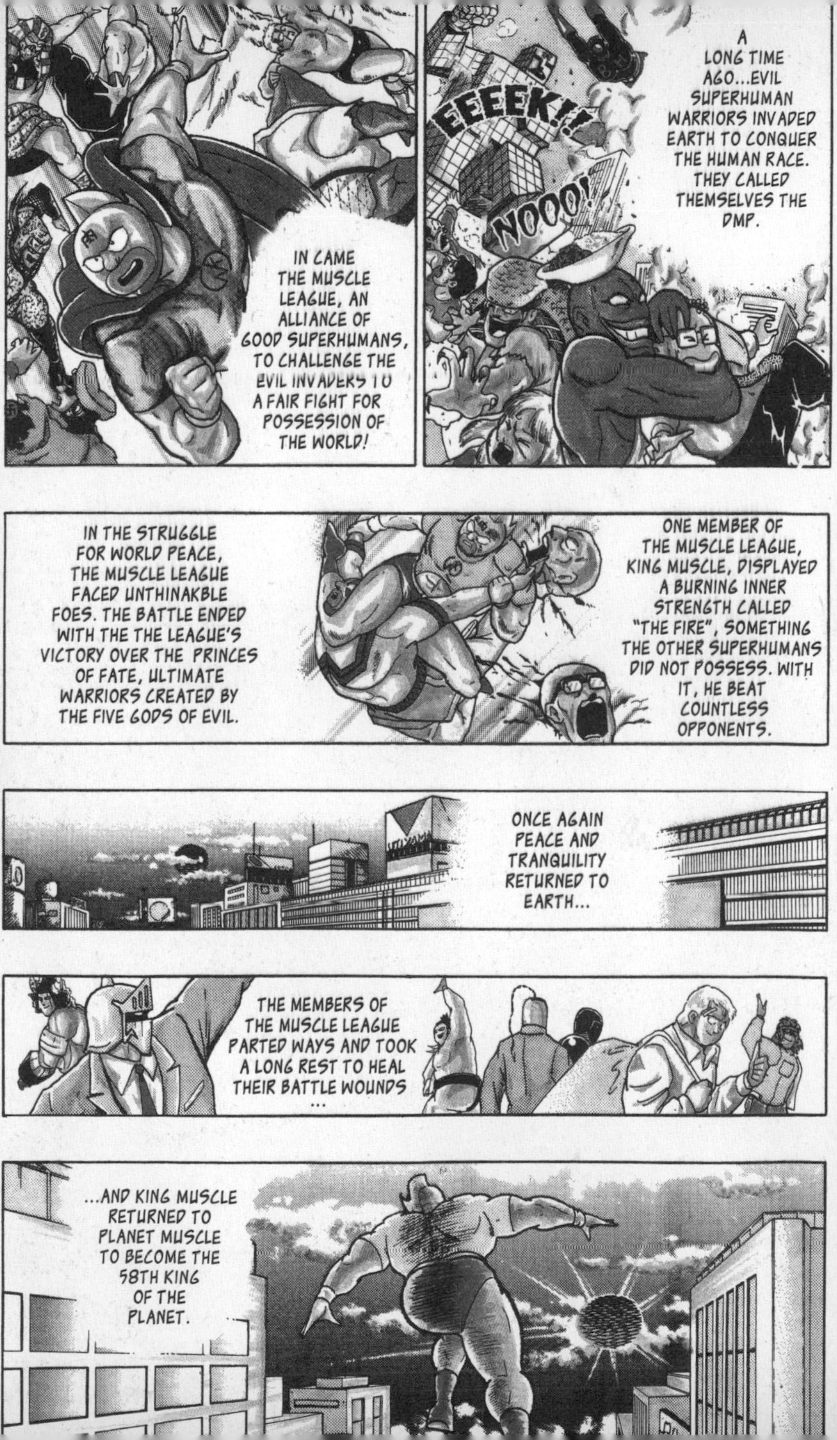
A LONG TIME AGO...EVIL SUPERHUMAN WARRIORS INVADED EARTH TO CONQUER THE HUMAN RACE. THEY CALLED THEMSELVES THE DMP.
EEEEK!!
NOOO!
IN CAME THE MUSCLE LEAGUE, AN ALLIANCE OF GOOD SUPERHUMANS, TO CHALLENGE THE EVIL INVADERS TO A FAIR FIGHT FOR POSSESSION OF THE WORLD!
ONE MEMBER OF THE MUSCLE LEAGUE, KING MUSCLE, DISPLAYED A BURNING INNER STRENGTH CALLED "THE FIRE", SOMETHING THE OTHER SUPERHUMANS DID NOT POSSESS. WITH IT, HE BEAT COUNTLESS OPPONENTS.
IN THE STRUGGLE FOR WORLD PEACE, THE MUSCLE LEAGUE FACED UNTHINAKBLE FOES. THE BATTLE ENDED WITH THE THE LEAGUE'S VICTORY OVER THE PRINCES OF FATE, ULTIMATE WARRIORS CREATED BY THE FIVE GODS OF EVIL.
ONCE AGAIN PEACE AND TRANQUILITY RETURNED TO EARTH...
THE MEMBERS OF THE MUSCLE LEAGUE PARTED WAYS AND TOOK A LONG REST TO HEAL THEIR BATTLE WOUNDS ...
...AND KING MUSCLE RETURNED TO PLANET MUSCLE TO BECOME THE 58TH KING OF THE PLANET.

## The Legend of Muscle ~1~

# THE BOUT

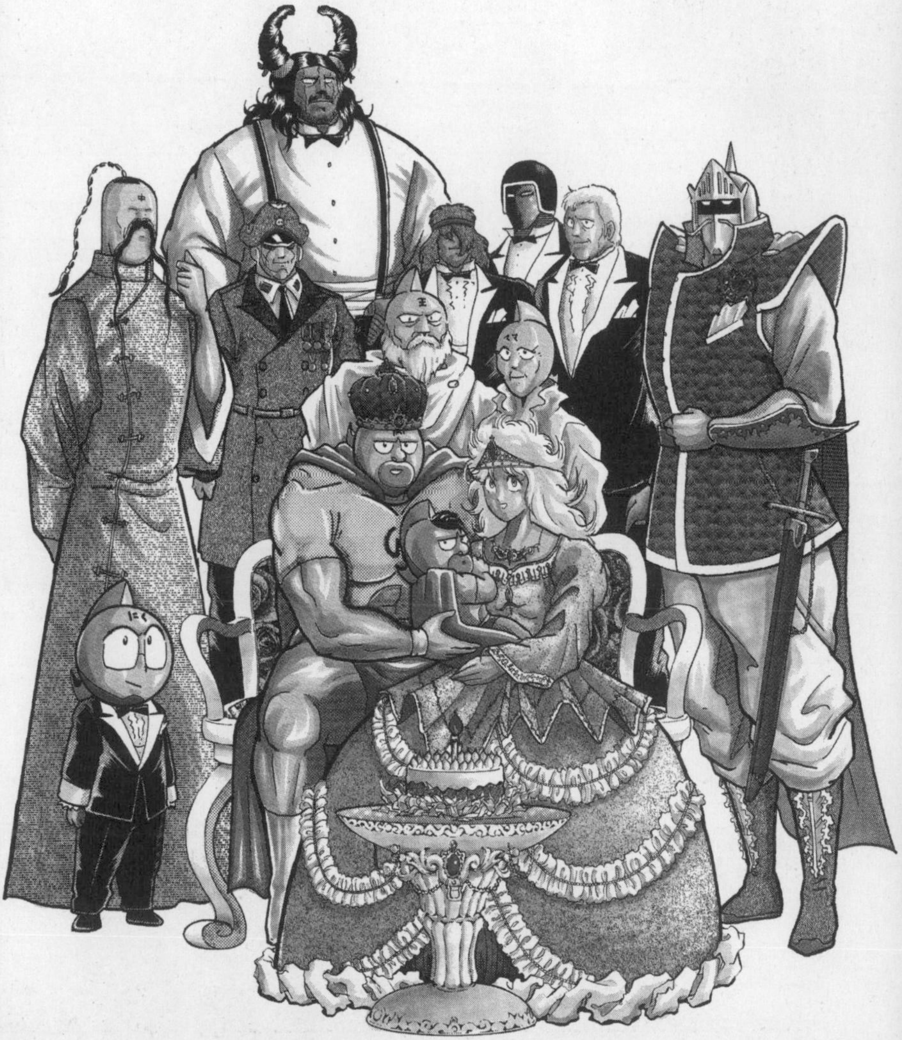

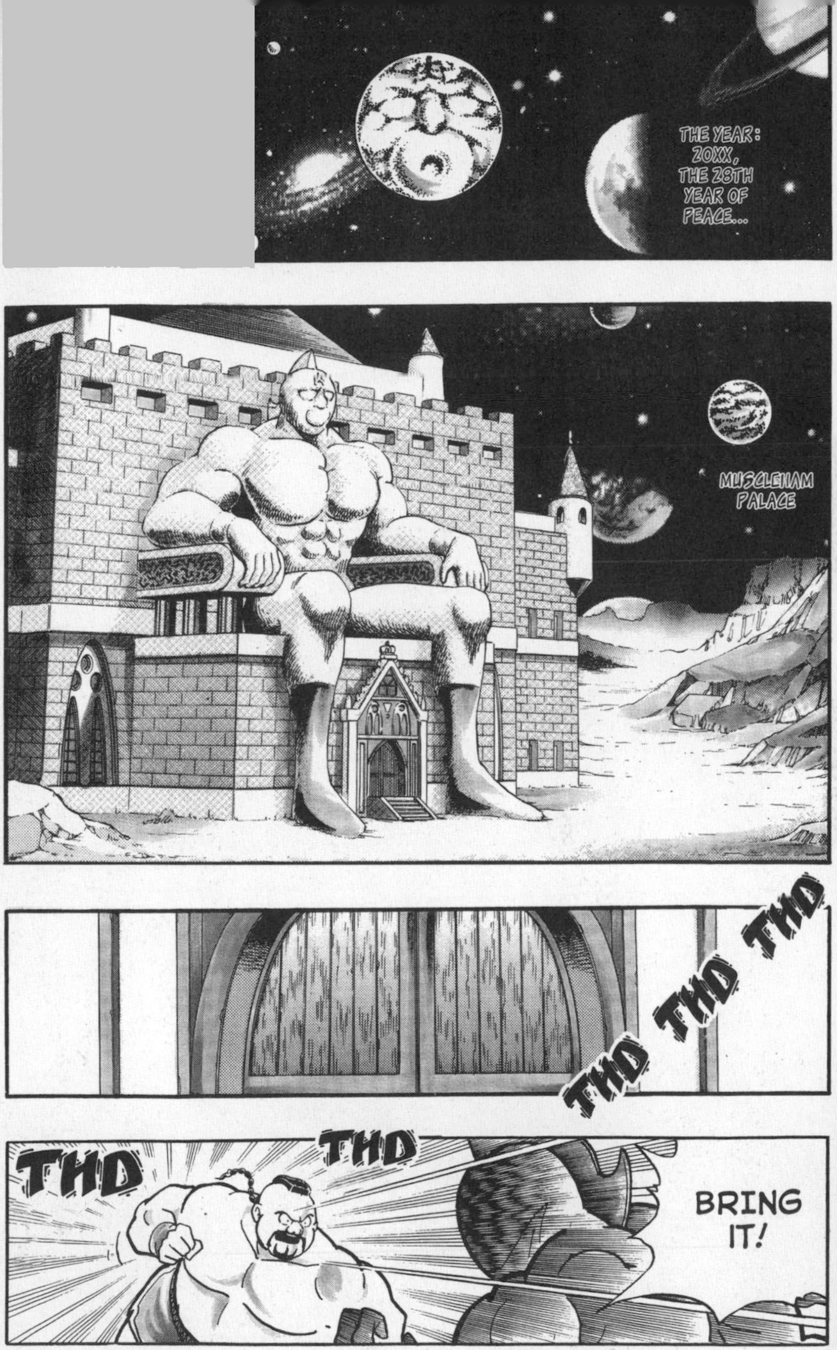
THE YEAR: 20XX, THE 28TH YEAR OF PEACE...
MUSCLEHAM PALACE
THD THD THD
BRING IT!
THD
THD

READ THIS WAY

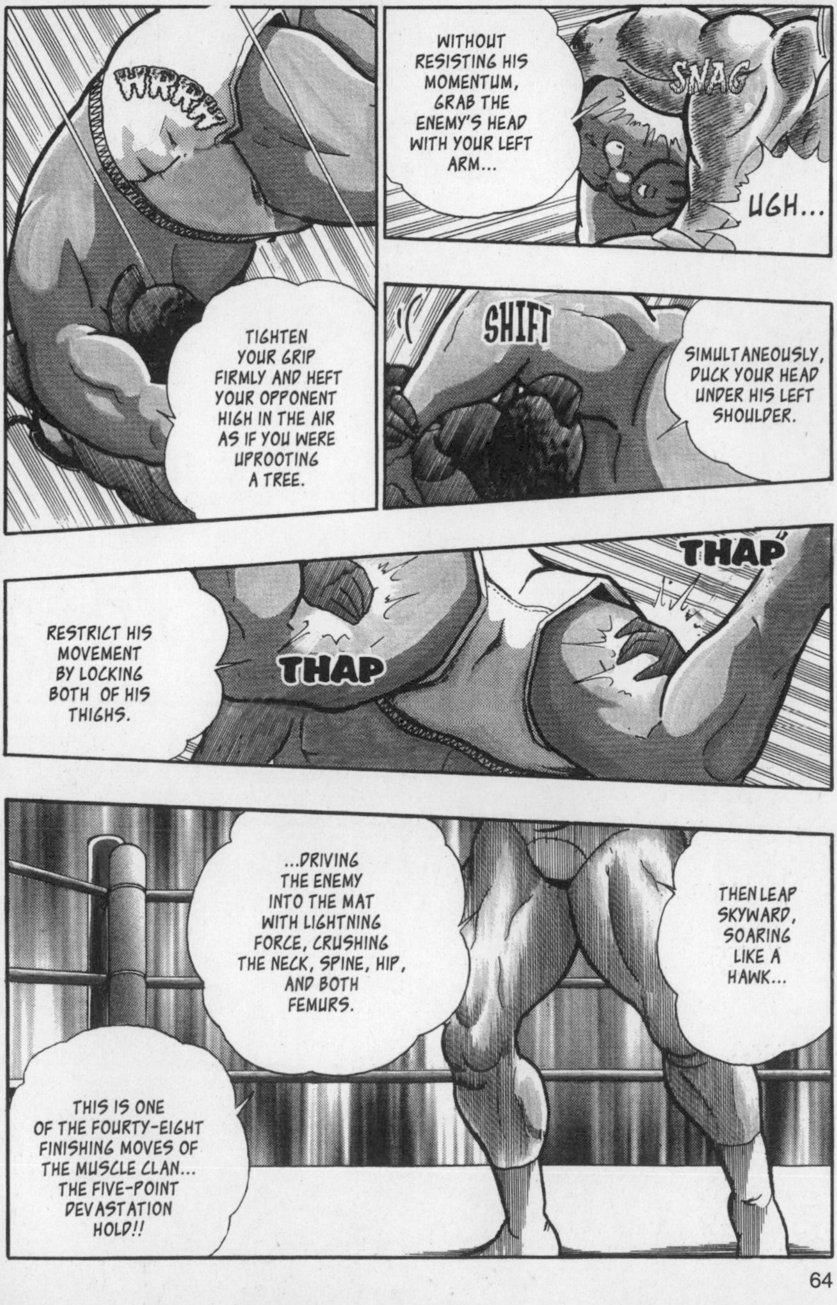

WITHOUT RESISTING HIS MOMENTUM, GRAB THE ENEMY'S HEAD WITH YOUR LEFT ARM...
SNAG
UGH...
SHIFT
SIMULTANEOUSLY, DUCK YOUR HEAD UNDER HIS LEFT SHOULDER.
WRRR
TIGHTEN YOUR GRIP FIRMLY AND HEFT YOUR OPPONENT HIGH IN THE AIR AS IF YOU WERE UPROOTING A TREE.
THAP
THAP
RESTRICT HIS MOVEMENT BY LOCKING BOTH OF HIS THIGHS.
THEN LEAP SKYWARD, SOARING LIKE A HAWK...
...DRIVING THE ENEMY INTO THE MAT WITH LIGHTNING FORCE, CRUSHING THE NECK, SPINE, HIP, AND BOTH FEMURS.
THIS IS ONE OF THE FOURTY-EIGHT FINISHING MOVES OF THE MUSCLE CLAN... THE FIVE-POINT DEVASTATION HOLD!!

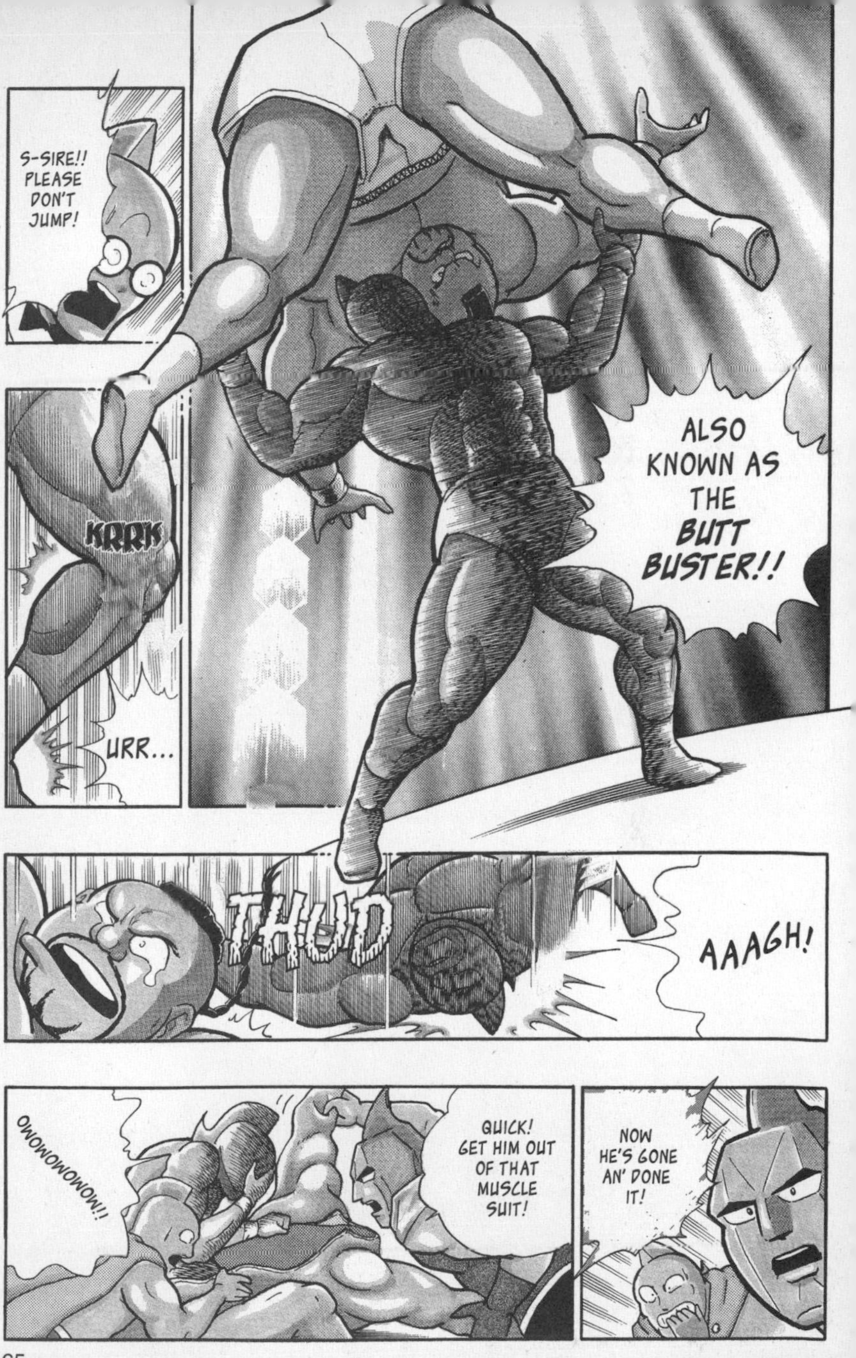
ALSO KNOWN AS THE BUTT BUSTER!!
S-SIRE!! PLEASE DON'T JUMP!
KRRK
URR...
AAAGH!
THUD
NOW HE'S GONE AN' DONE IT!
QUICK! GET HIM OUT OF THAT MUSCLE SUIT!
OWOWOWOWOW!!

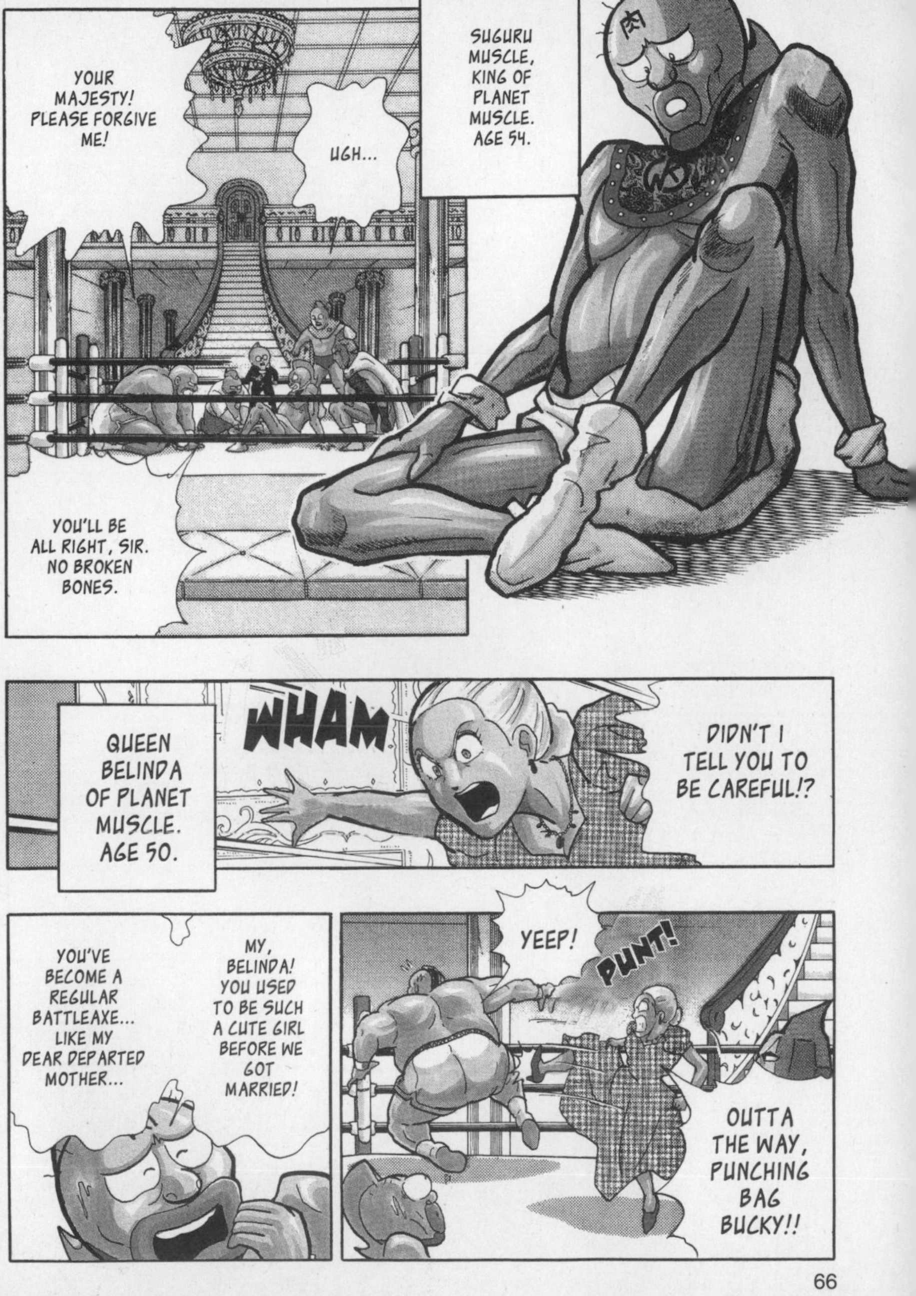

SUGURU MUSCLE, KING OF PLANET MUSCLE. AGE 54.
UGH...
YOUR MAJESTY! PLEASE FORGIVE ME!
YOU'LL BE ALL RIGHT, SIR. NO BROKEN BONES.
DIDN'T I TELL YOU TO BE CAREFUL!?
WHAM
QUEEN BELINDA OF PLANET MUSCLE. AGE 50.
YEEP!
PUNT!
OUTTA THE WAY, PUNCHING BAG BUCKY!!
MY, BELINDA! YOU USED TO BE SUCH A CUTE GIRL BEFORE WE GOT MARRIED!
YOU'VE BECOME A REGULAR BATTLEAXE... LIKE MY DEAR DEPARTED MOTHER...

READ THIS WAY

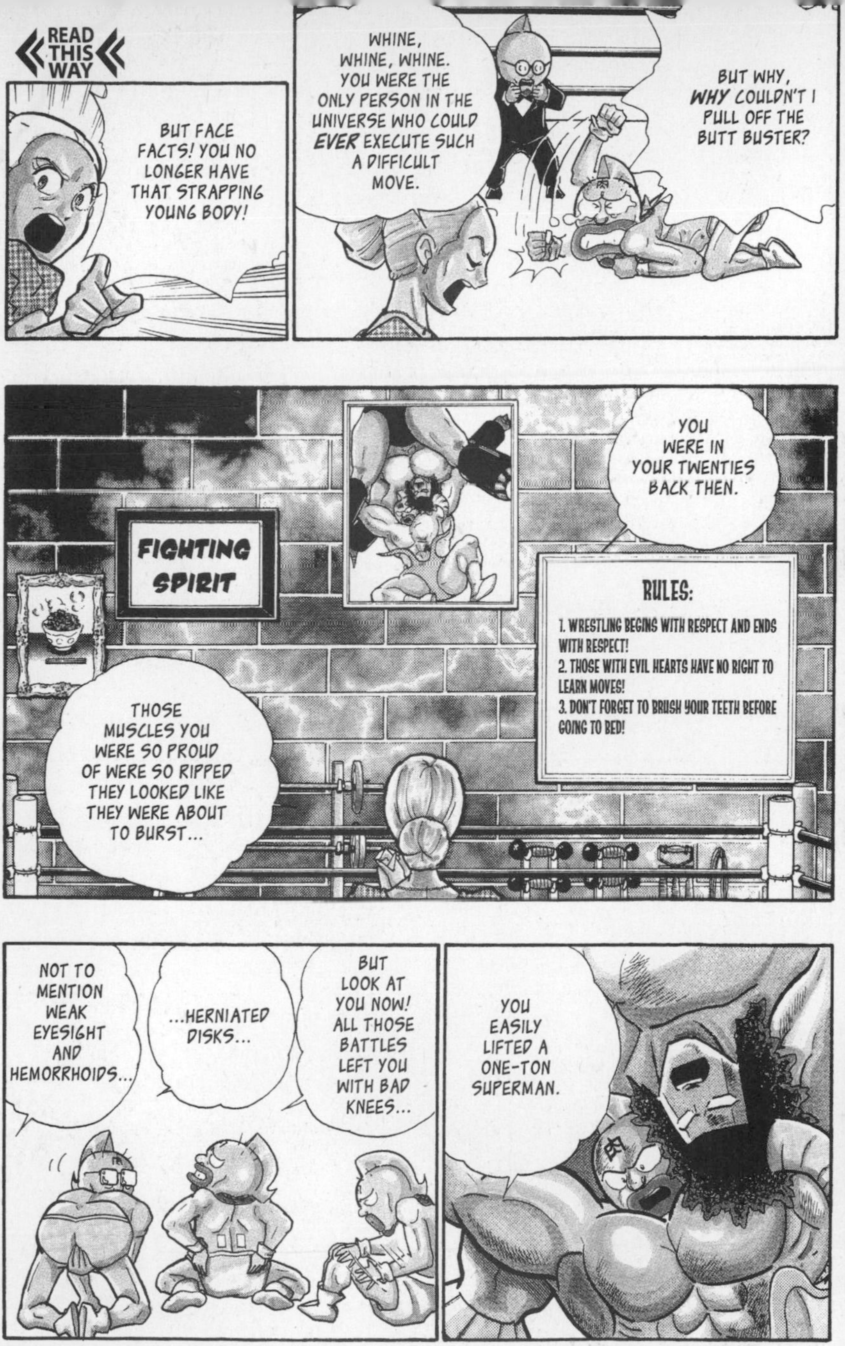

BUT WHY, *WHY* COULDN'T I PULL OFF THE BUTT BUSTER?
WHINE, WHINE, WHINE. YOU WERE THE ONLY PERSON IN THE UNIVERSE WHO COULD *EVER* EXECUTE SUCH A DIFFICULT MOVE.
BUT FACE FACTS! YOU NO LONGER HAVE THAT STRAPPING YOUNG BODY!
YOU WERE IN YOUR TWENTIES BACK THEN.
RULES:
1. WRESTLING BEGINS WITH RESPECT AND ENDS WITH RESPECT!
2. THOSE WITH EVIL HEARTS HAVE NO RIGHT TO LEARN MOVES!
3. DON'T FORGET TO BRUSH YOUR TEETH BEFORE GOING TO BED!
FIGHTING SPIRIT
THOSE MUSCLES YOU WERE SO PROUD OF WERE SO RIPPED THEY LOOKED LIKE THEY WERE ABOUT TO BURST...
YOU EASILY LIFTED A ONE-TON SUPERMAN.
BUT LOOK AT YOU NOW! ALL THOSE BATTLES LEFT YOU WITH BAD KNEES...
...HERNIATED DISKS...
NOT TO MENTION WEAK EYESIGHT AND HEMORRHOIDS...

READ THIS WAY

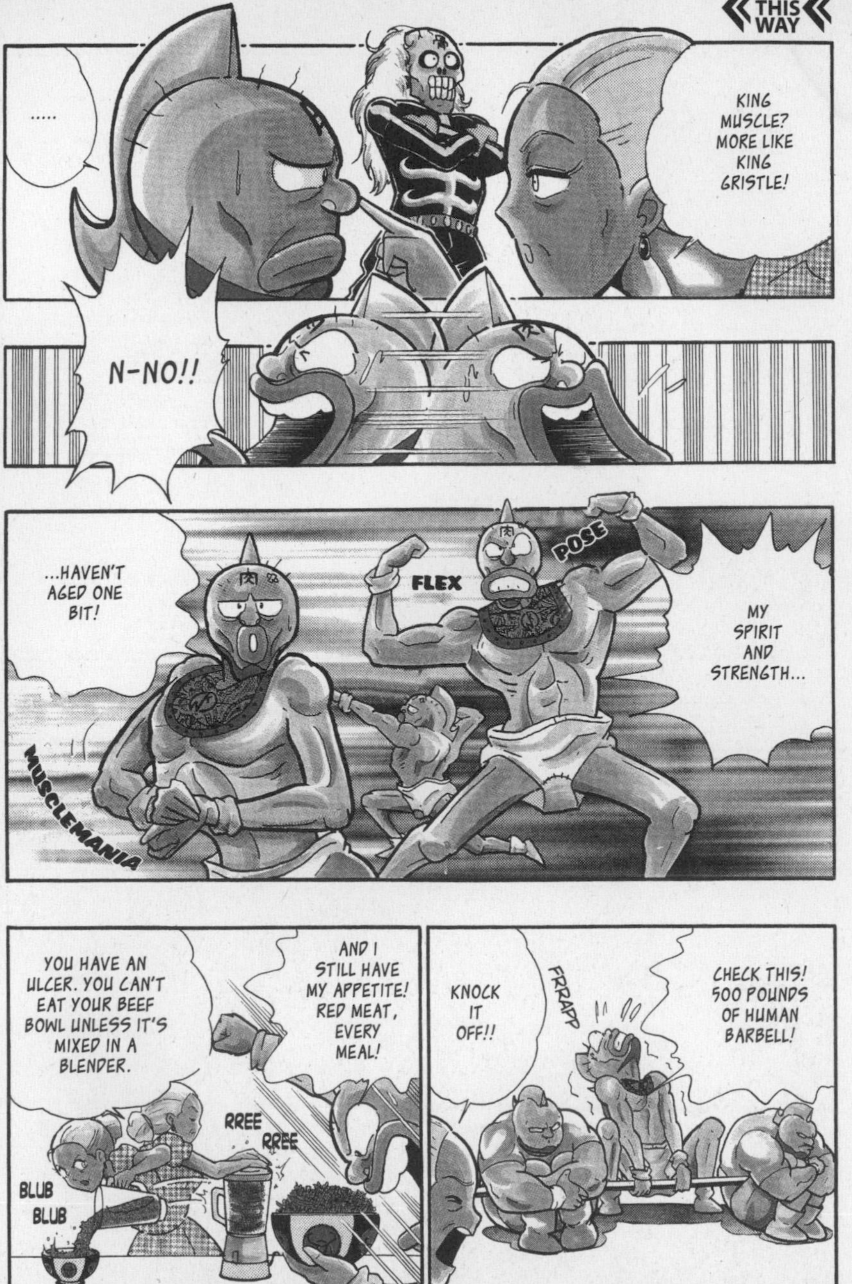
KING MUSCLE? MORE LIKE KING GRISTLE!
.....
N-NO!!
MY SPIRIT AND STRENGTH...
POSE
FLEX
...HAVEN'T AGED ONE BIT!
MUSCLEMANIA
CHECK THIS! 500 POUNDS OF HUMAN BARBELL!
FRRAPP
KNOCK IT OFF!!
AND I STILL HAVE MY APPETITE! RED MEAT, EVERY MEAL!
RREE
RREE
YOU HAVE AN ULCER. YOU CAN'T EAT YOUR BEEF BOWL UNLESS IT'S MIXED IN A BLENDER.
BLUB
BLUB

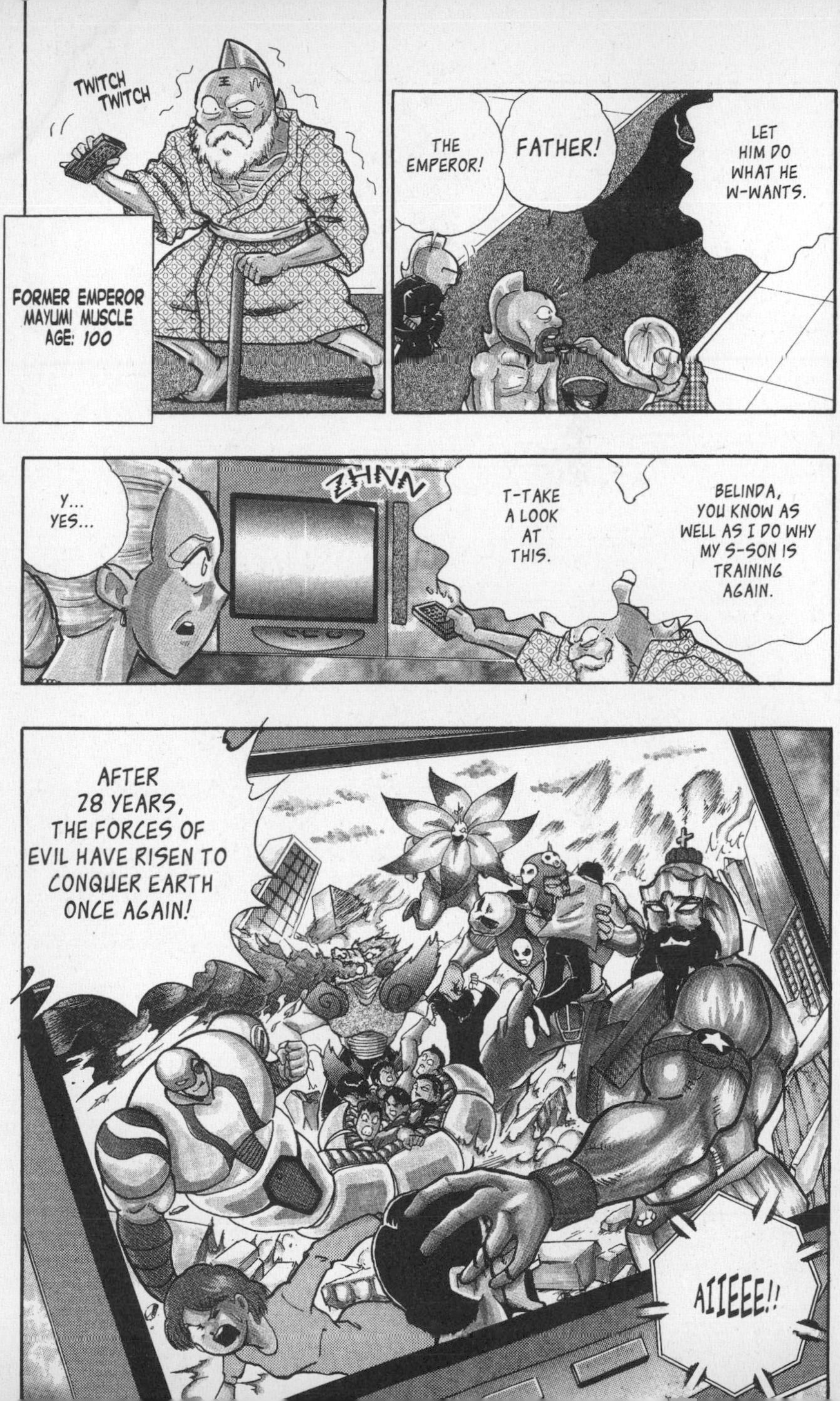
LET HIM DO WHAT HE W-WANTS.
FATHER!
THE EMPEROR!
TWITCH TWITCH
FORMER EMPEROR MAYUMI MUSCLE AGE: 100
BELINDA, YOU KNOW AS WELL AS I DO WHY MY S-SON IS TRAINING AGAIN.
T-TAKE A LOOK AT THIS.
ZHNN
Y... YES...
AFTER 28 YEARS, THE FORCES OF EVIL HAVE RISEN TO CONQUER EARTH ONCE AGAIN!
AIIEEE!!

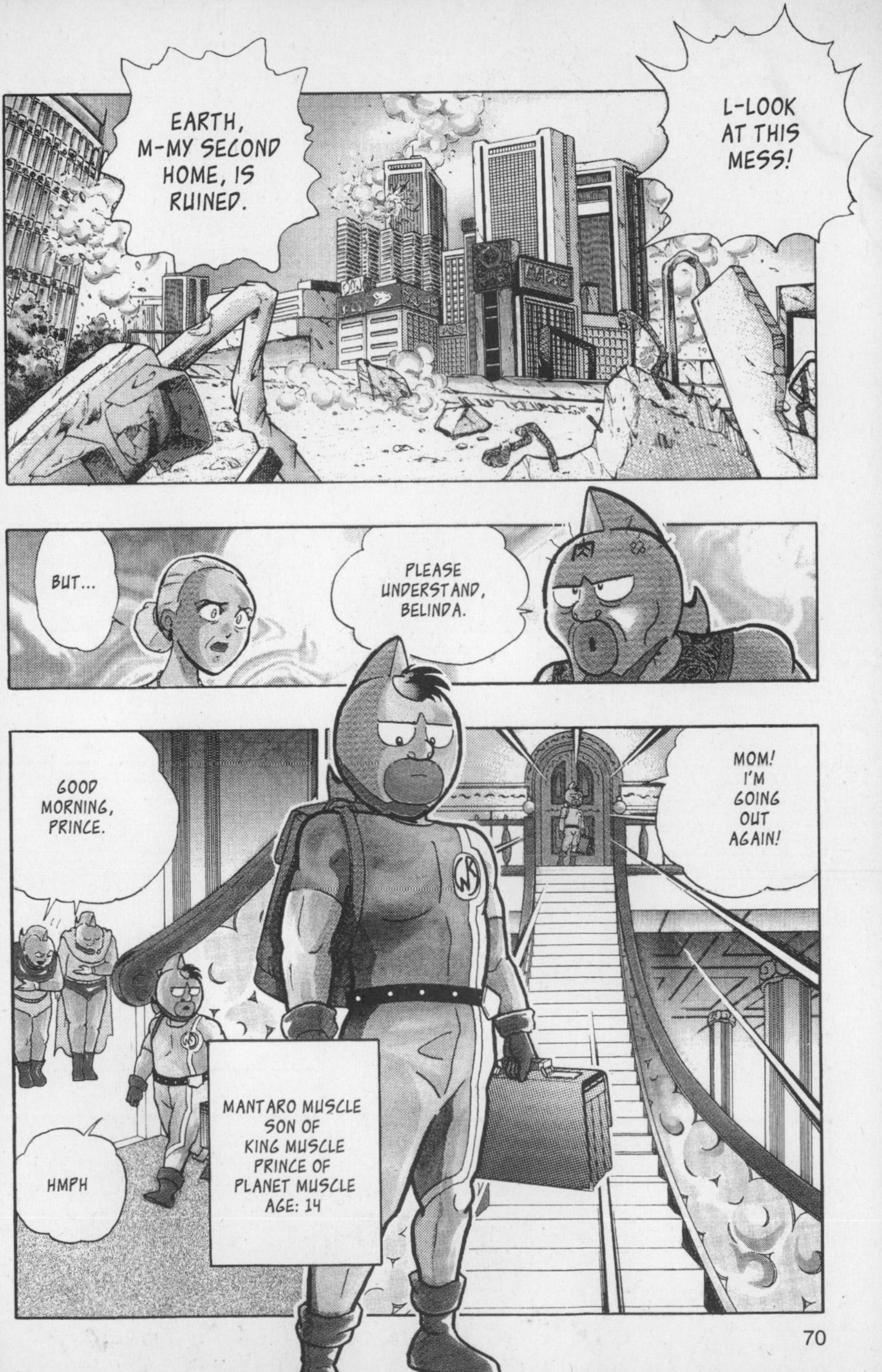
L-LOOK AT THIS MESS!
EARTH, M-MY SECOND HOME, IS RUINED.
PLEASE UNDERSTAND, BELINDA.
BUT...
MOM! I'M GOING OUT AGAIN!
GOOD MORNING, PRINCE.
MANTARO MUSCLE SON OF KING MUSCLE PRINCE OF PLANET MUSCLE AGE: 14
HMPH

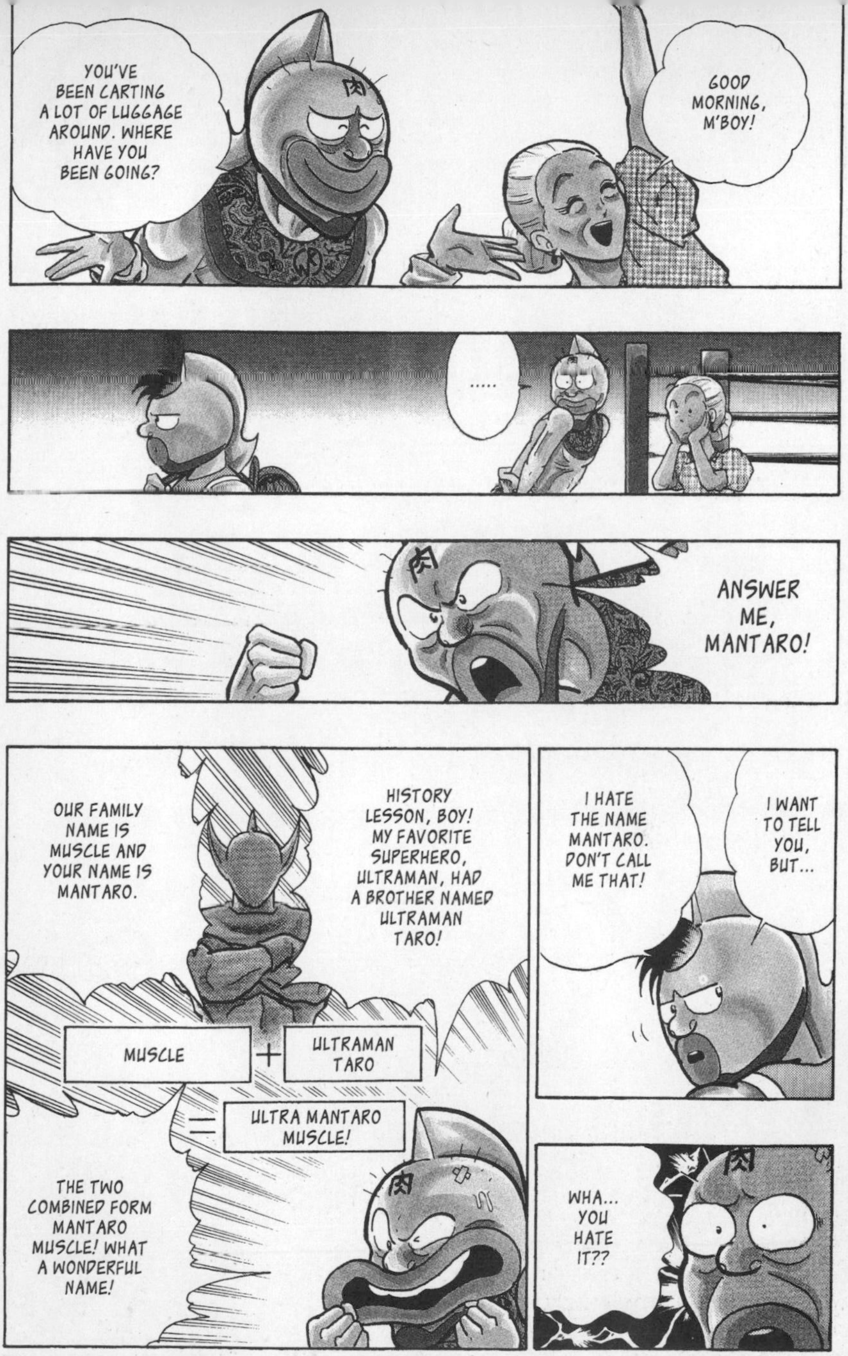
GOOD MORNING, M'BOY!
YOU'VE BEEN CARTING A LOT OF LUGGAGE AROUND. WHERE HAVE YOU BEEN GOING?
.....
ANSWER ME, MANTARO!
I WANT TO TELL YOU, BUT...
I HATE THE NAME MANTARO. DON'T CALL ME THAT!
WHA... YOU HATE IT??
HISTORY LESSON, BOY! MY FAVORITE SUPERHERO, ULTRAMAN, HAD A BROTHER NAMED ULTRAMAN TARO!
OUR FAMILY NAME IS MUSCLE AND YOUR NAME IS MANTARO.
MUSCLE
+
ULTRAMAN TARO
=
ULTRA MANTARO MUSCLE!
THE TWO COMBINED FORM MANTARO MUSCLE! WHAT A WONDERFUL NAME!

READ THIS WAY

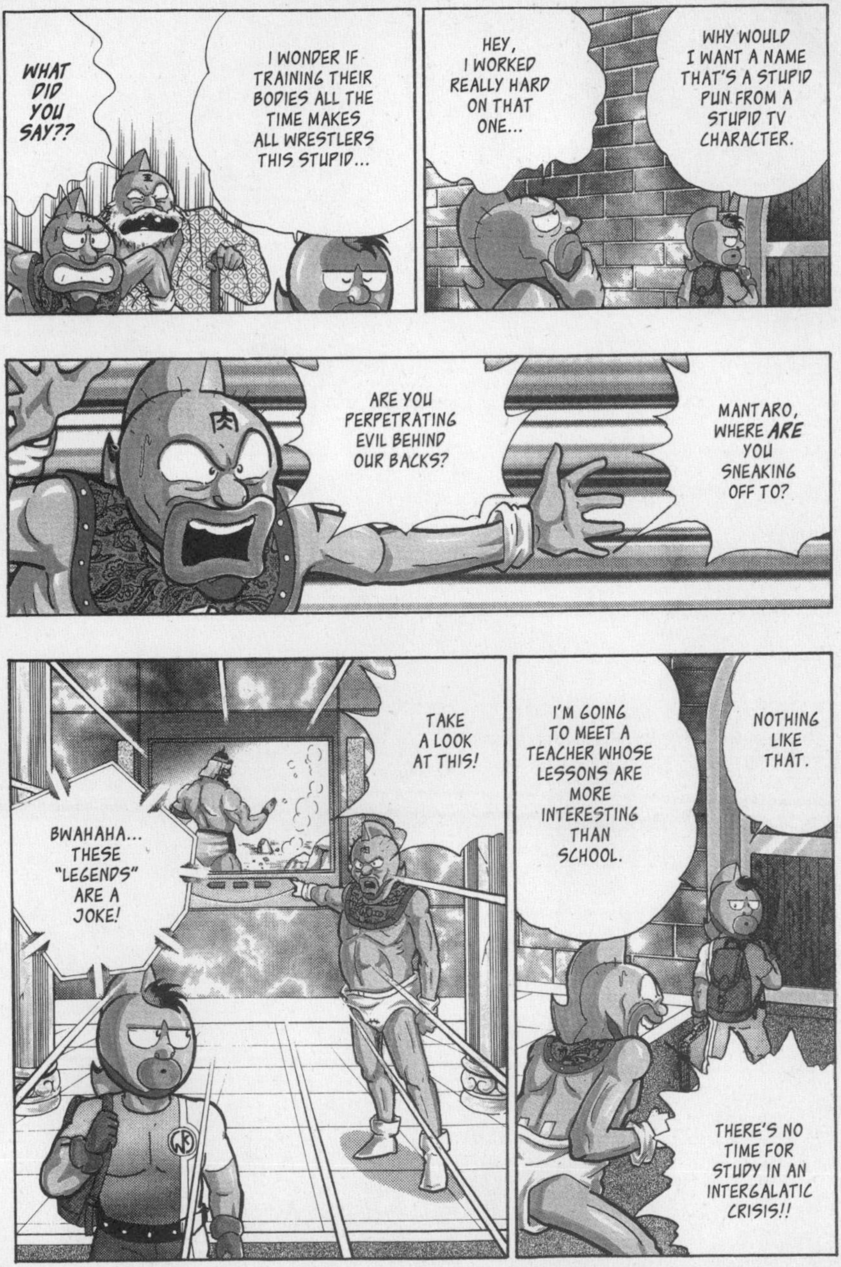
WHY WOULD I WANT A NAME THAT'S A STUPID PUN FROM A STUPID TV CHARACTER.
HEY, I WORKED REALLY HARD ON THAT ONE...
I WONDER IF TRAINING THEIR BODIES ALL THE TIME MAKES ALL WRESTLERS THIS STUPID...
WHAT DID YOU SAY??
MANTARO, WHERE **ARE** YOU SNEAKING OFF TO?
ARE YOU PERPETRATING EVIL BEHIND OUR BACKS?
NOTHING LIKE THAT.
I'M GOING TO MEET A TEACHER WHOSE LESSONS ARE MORE INTERESTING THAN SCHOOL.
THERE'S NO TIME FOR STUDY IN AN INTERGALATIC CRISIS!!
TAKE A LOOK AT THIS!
BWAHAHA... THESE "LEGENDS" ARE A JOKE!

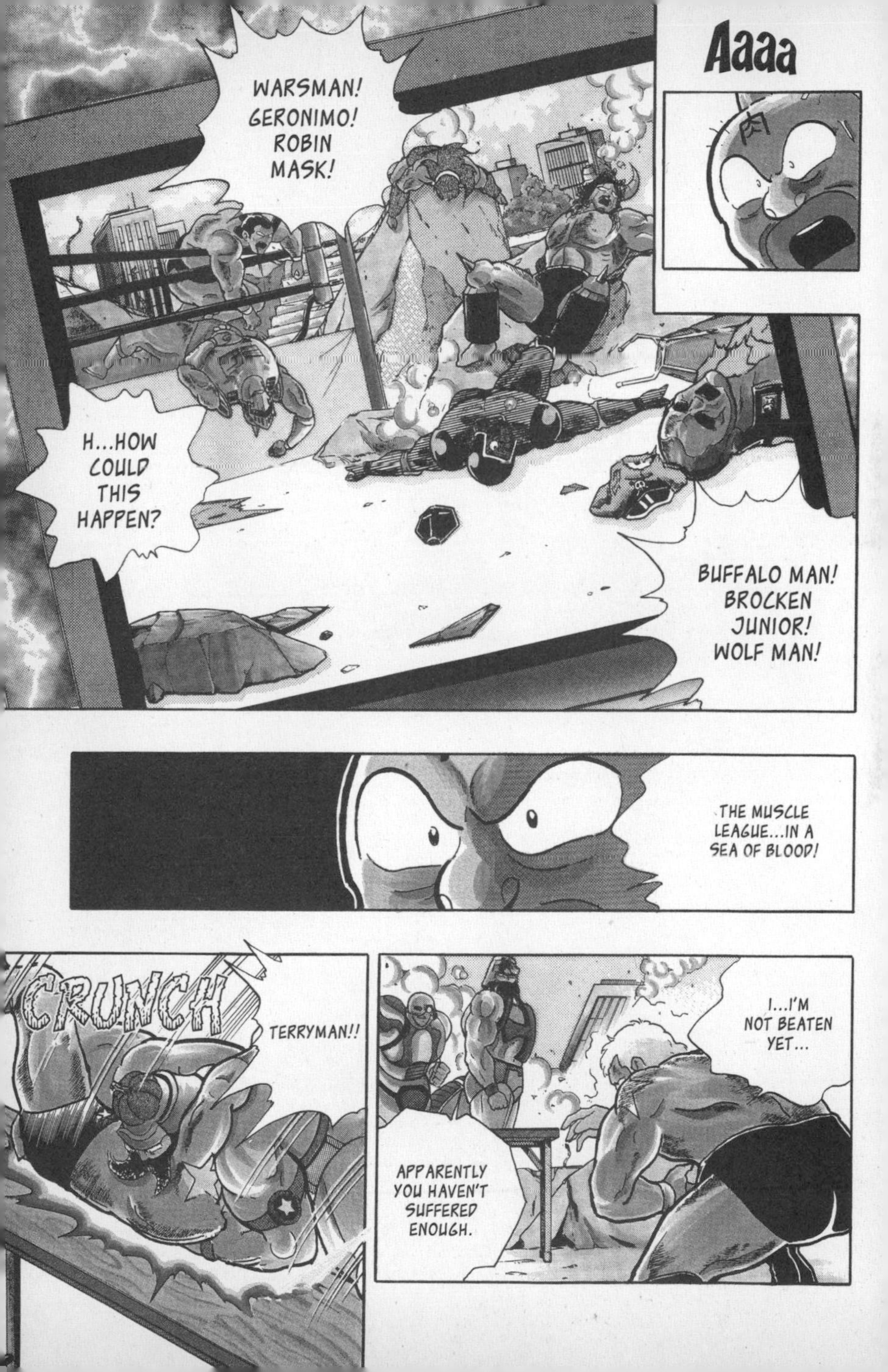
Aaaa
WARSMAN! GERONIMO! ROBIN MASK!
BUFFALO MAN! BROCKEN JUNIOR! WOLF MAN!
H...HOW COULD THIS HAPPEN?
THE MUSCLE LEAGUE...IN A SEA OF BLOOD!
I...I'M NOT BEATEN YET...
APPARENTLY YOU HAVEN'T SUFFERED ENOUGH.
CRUNCH
TERRYMAN!!

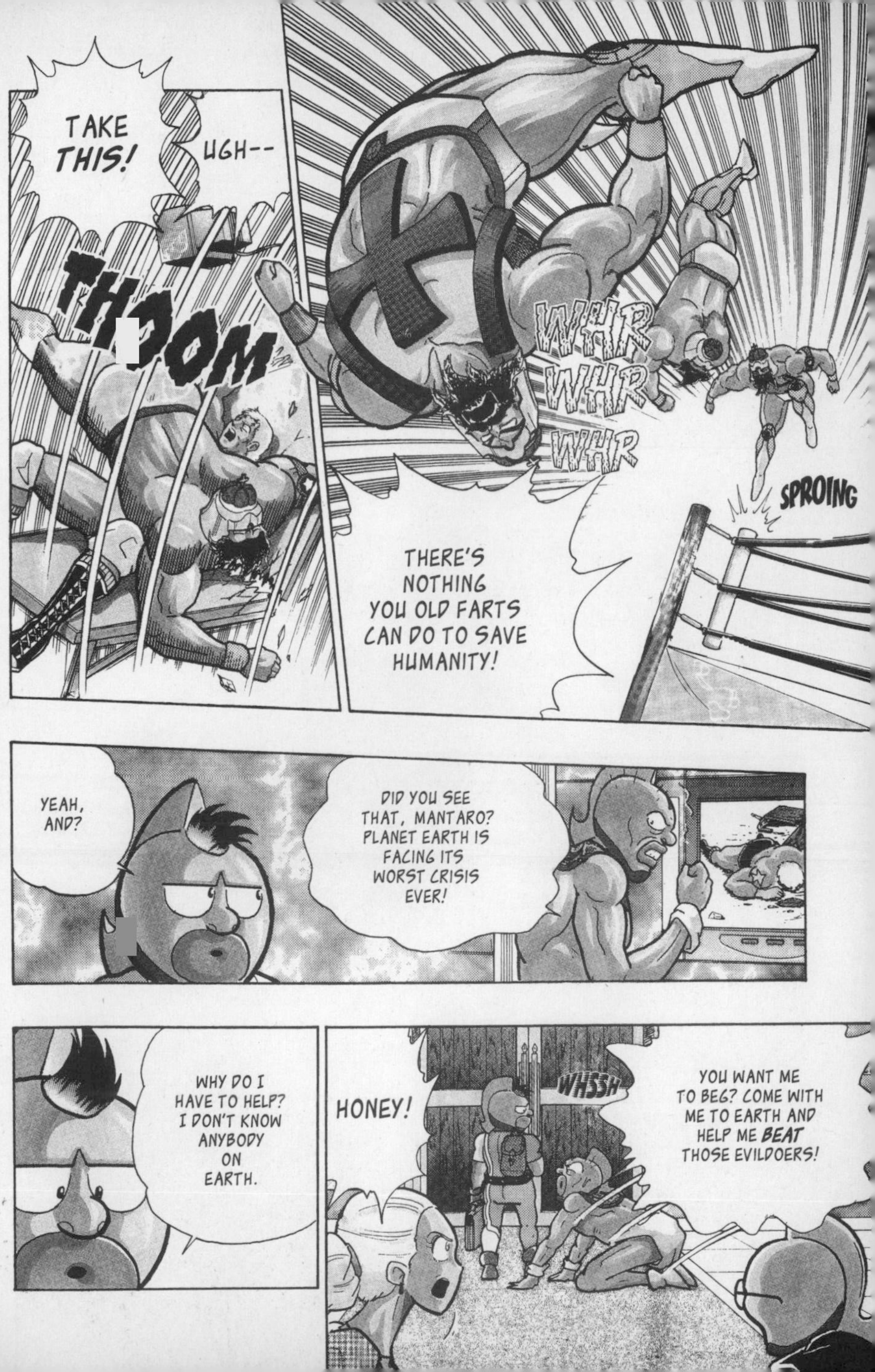
WHR
WHR
WHR
SPROING
THERE'S NOTHING YOU OLD FARTS CAN DO TO SAVE HUMANITY!
TAKE THIS!
UGH--
THOOM
DID YOU SEE THAT, MANTARO? PLANET EARTH IS FACING ITS WORST CRISIS EVER!
YEAH, AND?
YOU WANT ME TO BEG? COME WITH ME TO EARTH AND HELP ME BEAT THOSE EVILDOERS!
WHSSH
HONEY!
WHY DO I HAVE TO HELP? I DON'T KNOW ANYBODY ON EARTH.

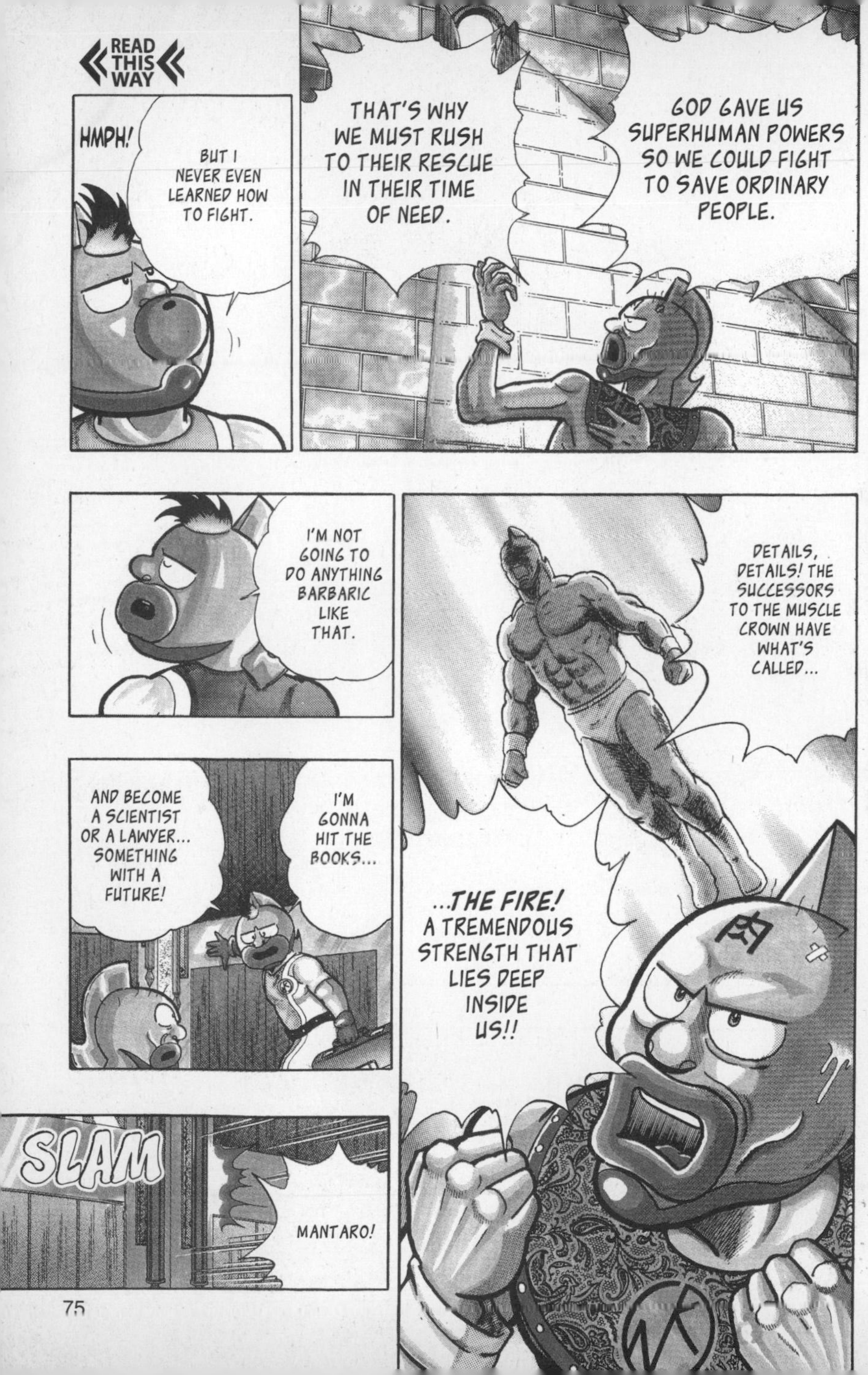
READ THIS WAY
GOD GAVE US SUPERHUMAN POWERS SO WE COULD FIGHT TO SAVE ORDINARY PEOPLE.
THAT'S WHY WE MUST RUSH TO THEIR RESCUE IN THEIR TIME OF NEED.
HMPH!
BUT I NEVER EVEN LEARNED HOW TO FIGHT.
DETAILS, DETAILS! THE SUCCESSORS TO THE MUSCLE CROWN HAVE WHAT'S CALLED...
...THE FIRE! A TREMENDOUS STRENGTH THAT LIES DEEP INSIDE US!!
I'M NOT GOING TO DO ANYTHING BARBARIC LIKE THAT.
I'M GONNA HIT THE BOOKS...
AND BECOME A SCIENTIST OR A LAWYER... SOMETHING WITH A FUTURE!
SLAM
MANTARO!

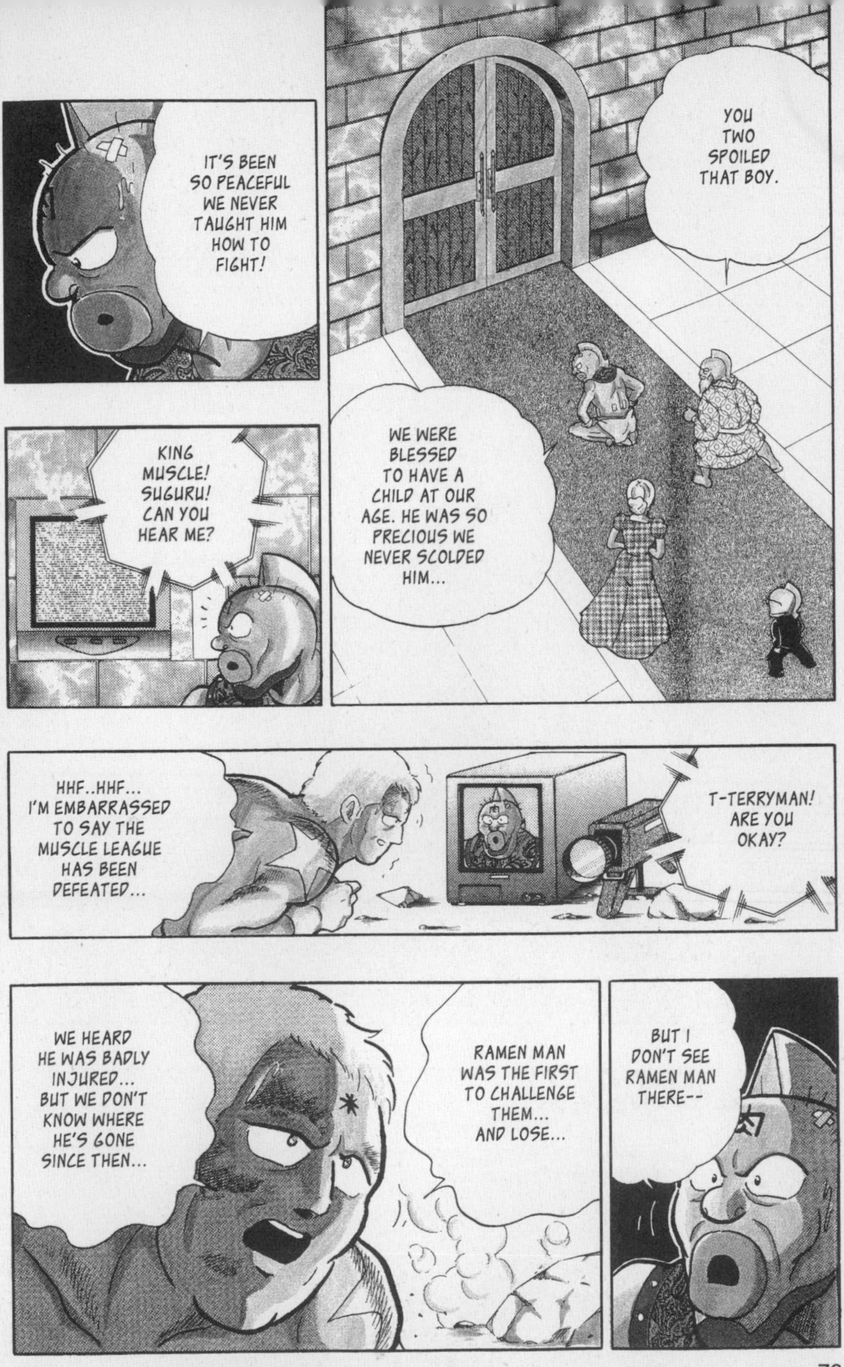
YOU TWO SPOILED THAT BOY.
WE WERE BLESSED TO HAVE A CHILD AT OUR AGE. HE WAS SO PRECIOUS WE NEVER SCOLDED HIM...
IT'S BEEN SO PEACEFUL WE NEVER TAUGHT HIM HOW TO FIGHT!
KING MUSCLE! SUGURU! CAN YOU HEAR ME?
T-TERRYMAN! ARE YOU OKAY?
HHF..HHF... I'M EMBARRASSED TO SAY THE MUSCLE LEAGUE HAS BEEN DEFEATED...
BUT I DON'T SEE RAMEN MAN THERE--
RAMEN MAN WAS THE FIRST TO CHALLENGE THEM... AND LOSE...
WE HEARD HE WAS BADLY INJURED... BUT WE DON'T KNOW WHERE HE'S GONE SINCE THEN...

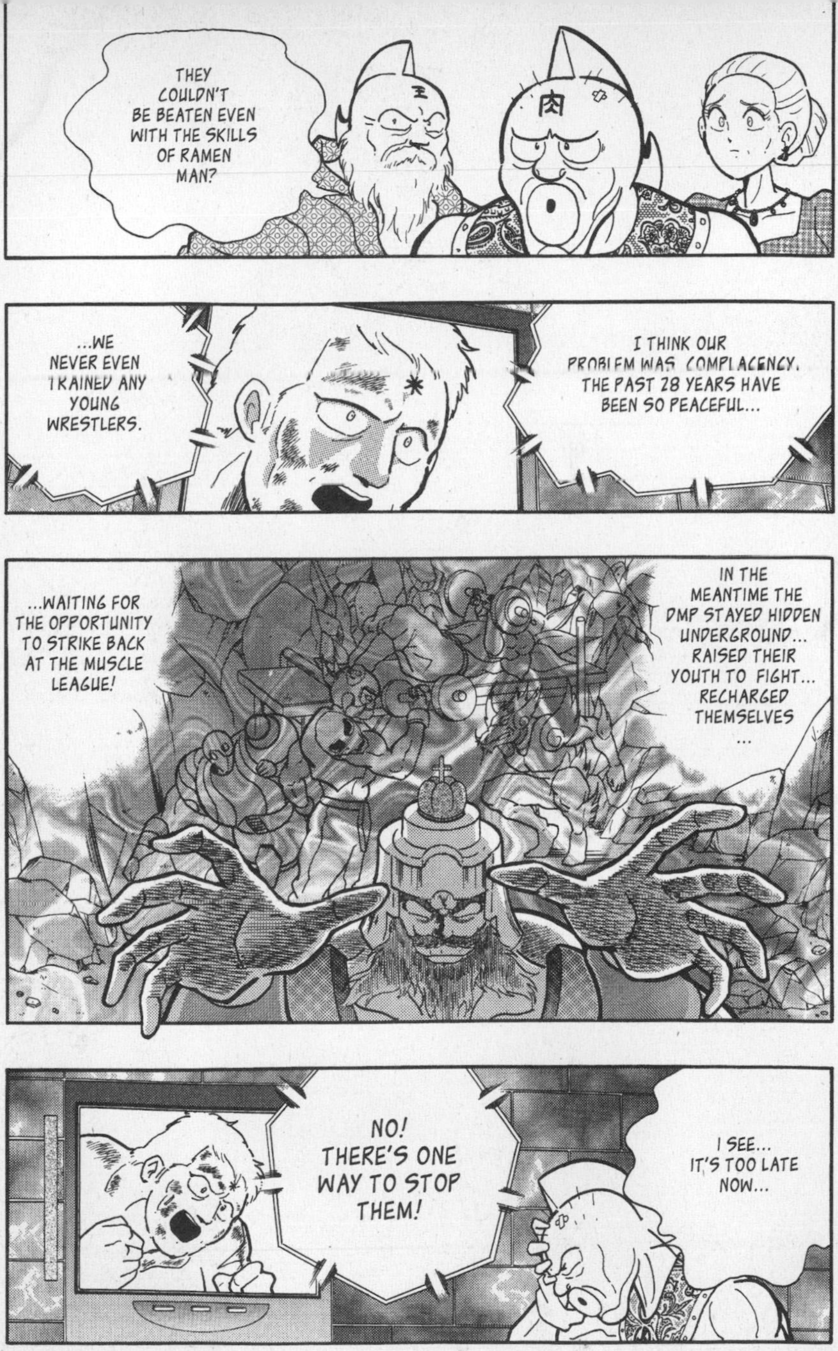
THEY COULDN'T BE BEATEN EVEN WITH THE SKILLS OF RAMEN MAN?
I THINK OUR PROBLEM WAS COMPLACENCY. THE PAST 28 YEARS HAVE BEEN SO PEACEFUL...
...WE NEVER EVEN TRAINED ANY YOUNG WRESTLERS.
IN THE MEANTIME THE DMP STAYED HIDDEN UNDERGROUND... RAISED THEIR YOUTH TO FIGHT... RECHARGED THEMSELVES ...
...WAITING FOR THE OPPORTUNITY TO STRIKE BACK AT THE MUSCLE LEAGUE!
I SEE... IT'S TOO LATE NOW...
NO! THERE'S ONE WAY TO STOP THEM!

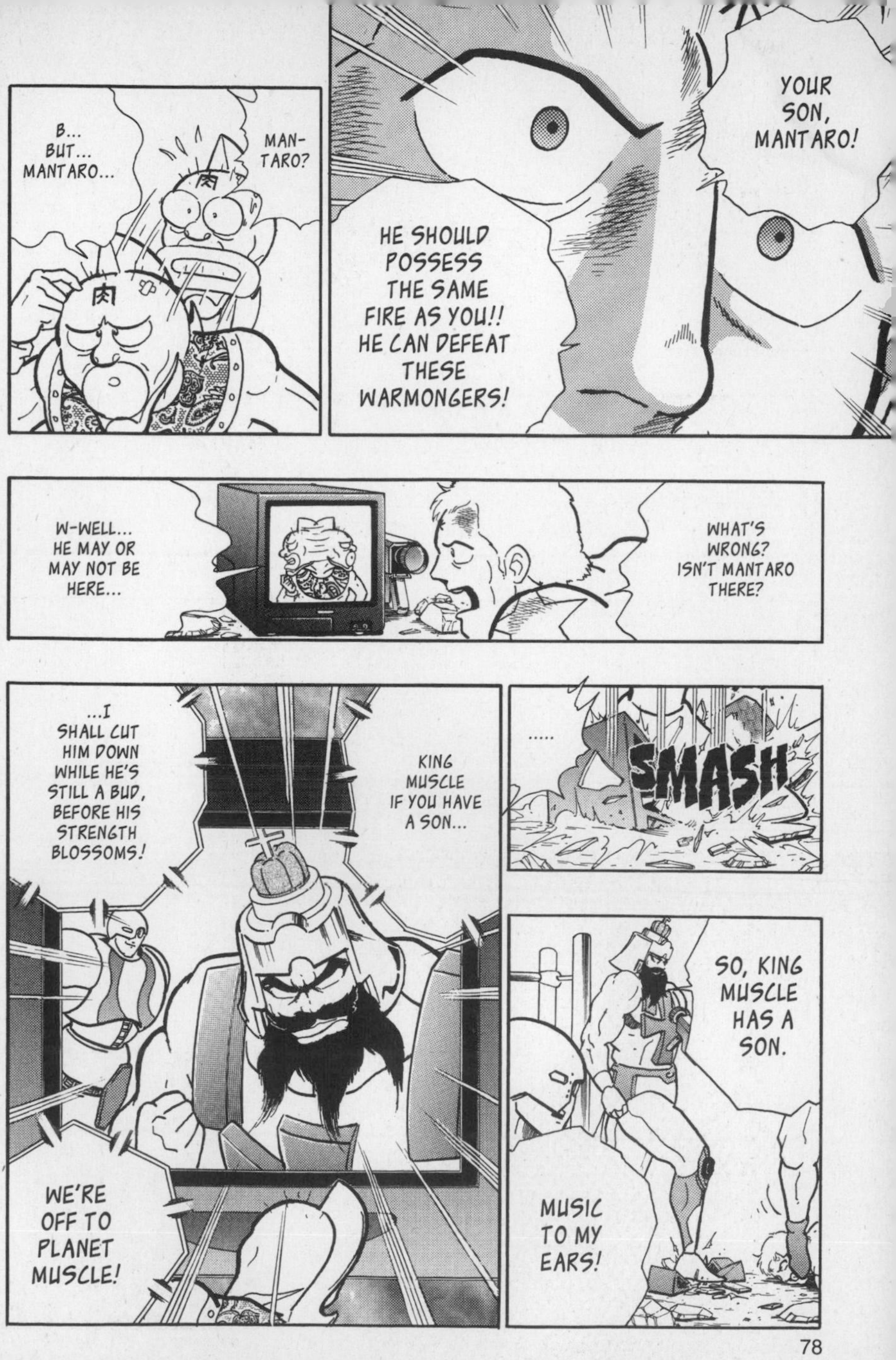
YOUR SON, MANTARO!
HE SHOULD POSSESS THE SAME FIRE AS YOU!! HE CAN DEFEAT THESE WARMONGERS!
MAN-TARO?
B... BUT... MANTARO...
WHAT'S WRONG? ISN'T MANTARO THERE?
W-WELL... HE MAY OR MAY NOT BE HERE...
.....
SMASH
SO, KING MUSCLE HAS A SON.
MUSIC TO MY EARS!
KING MUSCLE IF YOU HAVE A SON...
...I SHALL CUT HIM DOWN WHILE HE'S STILL A BUD, BEFORE HIS STRENGTH BLOSSOMS!
WE'RE OFF TO PLANET MUSCLE!

MANTARO
IS IN
DANGER!

"OLD MAN
OF THE
BRAID"...

...I'M HERE
TO LEARN
FROM YOU
AGAIN.

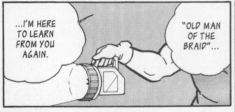

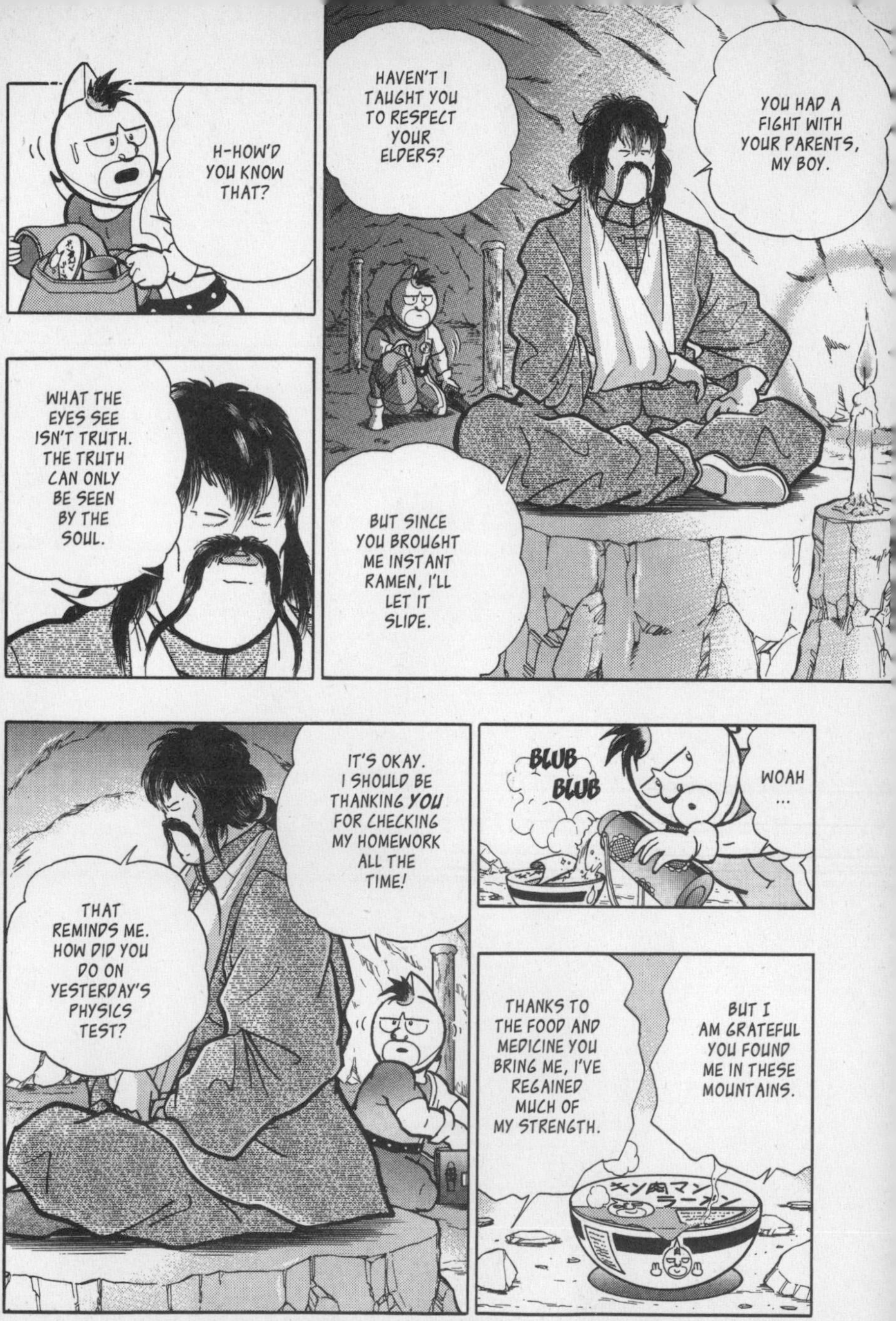
YOU HAD A FIGHT WITH YOUR PARENTS, MY BOY.
HAVEN'T I TAUGHT YOU TO RESPECT YOUR ELDERS?
BUT SINCE YOU BROUGHT ME INSTANT RAMEN, I'LL LET IT SLIDE.
H-HOW'D YOU KNOW THAT?
WHAT THE EYES SEE ISN'T TRUTH. THE TRUTH CAN ONLY BE SEEN BY THE SOUL.
WOAH ...
BLUB BLUB
BUT I AM GRATEFUL YOU FOUND ME IN THESE MOUNTAINS.
THANKS TO THE FOOD AND MEDICINE YOU BRING ME, I'VE REGAINED MUCH OF MY STRENGTH.
IT'S OKAY. I SHOULD BE THANKING *YOU* FOR CHECKING MY HOMEWORK ALL THE TIME!
THAT REMINDS ME. HOW DID YOU DO ON YESTERDAY'S PHYSICS TEST?

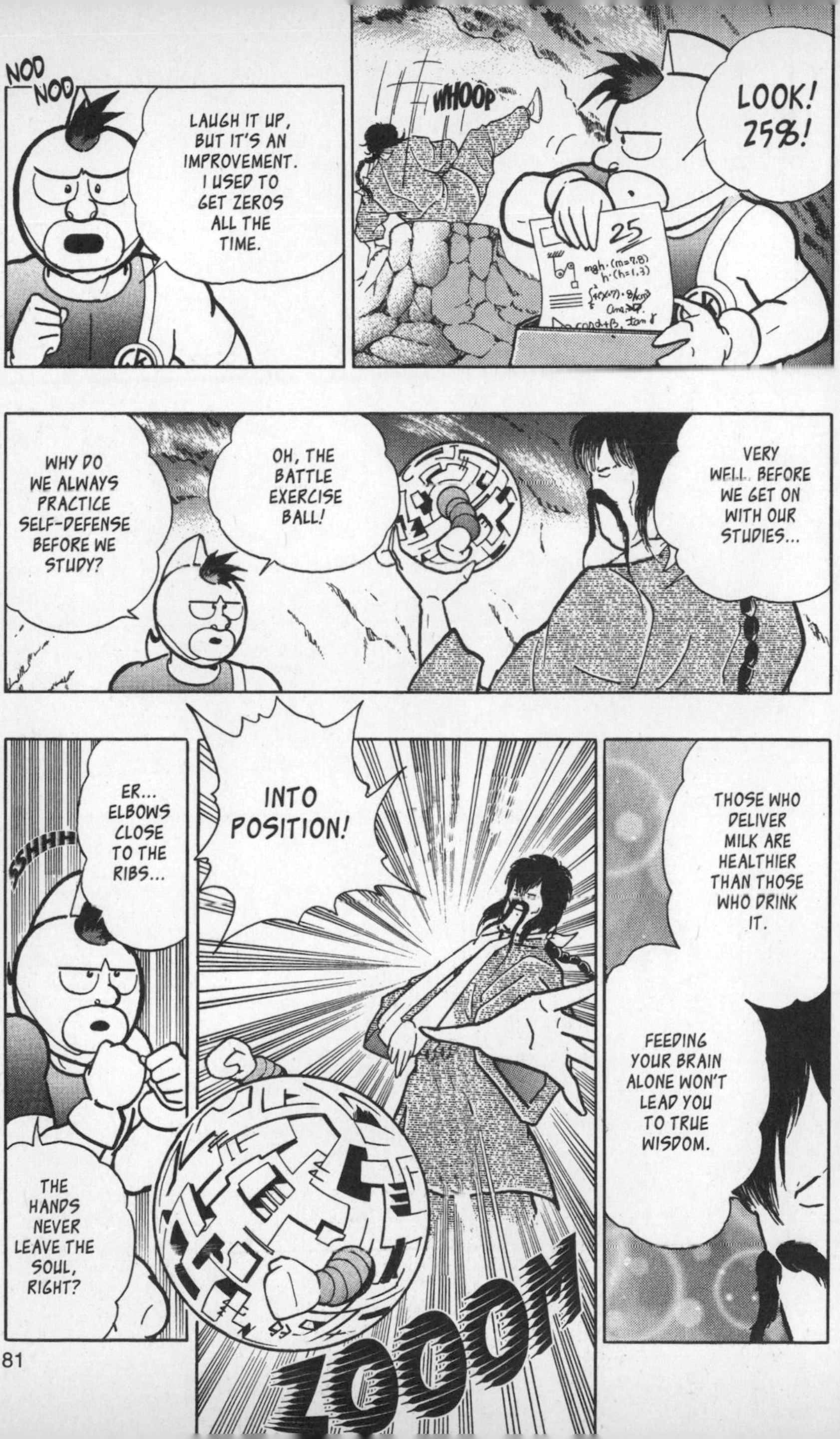
WHOOP
LOOK! 25%!
25
NOD NOD
LAUGH IT UP, BUT IT'S AN IMPROVEMENT. I USED TO GET ZEROS ALL THE TIME.
VERY WELL. BEFORE WE GET ON WITH OUR STUDIES...
OH, THE BATTLE EXERCISE BALL!
WHY DO WE ALWAYS PRACTICE SELF-DEFENSE BEFORE WE STUDY?
THOSE WHO DELIVER MILK ARE HEALTHIER THAN THOSE WHO DRINK IT.
FEEDING YOUR BRAIN ALONE WON'T LEAD YOU TO TRUE WISDOM.
INTO POSITION!
ZOOOM
SSHHH
ER... ELBOWS CLOSE TO THE RIBS...
THE HANDS NEVER LEAVE THE SOUL, RIGHT?

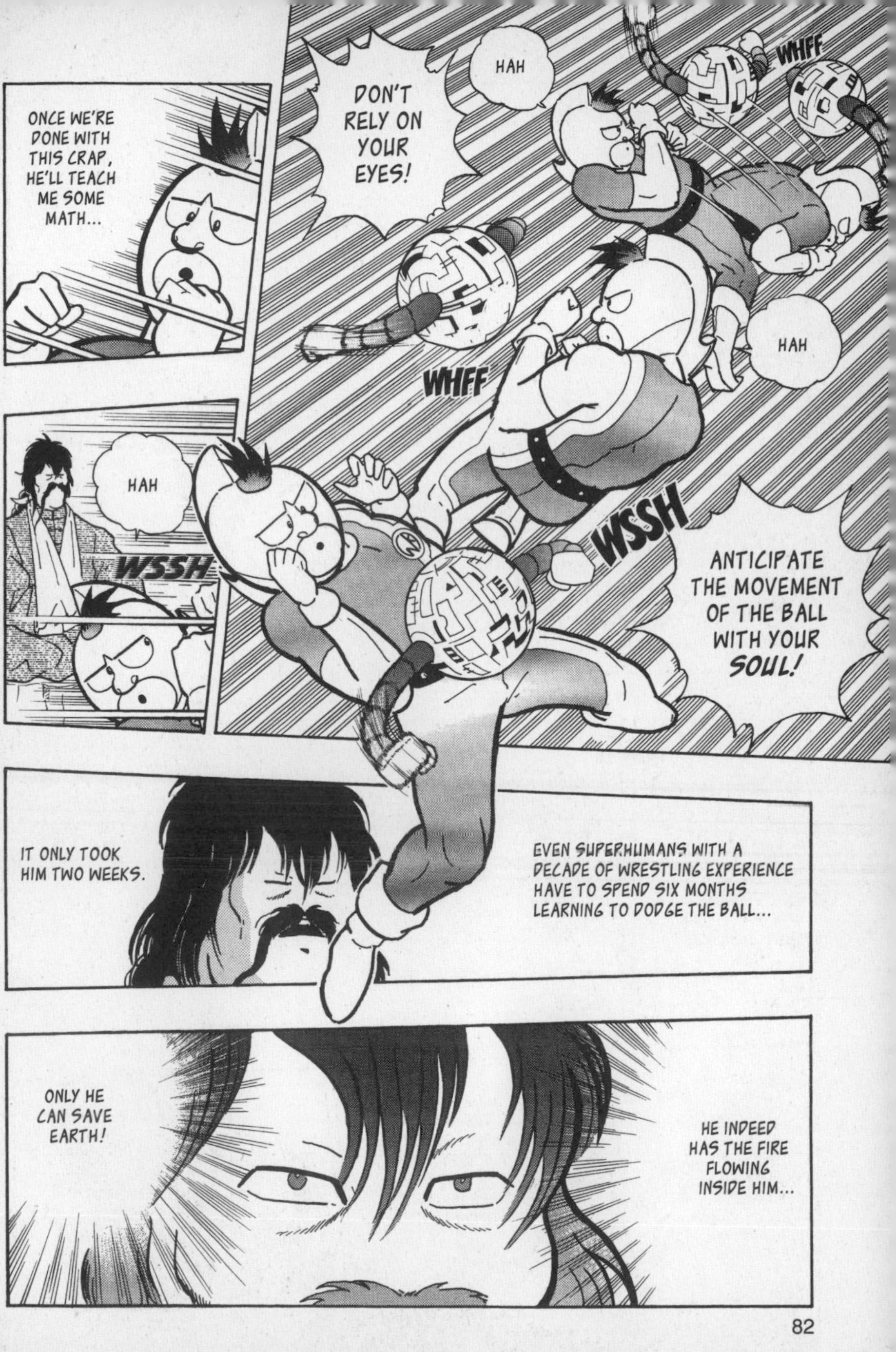
WHFF
HAH
DON'T RELY ON YOUR EYES!
HAH
ANTICIPATE THE MOVEMENT OF THE BALL WITH YOUR SOUL!
WSSH
WHFF
ONCE WE'RE DONE WITH THIS CRAP, HE'LL TEACH ME SOME MATH...
HAH
WSSH
EVEN SUPERHUMANS WITH A DECADE OF WRESTLING EXPERIENCE HAVE TO SPEND SIX MONTHS LEARNING TO DODGE THE BALL...
IT ONLY TOOK HIM TWO WEEKS.
HE INDEED HAS THE FIRE FLOWING INSIDE HIM...
ONLY HE CAN SAVE EARTH!

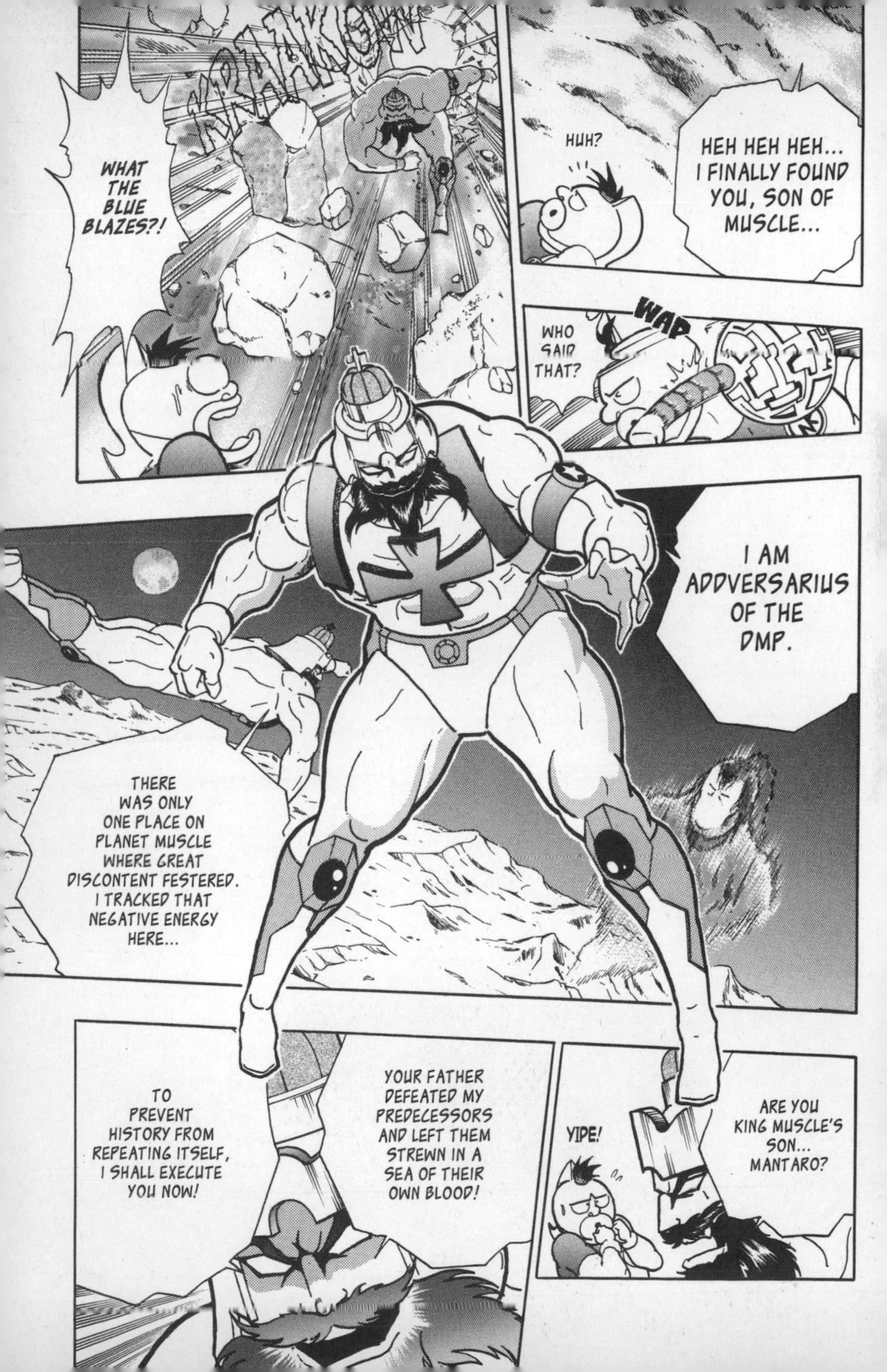
HEH HEH HEH... I FINALLY FOUND YOU, SON OF MUSCLE...
HUH?
WAP
WHO SAID THAT?
WHAT THE BLUE BLAZES?!
I AM ADDVERSARIUS OF THE DMP.
THERE WAS ONLY ONE PLACE ON PLANET MUSCLE WHERE GREAT DISCONTENT FESTERED. I TRACKED THAT NEGATIVE ENERGY HERE...
ARE YOU KING MUSCLE'S SON... MANTARO?
YIPE!
YOUR FATHER DEFEATED MY PREDECESSORS AND LEFT THEM STREWN IN A SEA OF THEIR OWN BLOOD!
TO PREVENT HISTORY FROM REPEATING ITSELF, I SHALL EXECUTE YOU NOW!

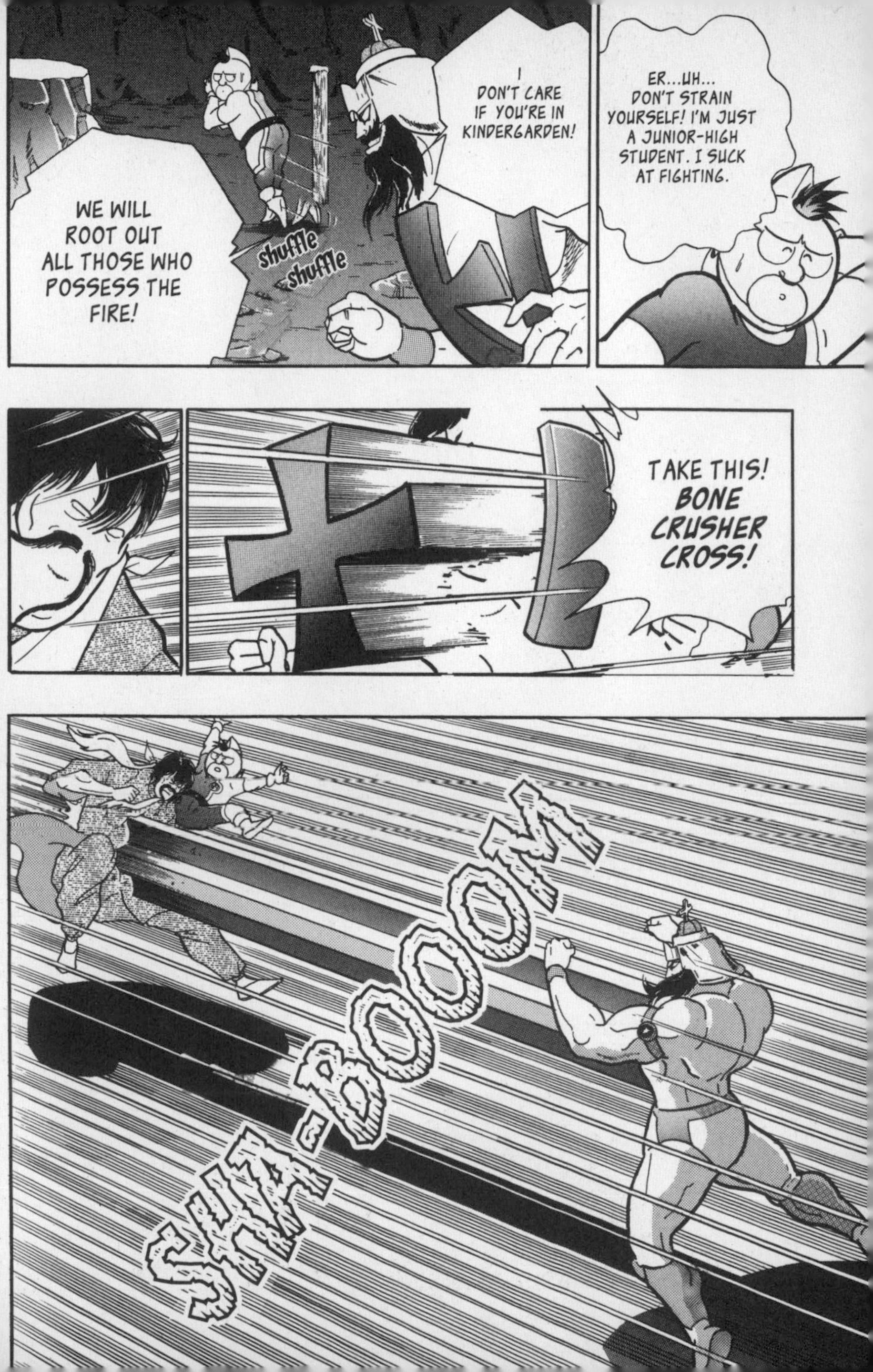
ER...UH... DON'T STRAIN YOURSELF! I'M JUST A JUNIOR-HIGH STUDENT. I SUCK AT FIGHTING.
I DON'T CARE IF YOU'RE IN KINDERGARDEN!
shuffle shuffle
WE WILL ROOT OUT ALL THOSE WHO POSSESS THE FIRE!
TAKE THIS! BONE CRUSHER CROSS!
SHA-BOOOOM

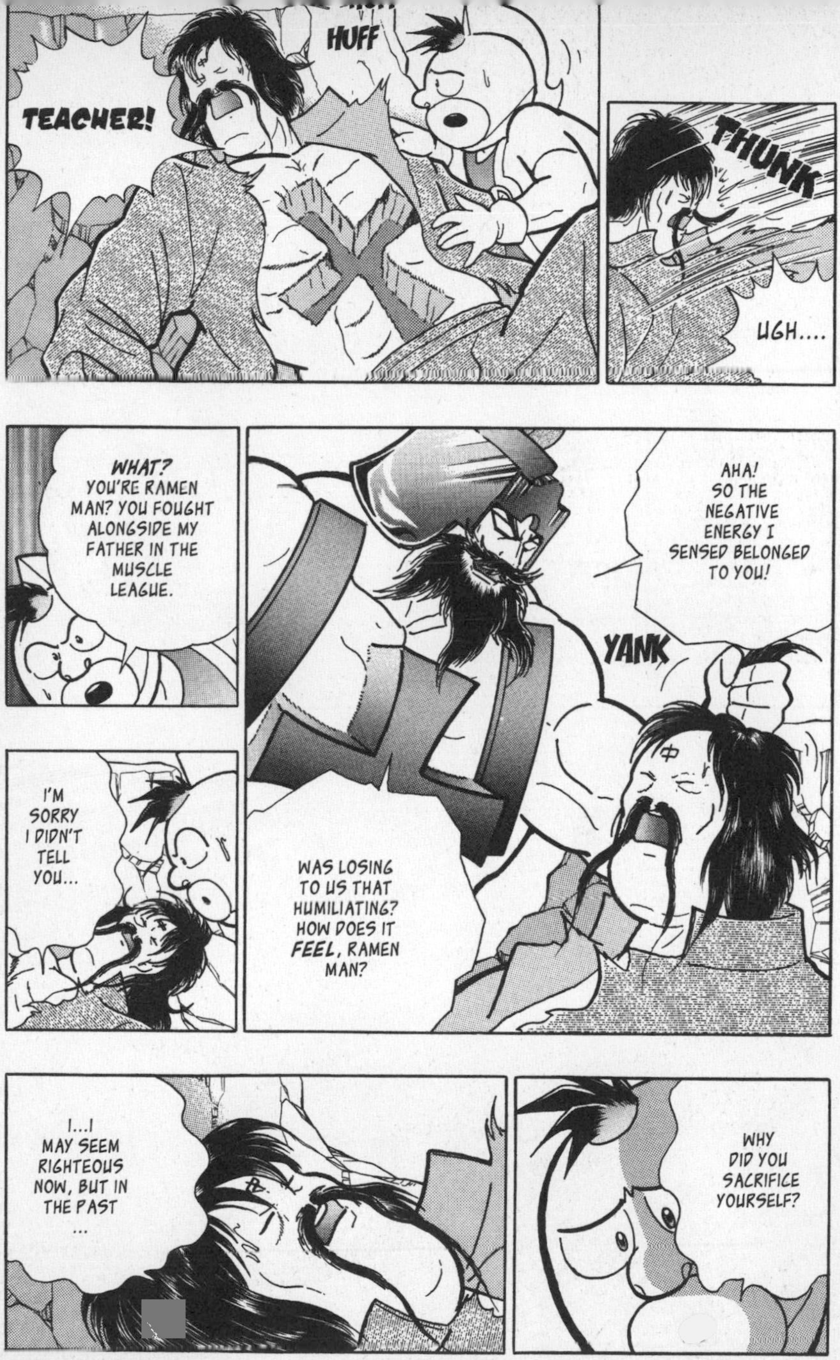
THUNK
UGH....
HUFF
TEACHER!
AHA! SO THE NEGATIVE ENERGY I SENSED BELONGED TO YOU!
YANK
WAS LOSING TO US THAT HUMILIATING? HOW DOES IT *FEEL*, RAMEN MAN?
*WHAT?* YOU'RE RAMEN MAN? YOU FOUGHT ALONGSIDE MY FATHER IN THE MUSCLE LEAGUE.
I'M SORRY I DIDN'T TELL YOU...
WHY DID YOU SACRIFICE YOURSELF?
I...I MAY SEEM RIGHTEOUS NOW, BUT IN THE PAST ...

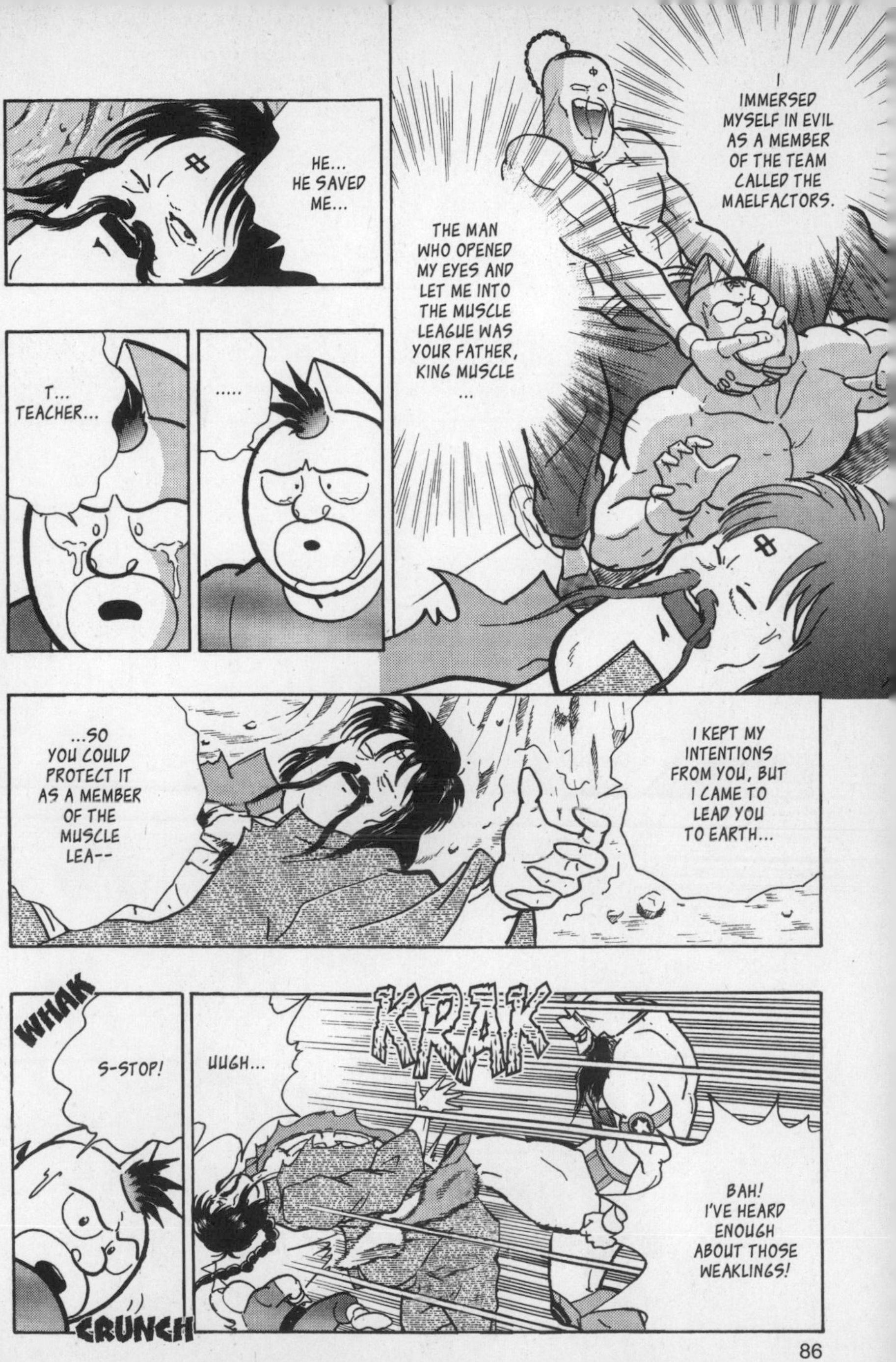

I IMMERSED MYSELF IN EVIL AS A MEMBER OF THE TEAM CALLED THE MAELFACTORS.
THE MAN WHO OPENED MY EYES AND LET ME INTO THE MUSCLE LEAGUE WAS YOUR FATHER, KING MUSCLE ...
HE... HE SAVED ME...
.....
T... TEACHER...
I KEPT MY INTENTIONS FROM YOU, BUT I CAME TO LEAD YOU TO EARTH...
...SO YOU COULD PROTECT IT AS A MEMBER OF THE MUSCLE LEA--
KRAK
UUGH...
BAH! I'VE HEARD ENOUGH ABOUT THOSE WEAKLINGS!
WHAK
S-STOP!
CRUNCH

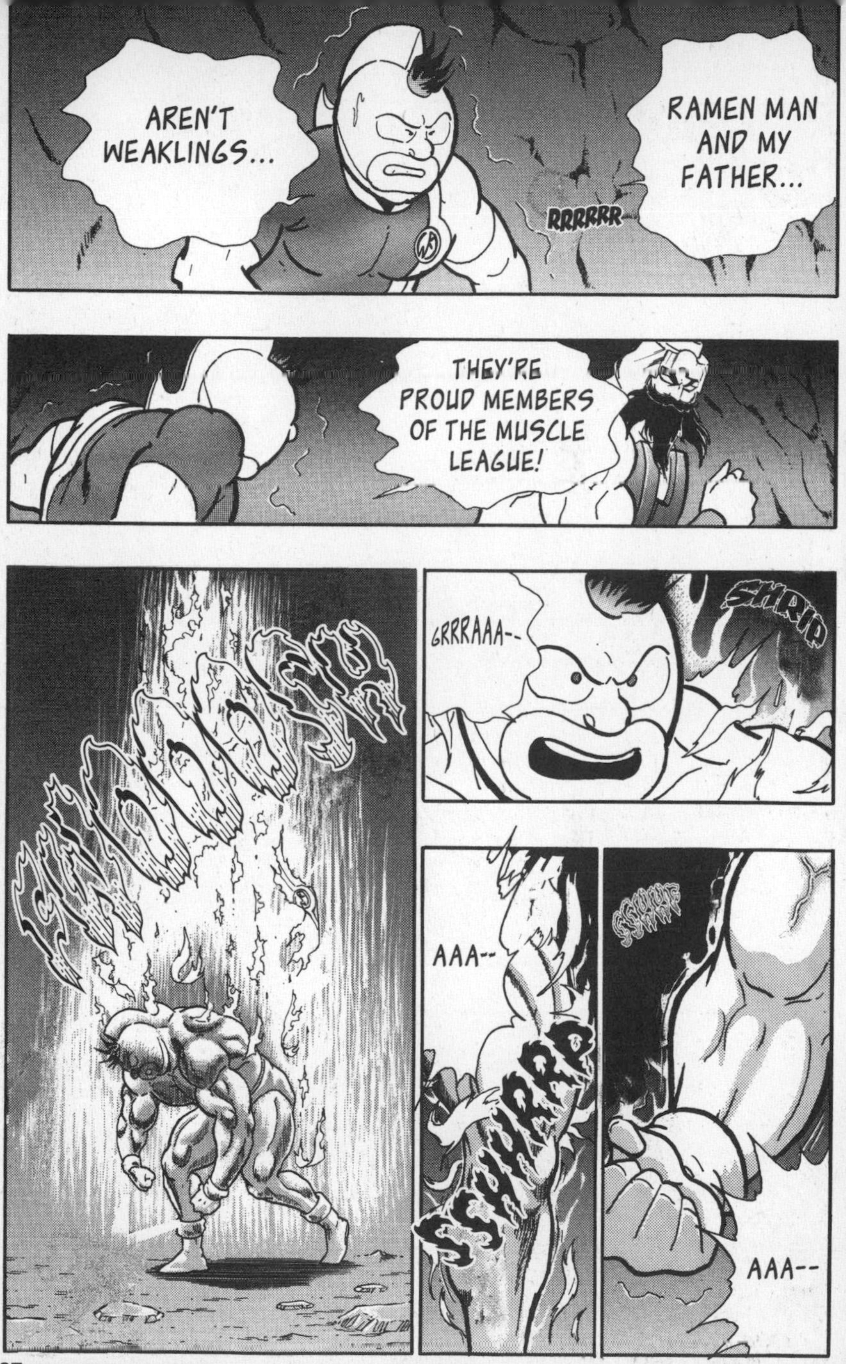
RAMEN MAN AND MY FATHER...
RRRRRR
AREN'T WEAKLINGS...
THEY'RE PROUD MEMBERS OF THE MUSCLE LEAGUE!
SHRIP
GRRRAAA--
AAA--
AAA--

READ THIS WAY

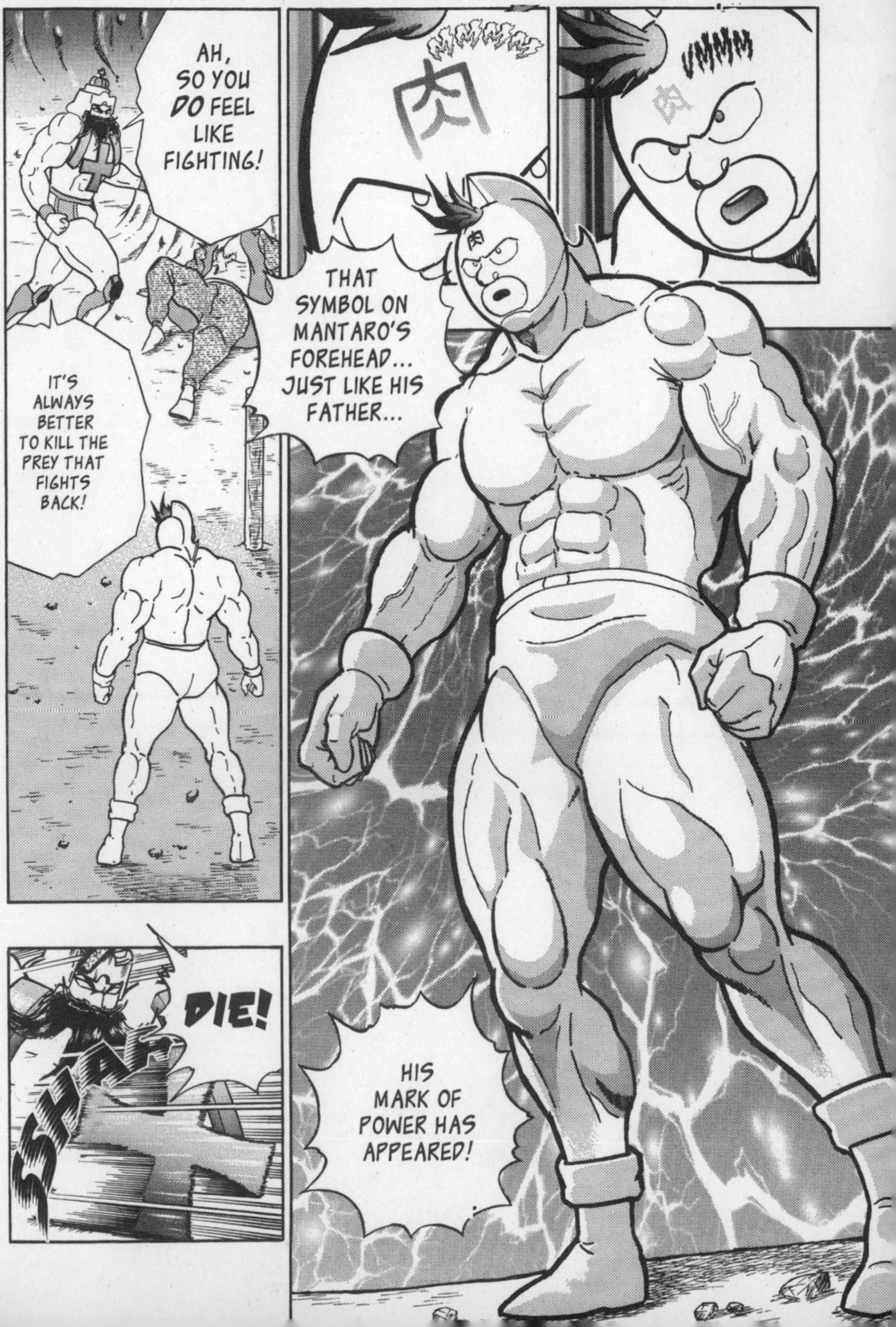

UMMM
UMMM
肉
THAT SYMBOL ON MANTARO'S FOREHEAD... JUST LIKE HIS FATHER...
HIS MARK OF POWER HAS APPEARED!
AH, SO YOU DO FEEL LIKE FIGHTING!
IT'S ALWAYS BETTER TO KILL THE PREY THAT FIGHTS BACK!
DIE!

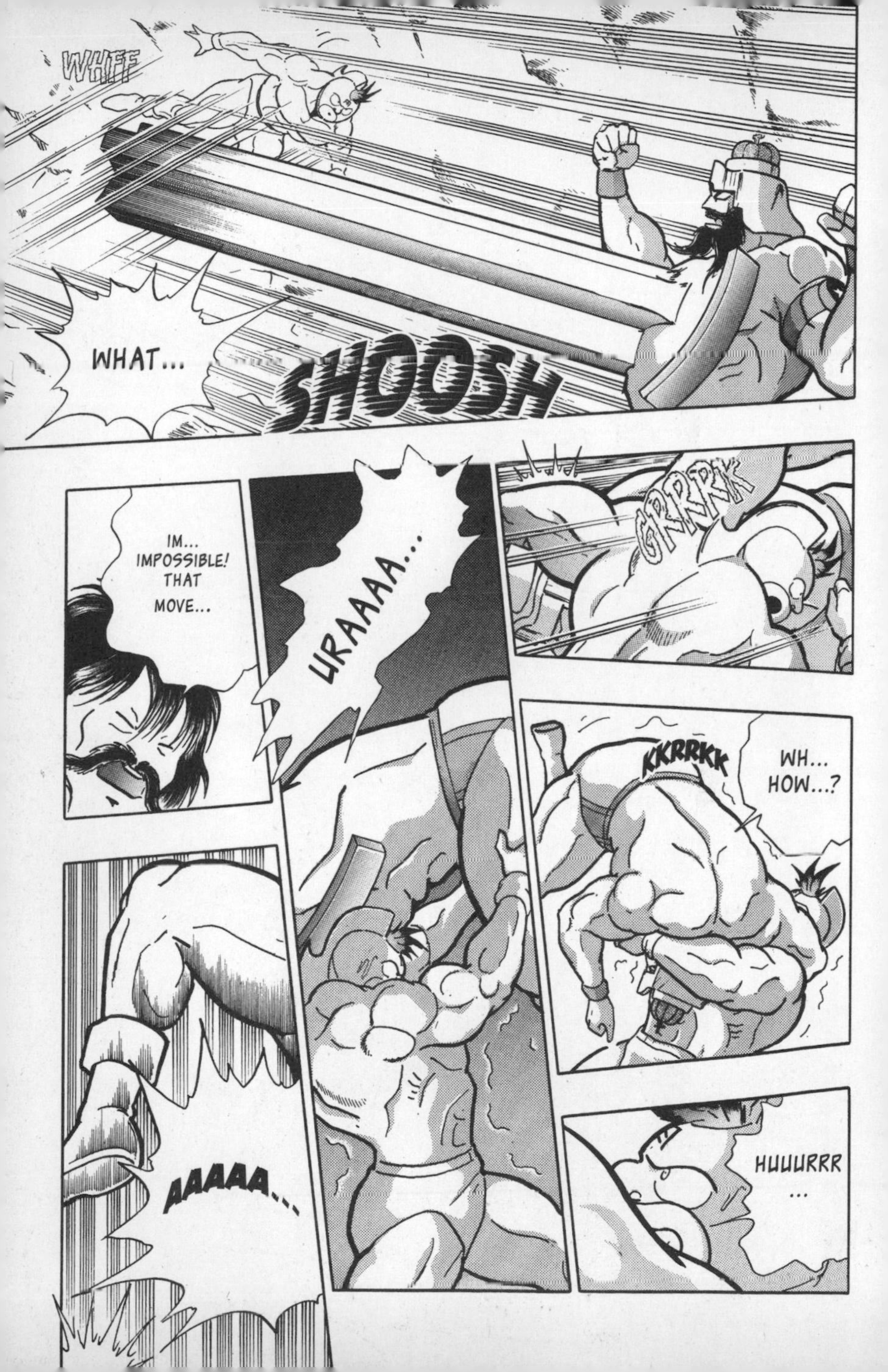
WHIFF
WHAT...
SHOOSH
GRRRK
KKRRKK
WH... HOW...?
HUUURRR ...
URAAAA...
IM... IMPOSSIBLE! THAT MOVE...
AAAAA...

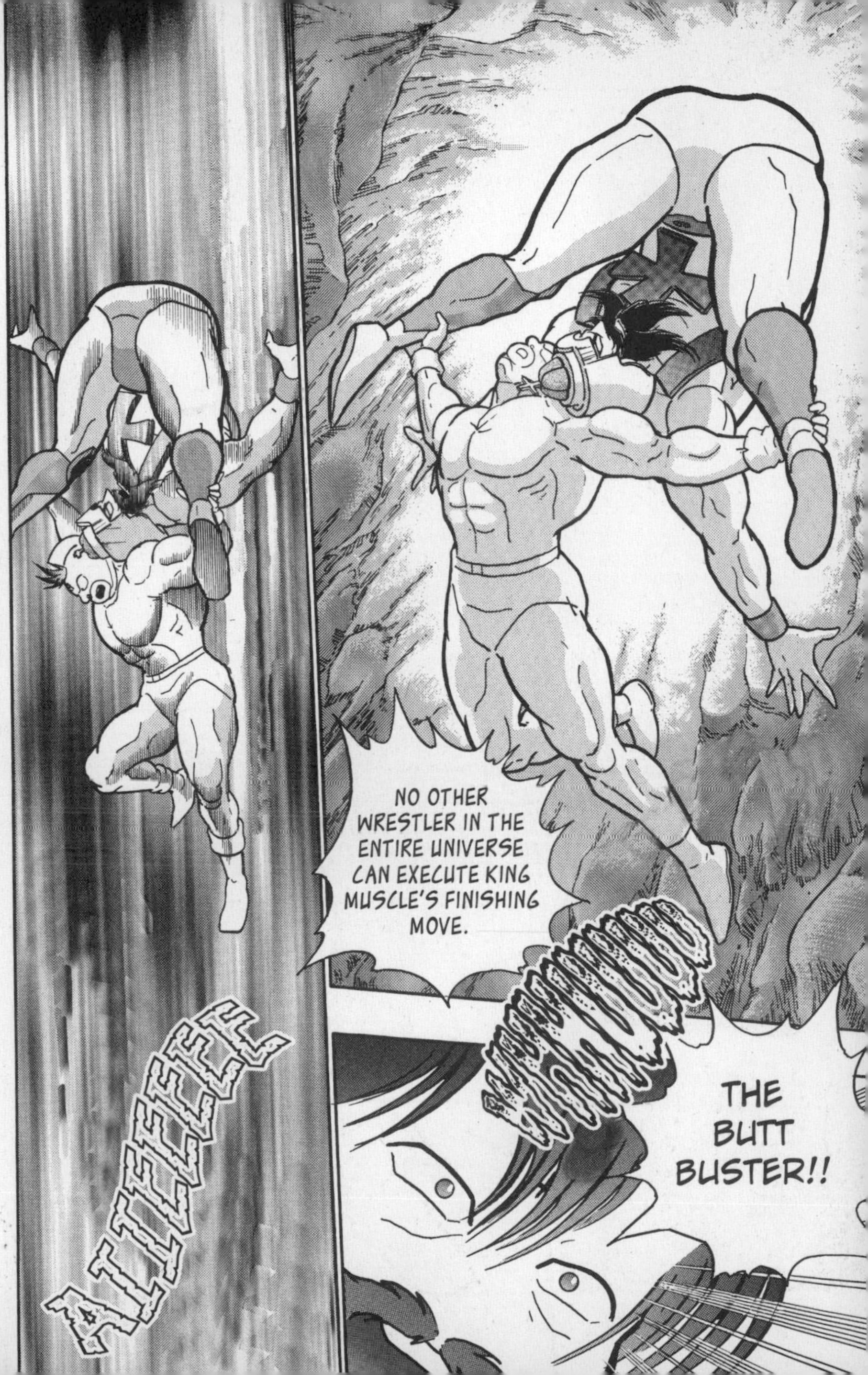
NO OTHER WRESTLER IN THE ENTIRE UNIVERSE CAN EXECUTE KING MUSCLE'S FINISHING MOVE.
THE BUTT BUSTER!!

READ THIS WAY

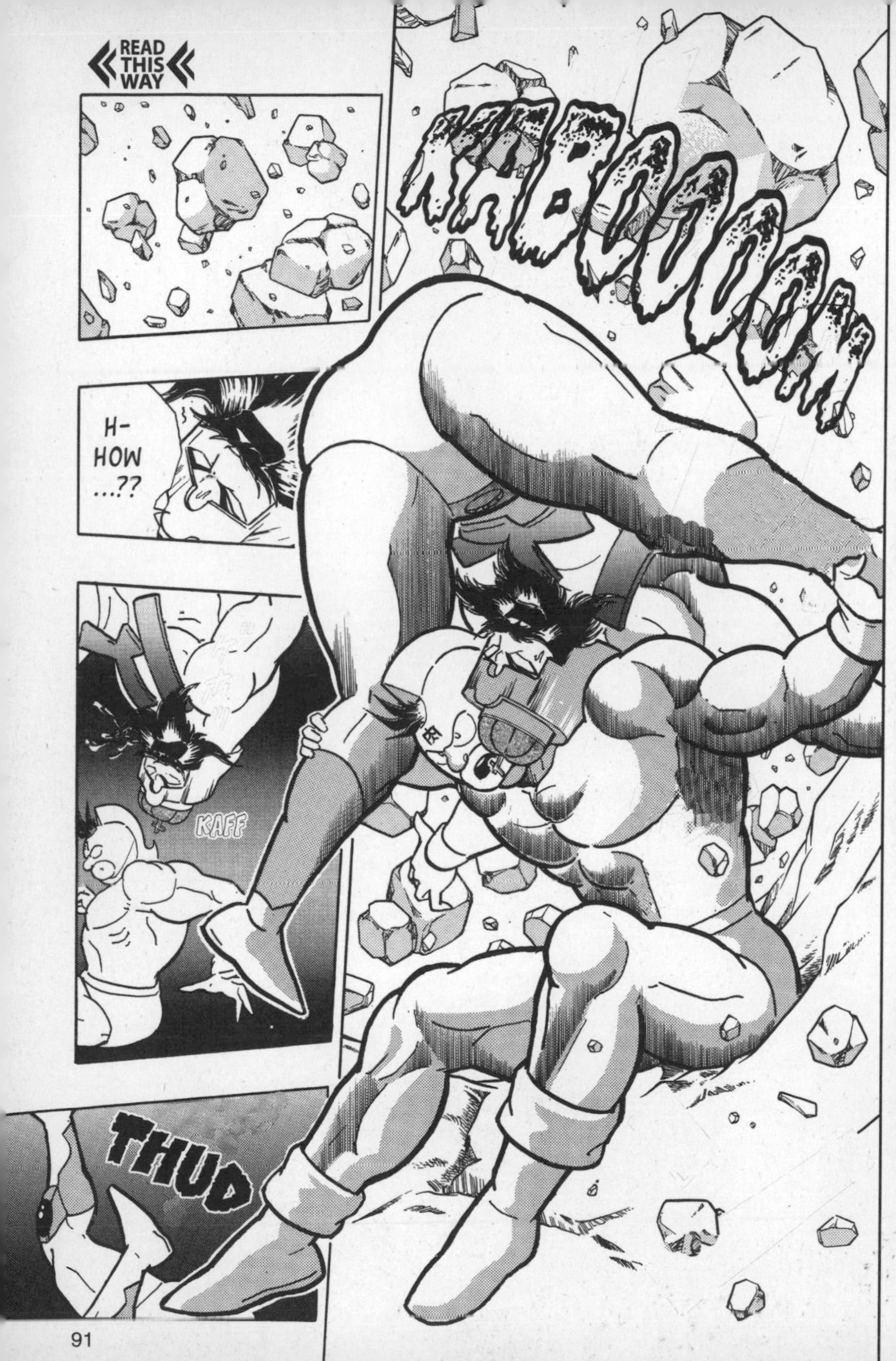
KABOOOOM
H-
HOW
...??
KAFF
THUD

READ THIS WAY

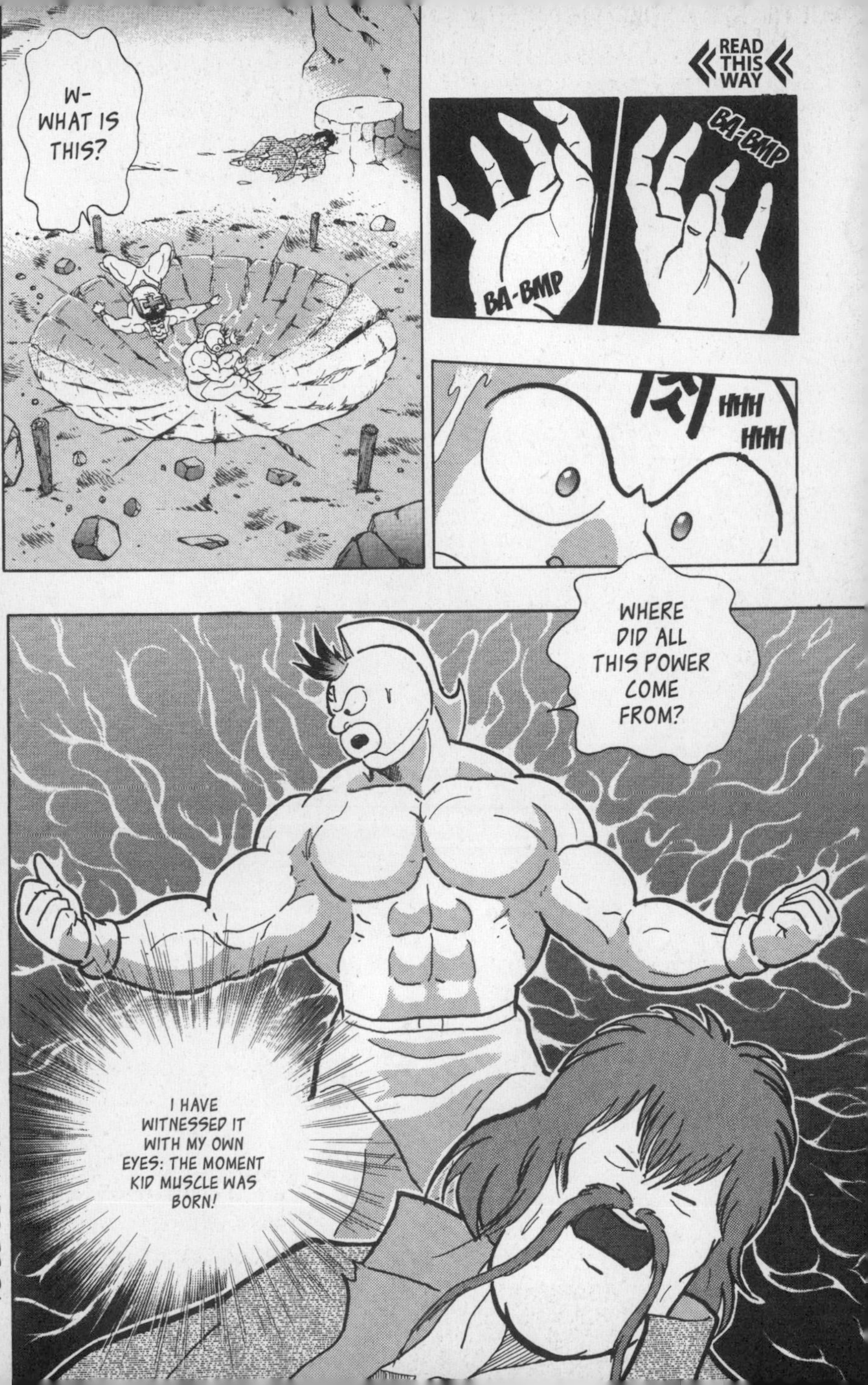
BA-BMP
BA-BMP
HHH
HHH
W-WHAT IS THIS?
WHERE DID ALL THIS POWER COME FROM?
I HAVE WITNESSED IT WITH MY OWN EYES: THE MOMENT KID MUSCLE WAS BORN!

TO BE CONTINUED IN **ULTIMATE MUSCLE** VOL. 1 ON SALE APRIL 14!

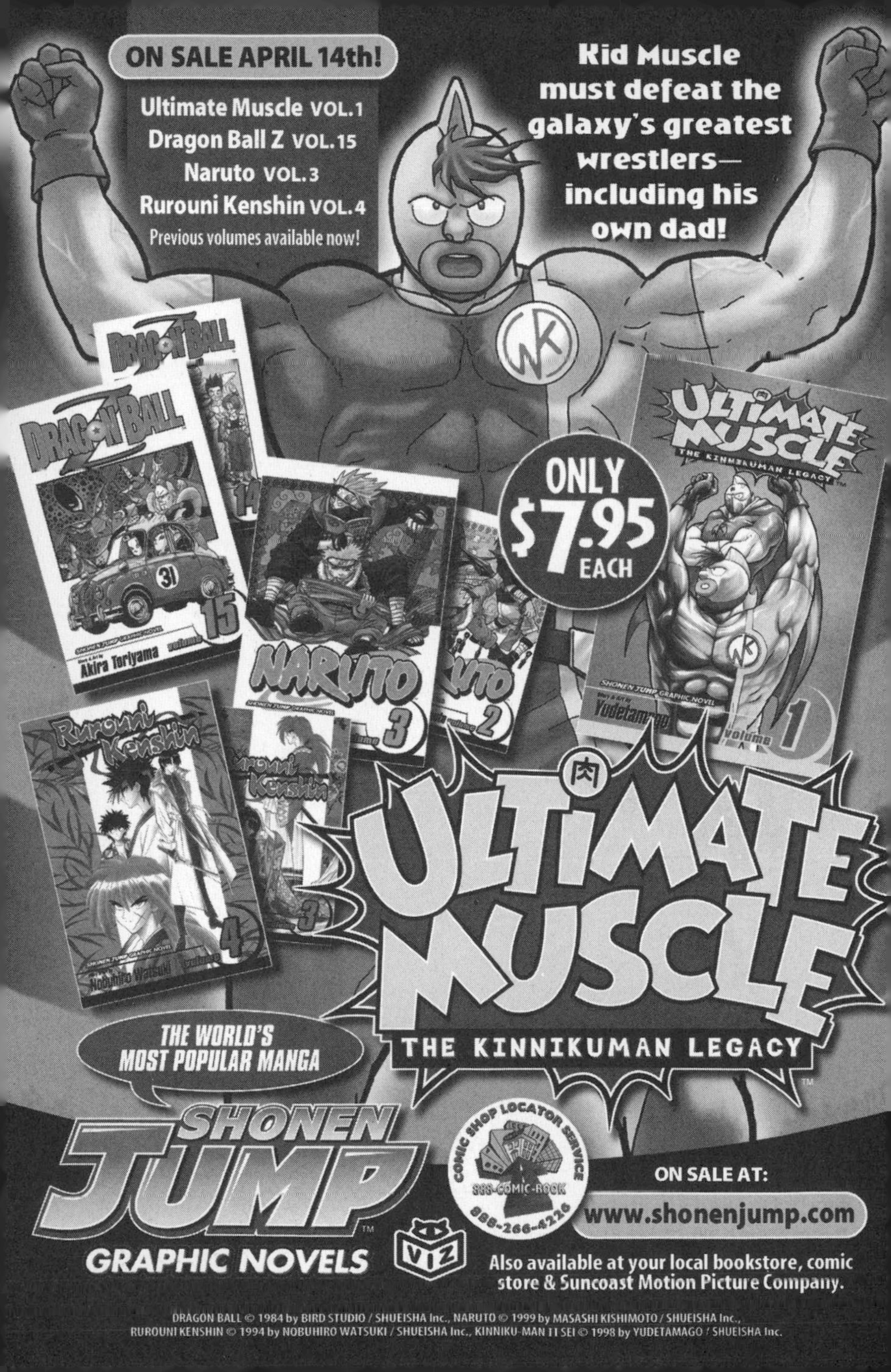

ON SALE APRIL 14th!
Ultimate Muscle VOL.1
Dragon Ball Z VOL.15
Naruto VOL.3
Rurouni Kenshin VOL.4
Previous volumes available now!
Kid Muscle must defeat the galaxy's greatest wrestlers—including his own dad!
ONLY $7.95 EACH
ULTIMATE MUSCLE
THE KINNIKUMAN LEGACY
THE WORLD'S MOST POPULAR MANGA
SHONEN JUMP GRAPHIC NOVELS
VIZ
COMIC SHOP LOCATOR SERVICE
888-COMIC-BOOK
888-266-4226
ON SALE AT:
www.shonenjump.com
Also available at your local bookstore, comic store & Suncoast Motion Picture Company.
DRAGON BALL © 1984 by BIRD STUDIO / SHUEISHA Inc., NARUTO © 1999 by MASASHI KISHIMOTO / SHUEISHA Inc., RUROUNI KENSHIN © 1994 by NOBUHIRO WATSUKI / SHUEISHA Inc., KINNIKU-MAN II SEI © 1998 by YUDETAMAGO / SHUEISHA Inc.

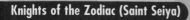

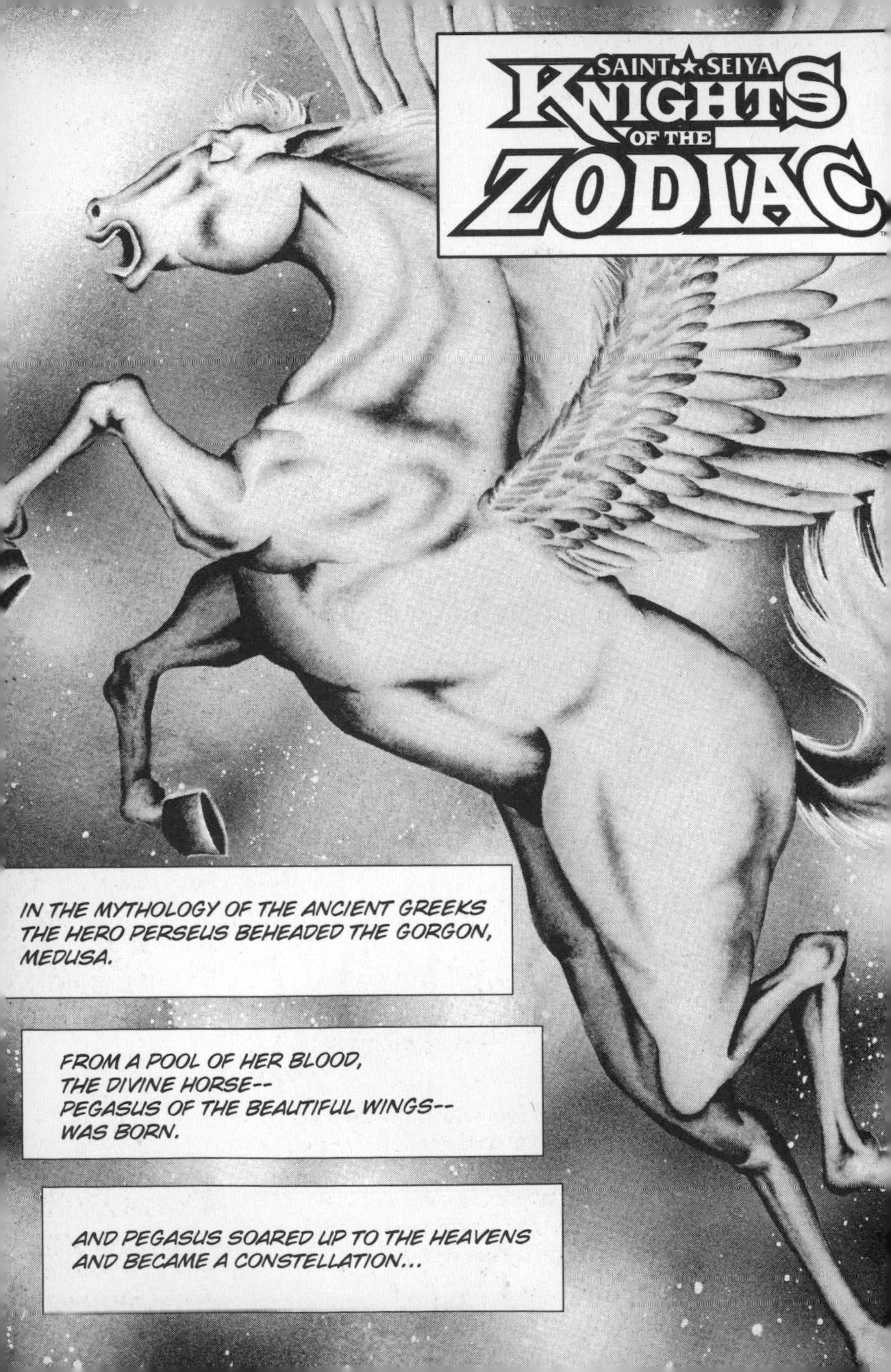
SAINT★SEIYA KNIGHTS OF THE ZODIAC
IN THE MYTHOLOGY OF THE ANCIENT GREEKS THE HERO PERSEUS BEHEADED THE GORGON, MEDUSA.
FROM A POOL OF HER BLOOD, THE DIVINE HORSE-- PEGASUS OF THE BEAUTIFUL WINGS-- WAS BORN.
AND PEGASUS SOARED UP TO THE HEAVENS AND BECAME A CONSTELLATION...

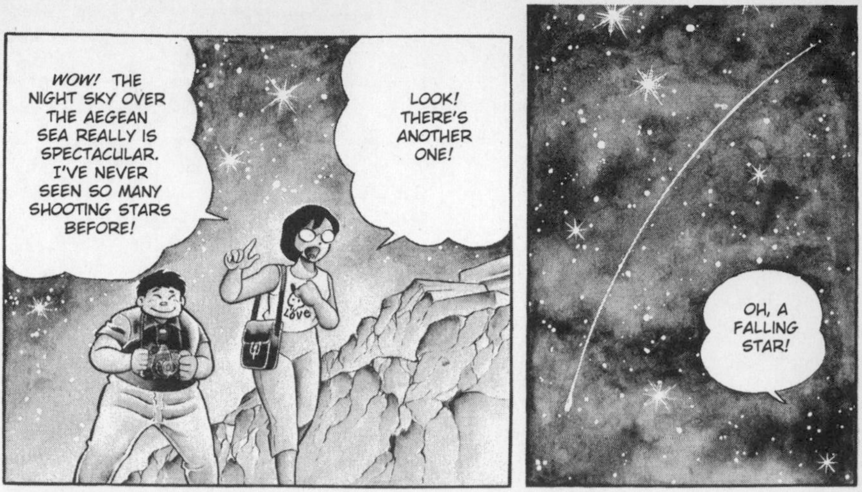
OH, A FALLING STAR!
LOOK! THERE'S ANOTHER ONE!
WOW! THE NIGHT SKY OVER THE AEGEAN SEA REALLY IS SPECTACULAR. I'VE NEVER SEEN SO MANY SHOOTING STARS BEFORE!

# CHAPTER 1: THE KNIGHTS OF ATHENA

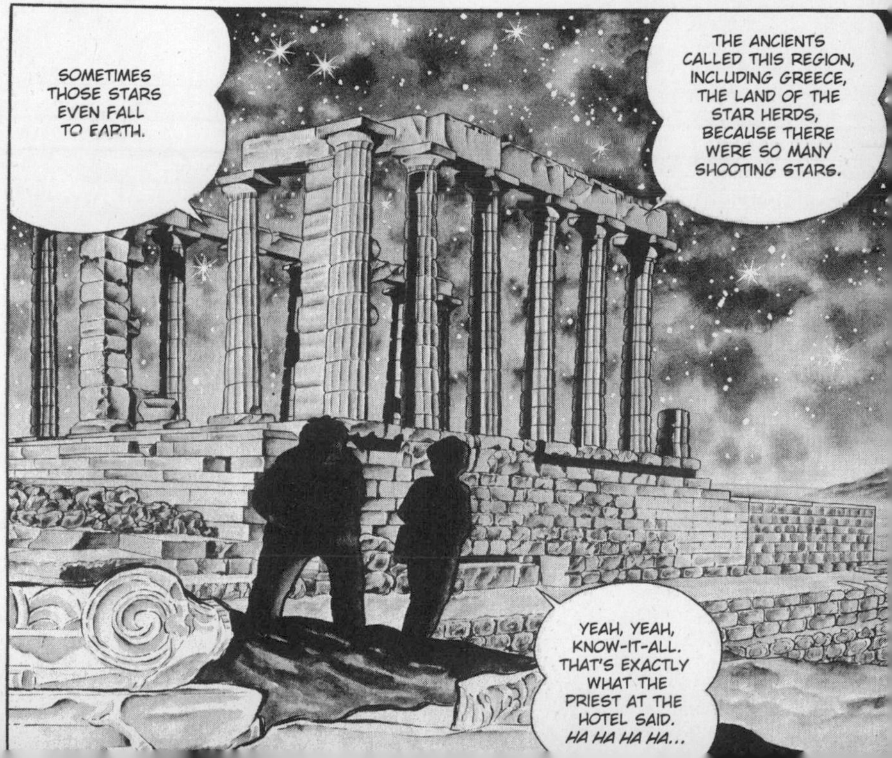
THE ANCIENTS CALLED THIS REGION, INCLUDING GREECE, THE LAND OF THE STAR HERDS, BECAUSE THERE WERE SO MANY SHOOTING STARS.
SOMETIMES THOSE STARS EVEN FALL TO EARTH.
YEAH, YEAH, KNOW-IT-ALL. THAT'S EXACTLY WHAT THE PRIEST AT THE HOTEL SAID. HA HA HA HA...

READ THIS WAY

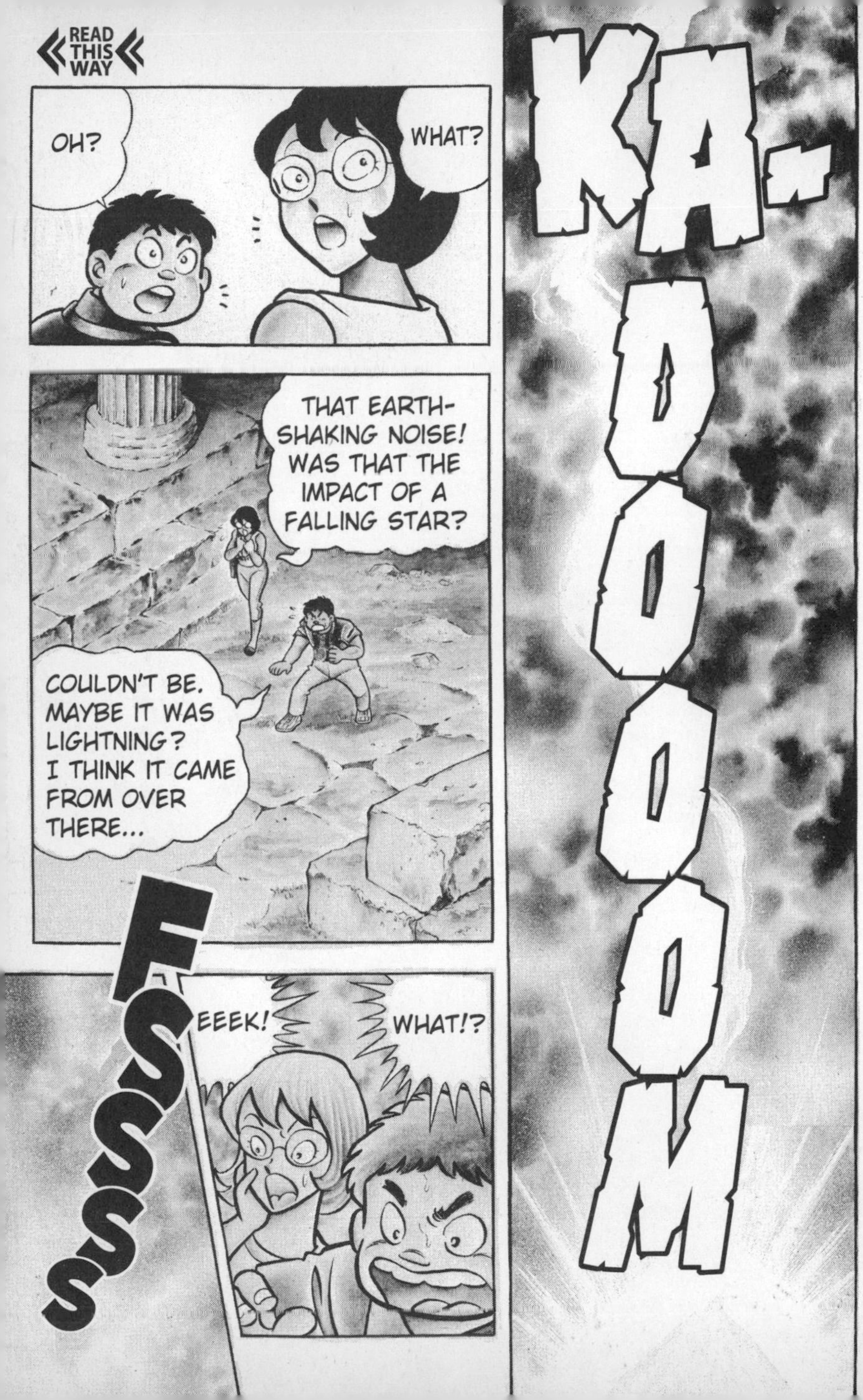
KA-DOOOOOM
WHAT?
OH?
THAT EARTH-SHAKING NOISE! WAS THAT THE IMPACT OF A FALLING STAR?
COULDN'T BE. MAYBE IT WAS LIGHTNING? I THINK IT CAME FROM OVER THERE...
WHAT!?
EEEK!
FSSSS

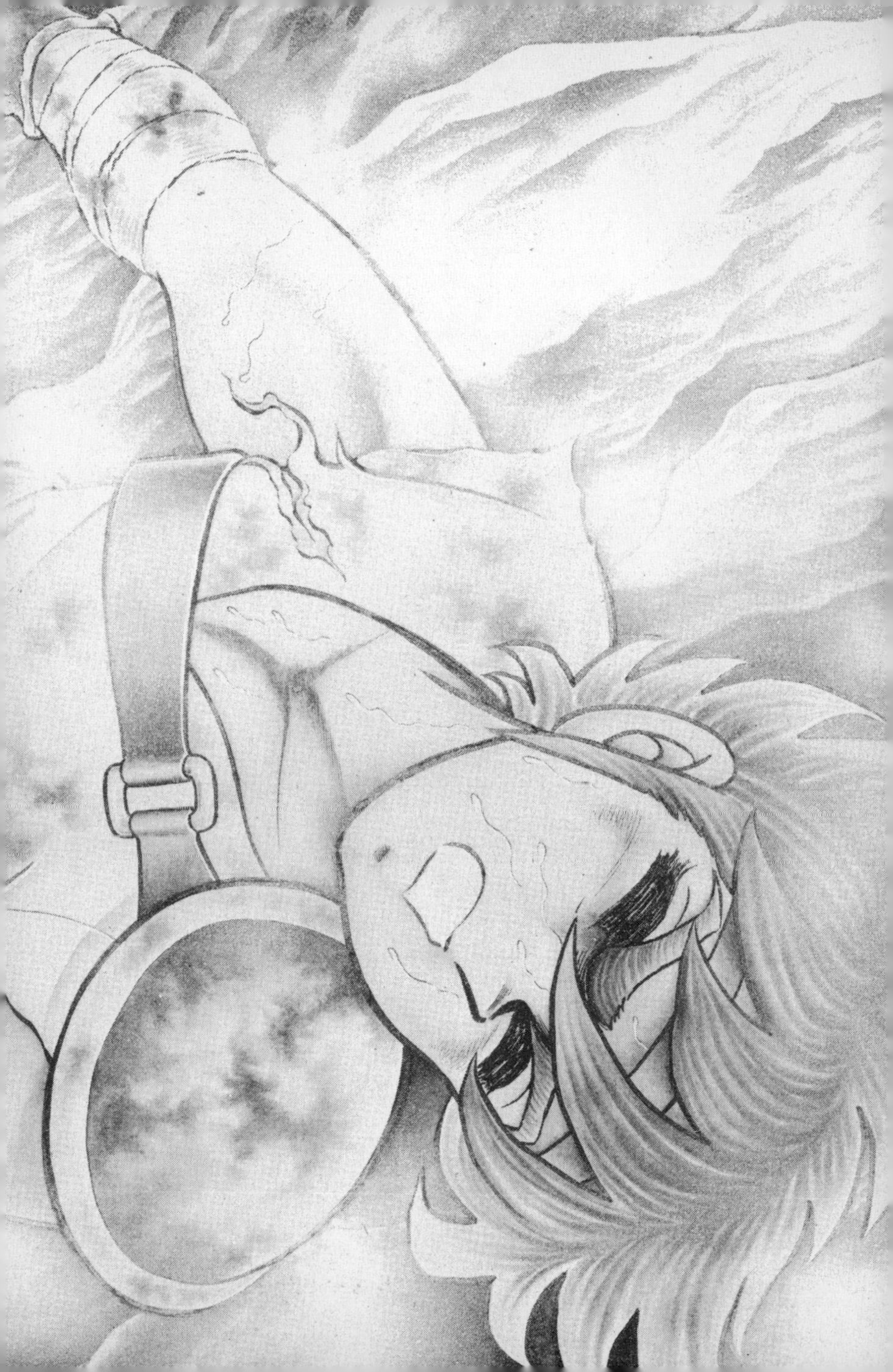

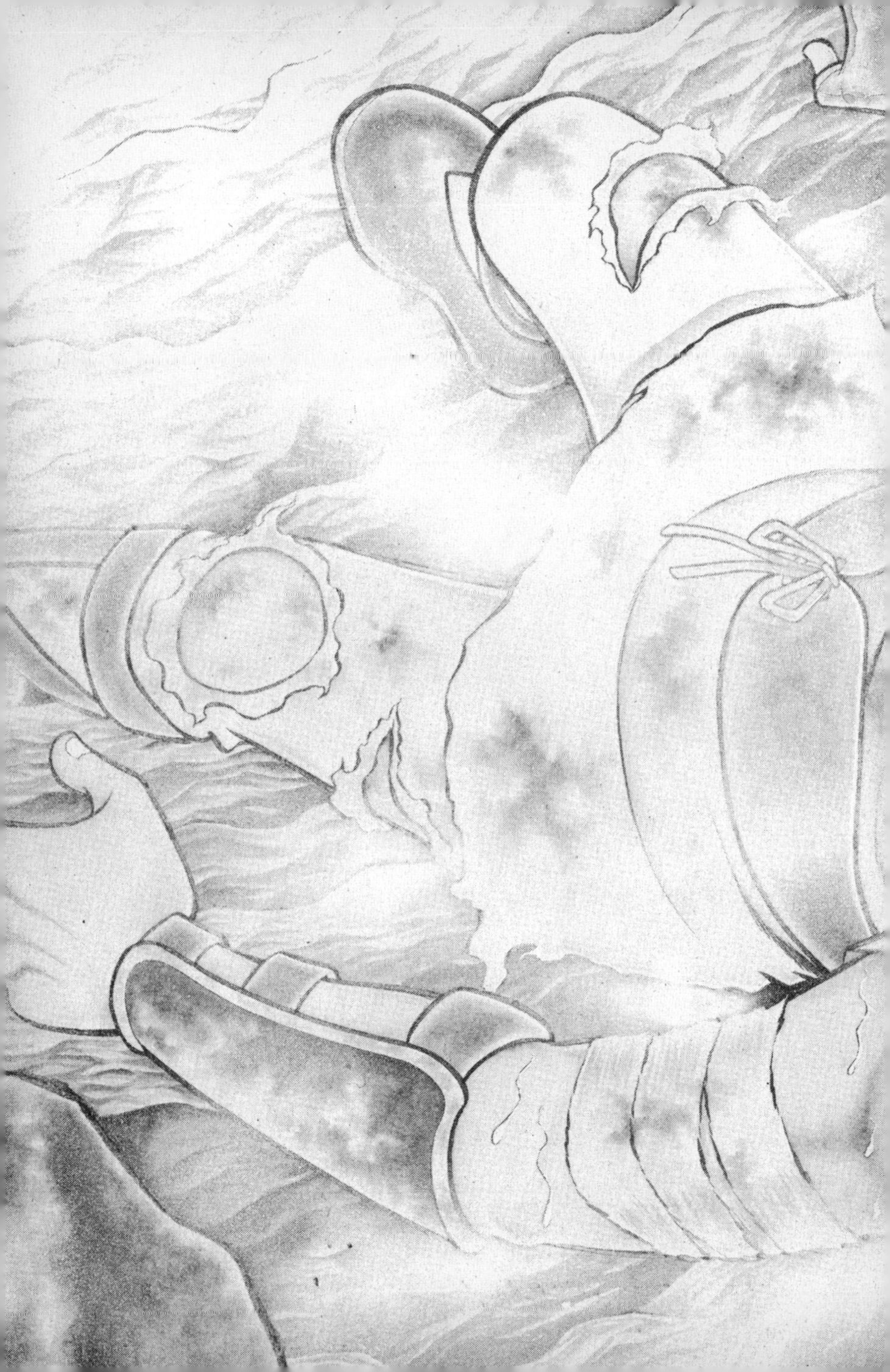

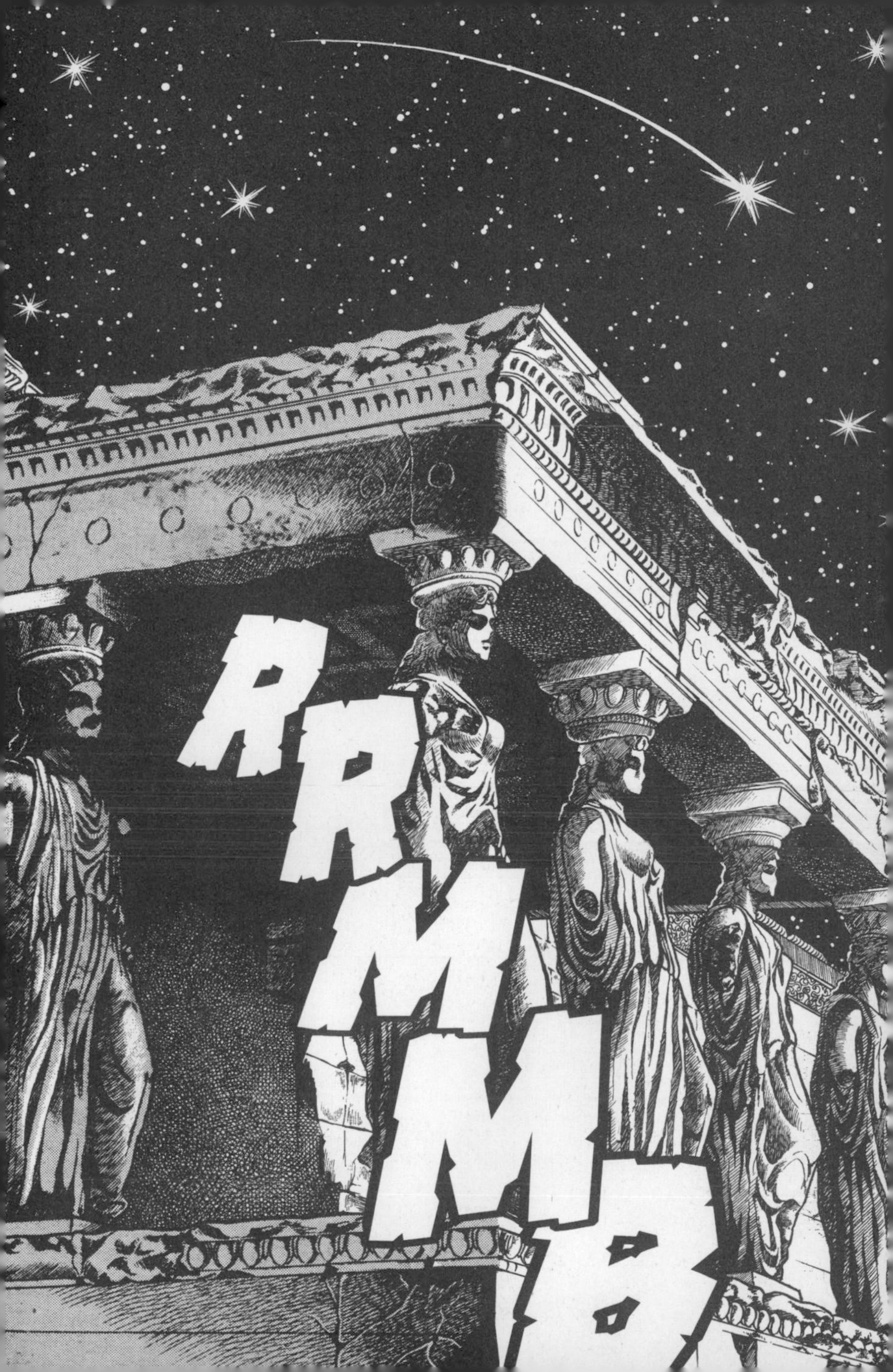
RRMMB

READ THIS WAY

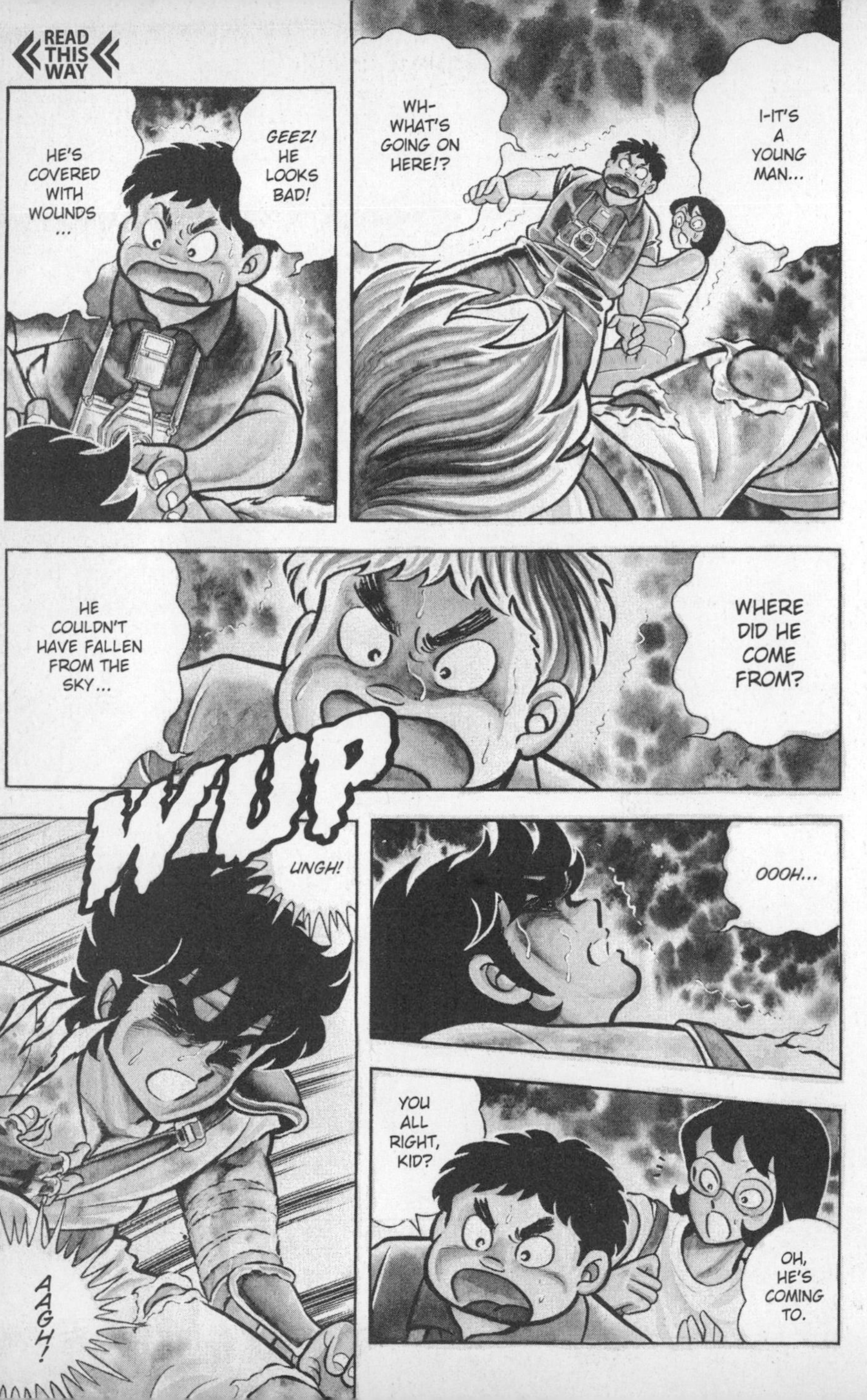
WH-WHAT'S GOING ON HERE!?
I-IT'S A YOUNG MAN...
GEEZ! HE LOOKS BAD!
HE'S COVERED WITH WOUNDS ...
WHERE DID HE COME FROM?
HE COULDN'T HAVE FALLEN FROM THE SKY...
OOOH...
OH, HE'S COMING TO.
YOU ALL RIGHT, KID?
WUP
UNGH!
AAGH!

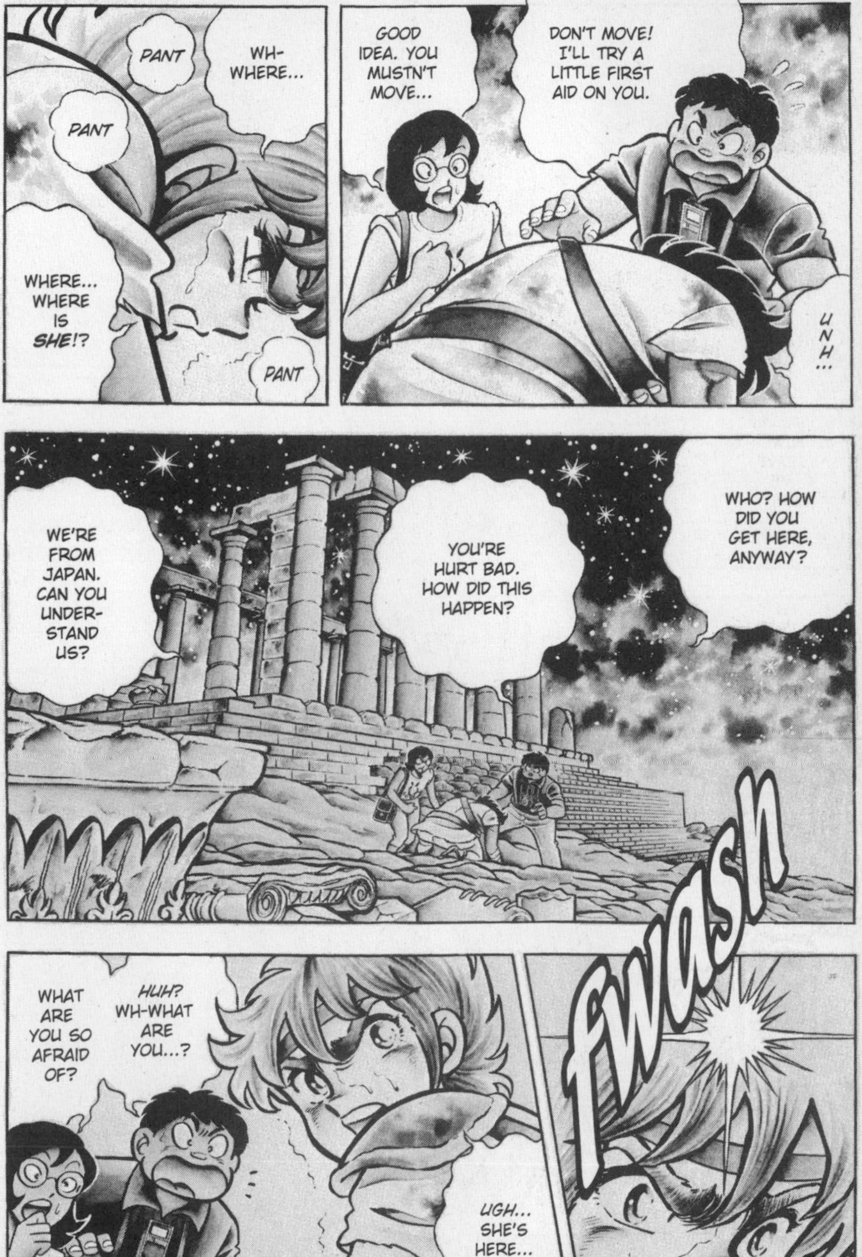
DON'T MOVE! I'LL TRY A LITTLE FIRST AID ON YOU.
GOOD IDEA. YOU MUSTN'T MOVE...
UNH...
WH- WHERE...
PANT
PANT
WHERE... WHERE IS SHE!?
PANT
WHO? HOW DID YOU GET HERE, ANYWAY?
YOU'RE HURT BAD. HOW DID THIS HAPPEN?
WE'RE FROM JAPAN. CAN YOU UNDER-STAND US?
fwash
HUH? WH-WHAT ARE YOU...?
WHAT ARE YOU SO AFRAID OF?
UGH... SHE'S HERE...

READ THIS WAY

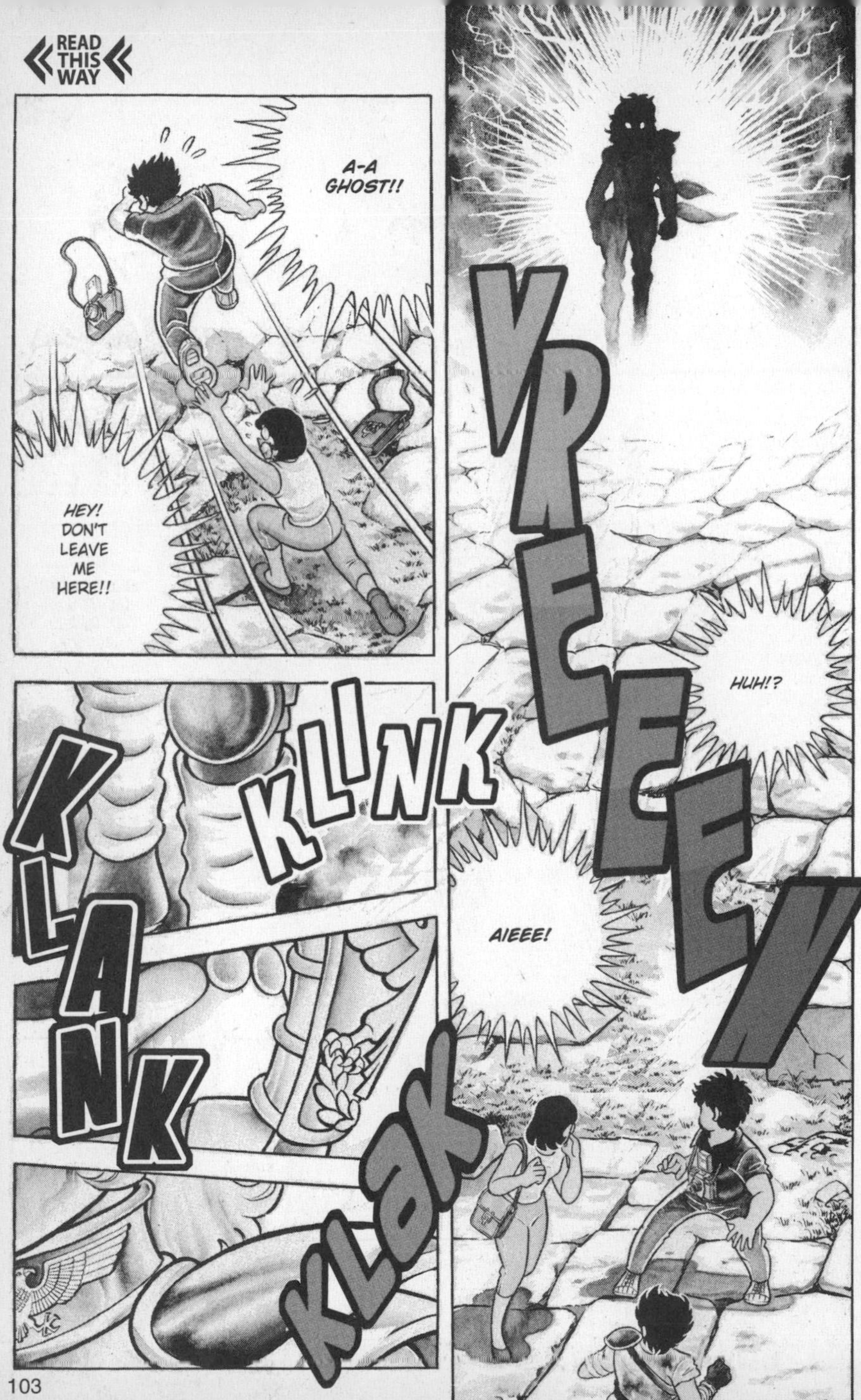
VREEEN
HUH!?
AIEEE!
A-A GHOST!!
HEY! DON'T LEAVE ME HERE!!
KLINK
KLANK
KLAK

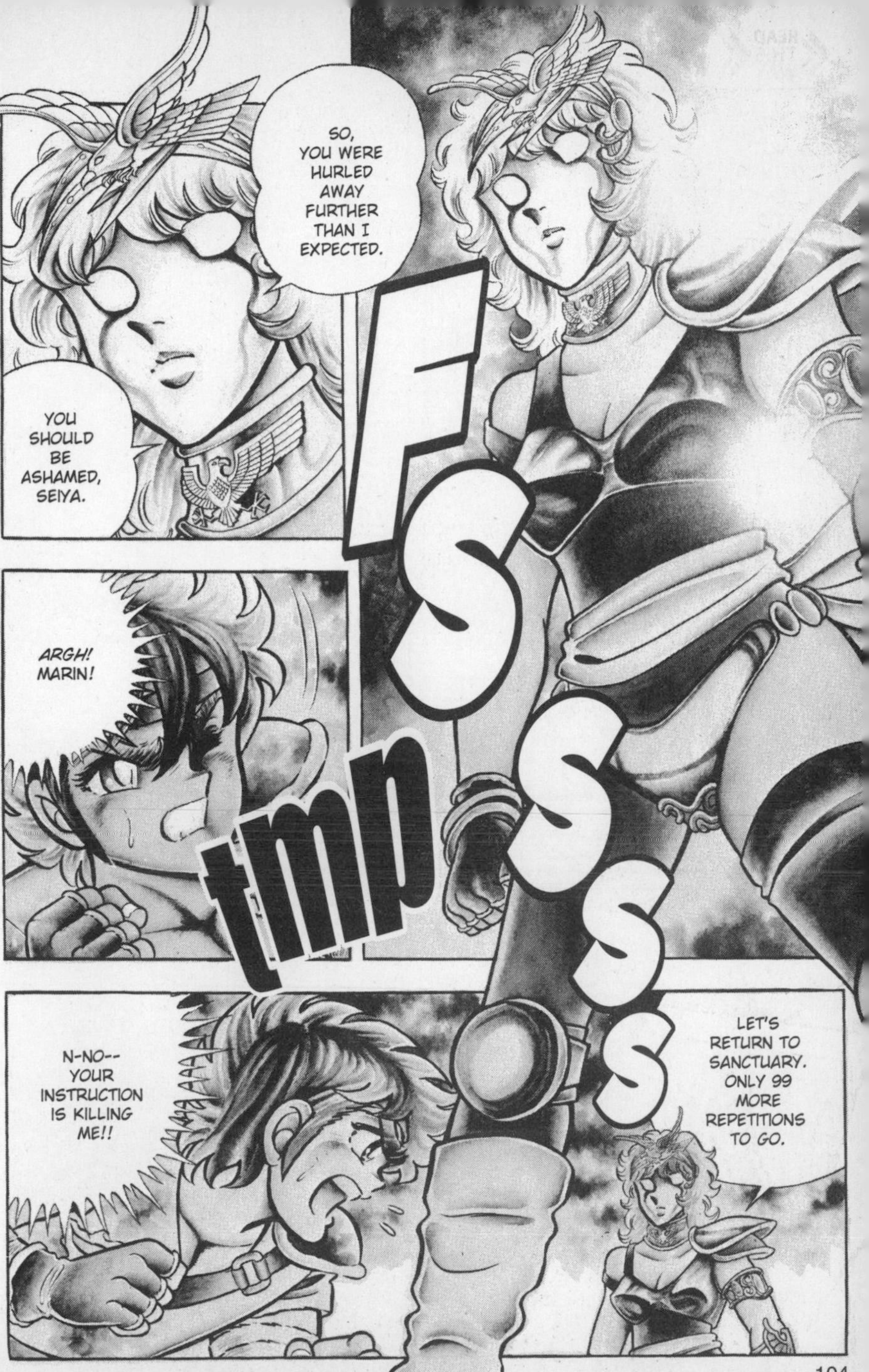
FSSSSS
SO, YOU WERE HURLED AWAY FURTHER THAN I EXPECTED.
YOU SHOULD BE ASHAMED, SEIYA.
ARGH! MARIN!
tmp
LET'S RETURN TO SANCTUARY. ONLY 99 MORE REPETITIONS TO GO.
N-NO-- YOUR INSTRUCTION IS KILLING ME!!

READ THIS WAY

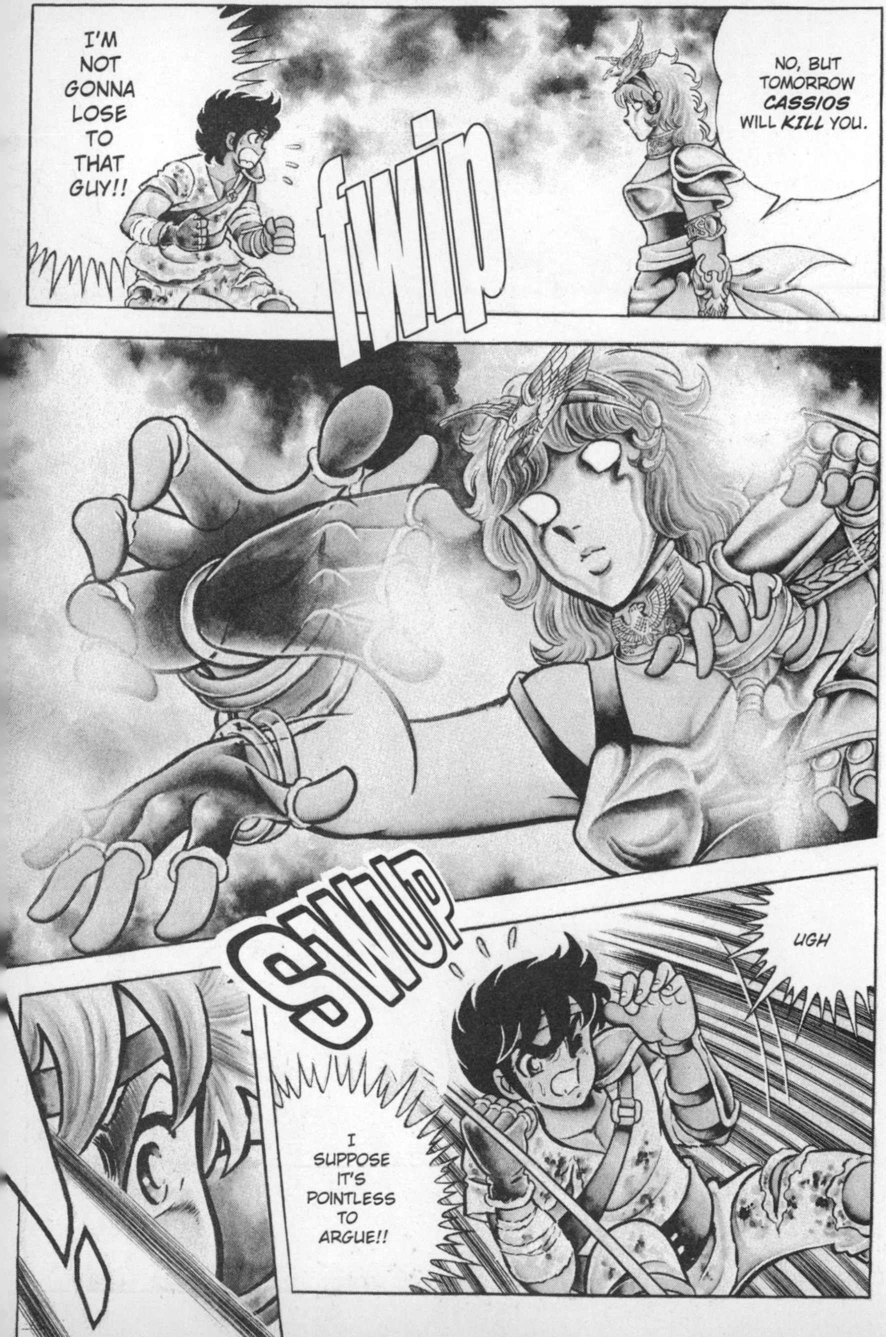
NO, BUT TOMORROW CASSIOS WILL KILL YOU.
I'M NOT GONNA LOSE TO THAT GUY!!
fwip
UGH
SWUP
I SUPPOSE IT'S POINTLESS TO ARGUE!!

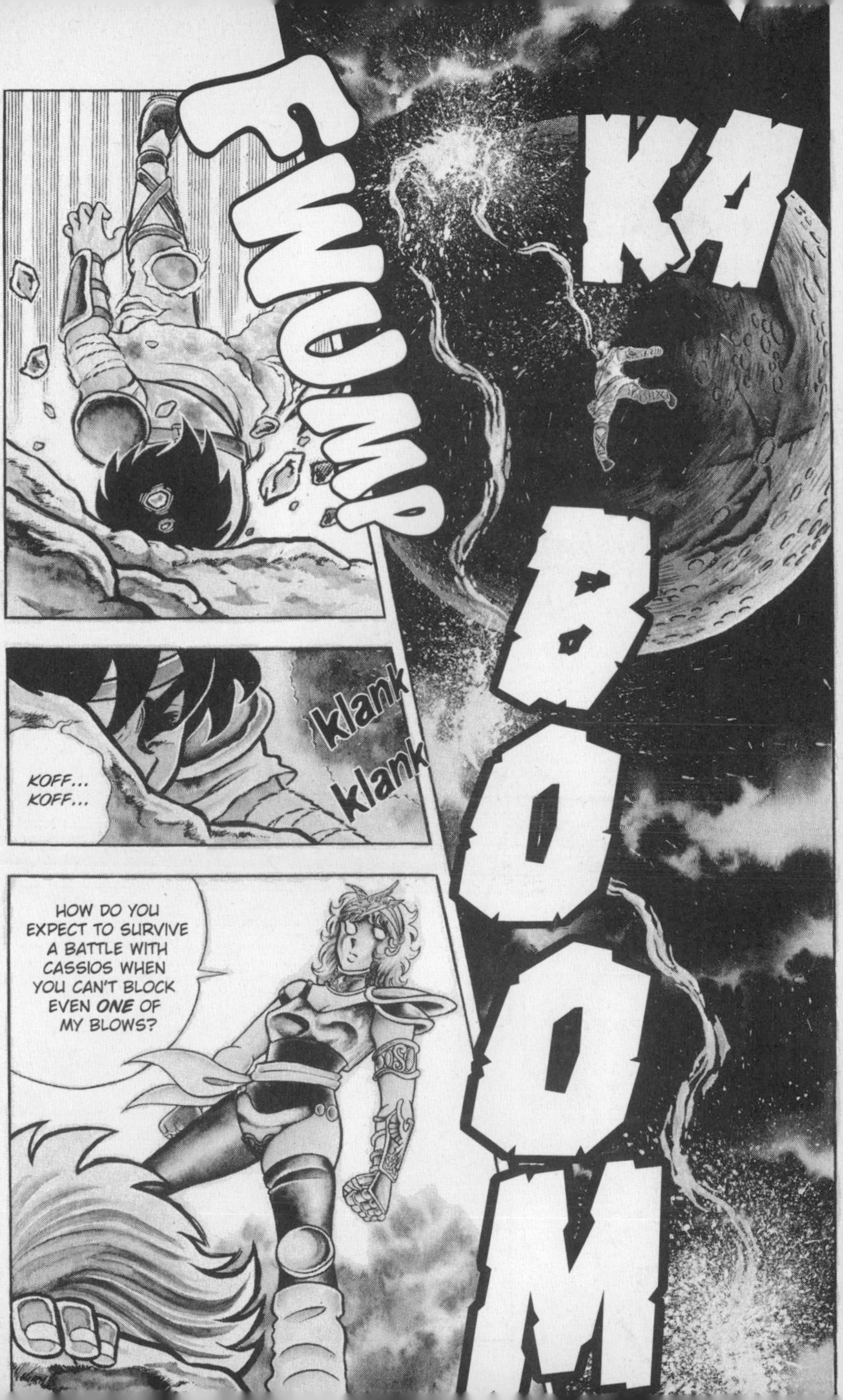
KA BOOM
FWUMP
klank klank
KOFF... KOFF...
HOW DO YOU EXPECT TO SURVIVE A BATTLE WITH CASSIOS WHEN YOU CAN'T BLOCK EVEN *ONE* OF MY BLOWS?

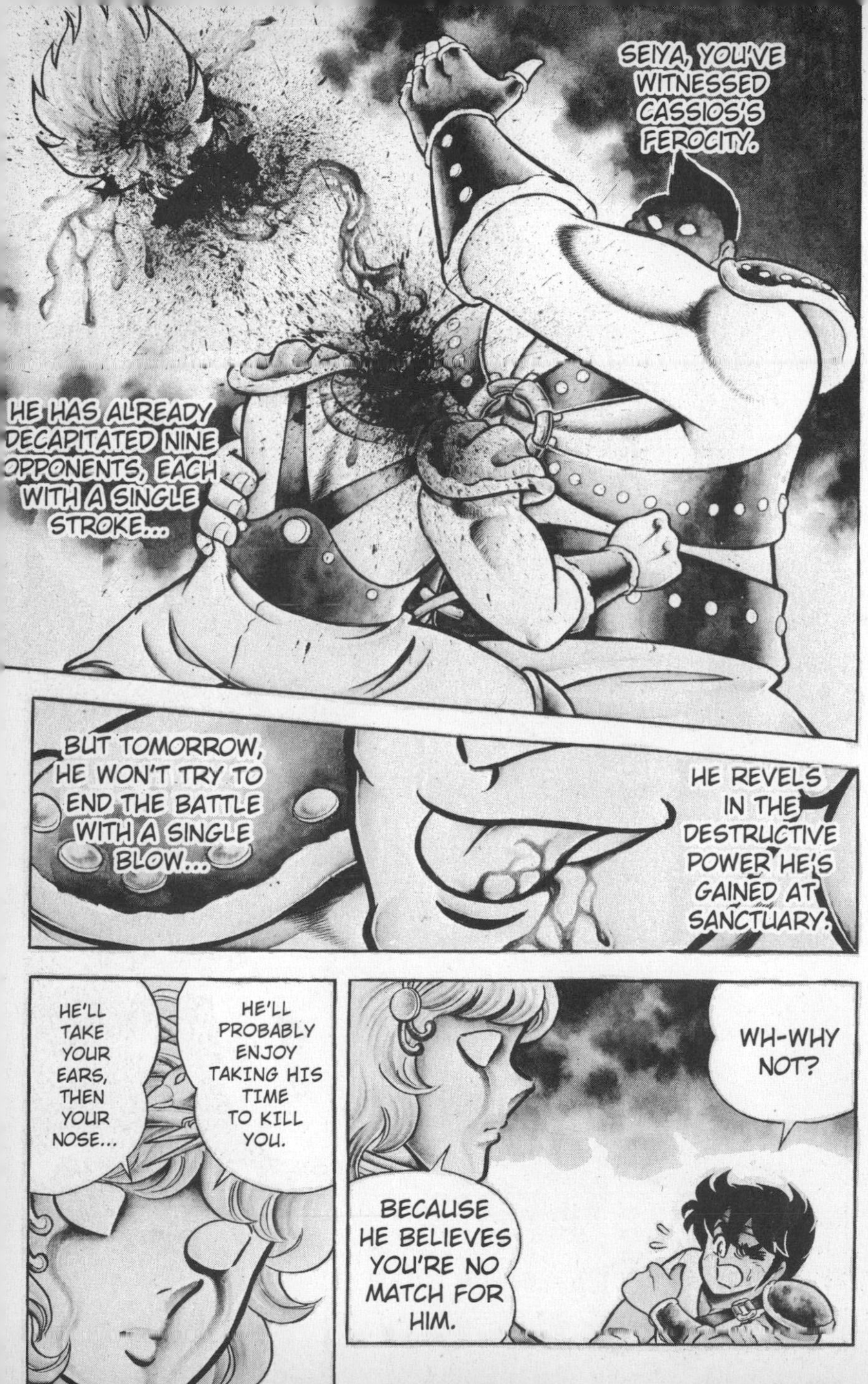
SEIYA, YOU'VE WITNESSED CASSIOS'S FEROCITY.
HE HAS ALREADY DECAPITATED NINE OPPONENTS, EACH WITH A SINGLE STROKE...
HE REVELS IN THE DESTRUCTIVE POWER HE'S GAINED AT SANCTUARY.
BUT TOMORROW, HE WON'T TRY TO END THE BATTLE WITH A SINGLE BLOW...
WH-WHY NOT?
BECAUSE HE BELIEVES YOU'RE NO MATCH FOR HIM.
HE'LL PROBABLY ENJOY TAKING HIS TIME TO KILL YOU.
HE'LL TAKE YOUR EARS, THEN YOUR NOSE...

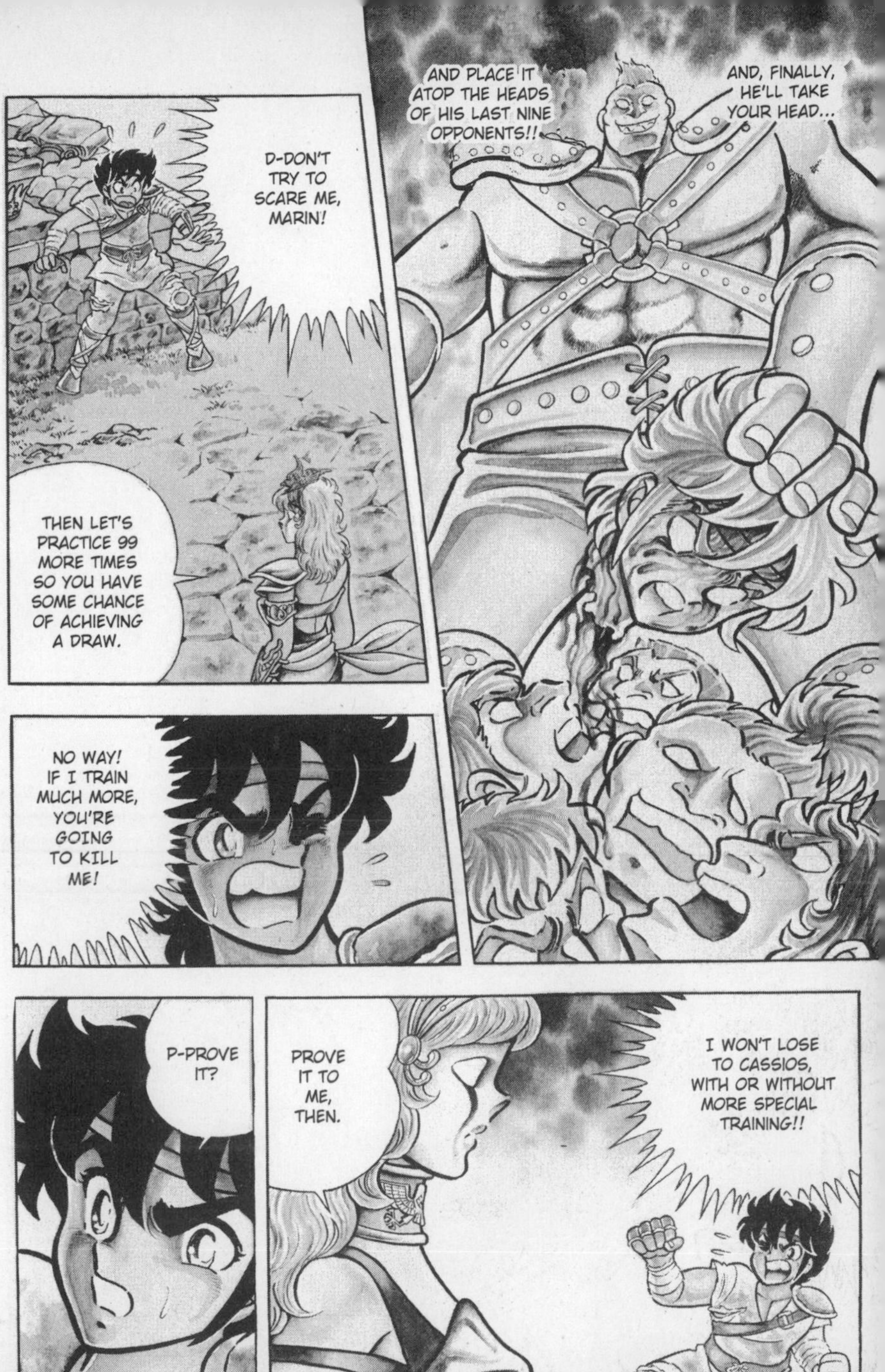
AND PLACE IT ATOP THE HEADS OF HIS LAST NINE OPPONENTS!!
AND, FINALLY, HE'LL TAKE YOUR HEAD...
D-DON'T TRY TO SCARE ME, MARIN!
THEN LET'S PRACTICE 99 MORE TIMES SO YOU HAVE SOME CHANCE OF ACHIEVING A DRAW.
NO WAY! IF I TRAIN MUCH MORE, YOU'RE GOING TO KILL ME!
I WON'T LOSE TO CASSIOS, WITH OR WITHOUT MORE SPECIAL TRAINING!!
PROVE IT TO ME, THEN.
P-PROVE IT?

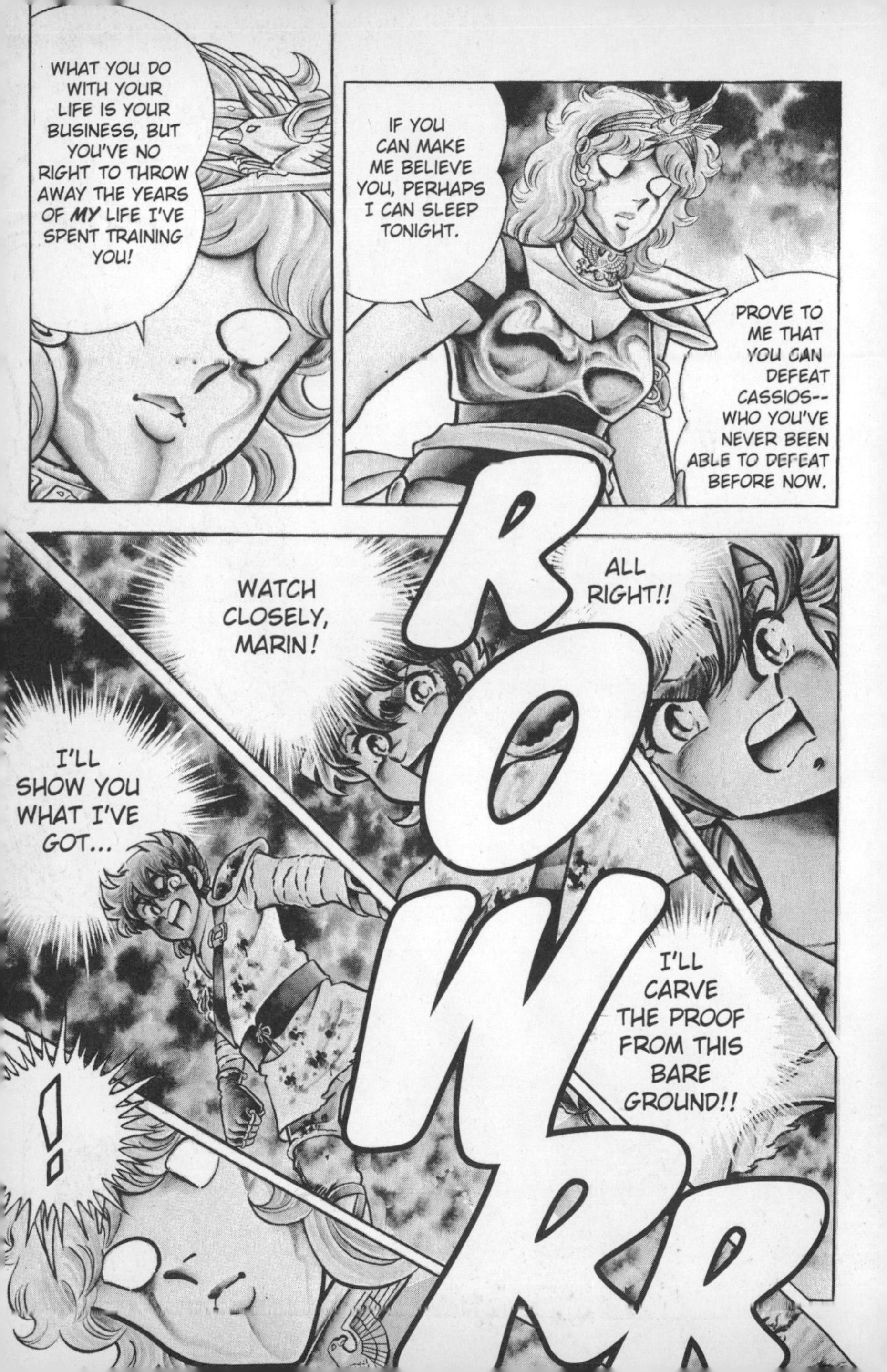
IF YOU CAN MAKE ME BELIEVE YOU, PERHAPS I CAN SLEEP TONIGHT.
PROVE TO ME THAT YOU CAN DEFEAT CASSIOS-- WHO YOU'VE NEVER BEEN ABLE TO DEFEAT BEFORE NOW.
WHAT YOU DO WITH YOUR LIFE IS YOUR BUSINESS, BUT YOU'VE NO RIGHT TO THROW AWAY THE YEARS OF *MY* LIFE I'VE SPENT TRAINING YOU!
ALL RIGHT!!
ROWRR
WATCH CLOSELY, MARIN!
I'LL CARVE THE PROOF FROM THIS BARE GROUND!!
I'LL SHOW YOU WHAT I'VE GOT...
!

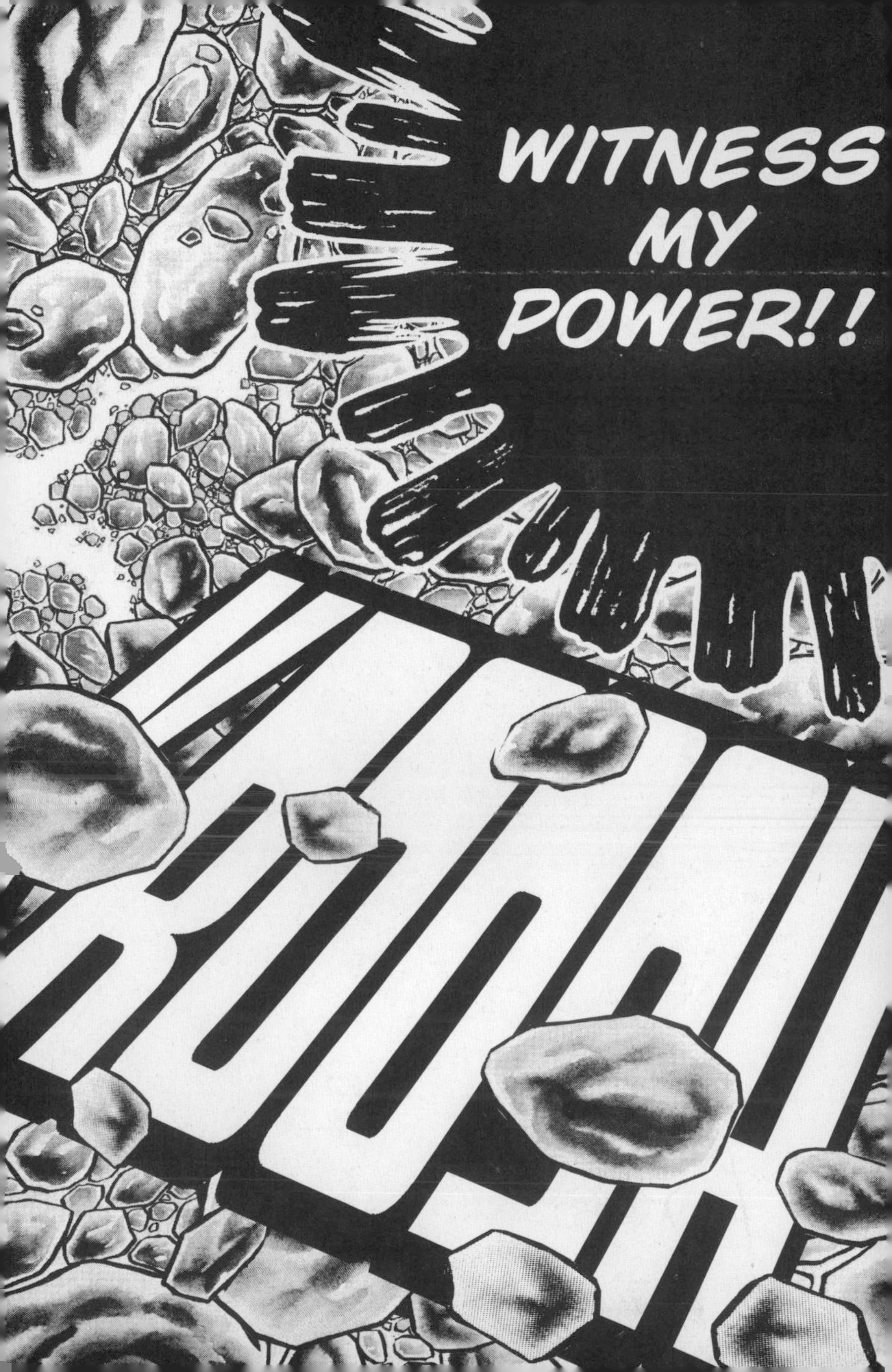
WITNESS MY POWER!!

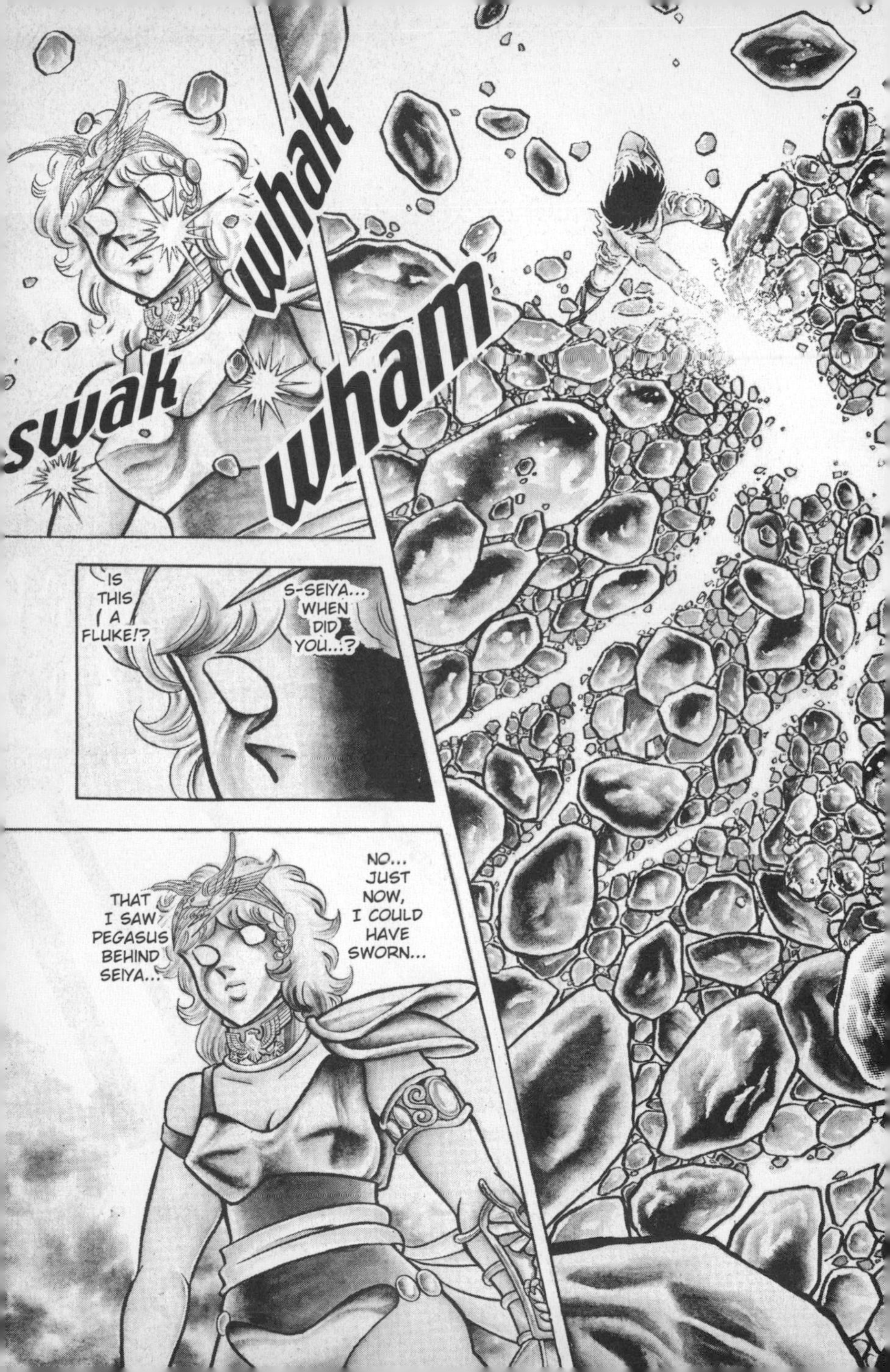
whak
wham
swak
S-SEIYA... WHEN DID YOU...?
IS THIS A FLUKE!?
NO... JUST NOW, I COULD HAVE SWORN...
THAT I SAW PEGASUS BEHIND SEIYA...

READ THIS WAY

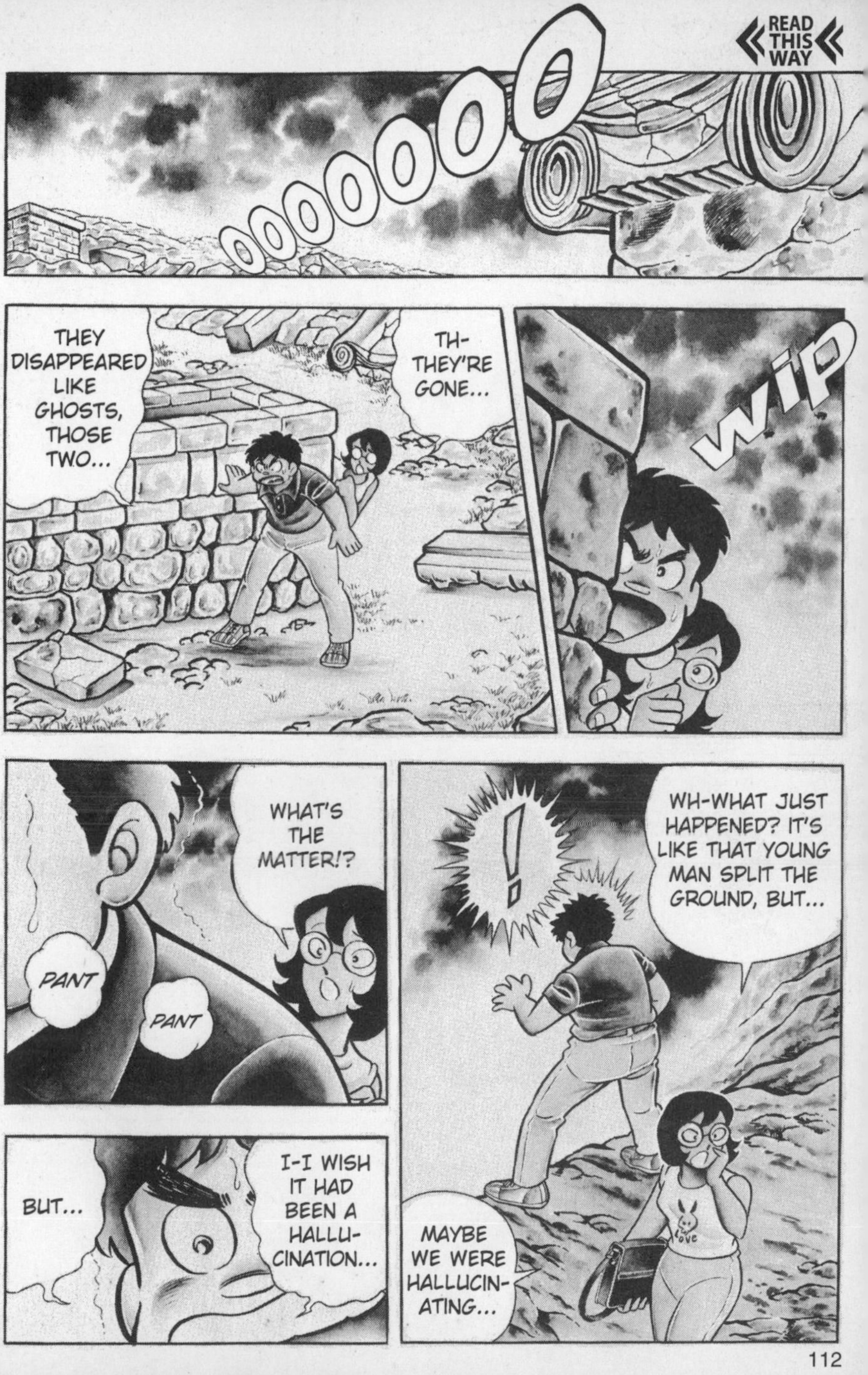
OOOOOOOO
WIP
TH- THEY'RE GONE...
THEY DISAPPEARED LIKE GHOSTS, THOSE TWO...
!
WH-WHAT JUST HAPPENED? IT'S LIKE THAT YOUNG MAN SPLIT THE GROUND, BUT...
MAYBE WE WERE HALLUCINATING...
WHAT'S THE MATTER!?
PANT
PANT
I-I WISH IT HAD BEEN A HALLUCINATION...
BUT...

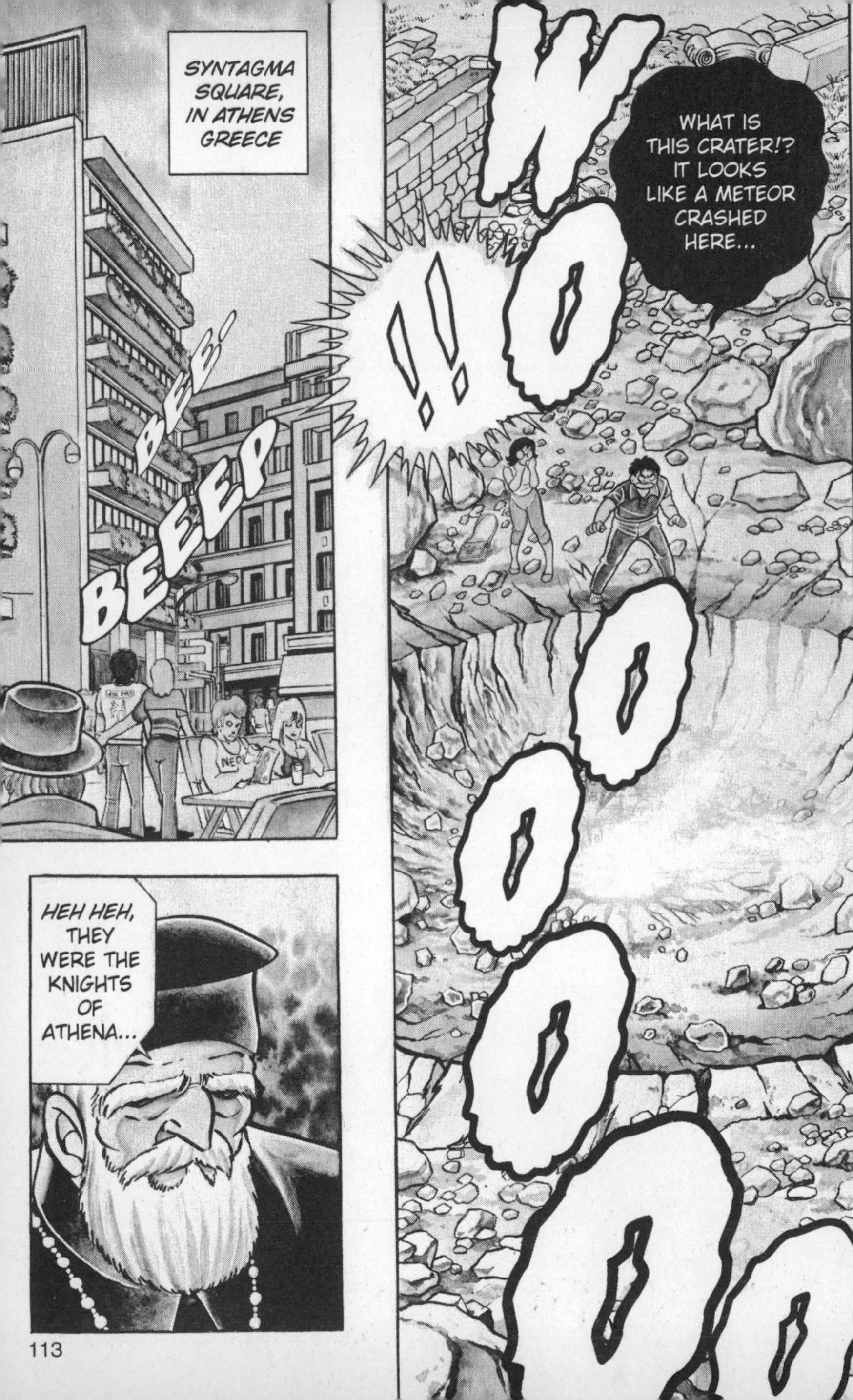
WHAT IS THIS CRATER!? IT LOOKS LIKE A METEOR CRASHED HERE...
WOOOOOOOO
!!
SYNTAGMA SQUARE, IN ATHENS GREECE
BEE BEEEP
HEH HEH, THEY WERE THE KNIGHTS OF ATHENA...

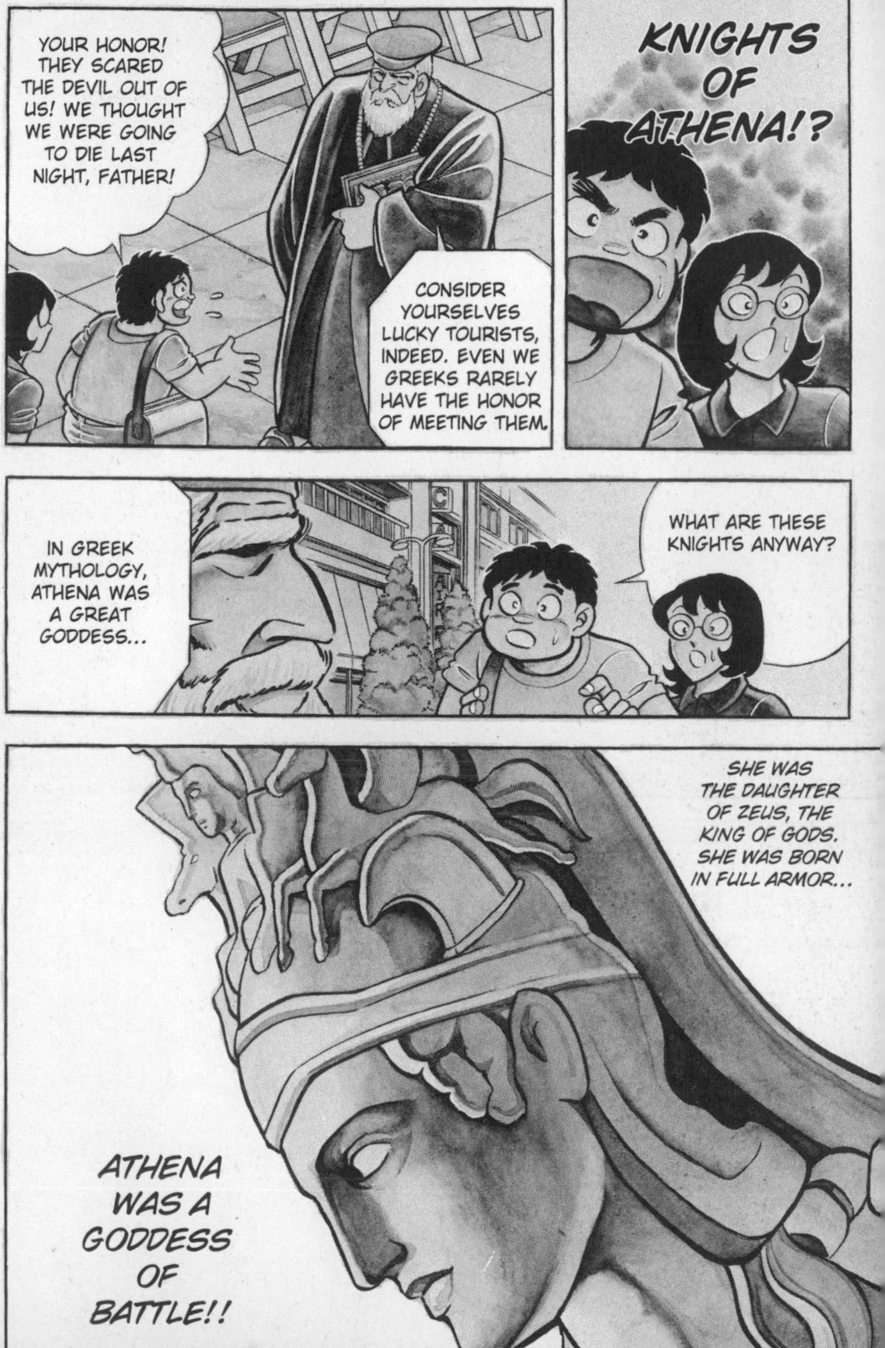
YOUR HONOR! THEY SCARED THE DEVIL OUT OF US! WE THOUGHT WE WERE GOING TO DIE LAST NIGHT, FATHER!
CONSIDER YOURSELVES LUCKY TOURISTS, INDEED. EVEN WE GREEKS RARELY HAVE THE HONOR OF MEETING THEM.
KNIGHTS OF ATHENA!?
WHAT ARE THESE KNIGHTS ANYWAY?
IN GREEK MYTHOLOGY, ATHENA WAS A GREAT GODDESS...
SHE WAS THE DAUGHTER OF ZEUS, THE KING OF GODS. SHE WAS BORN IN FULL ARMOR...
ATHENA WAS A GODDESS OF BATTLE!!

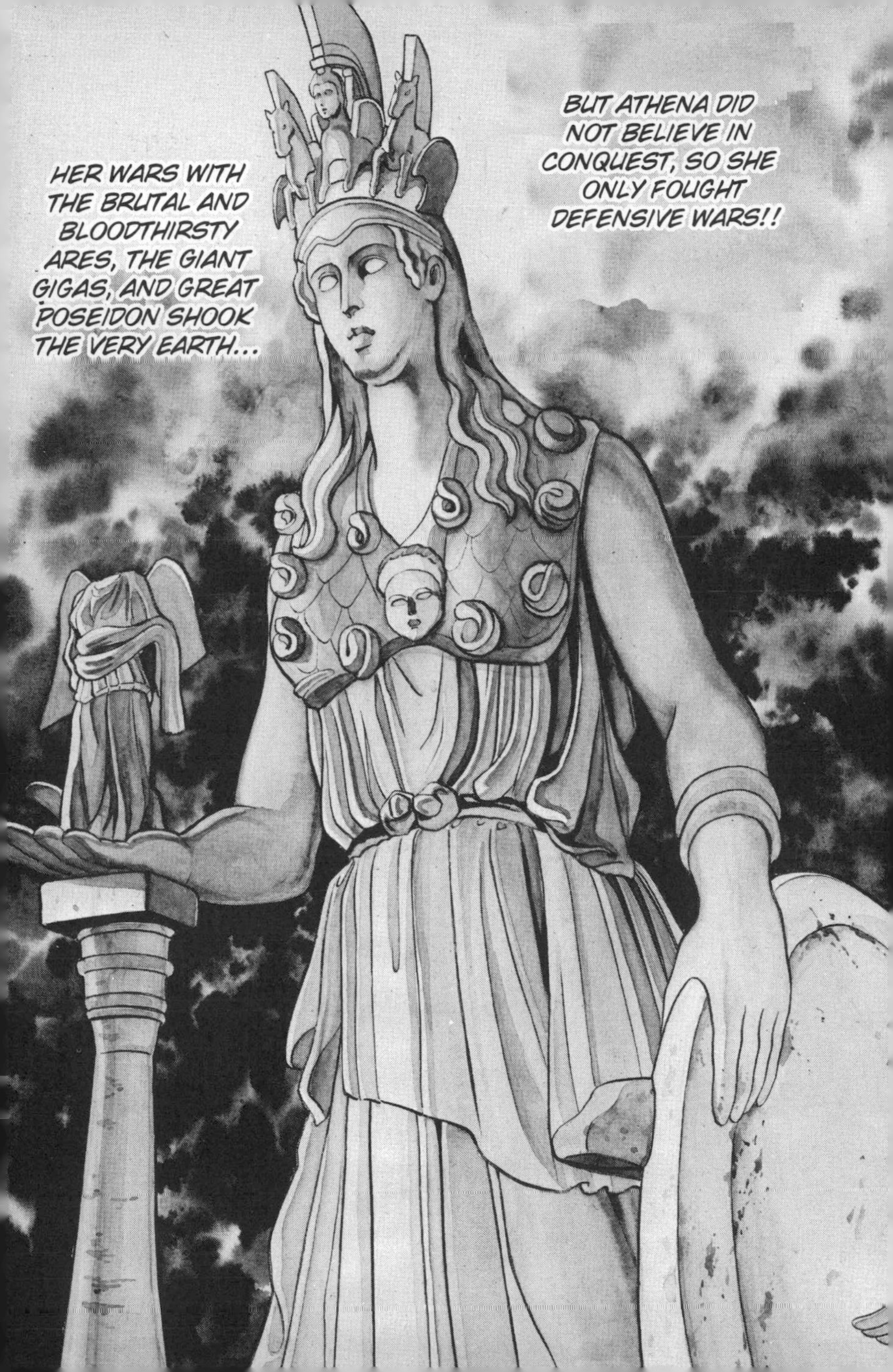

HER WARS WITH THE BRUTAL AND BLOODTHIRSTY ARES, THE GIANT GIGAS, AND GREAT POSEIDON SHOOK THE VERY EARTH...
BUT ATHENA DID NOT BELIEVE IN CONQUEST, SO SHE ONLY FOUGHT DEFENSIVE WARS!!

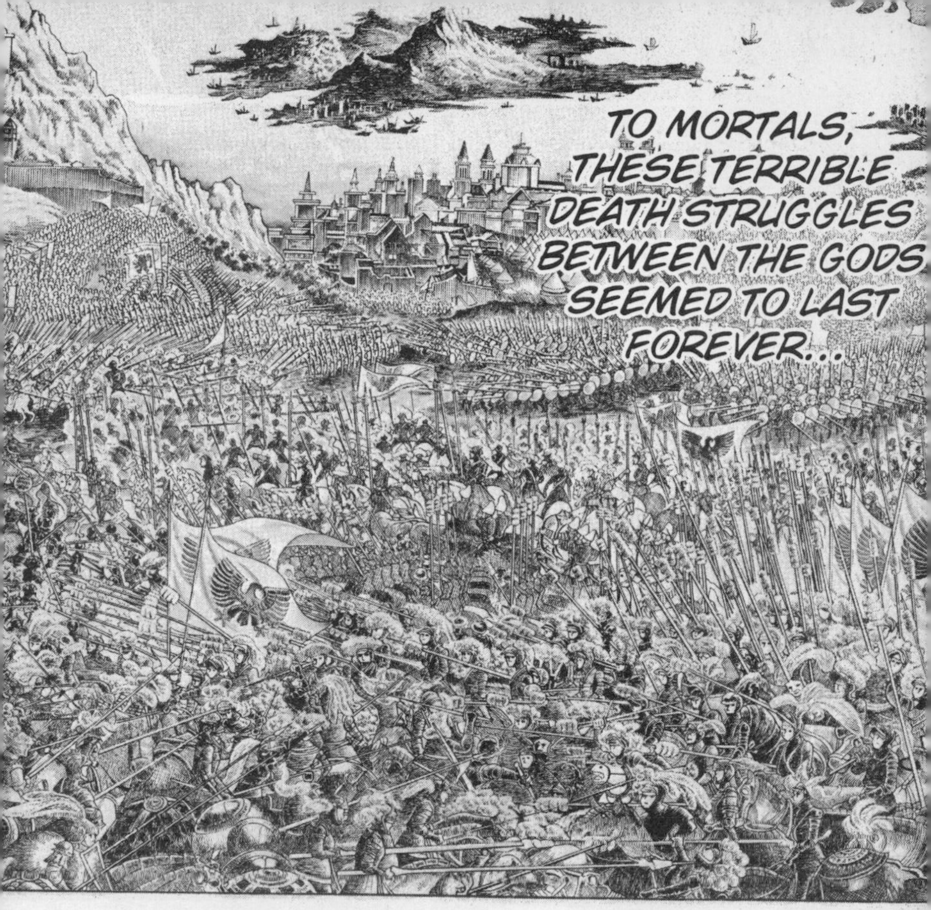
TO MORTALS, THESE TERRIBLE DEATH STRUGGLES BETWEEN THE GODS SEEMED TO LAST FOREVER...
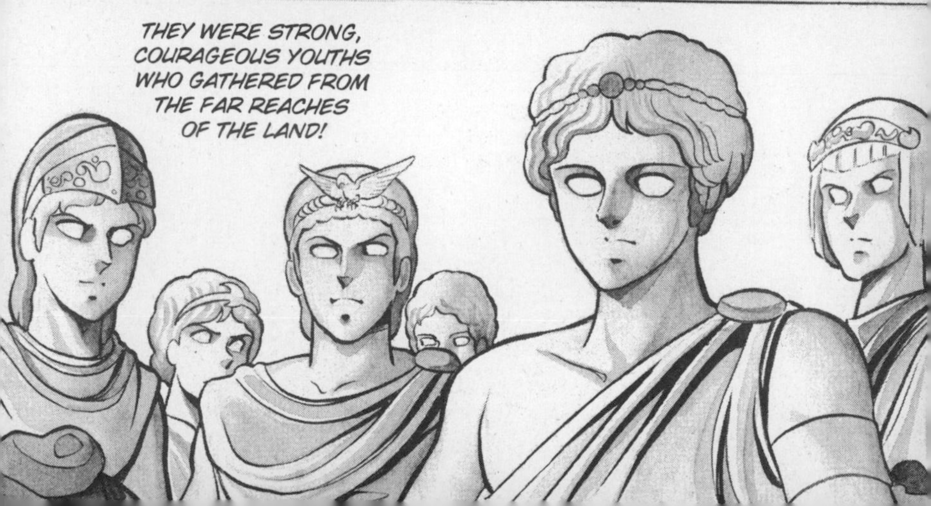
THEY WERE STRONG, COURAGEOUS YOUTHS WHO GATHERED FROM THE FAR REACHES OF THE LAND!

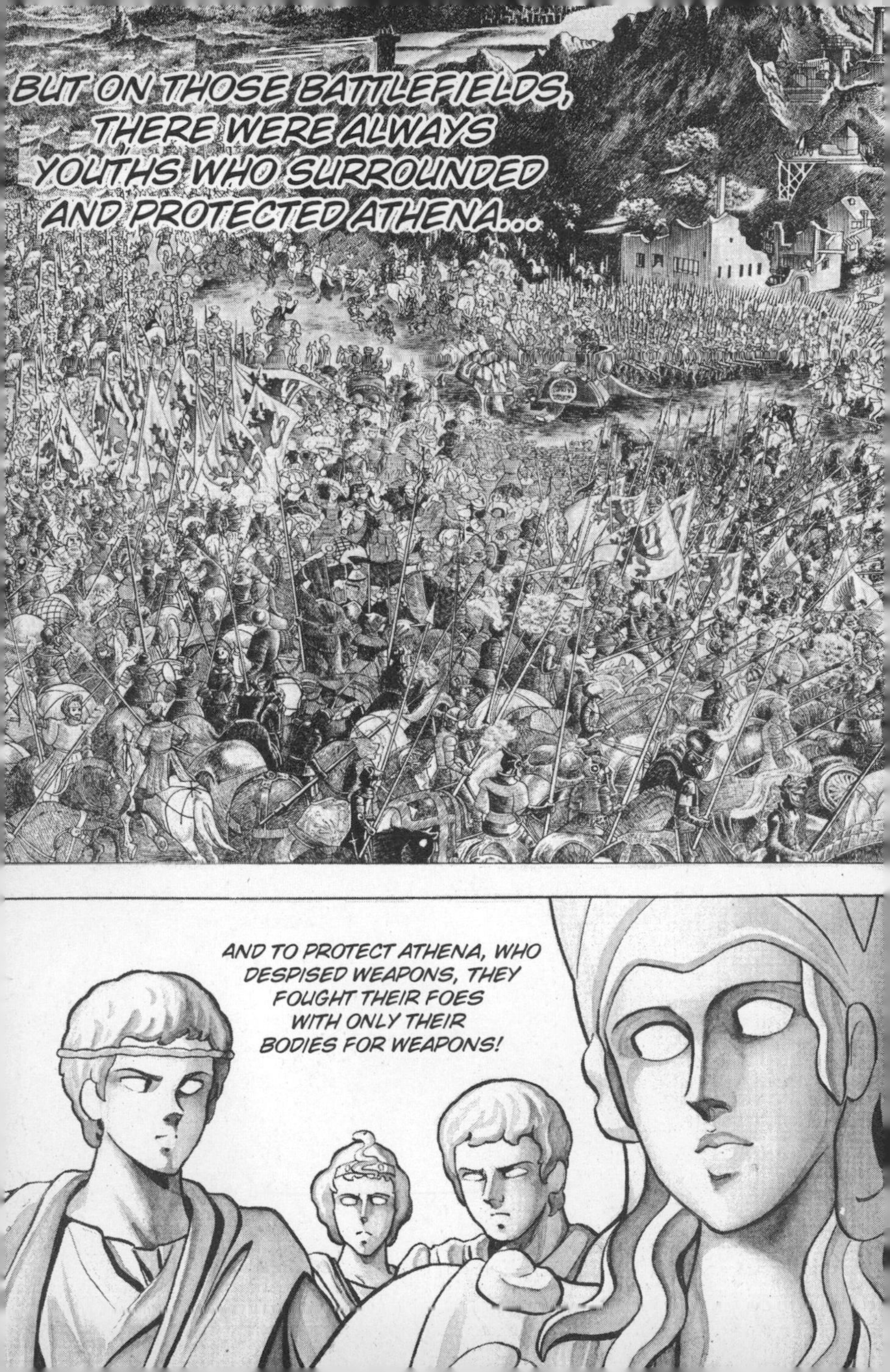
BUT ON THOSE BATTLEFIELDS, THERE WERE ALWAYS YOUTHS WHO SURROUNDED AND PROTECTED ATHENA...
AND TO PROTECT ATHENA, WHO DESPISED WEAPONS, THEY FOUGHT THEIR FOES WITH ONLY THEIR BODIES FOR WEAPONS!

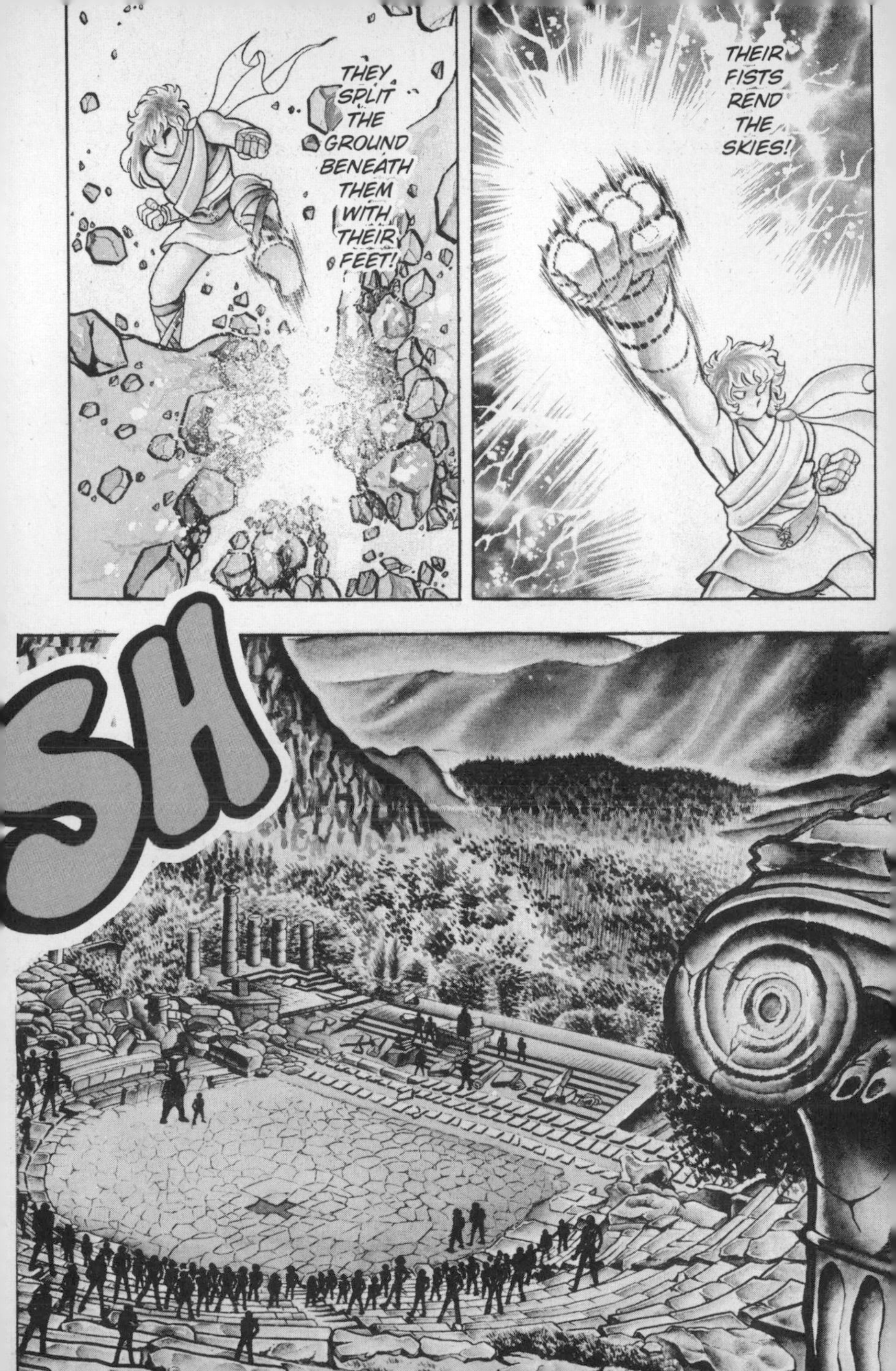
THEIR FISTS REND THE SKIES!
THEY SPLIT THE GROUND BENEATH THEM WITH THEIR FEET!
SH

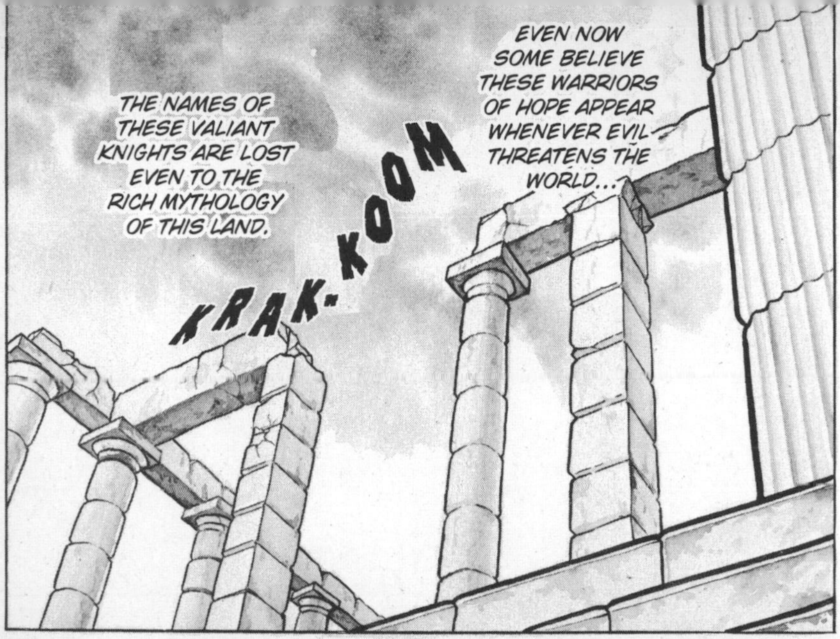
EVEN NOW SOME BELIEVE THESE WARRIORS OF HOPE APPEAR WHENEVER EVIL THREATENS THE WORLD...
THE NAMES OF THESE VALIANT KNIGHTS ARE LOST EVEN TO THE RICH MYTHOLOGY OF THIS LAND.
KRAK-KOOM
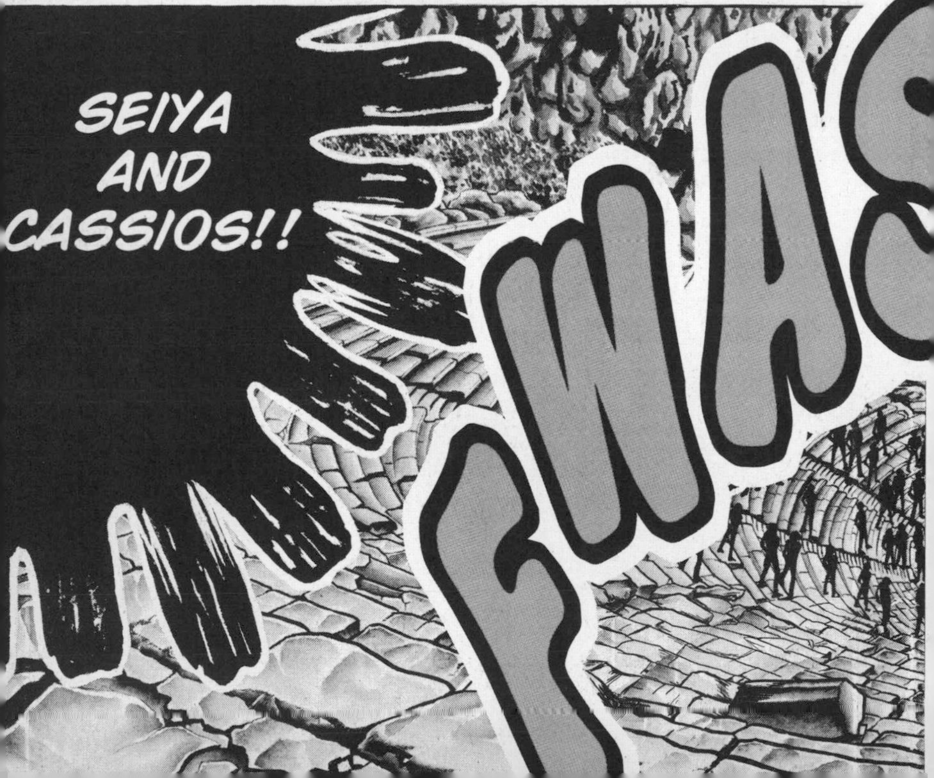
FWAS
SEIYA AND CASSIOS!!

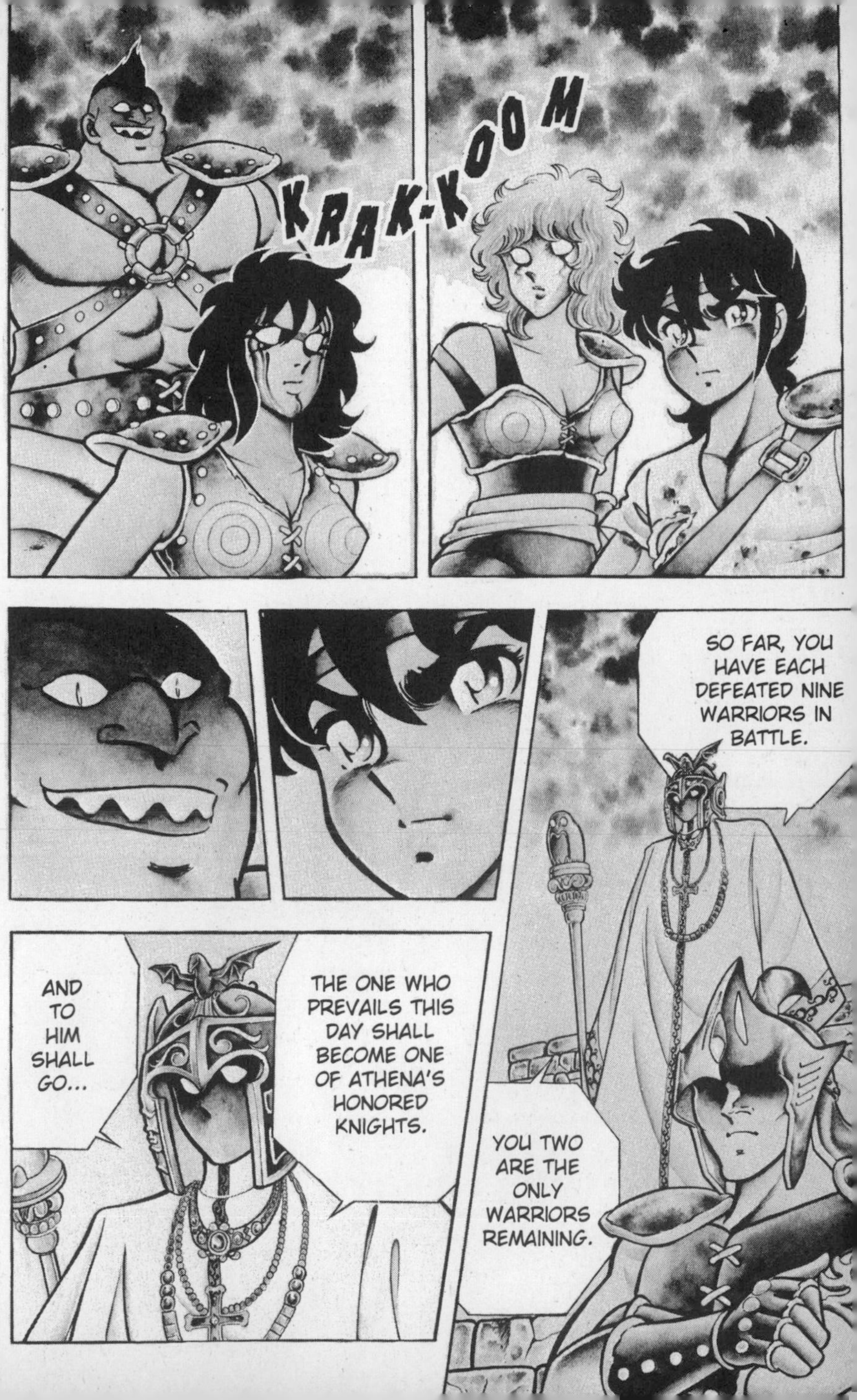
KRAK-KOOM
SO FAR, YOU HAVE EACH DEFEATED NINE WARRIORS IN BATTLE.
YOU TWO ARE THE ONLY WARRIORS REMAINING.
THE ONE WHO PREVAILS THIS DAY SHALL BECOME ONE OF ATHENA'S HONORED KNIGHTS.
AND TO HIM SHALL GO...

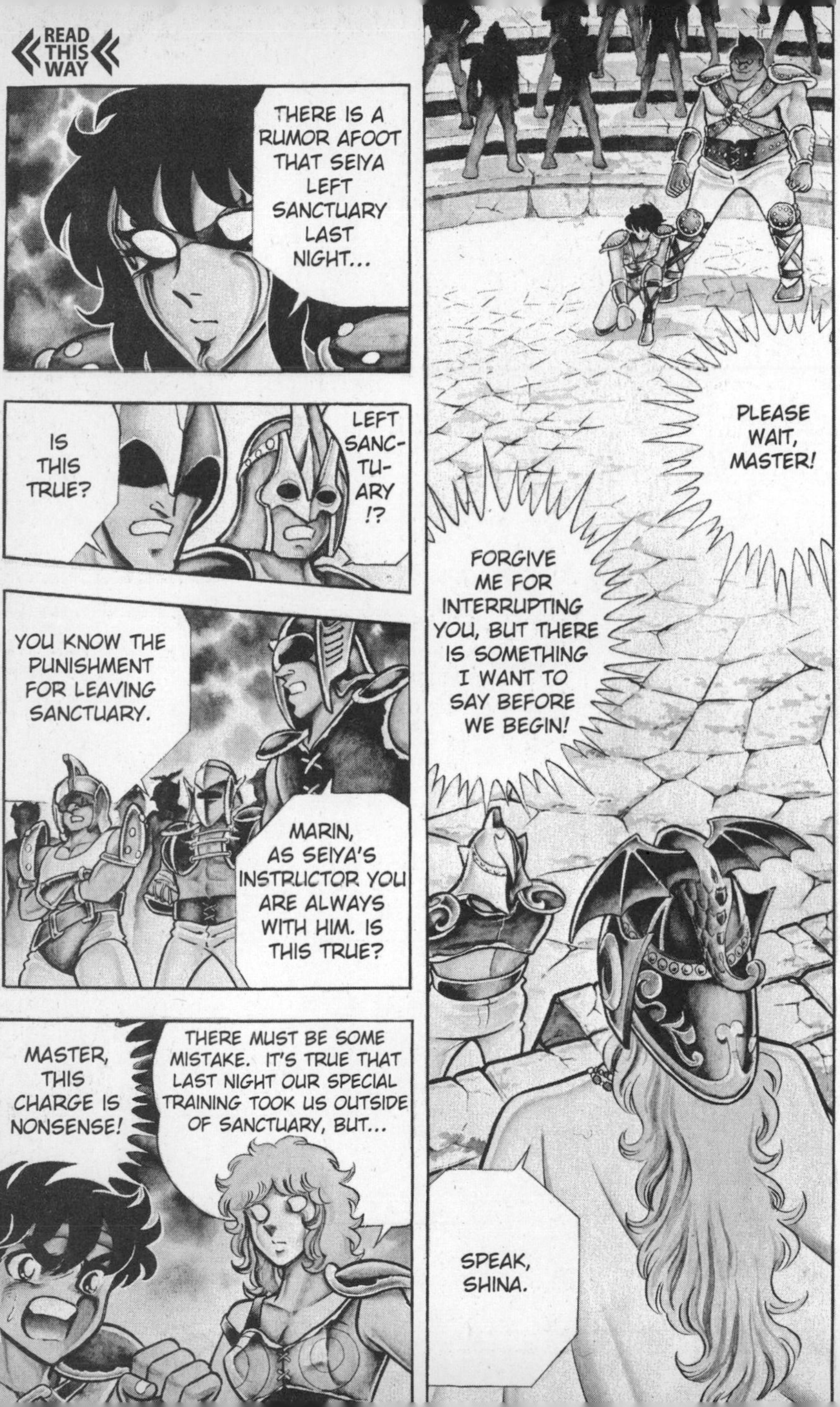
READ THIS WAY
PLEASE WAIT, MASTER!
FORGIVE ME FOR INTERRUPTING YOU, BUT THERE IS SOMETHING I WANT TO SAY BEFORE WE BEGIN!
SPEAK, SHINA.
THERE IS A RUMOR AFOOT THAT SEIYA LEFT SANCTUARY LAST NIGHT...
LEFT SANCTUARY!?
IS THIS TRUE?
YOU KNOW THE PUNISHMENT FOR LEAVING SANCTUARY.
MARIN, AS SEIYA'S INSTRUCTOR YOU ARE ALWAYS WITH HIM. IS THIS TRUE?
THERE MUST BE SOME MISTAKE. IT'S TRUE THAT LAST NIGHT OUR SPECIAL TRAINING TOOK US OUTSIDE OF SANCTUARY, BUT...
MASTER, THIS CHARGE IS NONSENSE!

READ THIS WAY

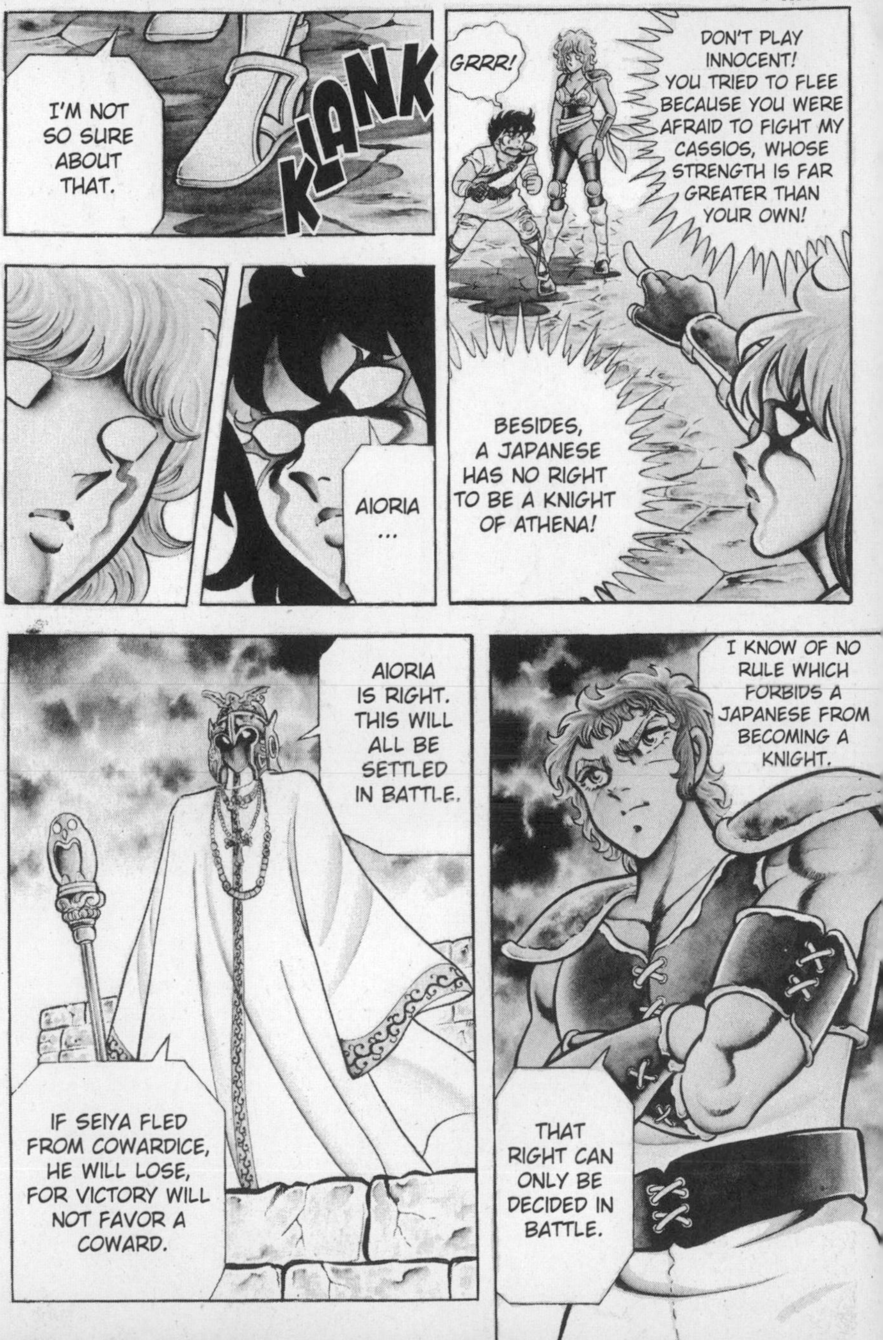
DON'T PLAY INNOCENT! YOU TRIED TO FLEE BECAUSE YOU WERE AFRAID TO FIGHT MY CASSIOS, WHOSE STRENGTH IS FAR GREATER THAN YOUR OWN!
GRRR!
BESIDES, A JAPANESE HAS NO RIGHT TO BE A KNIGHT OF ATHENA!
I'M NOT SO SURE ABOUT THAT.
K'LANK
AIORIA ...
I KNOW OF NO RULE WHICH FORBIDS A JAPANESE FROM BECOMING A KNIGHT.
THAT RIGHT CAN ONLY BE DECIDED IN BATTLE.
AIORIA IS RIGHT. THIS WILL ALL BE SETTLED IN BATTLE.
IF SEIYA FLED FROM COWARDICE, HE WILL LOSE, FOR VICTORY WILL NOT FAVOR A COWARD.

READ THIS WAY

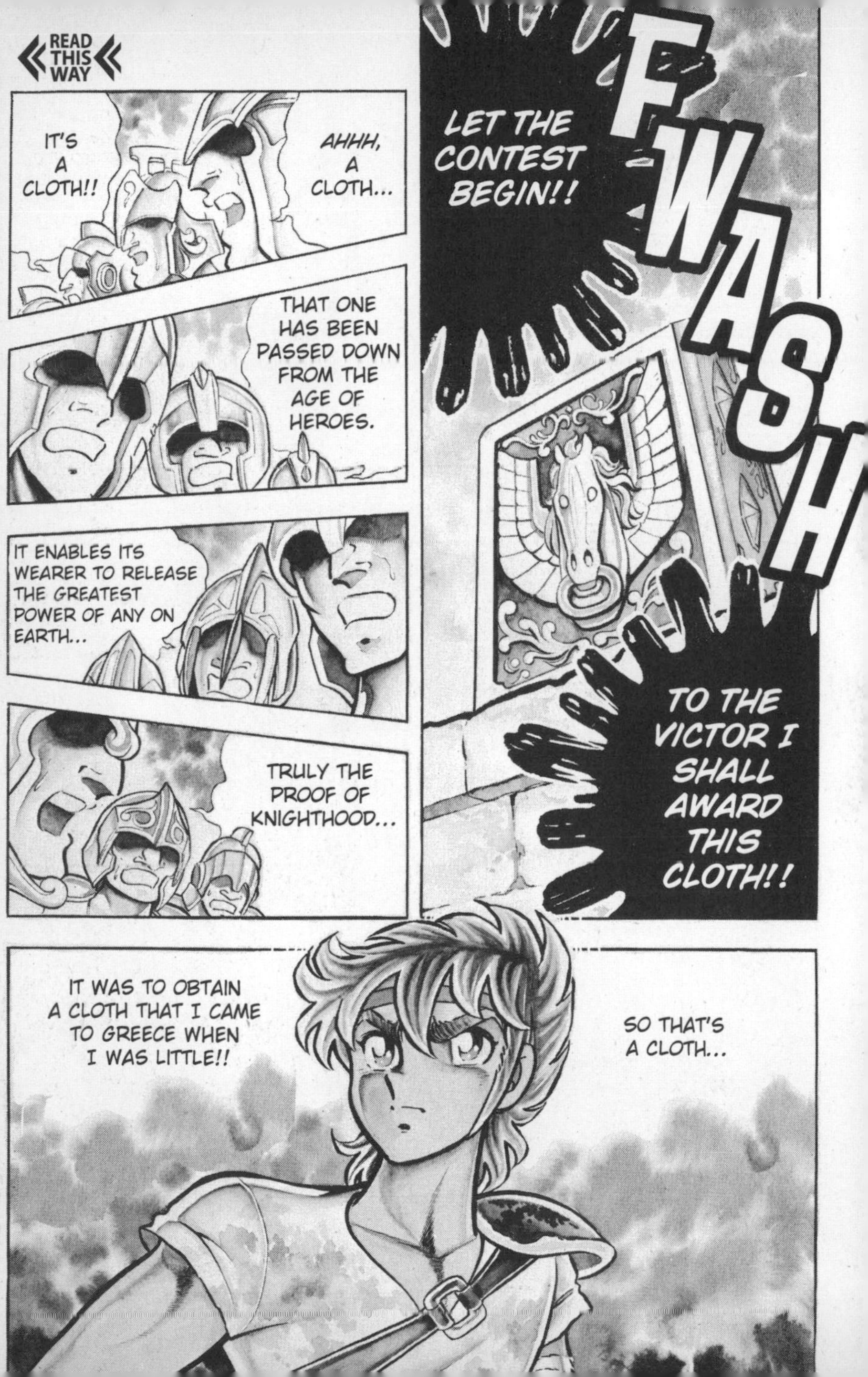
LET THE CONTEST BEGIN!!
FWASH
TO THE VICTOR I SHALL AWARD THIS CLOTH!!
AHHH, A CLOTH...
IT'S A CLOTH!!
THAT ONE HAS BEEN PASSED DOWN FROM THE AGE OF HEROES.
IT ENABLES ITS WEARER TO RELEASE THE GREATEST POWER OF ANY ON EARTH...
TRULY THE PROOF OF KNIGHTHOOD...
SO THAT'S A CLOTH...
IT WAS TO OBTAIN A CLOTH THAT I CAME TO GREECE WHEN I WAS LITTLE!!

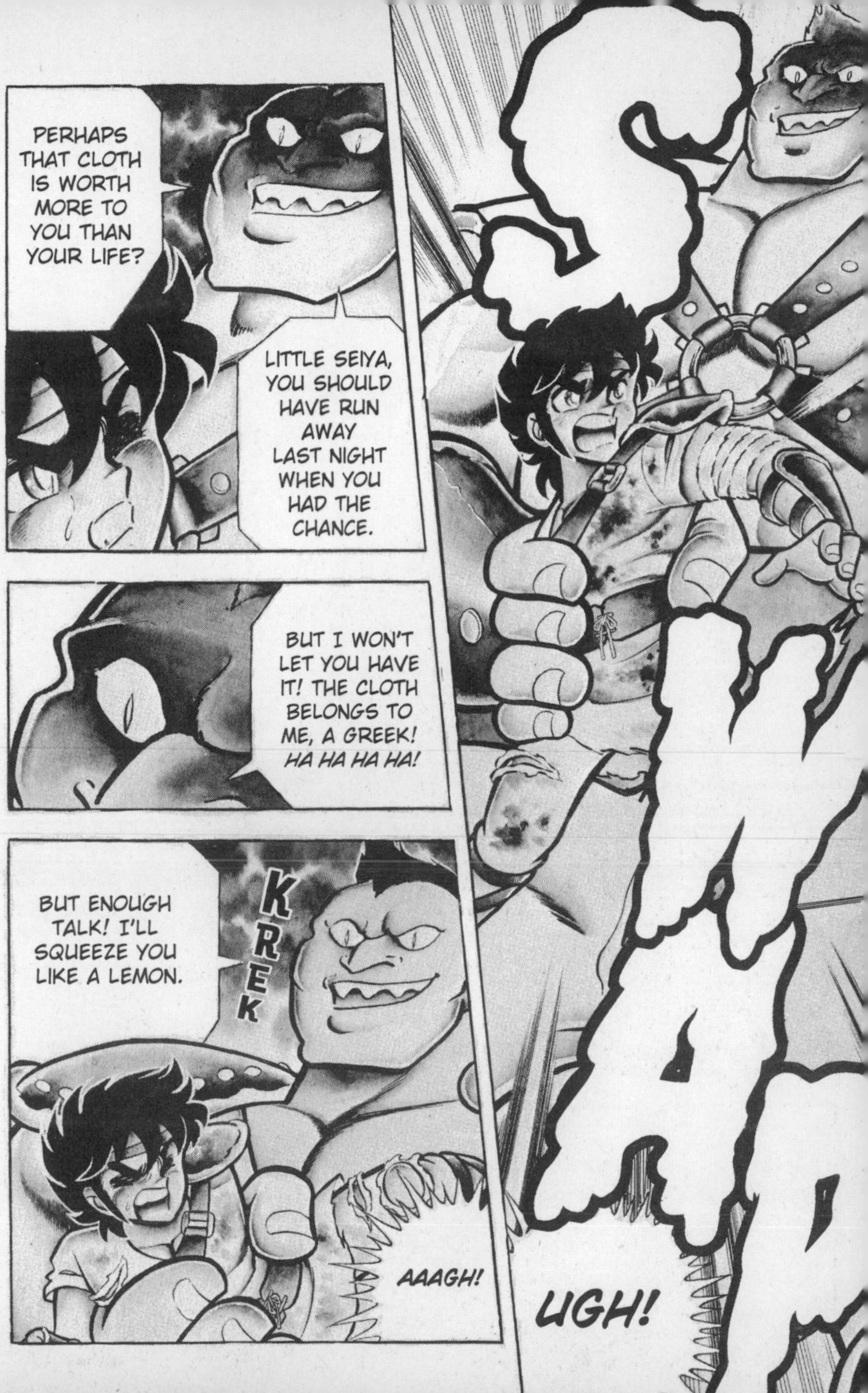
UGH!
PERHAPS THAT CLOTH IS WORTH MORE TO YOU THAN YOUR LIFE?
LITTLE SEIYA, YOU SHOULD HAVE RUN AWAY LAST NIGHT WHEN YOU HAD THE CHANCE.
BUT I WON'T LET YOU HAVE IT! THE CLOTH BELONGS TO ME, A GREEK! HA HA HA HA!
KREK
BUT ENOUGH TALK! I'LL SQUEEZE YOU LIKE A LEMON.
AAAGH!

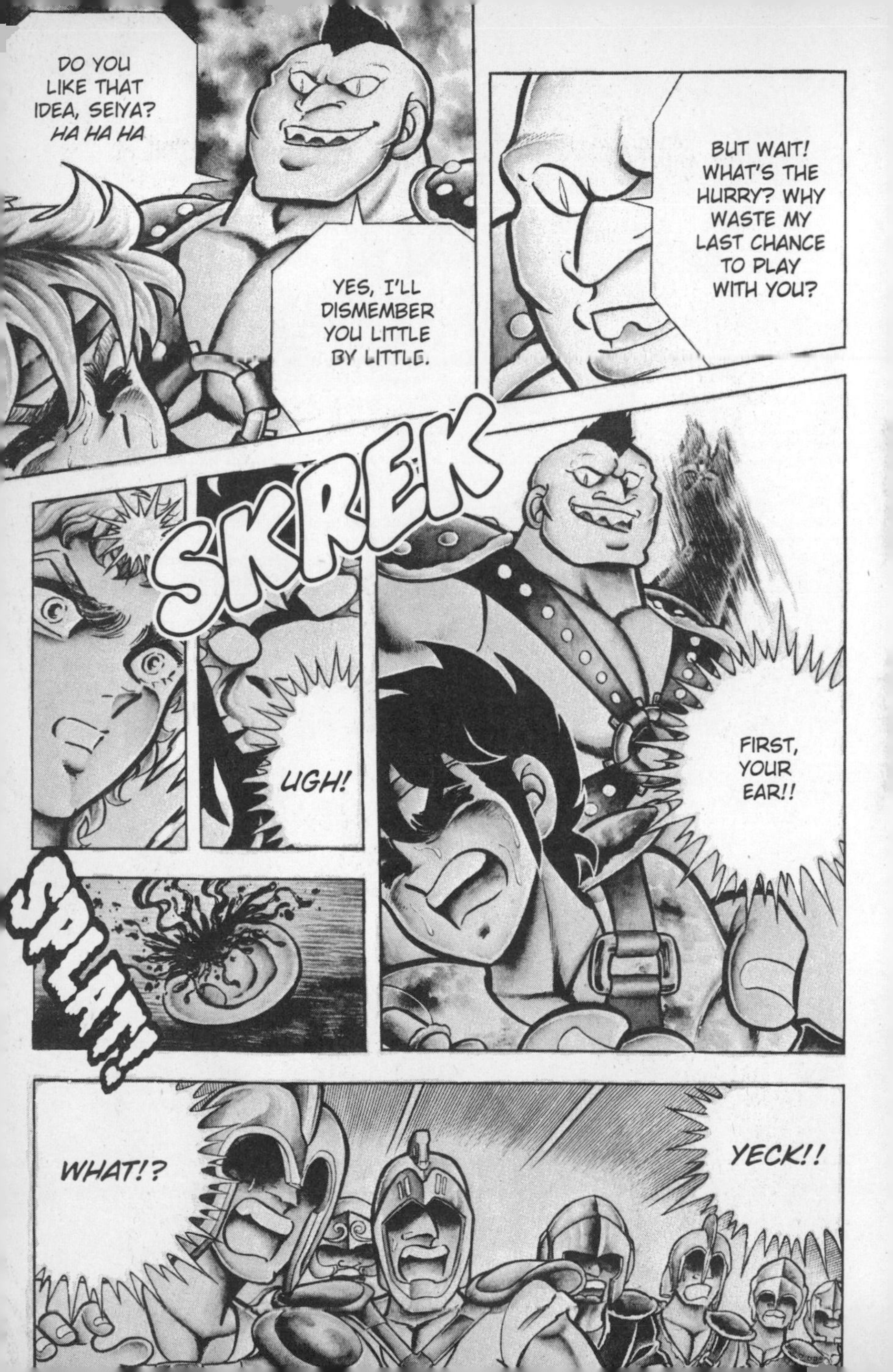

BUT WAIT! WHAT'S THE HURRY? WHY WASTE MY LAST CHANCE TO PLAY WITH YOU?
DO YOU LIKE THAT IDEA, SEIYA? HA HA HA
YES, I'LL DISMEMBER YOU LITTLE BY LITTLE.
FIRST, YOUR EAR!!
SKREK
UGH!
SPLAT!!
YECK!!
WHAT!?

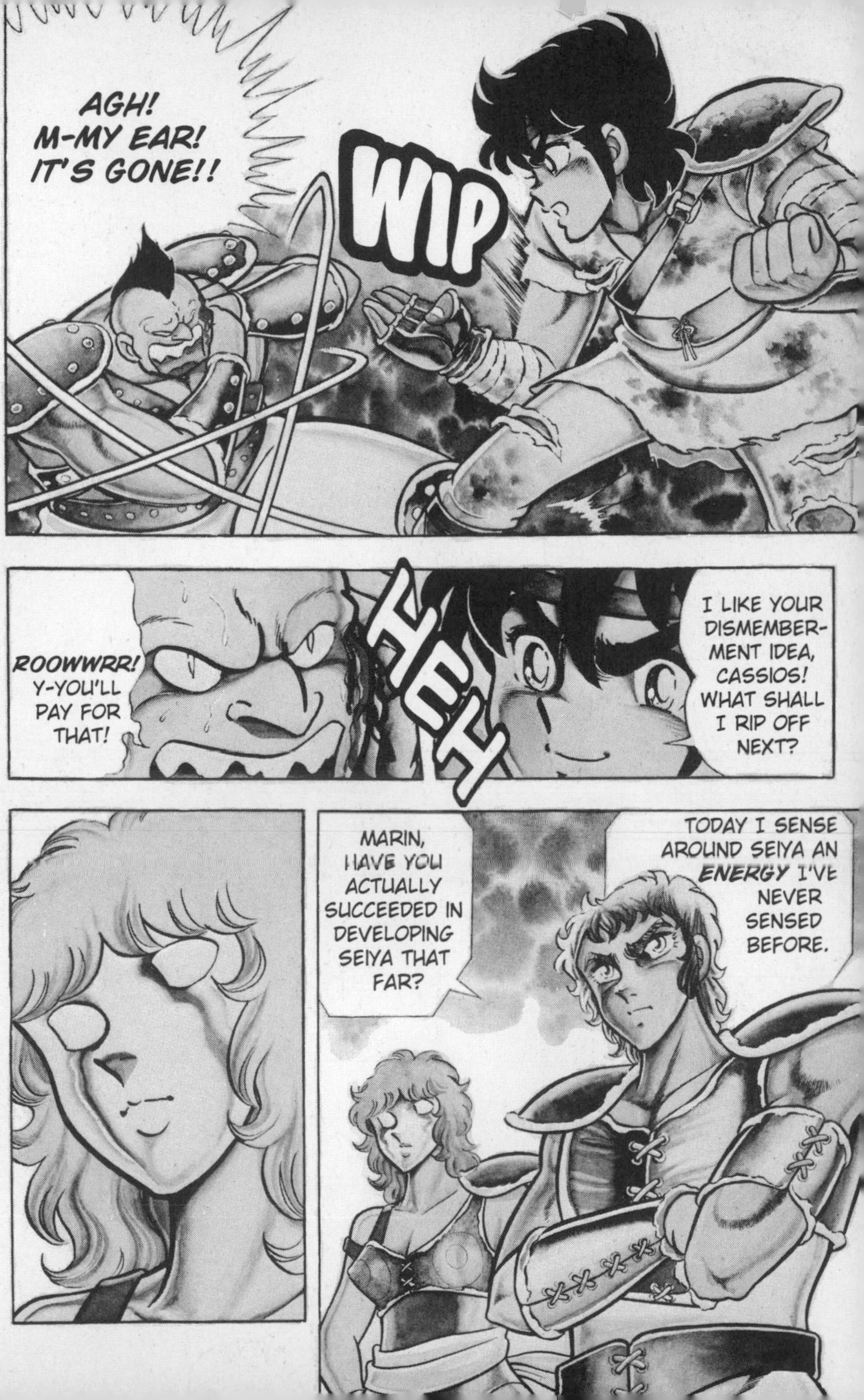
WIP
AGH! M-MY EAR! IT'S GONE!!
I LIKE YOUR DISMEMBER-MENT IDEA, CASSIOS! WHAT SHALL I RIP OFF NEXT?
HEH
ROOWWRR! Y-YOU'LL PAY FOR THAT!
TODAY I SENSE AROUND SEIYA AN ENERGY I'VE NEVER SENSED BEFORE.
MARIN, HAVE YOU ACTUALLY SUCCEEDED IN DEVELOPING SEIYA THAT FAR?

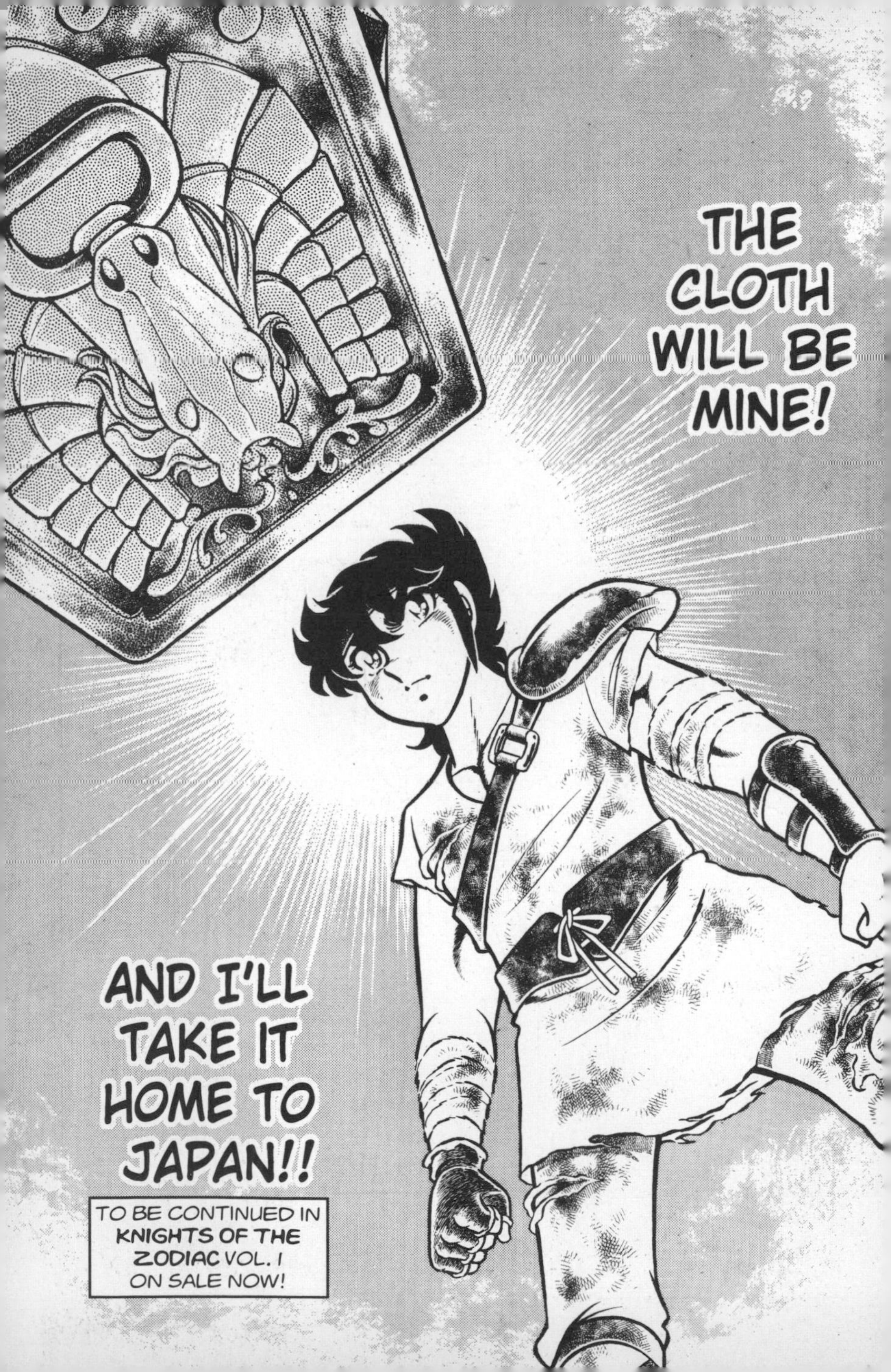
THE CLOTH WILL BE MINE!
AND I'LL TAKE IT HOME TO JAPAN!!
TO BE CONTINUED IN KNIGHTS OF THE ZODIAC VOL. 1 ON SALE NOW!

## The Prince of Tennis

Story and Art by Takeshi Konomi

# Hot fiery determination to be the best in the world!

THE PRINCE OF TENNIS
HONEN JUMP GRAPHIC NOVEL
& Art by
Takeshi Konomi
volume 1

TENNIS PLAYERS AROUND THE WORLD WILL LOVE THIS MANGA!

ADAPTED INTO A JAPANESE ANIME SERIES AND VIDEO GAMES!

What would a 12-year-old boy know about tennis anyway? How could he possibly compete with players who are older, bigger, and more experienced? But this cool, collected 12-year-old has the determination deep down in his heart to be the best tennis player in all of Japan…and, maybe, help create a group of players such as the world has never seen. Tennis action has never been so intense and cool! There can only be one Prince of Tennis!

RATED A FOR ALL AGES

Bimonthly

$7.95

Available in May



Cover art subject to change.

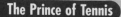

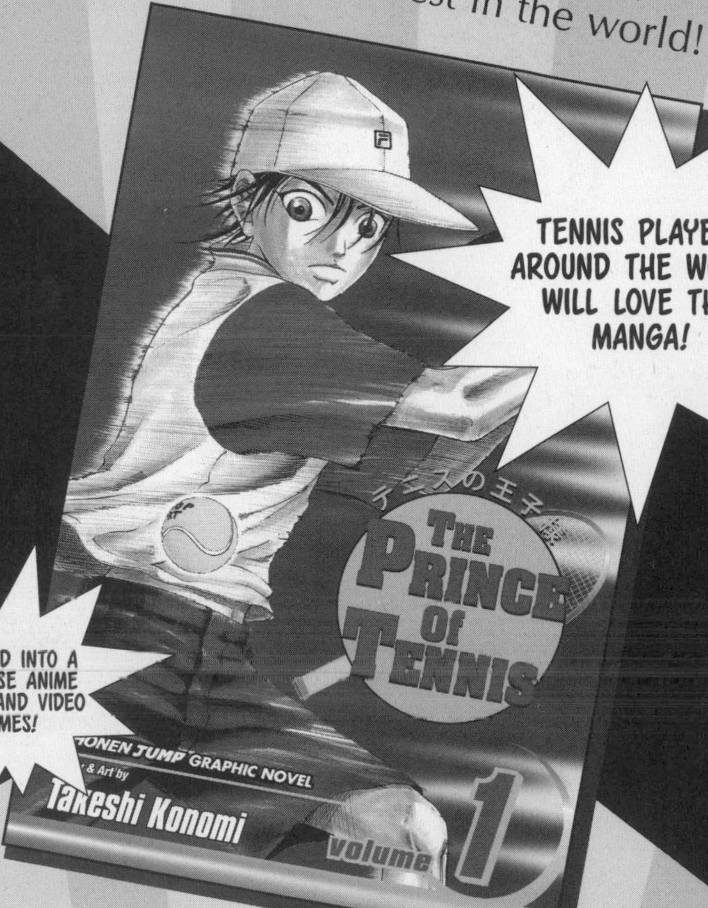

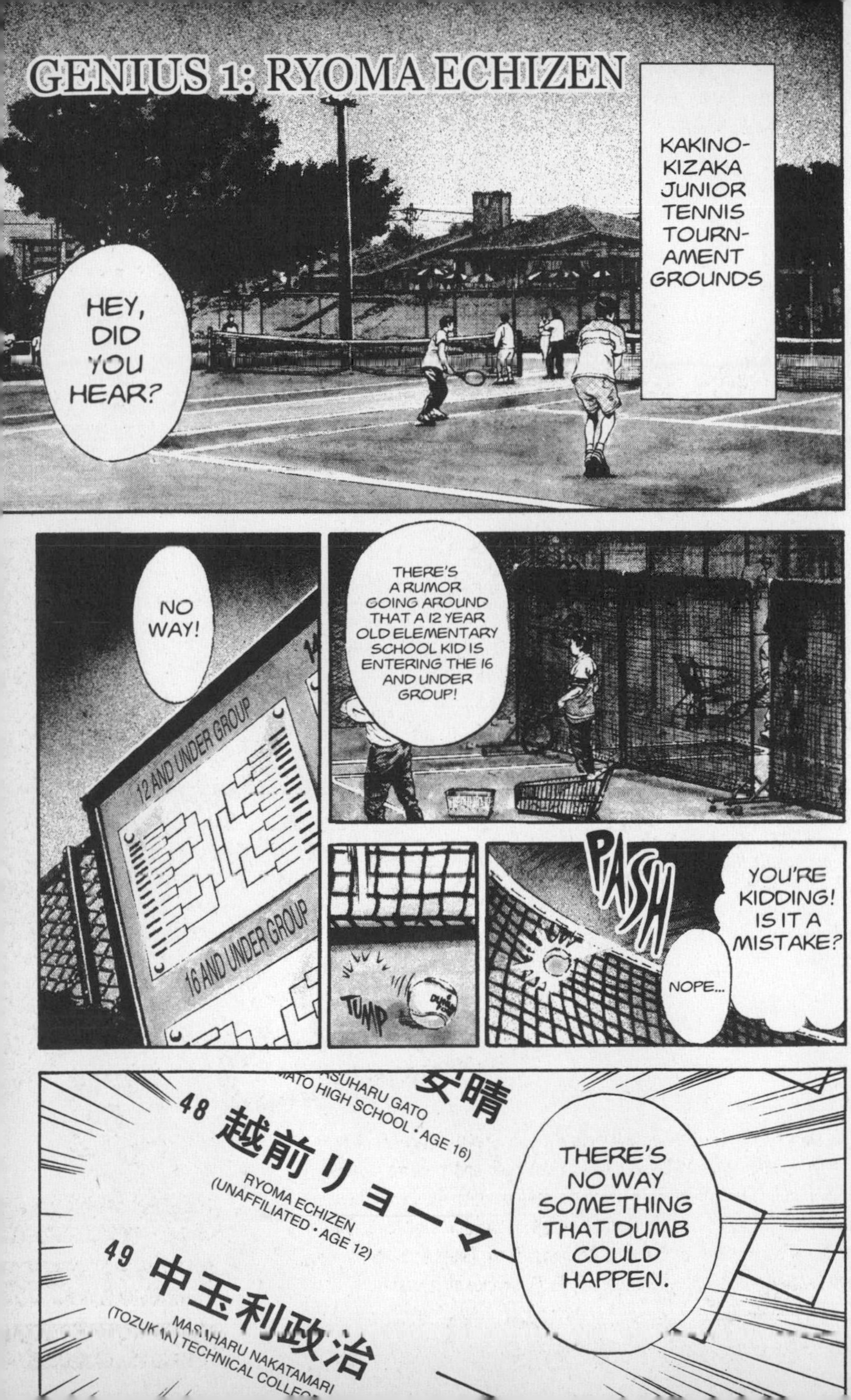
GENIUS 1: RYOMA ECHIZEN
KAKINO-KIZAKA JUNIOR TENNIS TOURN-AMENT GROUNDS
HEY, DID YOU HEAR?
THERE'S A RUMOR GOING AROUND THAT A 12 YEAR OLD ELEMENTARY SCHOOL KID IS ENTERING THE 16 AND UNDER GROUP!
YOU'RE KIDDING! IS IT A MISTAKE?
PASH
NOPE...
TUMP
NO WAY!
12 AND UNDER GROUP
16 AND UNDER GROUP
THERE'S NO WAY SOMETHING THAT DUMB COULD HAPPEN.
安晴
48 越前リョーマ
RYOMA ECHIZEN
(UNAFFILIATED · AGE 12)
49 中玉利政治
MASAHARU NAKATAMARI

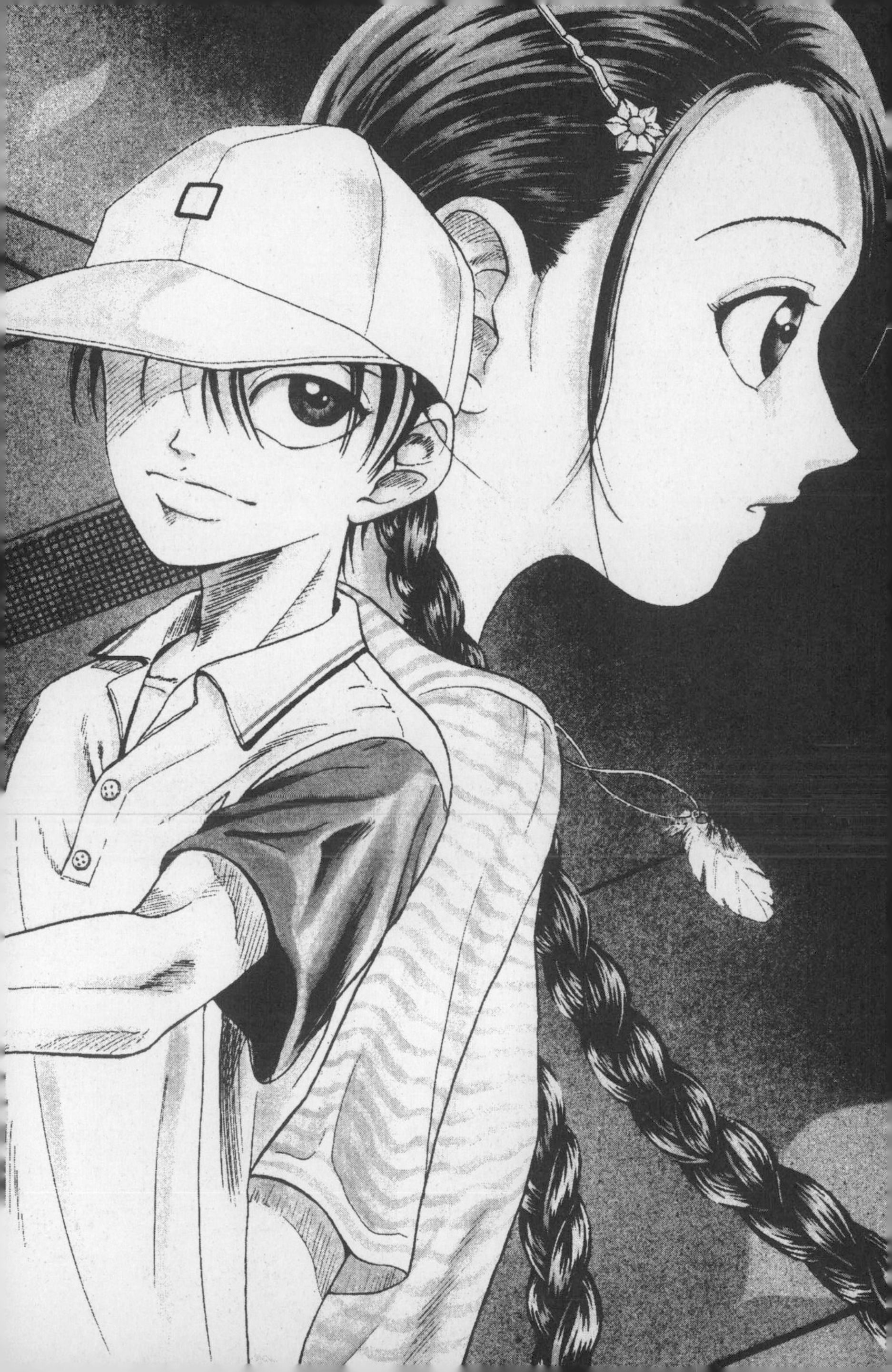

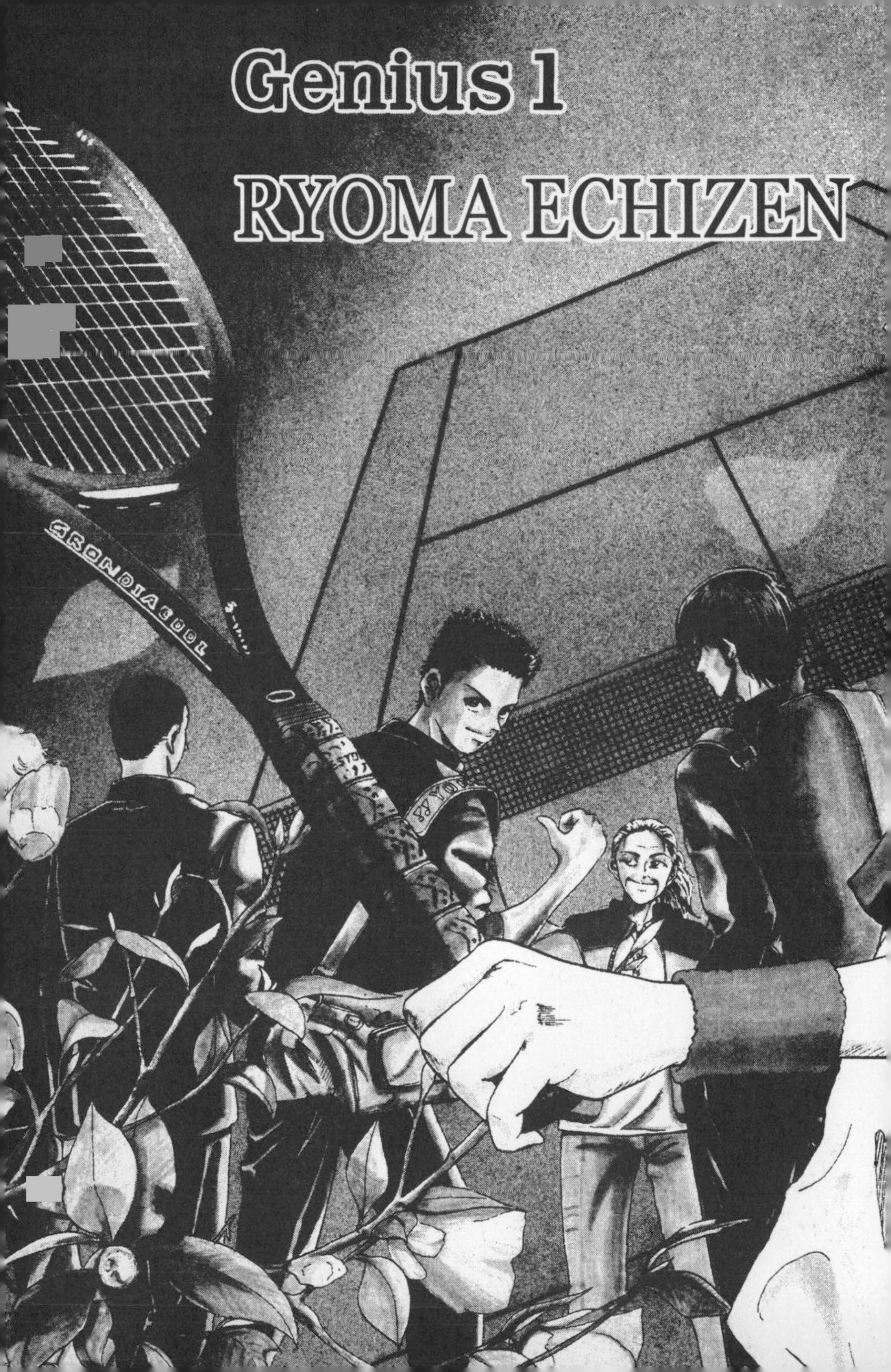
Genius 1
RYOMA ECHIZEN

# テニスの王子様
# THE PRINCE OF TENNIS™

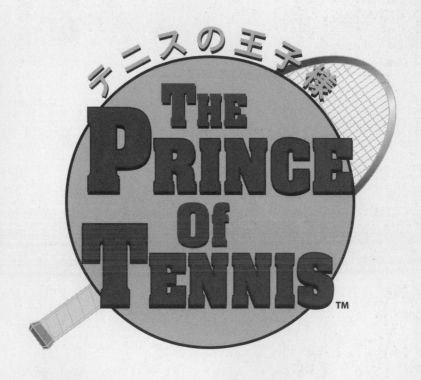

READ THIS WAY

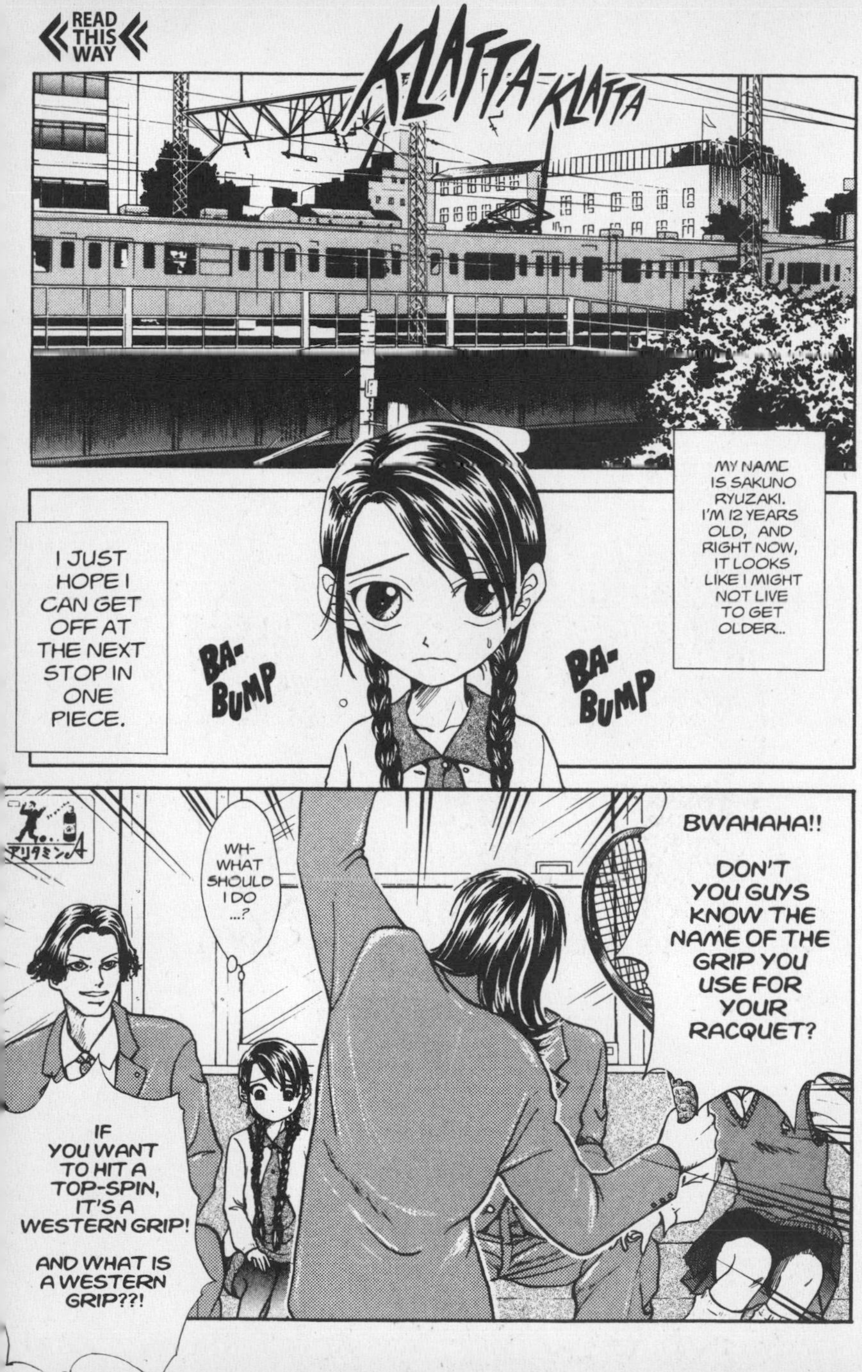
KLATTA KLATTA
MY NAME IS SAKUNO RYUZAKI. I'M 12 YEARS OLD, AND RIGHT NOW, IT LOOKS LIKE I MIGHT NOT LIVE TO GET OLDER...
BA-BUMP
BA-BUMP
I JUST HOPE I CAN GET OFF AT THE NEXT STOP IN ONE PIECE.
BWAHAHA!!
DON'T YOU GUYS KNOW THE NAME OF THE GRIP YOU USE FOR YOUR RACQUET?
WH-WHAT SHOULD I DO ...?
IF YOU WANT TO HIT A TOP-SPIN, IT'S A WESTERN GRIP!
AND WHAT IS A WESTERN GRIP??!

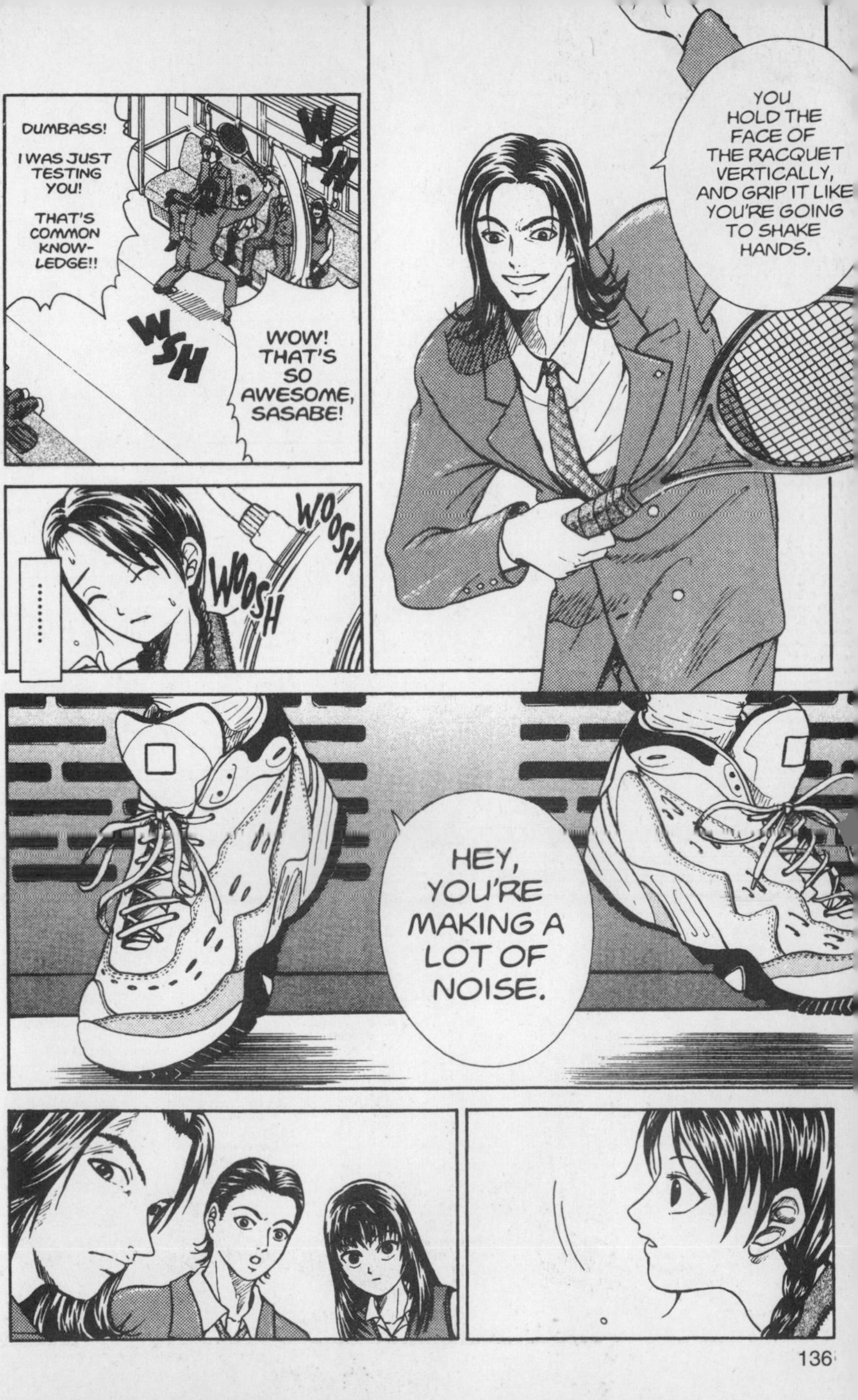
YOU HOLD THE FACE OF THE RACQUET VERTICALLY, AND GRIP IT LIKE YOU'RE GOING TO SHAKE HANDS.
WSH
WOW! THAT'S SO AWESOME, SASABE!
WSH
DUMBASS! I WAS JUST TESTING YOU! THAT'S COMMON KNOW-LEDGE!!
WOOSH
WOOSH
........
HEY, YOU'RE MAKING A LOT OF NOISE.

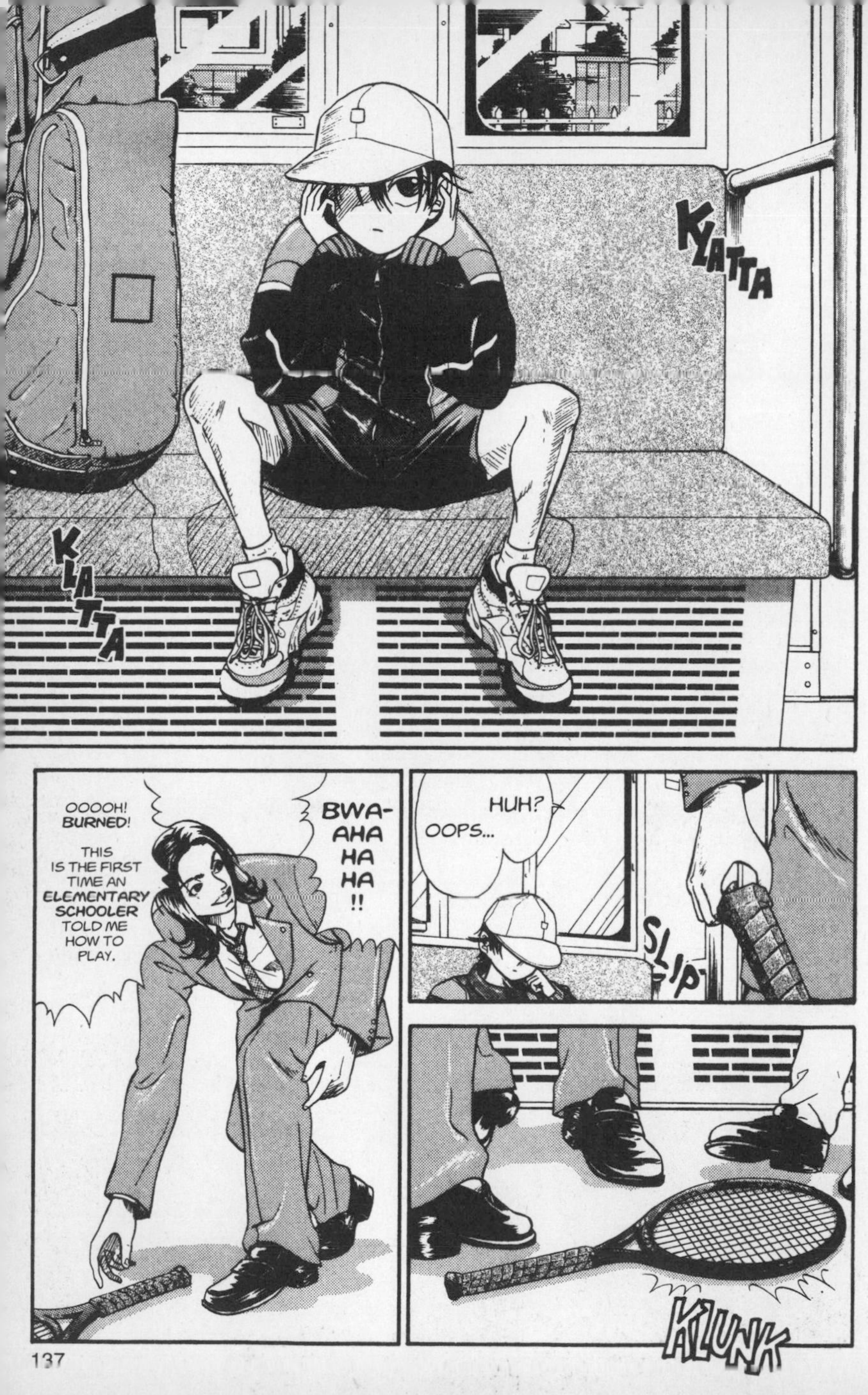
KYATTA
KLATTA
HUH?
OOPS...
SLIP
KLUNK
BWA-AHA HA HA !!
OOOOH! BURNED!
THIS IS THE FIRST TIME AN **ELEMENTARY SCHOOLER** TOLD ME HOW TO PLAY.

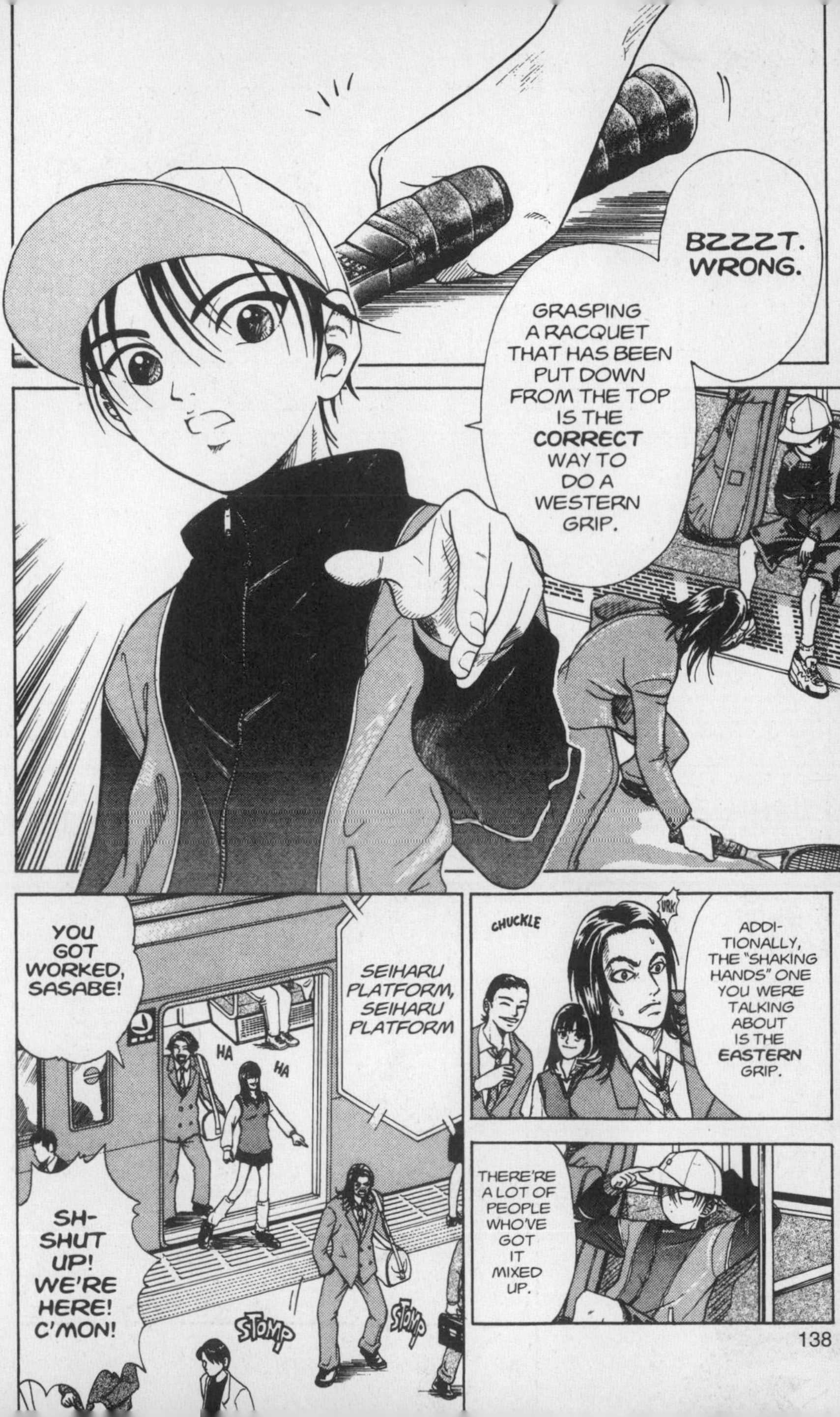

BZZZT. WRONG.
GRASPING A RACQUET THAT HAS BEEN PUT DOWN FROM THE TOP IS THE **CORRECT** WAY TO DO A WESTERN GRIP.
URK
ADDI-TIONALLY, THE "SHAKING HANDS" ONE YOU WERE TALKING ABOUT IS THE **EASTERN** GRIP.
CHUCKLE
THERE'RE A LOT OF PEOPLE WHO'VE GOT IT MIXED UP.
SEIHARU PLATFORM, SEIHARU PLATFORM
YOU GOT WORKED, SASABE!
HA
HA
SH-SHUT UP! WE'RE HERE! C'MON!
STOMP
STOMP

READ THIS WAY

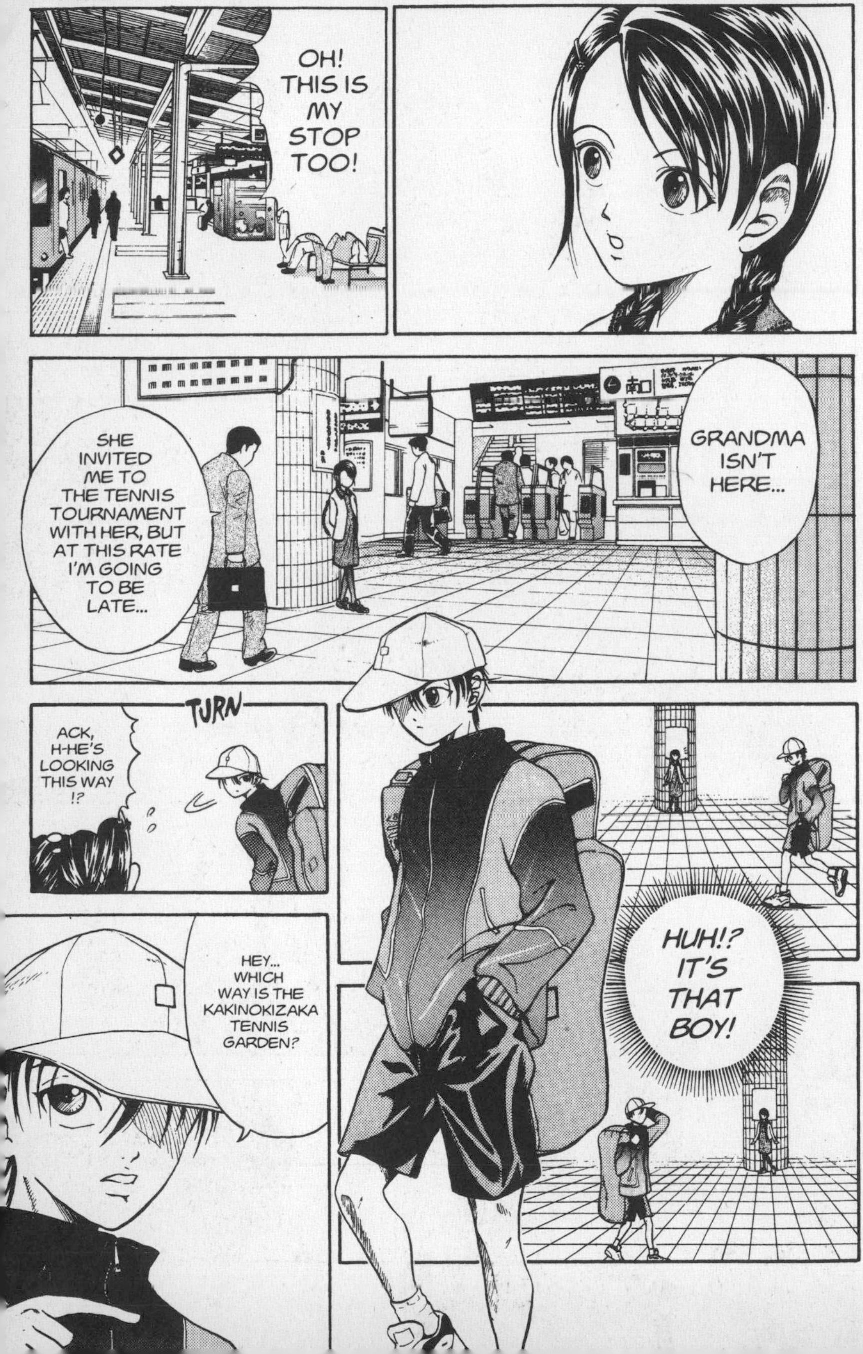
OH! THIS IS MY STOP TOO!
GRANDMA ISN'T HERE...
SHE INVITED ME TO THE TENNIS TOURNAMENT WITH HER, BUT AT THIS RATE I'M GOING TO BE LATE...
HUH!? IT'S THAT BOY!
TURN
ACK, H-HE'S LOOKING THIS WAY !?
HEY... WHICH WAY IS THE KAKINOKIZAKA TENNIS GARDEN?

READ THIS WAY

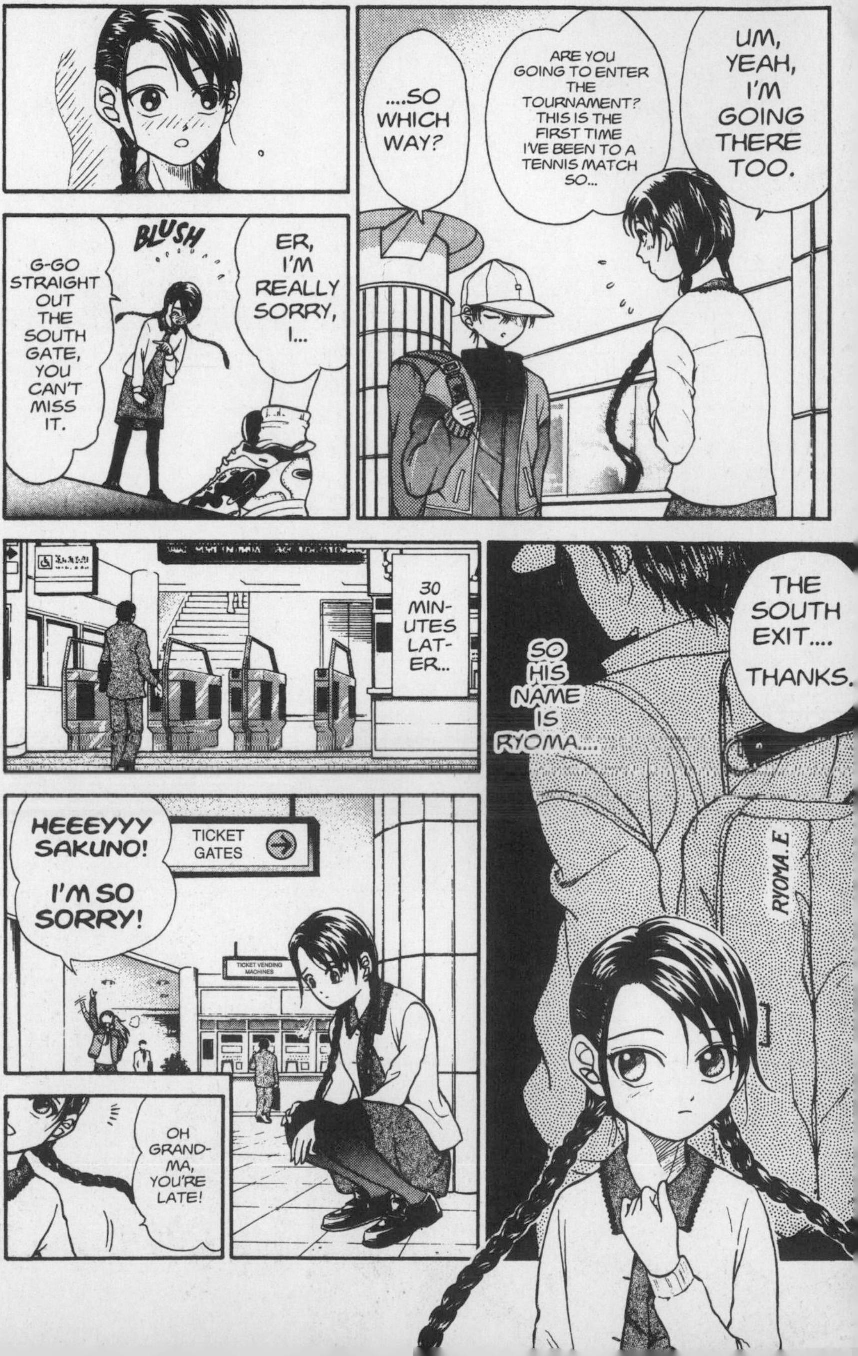
UM, YEAH, I'M GOING THERE TOO.
ARE YOU GOING TO ENTER THE TOURNAMENT? THIS IS THE FIRST TIME I'VE BEEN TO A TENNIS MATCH SO...
....SO WHICH WAY?
ER, I'M REALLY SORRY, I...
BLUSH
G-GO STRAIGHT OUT THE SOUTH GATE, YOU CAN'T MISS IT.
THE SOUTH EXIT.... THANKS.
SO HIS NAME IS RYOMA....
RYOMA.E
30 MINUTES LATER...
HEEEYYY SAKUNO! I'M SO SORRY!
TICKET GATES
TICKET VENDING MACHINES
OH GRANDMA, YOU'RE LATE!

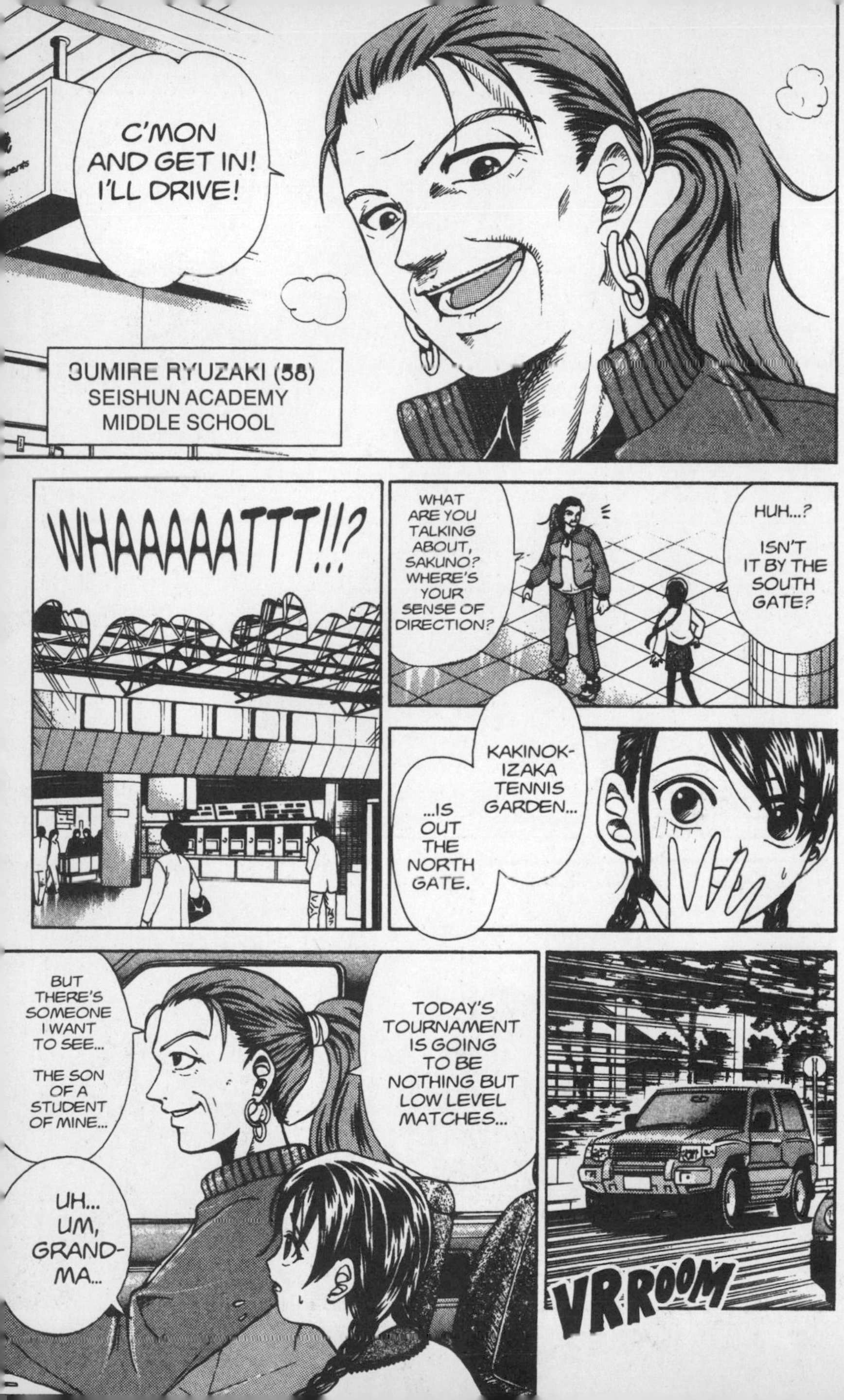
C'MON AND GET IN! I'LL DRIVE!
SUMIRE RYUZAKI (58) SEISHUN ACADEMY MIDDLE SCHOOL
HUH...? ISN'T IT BY THE SOUTH GATE?
WHAT ARE YOU TALKING ABOUT, SAKUNO? WHERE'S YOUR SENSE OF DIRECTION?
KAKINOK-IZAKA TENNIS GARDEN...
...IS OUT THE NORTH GATE.
WHAAAAATTT!!?
VRROOM
TODAY'S TOURNAMENT IS GOING TO BE NOTHING BUT LOW LEVEL MATCHES...
BUT THERE'S SOMEONE I WANT TO SEE... THE SON OF A STUDENT OF MINE...
UH... UM, GRAND-MA...

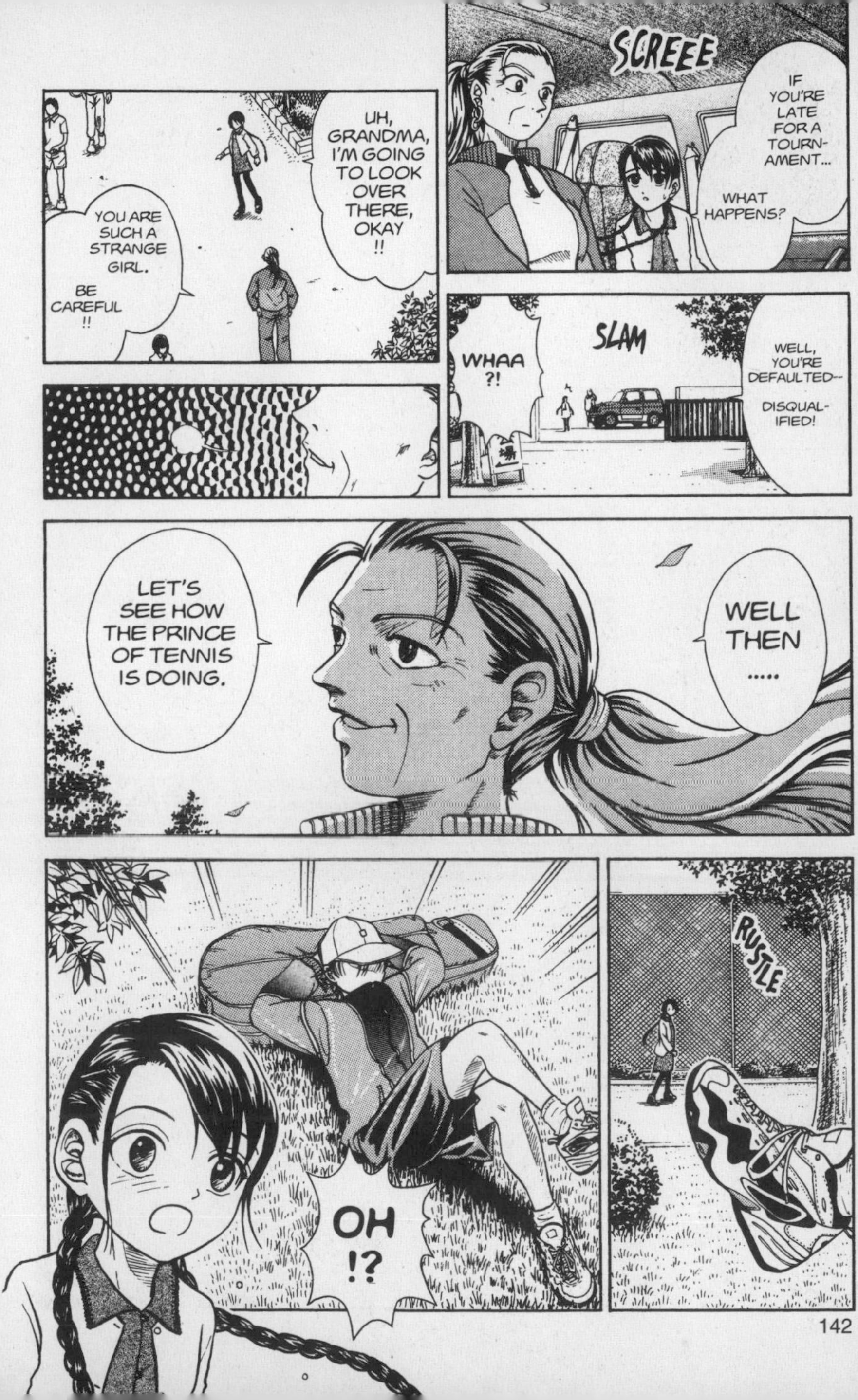
SCREEE
IF YOU'RE LATE FOR A TOURNAMENT...
WHAT HAPPENS?
SLAM
WELL, YOU'RE DEFAULTED--
DISQUALIFIED!
WHAA ?!
UH, GRANDMA, I'M GOING TO LOOK OVER THERE, OKAY !!
YOU ARE SUCH A STRANGE GIRL.
BE CAREFUL !!
WELL THEN .....
LET'S SEE HOW THE PRINCE OF TENNIS IS DOING.
RUSTLE
OH !?

READ THIS WAY

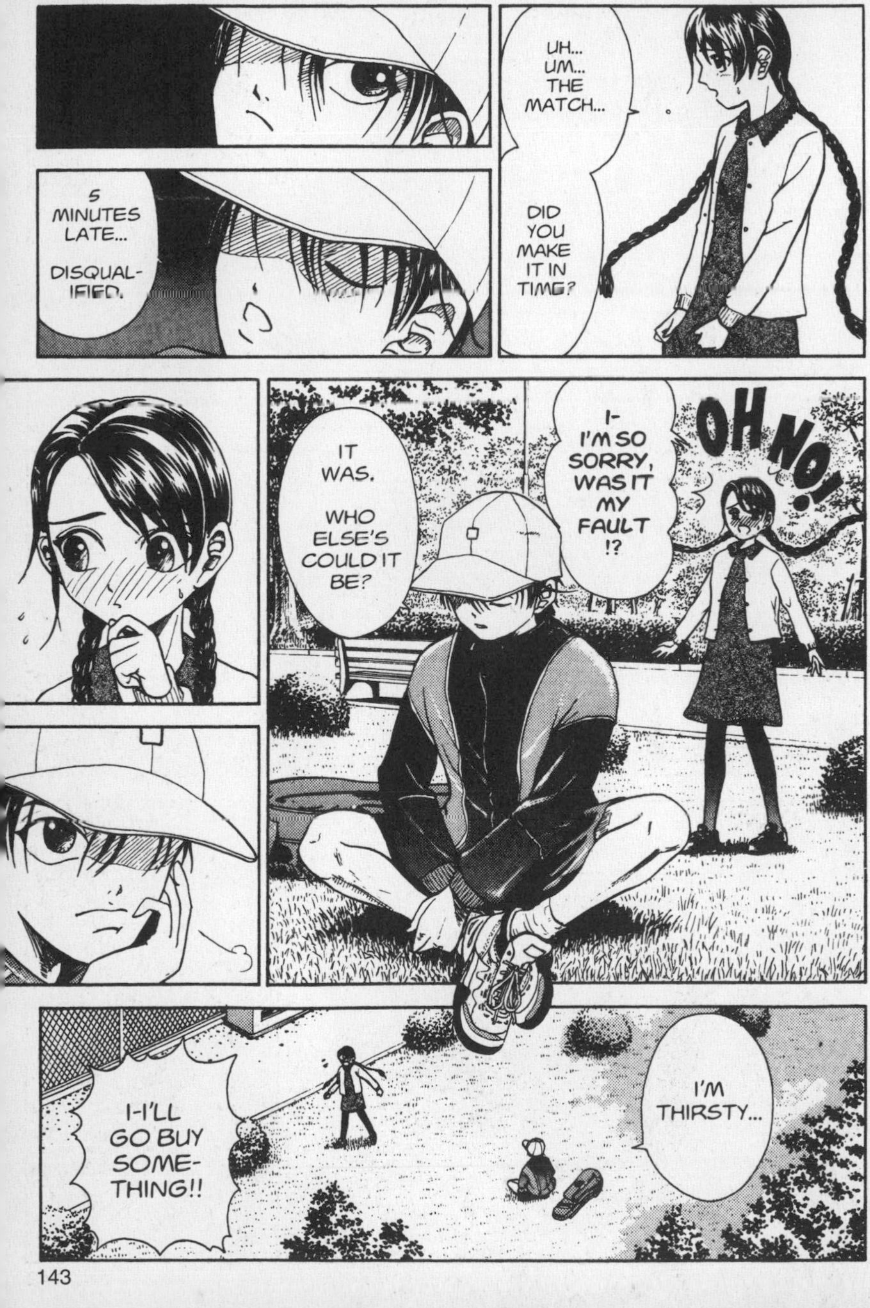
UH... UM... THE MATCH...
DID YOU MAKE IT IN TIME?
5 MINUTES LATE... DISQUALIFIED.
OH NO!
I- I'M SO SORRY, WAS IT MY FAULT !?
IT WAS.
WHO ELSE'S COULD IT BE?
I'M THIRSTY...
I-I'LL GO BUY SOME-THING!!

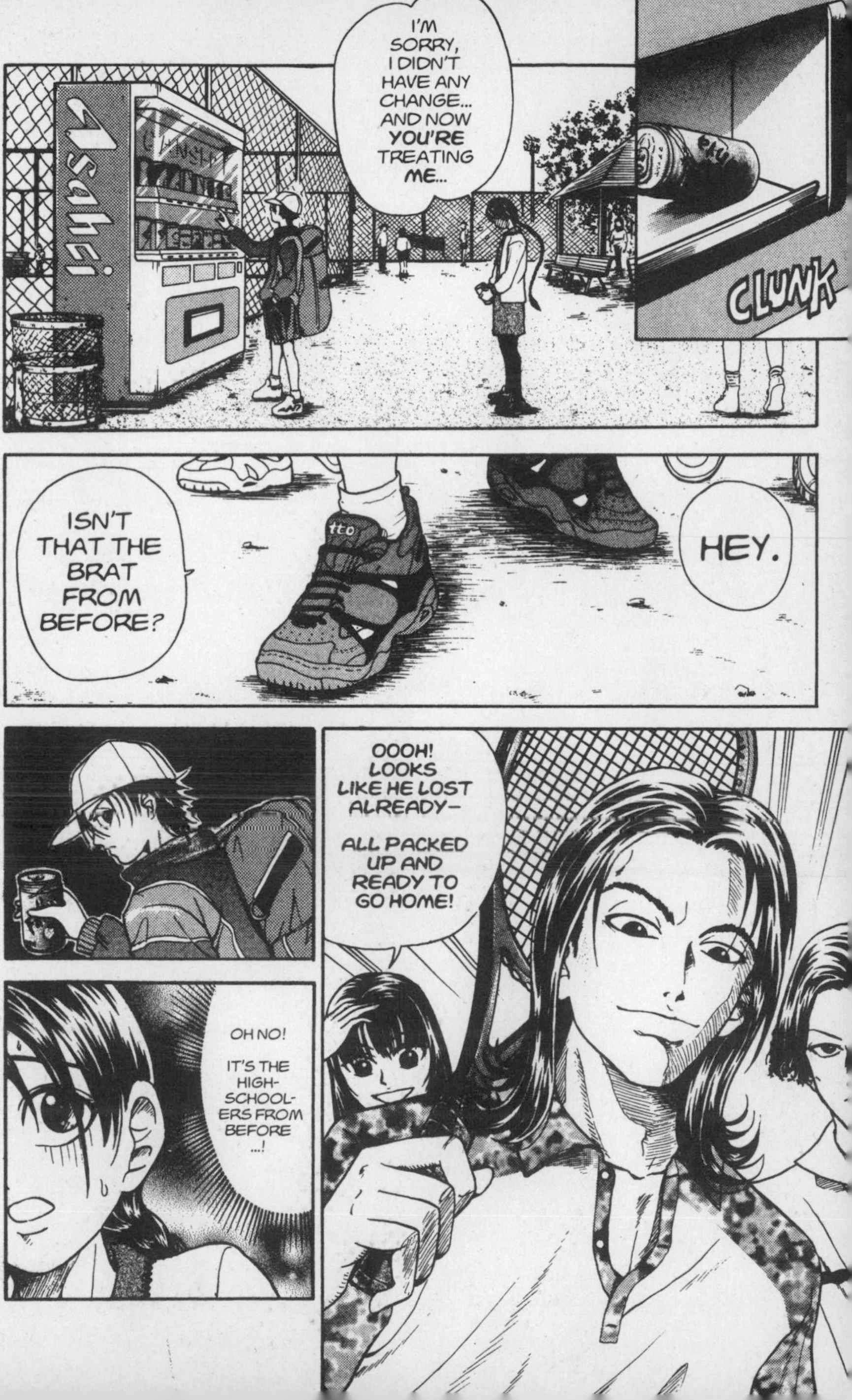
CLUNK
I'M SORRY, I DIDN'T HAVE ANY CHANGE... AND NOW **YOU'RE** TREATING ME...
Asahi
HEY.
ISN'T THAT THE BRAT FROM BEFORE?
OOOH! LOOKS LIKE HE LOST ALREADY—
ALL PACKED UP AND READY TO GO HOME!
OH NO!
IT'S THE HIGH-SCHOOLERS FROM BEFORE ...!

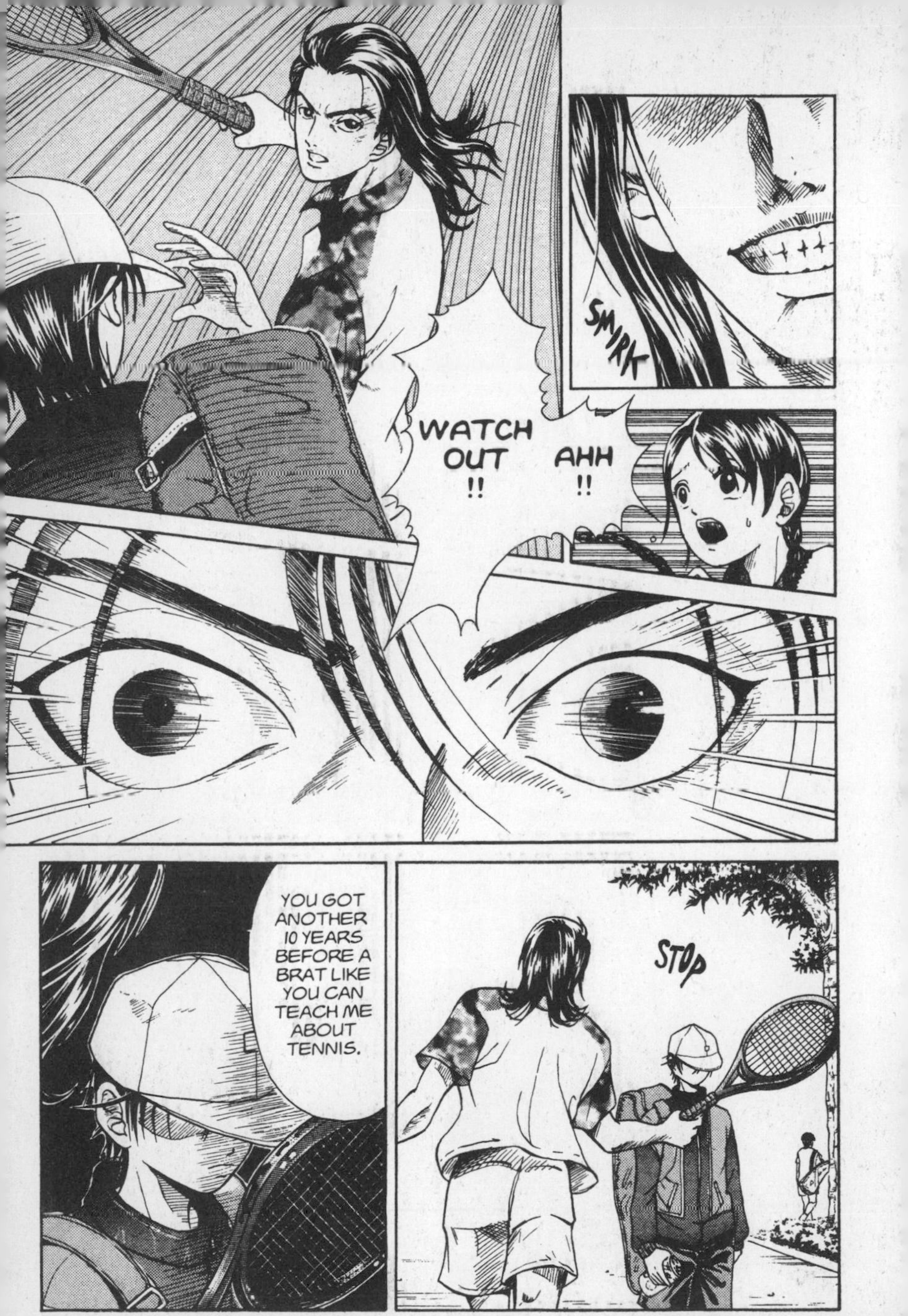
SMIRK
AHH !!
WATCH OUT !!
STOP
YOU GOT ANOTHER 10 YEARS BEFORE A BRAT LIKE YOU CAN TEACH ME ABOUT TENNIS.

READ THIS WAY

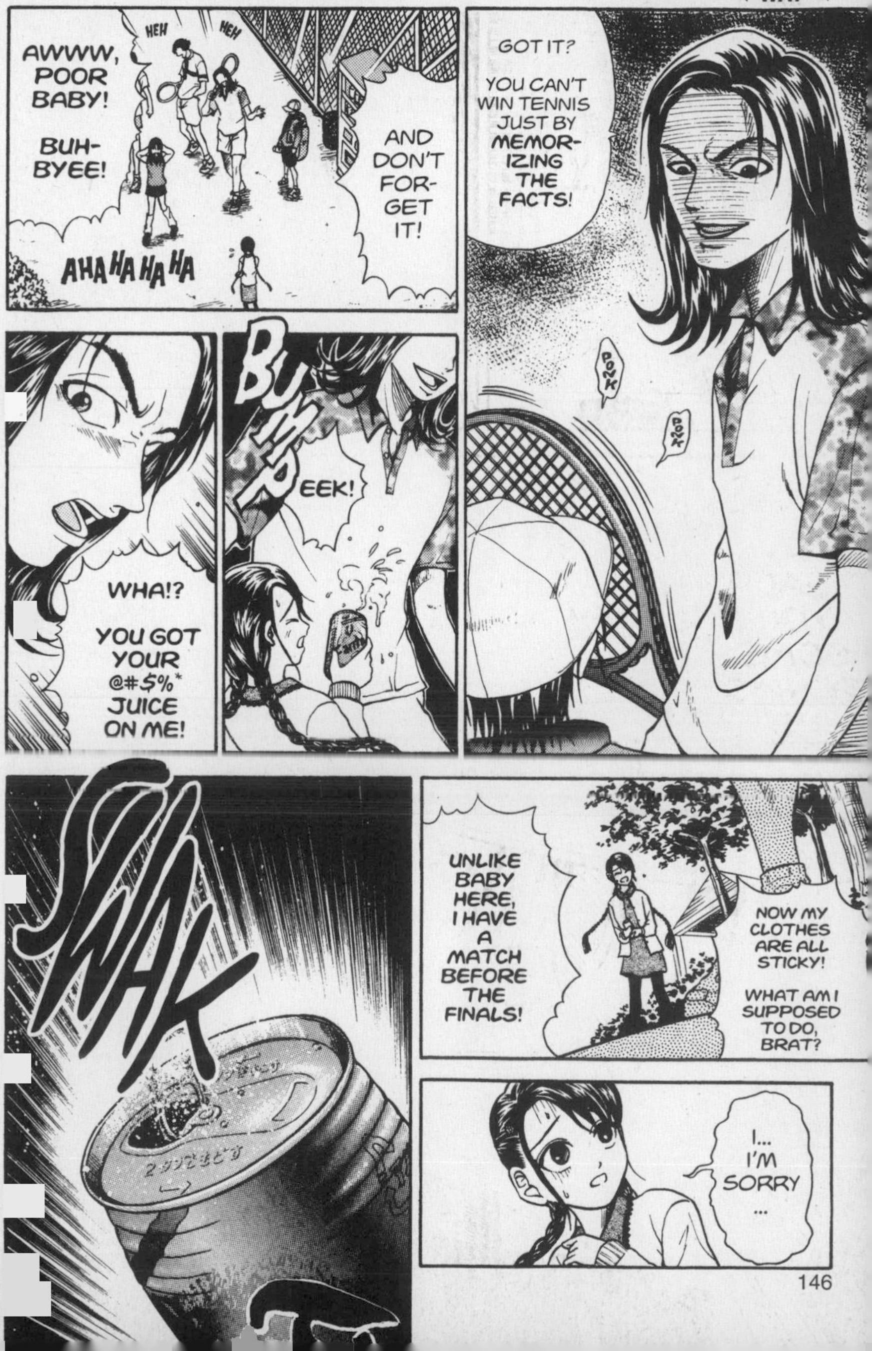
GOT IT?
YOU CAN'T WIN TENNIS JUST BY MEMORIZING THE FACTS!
POCK
POCK
AND DON'T FORGET IT!
HEH
HEH
AWWW, POOR BABY!
BUH-BYEE!
AHAHAHAHA
BUMP
EEK!
WHA!?
YOU GOT YOUR @#$%* JUICE ON ME!
NOW MY CLOTHES ARE ALL STICKY!
WHAT AM I SUPPOSED TO DO, BRAT?
UNLIKE BABY HERE, I HAVE A MATCH BEFORE THE FINALS!
I... I'M SORRY ...
SWAK

READ THIS WAY

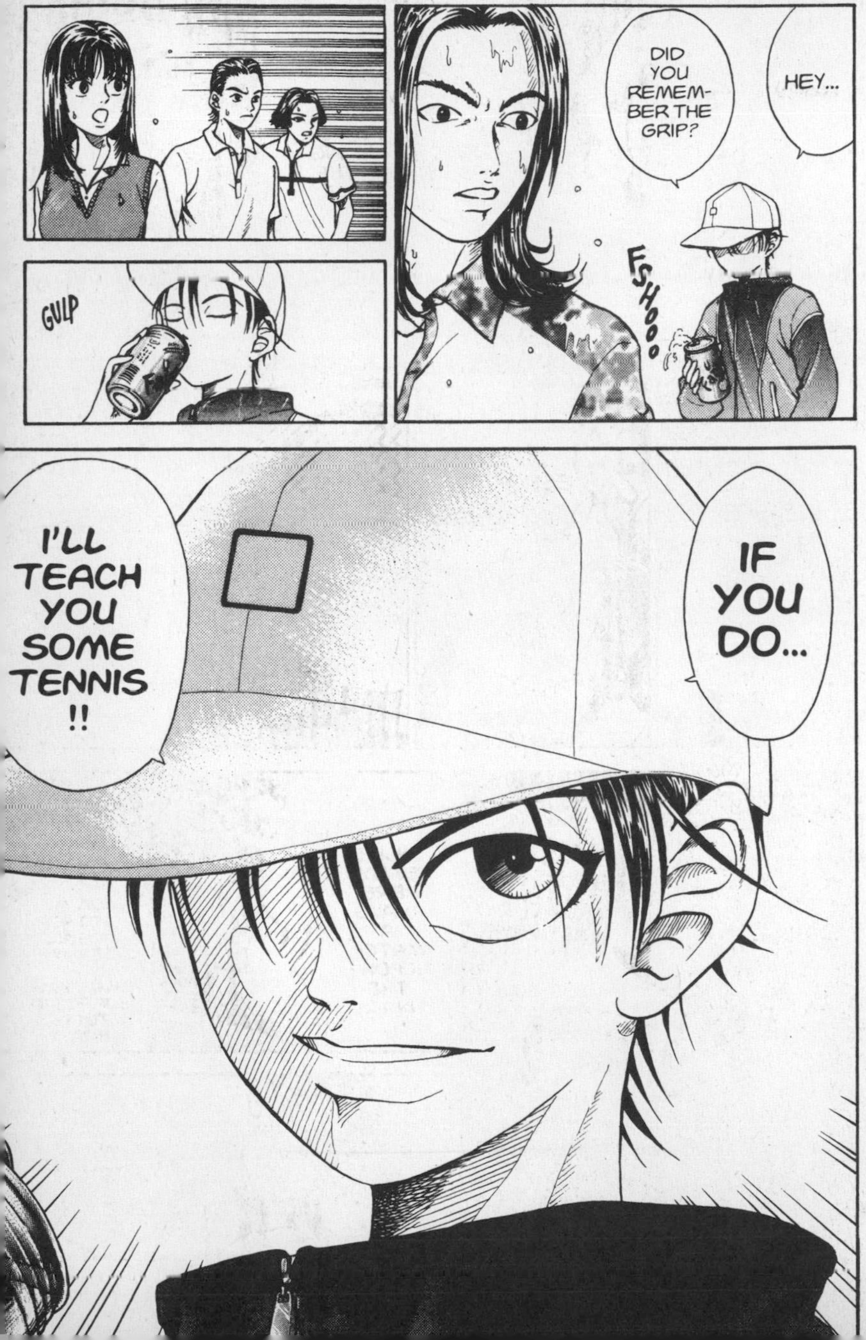
HEY...
DID YOU REMEMBER THE GRIP?
FSHOOO
GULP
IF YOU DO...
I'LL TEACH YOU SOME TENNIS!!

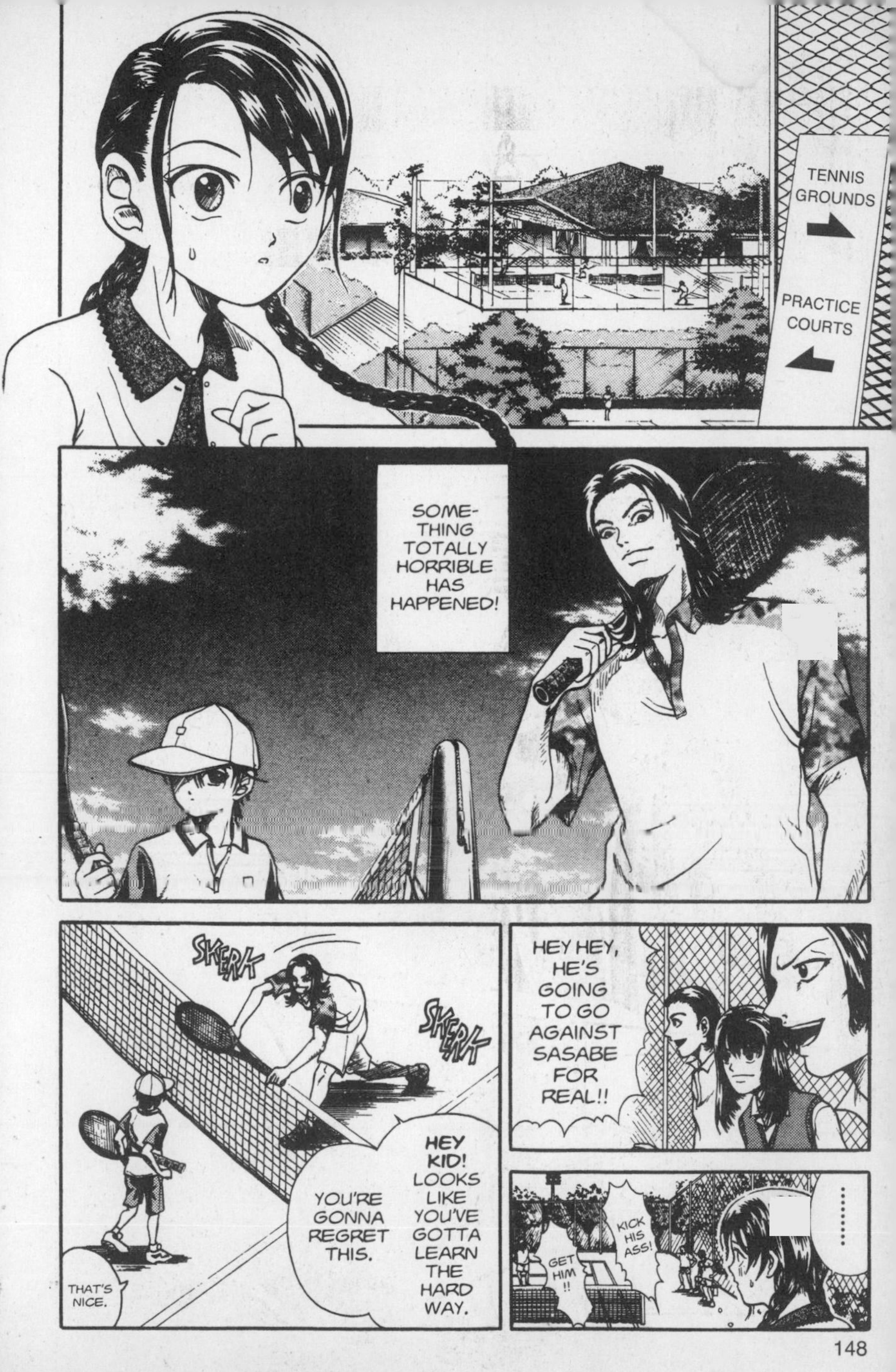
TENNIS GROUNDS
PRACTICE COURTS
SOMETHING TOTALLY HORRIBLE HAS HAPPENED!
HEY HEY, HE'S GOING TO GO AGAINST SASABE FOR REAL!!
......
KICK HIS ASS!
GET HIM !!
SKERK
SKERK
HEY KID! LOOKS LIKE YOU'VE GOTTA LEARN THE HARD WAY.
YOU'RE GONNA REGRET THIS.
THAT'S NICE.

READ THIS WAY

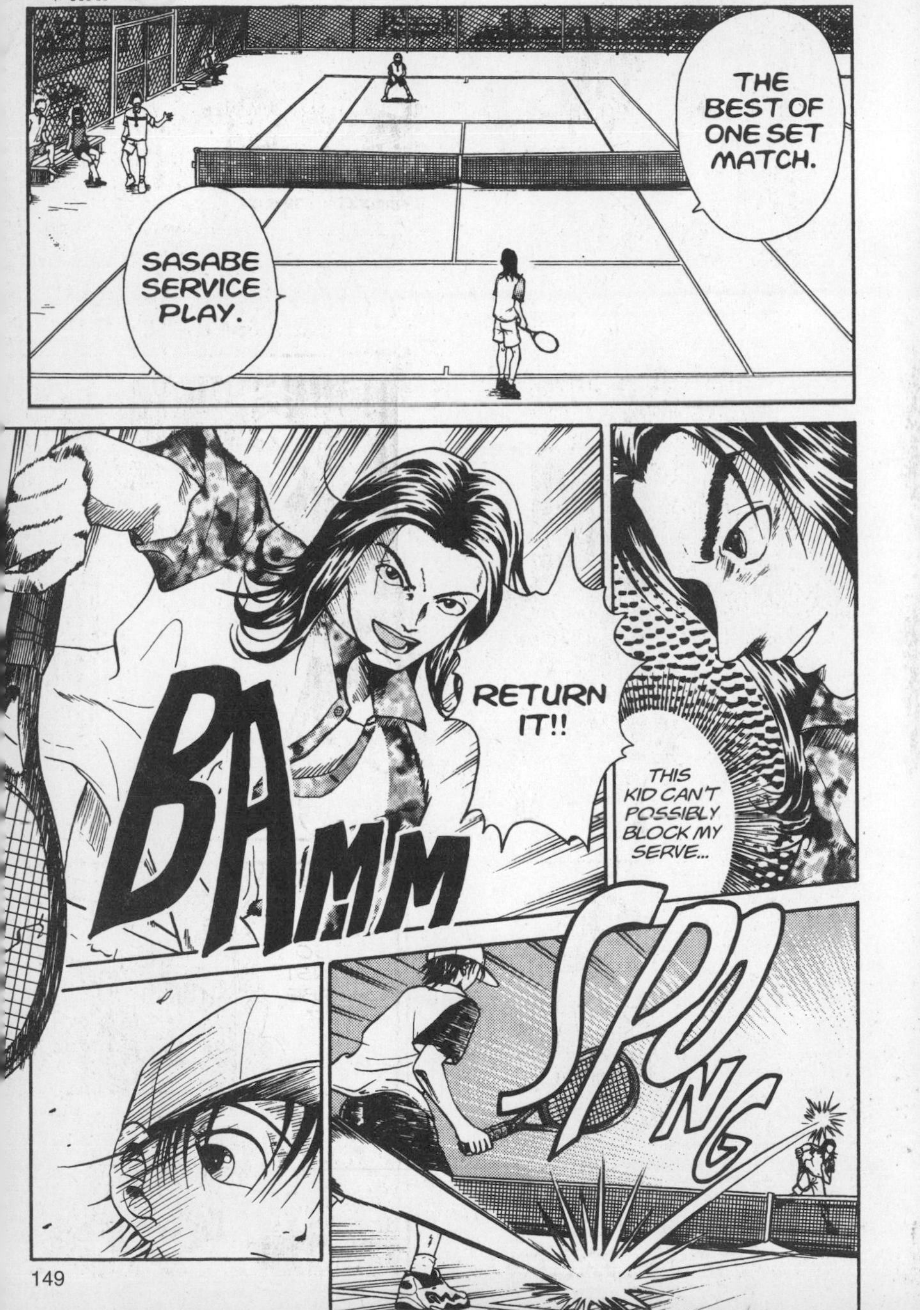
THE BEST OF ONE SET MATCH.
SASABE SERVICE PLAY.
THIS KID CAN'T POSSIBLY BLOCK MY SERVE...
RETURN IT!!
BAMM
SPONG

READ THIS WAY

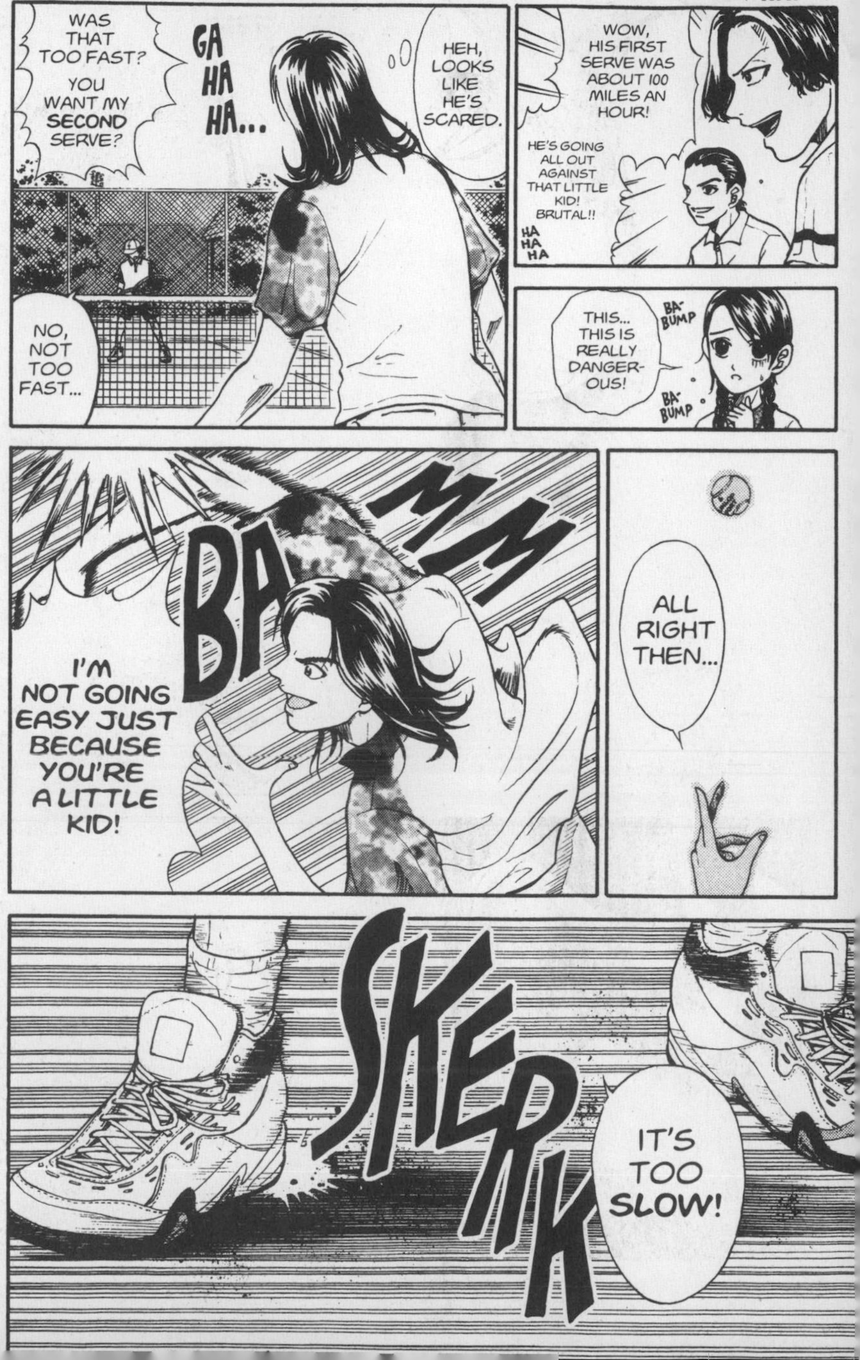
WOW, HIS FIRST SERVE WAS ABOUT 100 MILES AN HOUR!
HE'S GOING ALL OUT AGAINST THAT LITTLE KID! BRUTAL!!
HA HA HA
BA-BUMP
THIS... THIS IS REALLY DANGER-OUS!
BA-BUMP
HEH, LOOKS LIKE HE'S SCARED.
GA HA HA...
WAS THAT TOO FAST? YOU WANT MY SECOND SERVE?
NO, NOT TOO FAST...
ALL RIGHT THEN...
BAMMM
I'M NOT GOING EASY JUST BECAUSE YOU'RE A LITTLE KID!
IT'S TOO SLOW!
SKERK

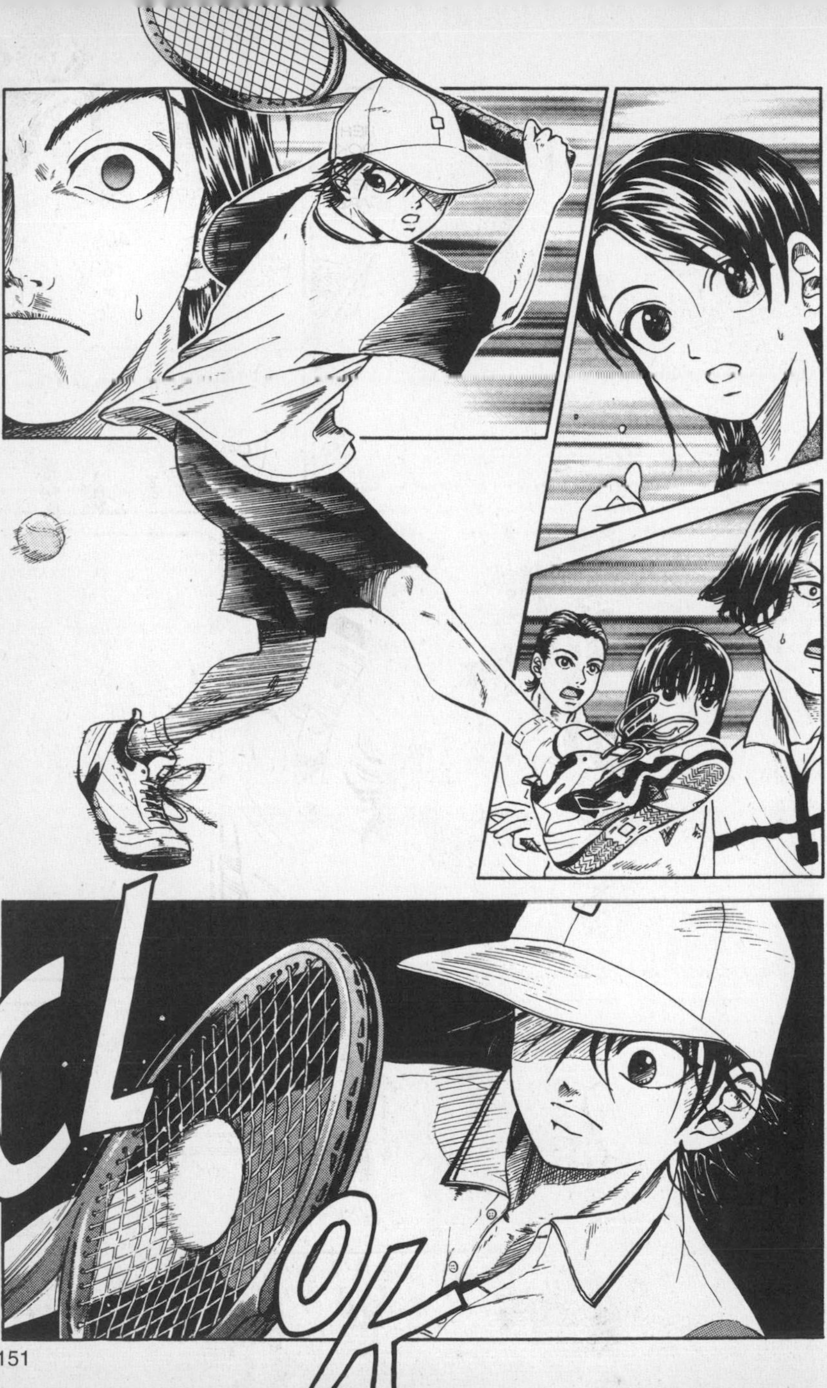
CLOK

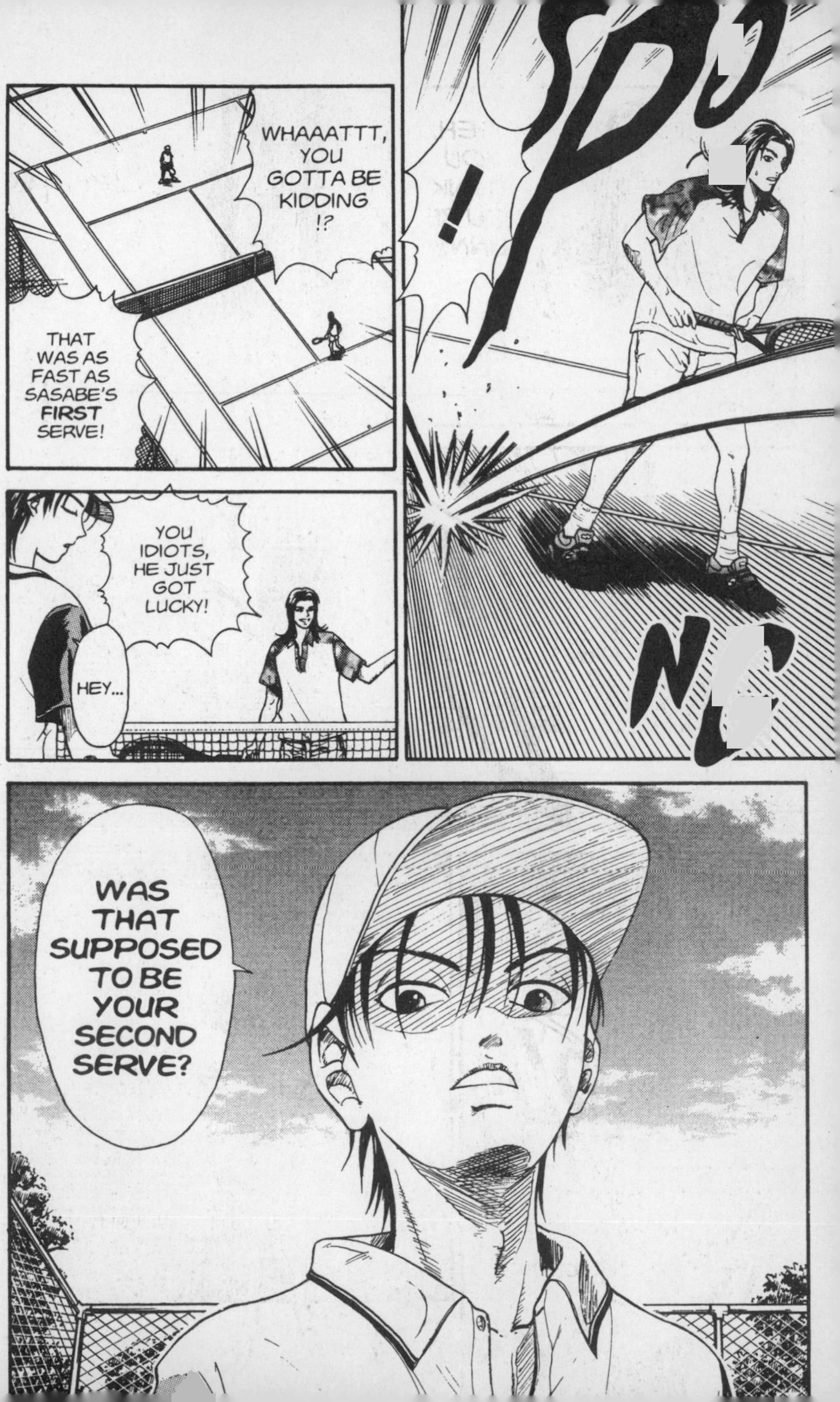
WHAAATTT, YOU GOTTA BE KIDDING !?
THAT WAS AS FAST AS SASABE'S **FIRST** SERVE!
YOU IDIOTS, HE JUST GOT LUCKY!
HEY...
WAS THAT SUPPOSED TO BE YOUR SECOND SERVE?

READ THIS WAY

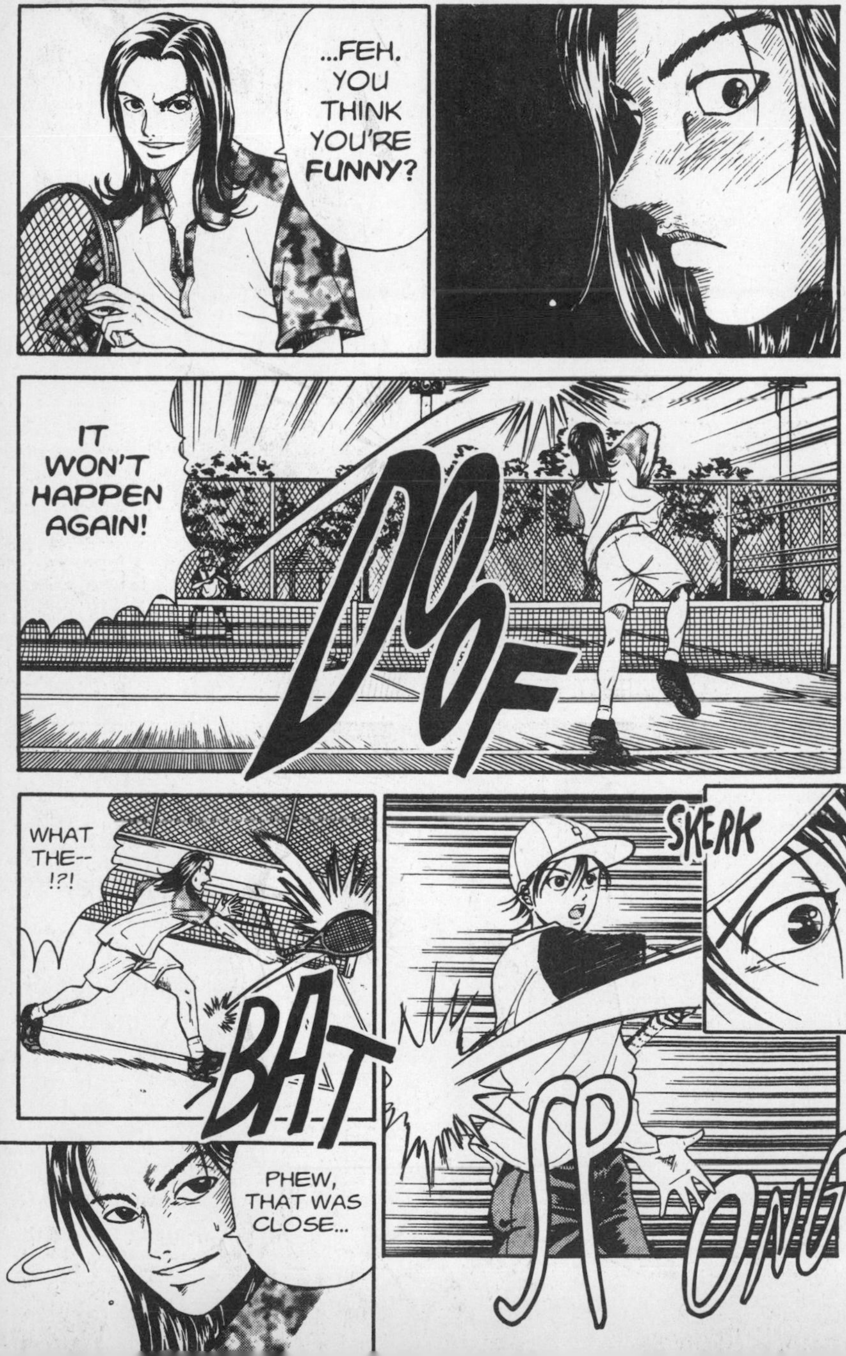

...FEH. YOU THINK YOU'RE FUNNY?
IT WON'T HAPPEN AGAIN!
DOOF
SKERK
SPONG
WHAT THE-- !?!
BAT
PHEW, THAT WAS CLOSE...

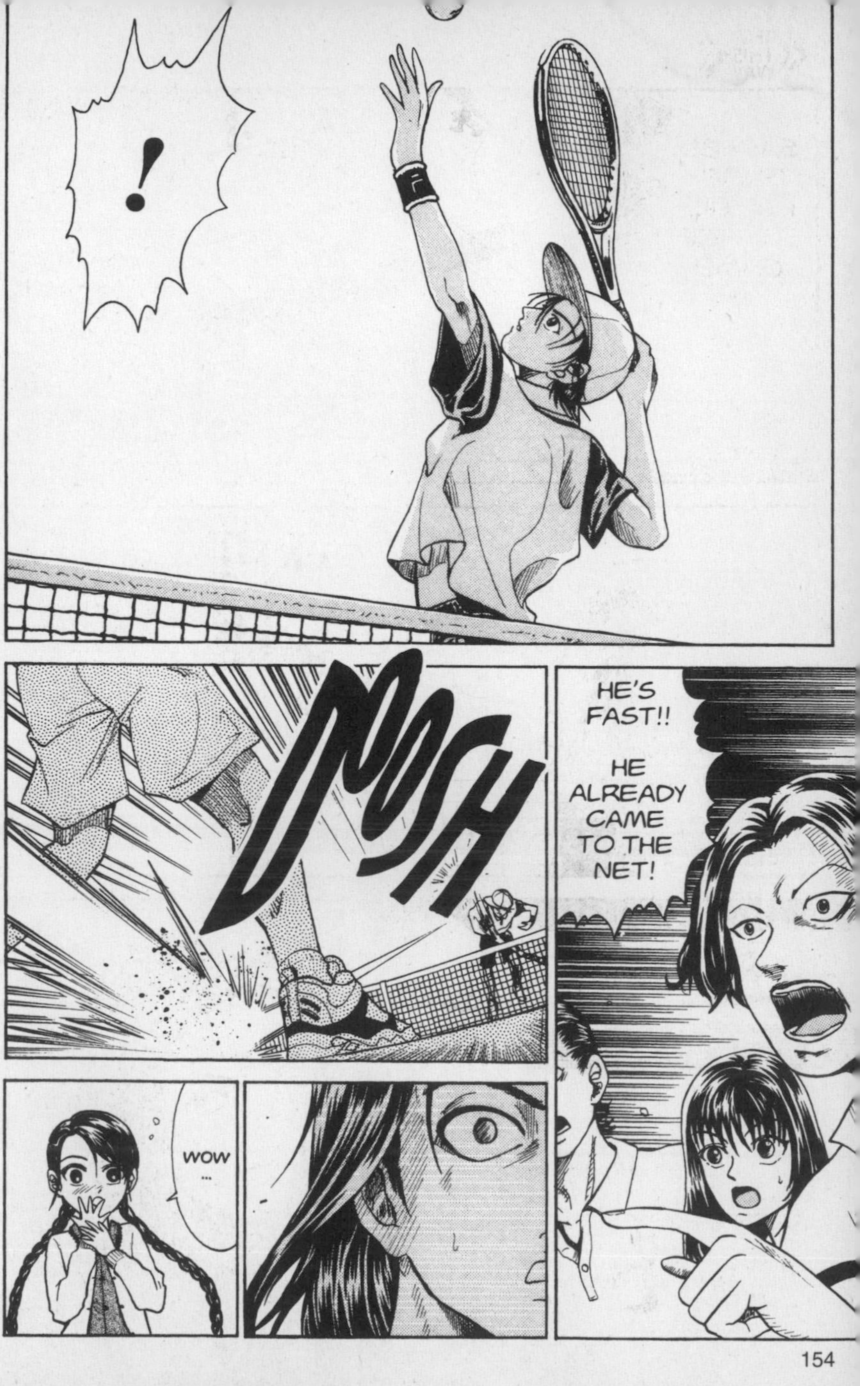
!
HE'S FAST!!
HE ALREADY CAME TO THE NET!
POSH
WOW ...

READ THIS WAY

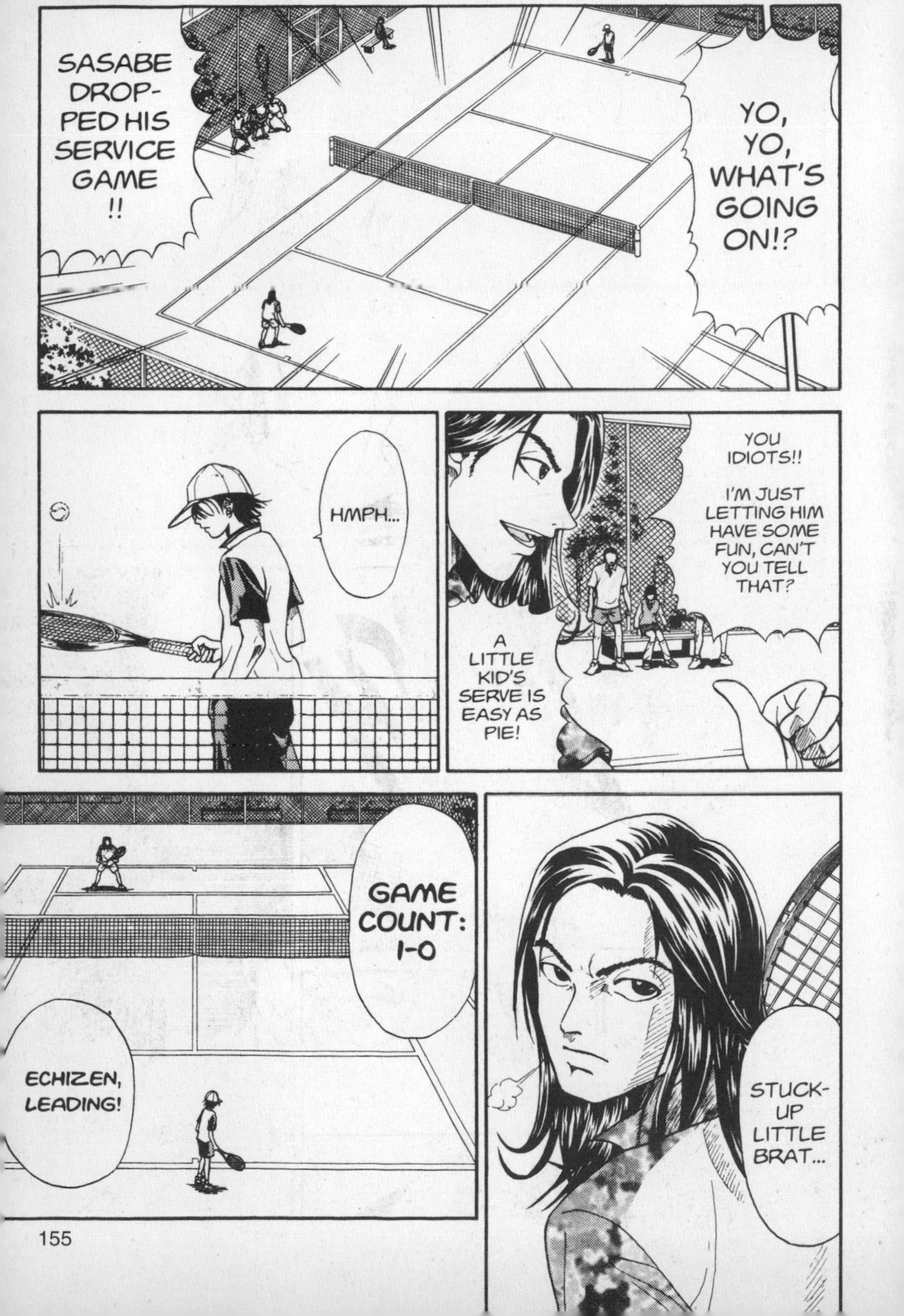

YO, YO, WHAT'S GOING ON!?
SASABE DROP-PED HIS SERVICE GAME !!
YOU IDIOTS!!
I'M JUST LETTING HIM HAVE SOME FUN, CAN'T YOU TELL THAT?
A LITTLE KID'S SERVE IS EASY AS PIE!
HMPH...
STUCK-UP LITTLE BRAT...
GAME COUNT: 1-0
ECHIZEN, LEADING!

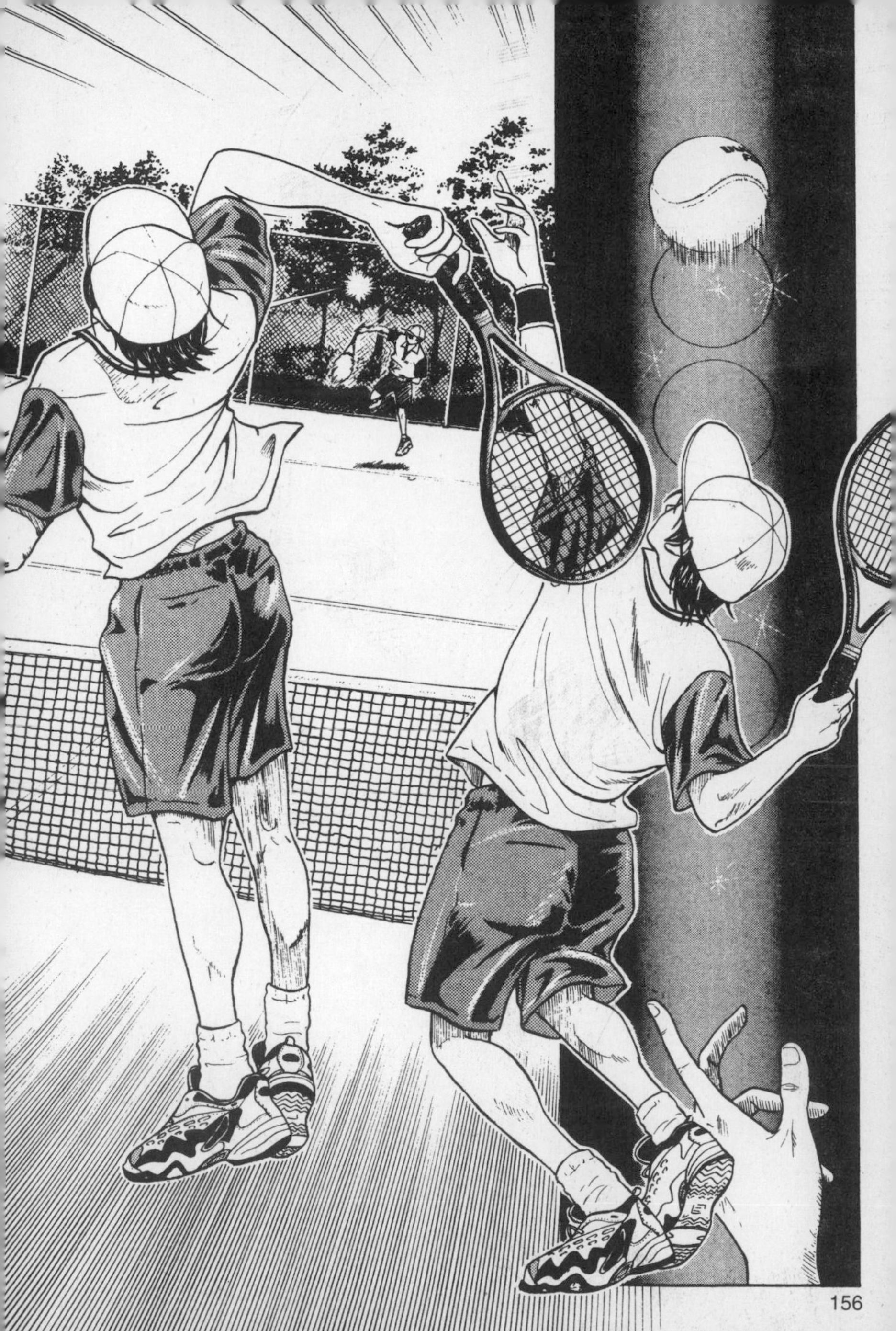

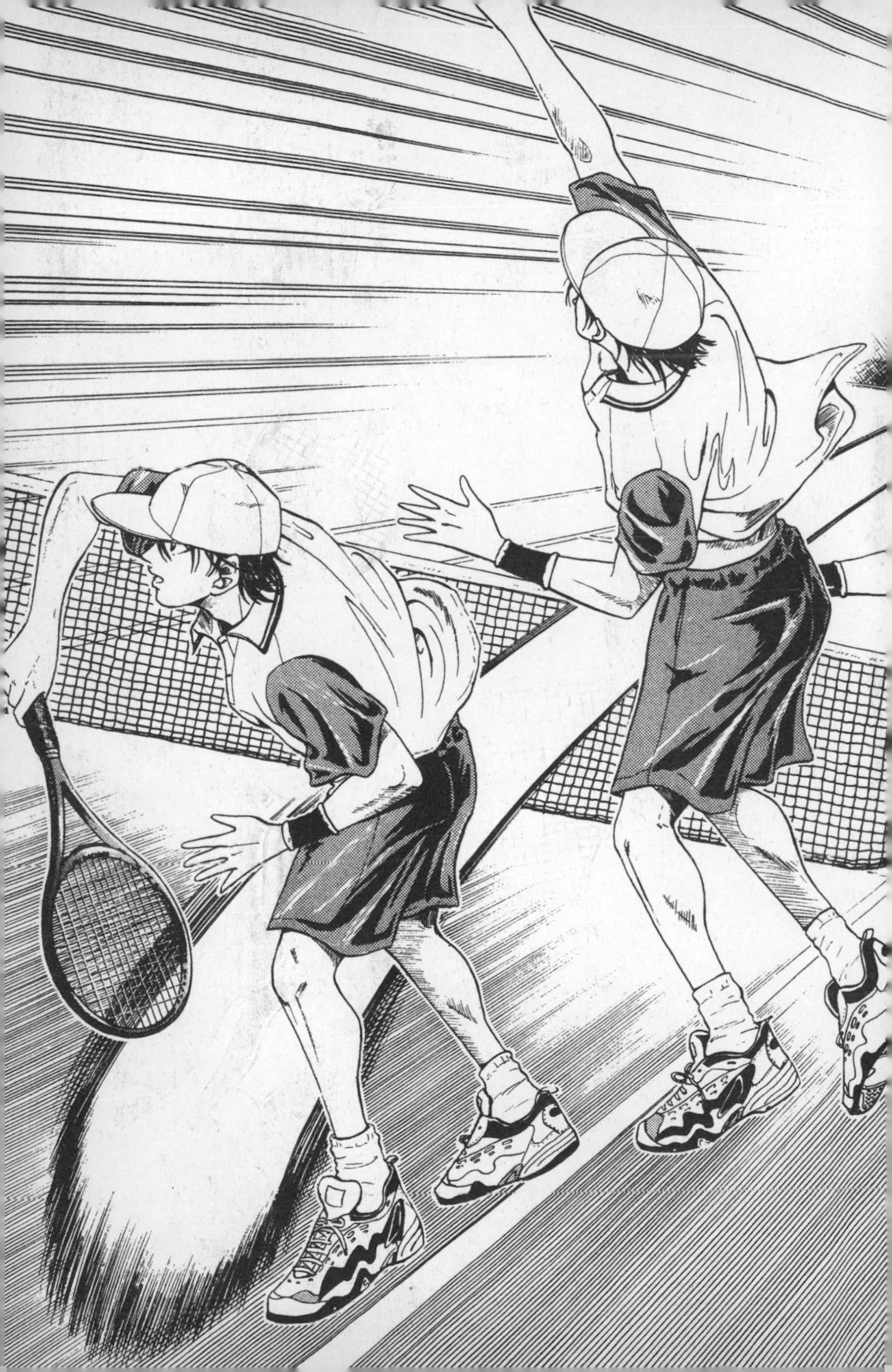

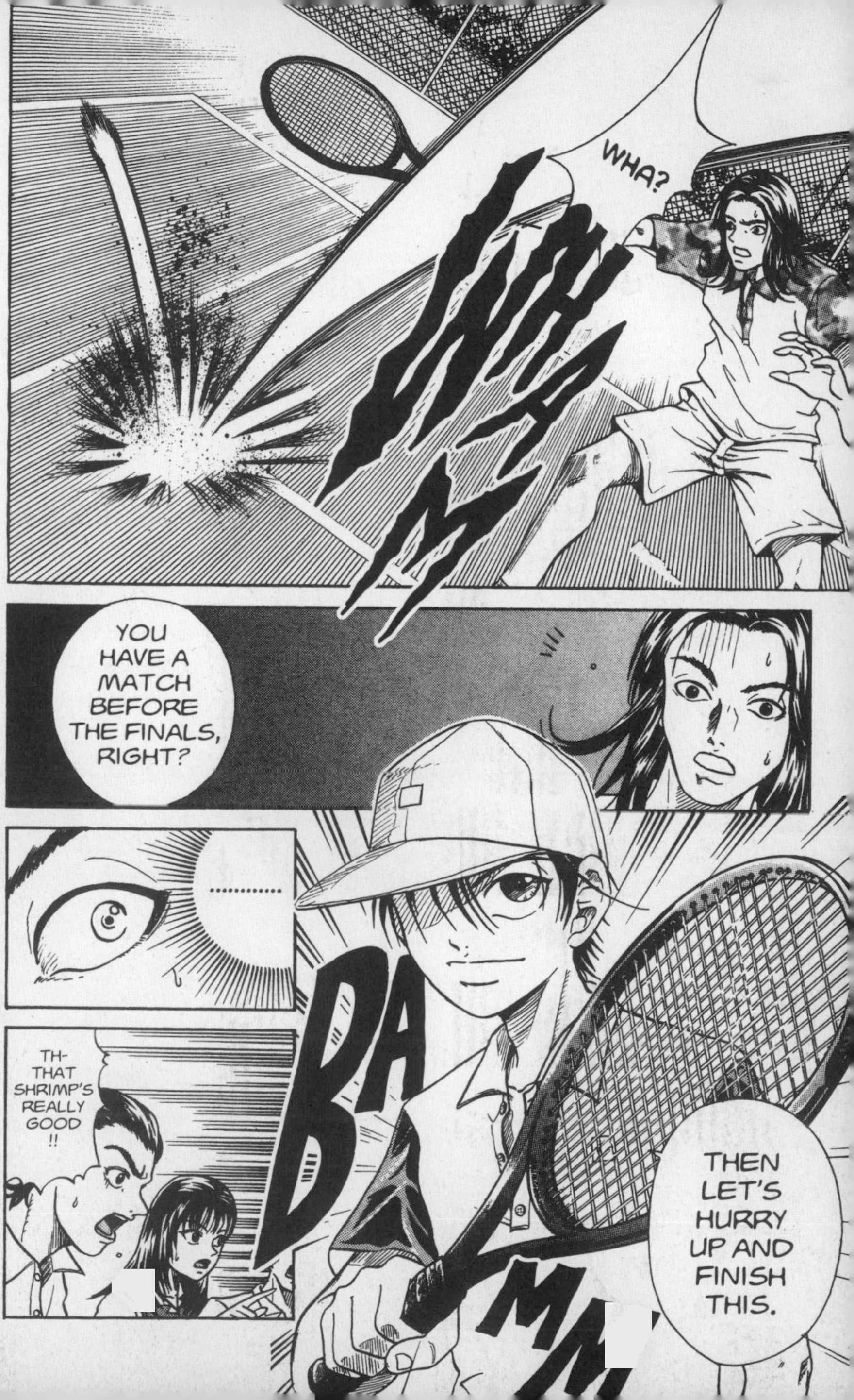
WHA?
YOU HAVE A MATCH BEFORE THE FINALS, RIGHT?
THEN LET'S HURRY UP AND FINISH THIS.
BAMM
...........
TH- THAT SHRIMP'S REALLY GOOD !!

TO BE CONTINUED IN **THE PRINCE OF TENNIS** VOL. 1 ON SALE NOW!

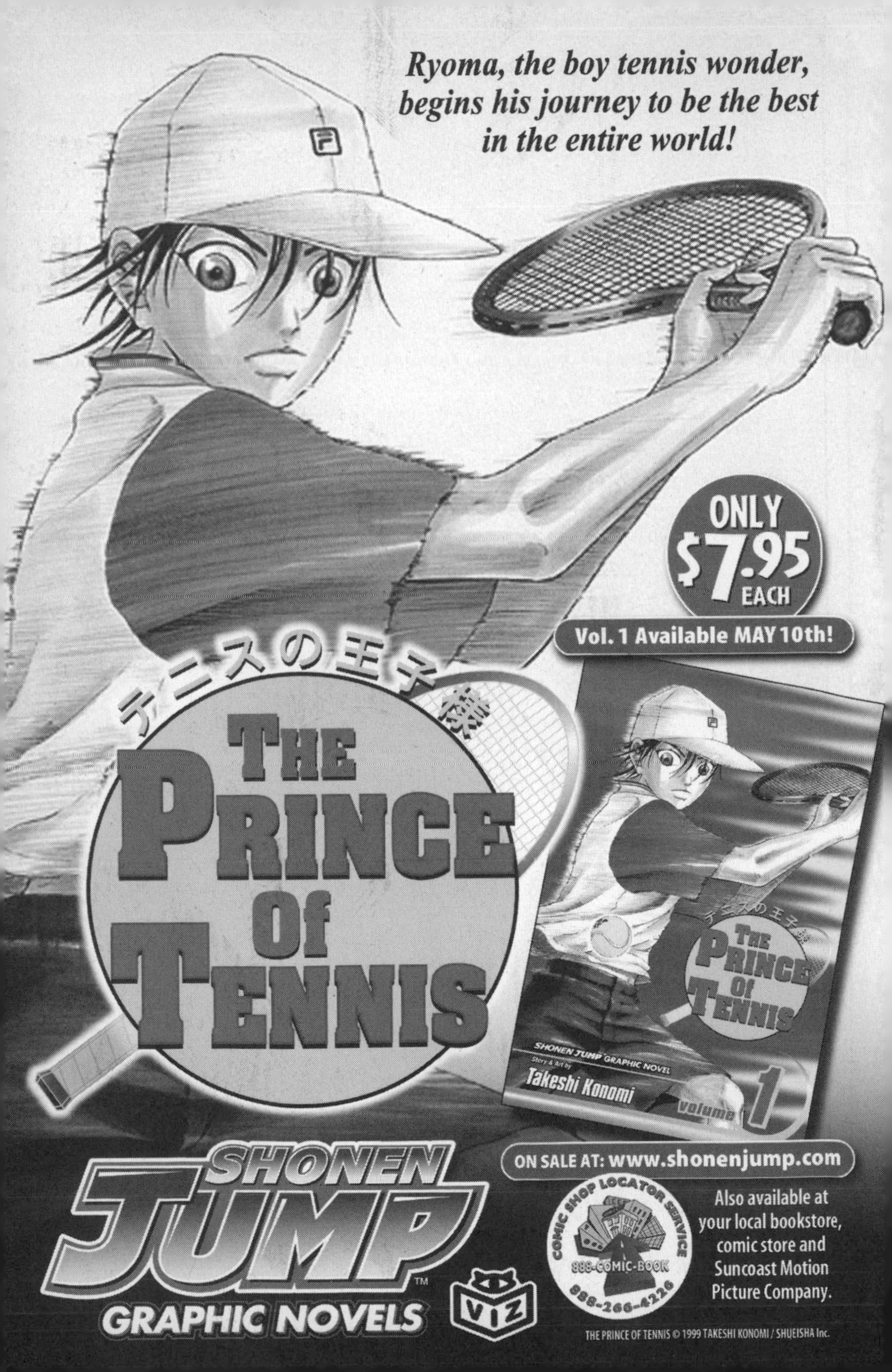
Ryoma, the boy tennis wonder, begins his journey to be the best in the entire world!
ONLY $7.95 EACH
Vol. 1 Available MAY 10th!
テニスの王子様
THE PRINCE Of TENNIS
SHONEN JUMP GRAPHIC NOVEL
Story & Art by
Takeshi Konomi
volume 1
ON SALE AT: www.shonenjump.com
SHONEN JUMP™
GRAPHIC NOVELS
VIZ
COMIC SHOP LOCATOR SERVICE
888-COMIC-BOOK
888-266-4226
Also available at your local bookstore, comic store and Suncoast Motion Picture Company.
THE PRINCE OF TENNIS © 1999 TAKESHI KONOMI / SHUEISHA Inc.

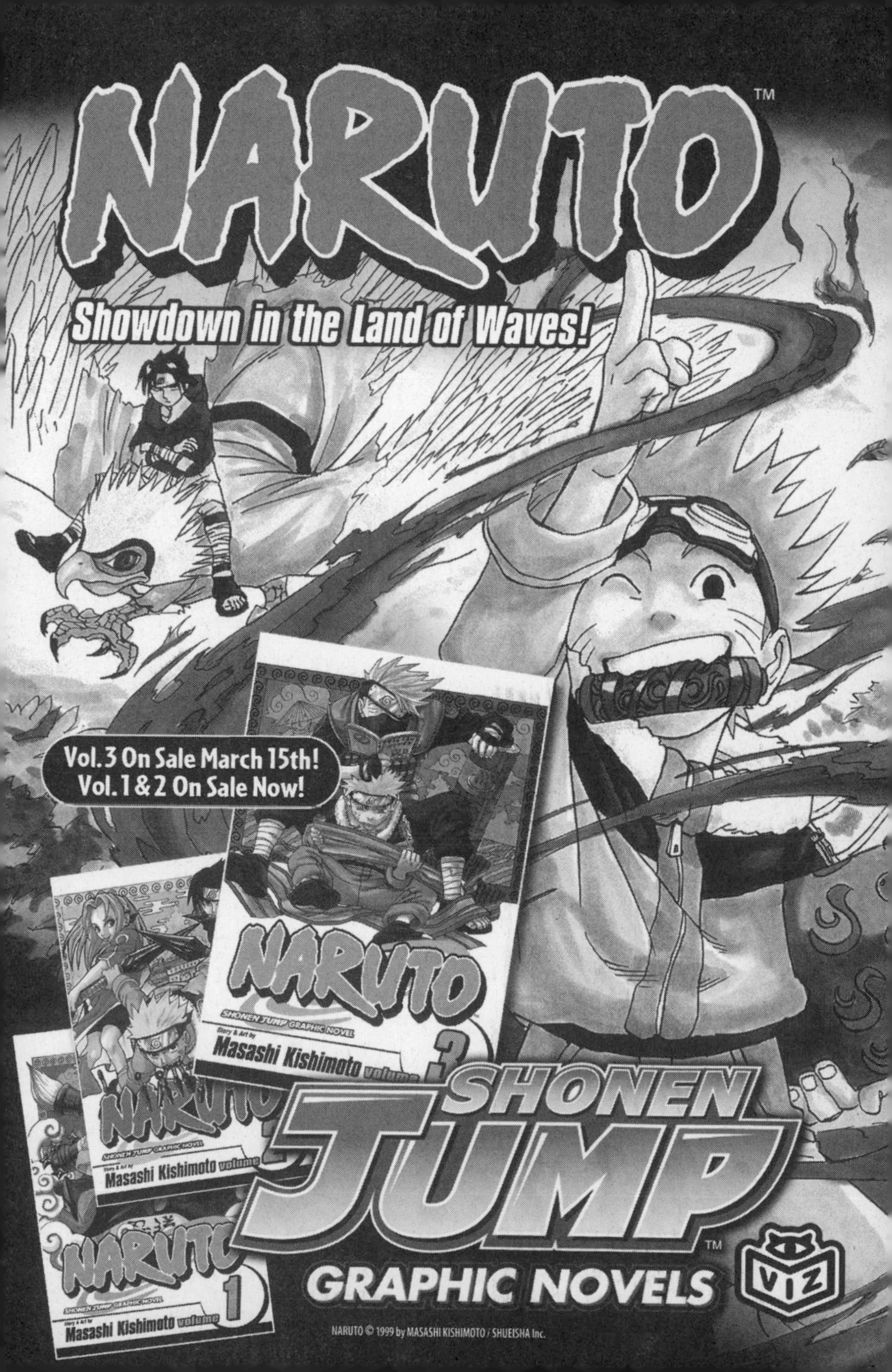

NARUTO™
Showdown in the Land of Waves!
Vol. 3 On Sale March 15th!
Vol. 1 & 2 On Sale Now!
NARUTO
SHONEN JUMP GRAPHIC NOVEL
Story & Art by
Masashi Kishimoto volume 3
SHONEN JUMP™
GRAPHIC NOVELS
VIZ
NARUTO © 1999 by MASASHI KISHIMOTO / SHUEISHA Inc.

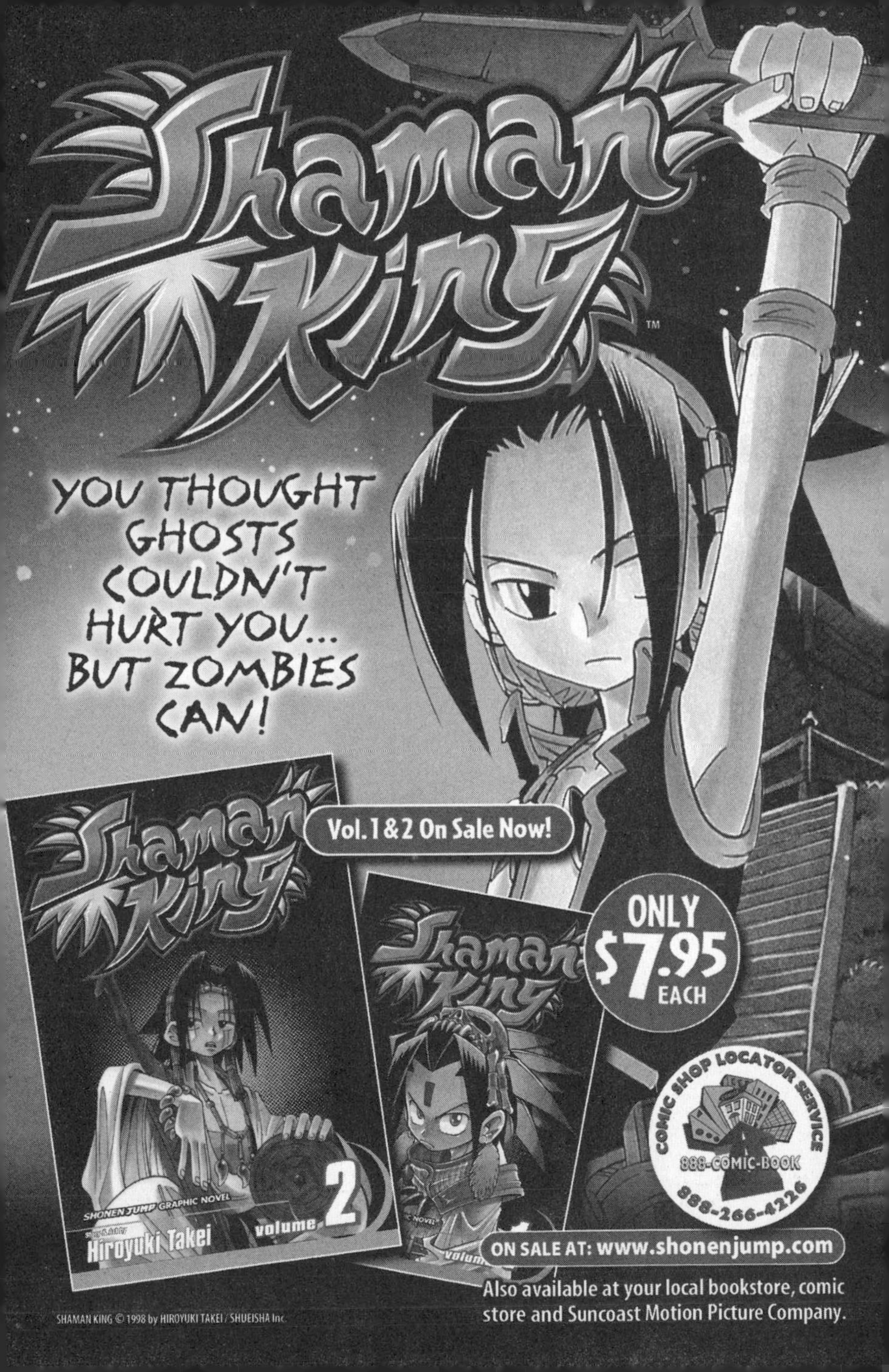

Shaman King™
YOU THOUGHT GHOSTS COULDN'T HURT YOU... BUT ZOMBIES CAN!
Vol. 1 & 2 On Sale Now!
Shaman King
SHONEN JUMP GRAPHIC NOVEL
Hiroyuki Takei
volume 2
Shaman King
ONLY $7.95 EACH
COMIC SHOP LOCATOR SERVICE
888-COMIC-BOOK
888-266-4226
ON SALE AT: www.shonenjump.com
Also available at your local bookstore, comic store and Suncoast Motion Picture Company.
SHAMAN KING © 1998 by HIROYUKI TAKEI / SHUEISHA Inc.

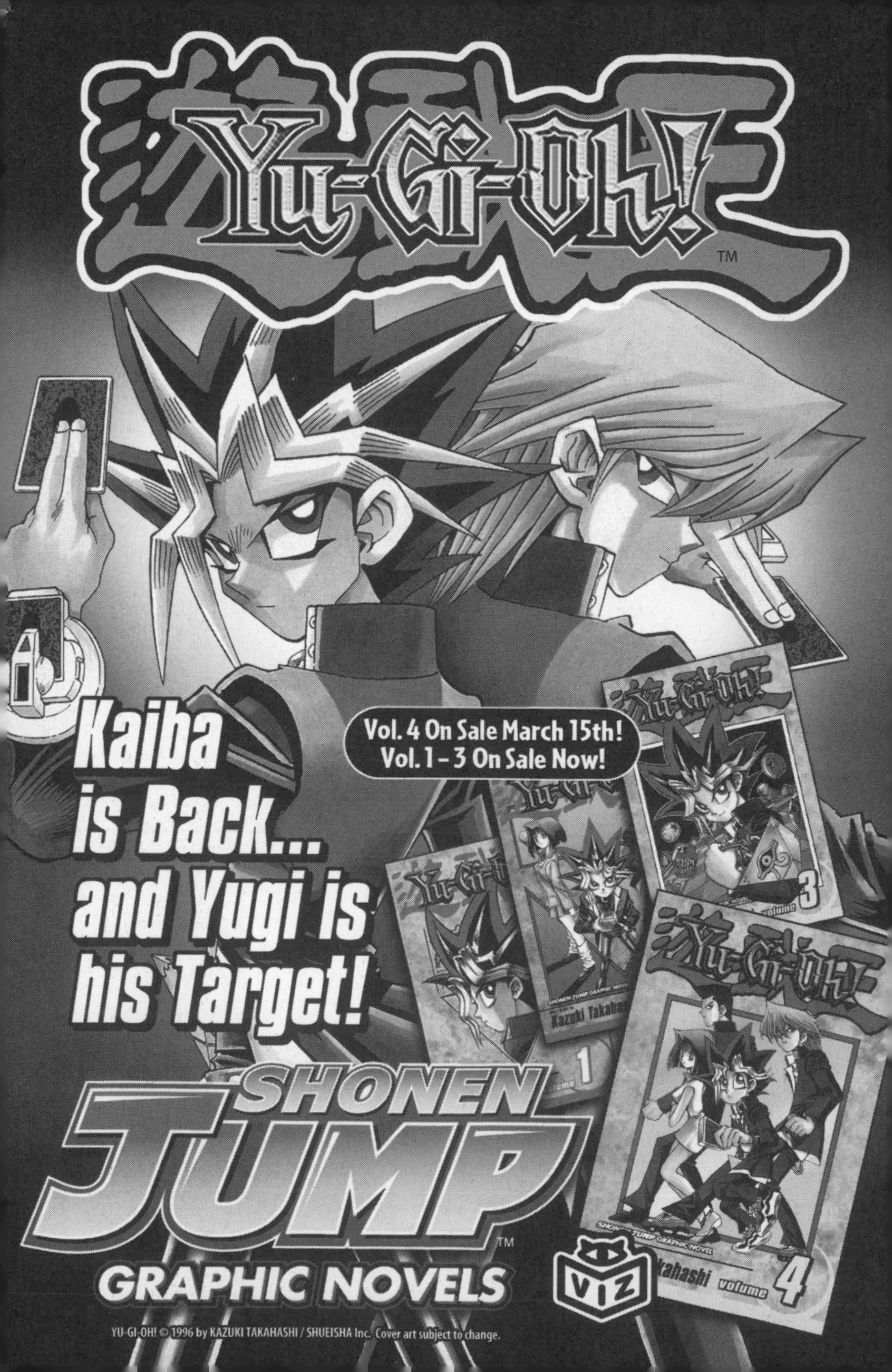

YU-GI-OH!™
Kaiba is Back... and Yugi is his Target!
Vol. 4 On Sale March 15th!
Vol. 1 - 3 On Sale Now!
SHONEN JUMP™
GRAPHIC NOVELS
VIZ
YU-GI-OH! © 1996 by KAZUKI TAKAHASHI / SHUEISHA Inc. Cover art subject to change.

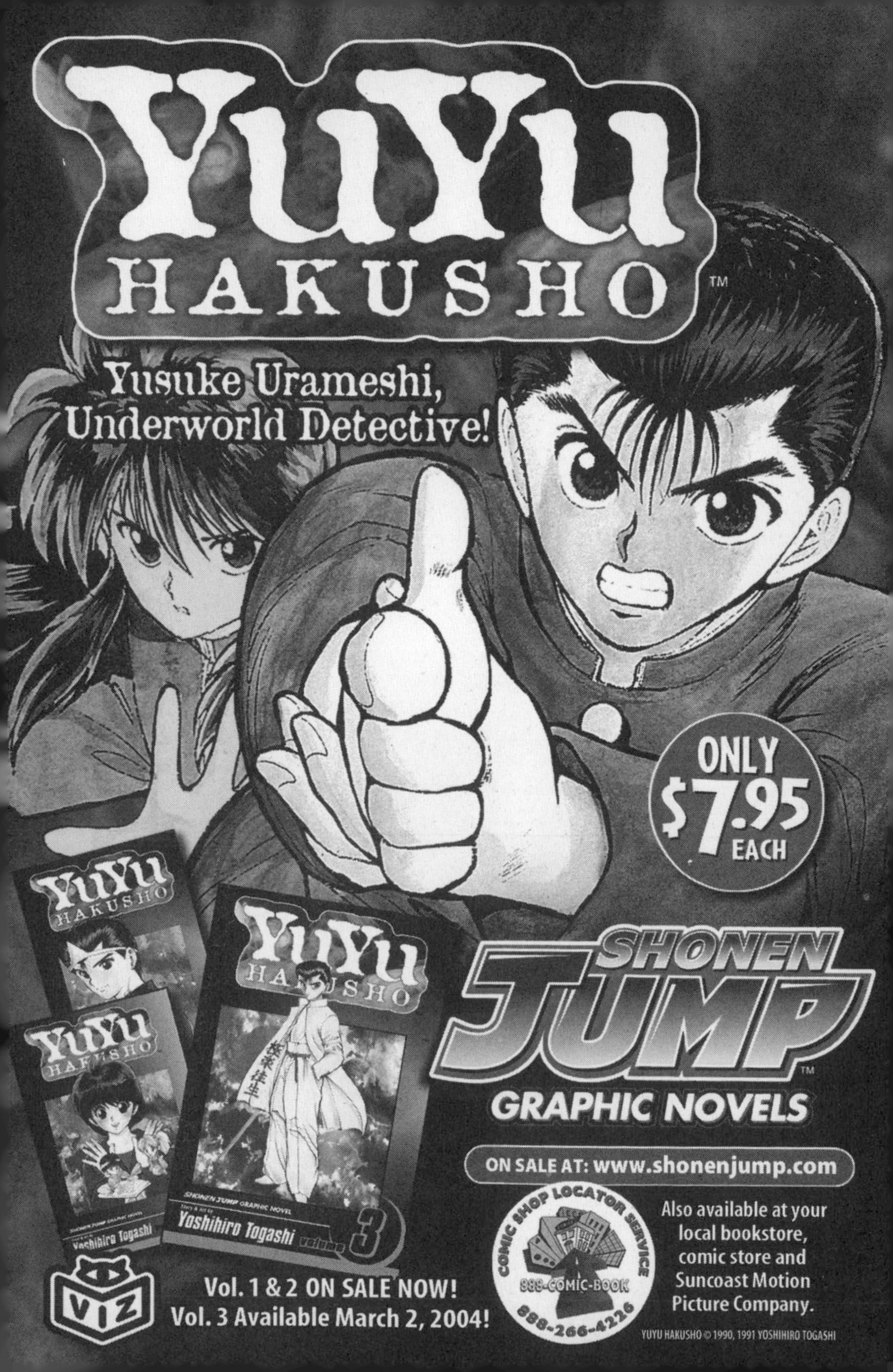

YuYu HAKUSHO™
Yusuke Urameshi, Underworld Detective!
ONLY $7.95 EACH
SHONEN JUMP™ GRAPHIC NOVELS
ON SALE AT: www.shonenjump.com
Also available at your local bookstore, comic store and Suncoast Motion Picture Company.
COMIC SHOP LOCATOR SERVICE
888-COMIC-BOOK
888-266-4226
VIZ
Vol. 1 & 2 ON SALE NOW!
Vol. 3 Available March 2, 2004!
Yoshihiro Togashi
YUYU HAKUSHO © 1990, 1991 YOSHIHIRO TOGASHI

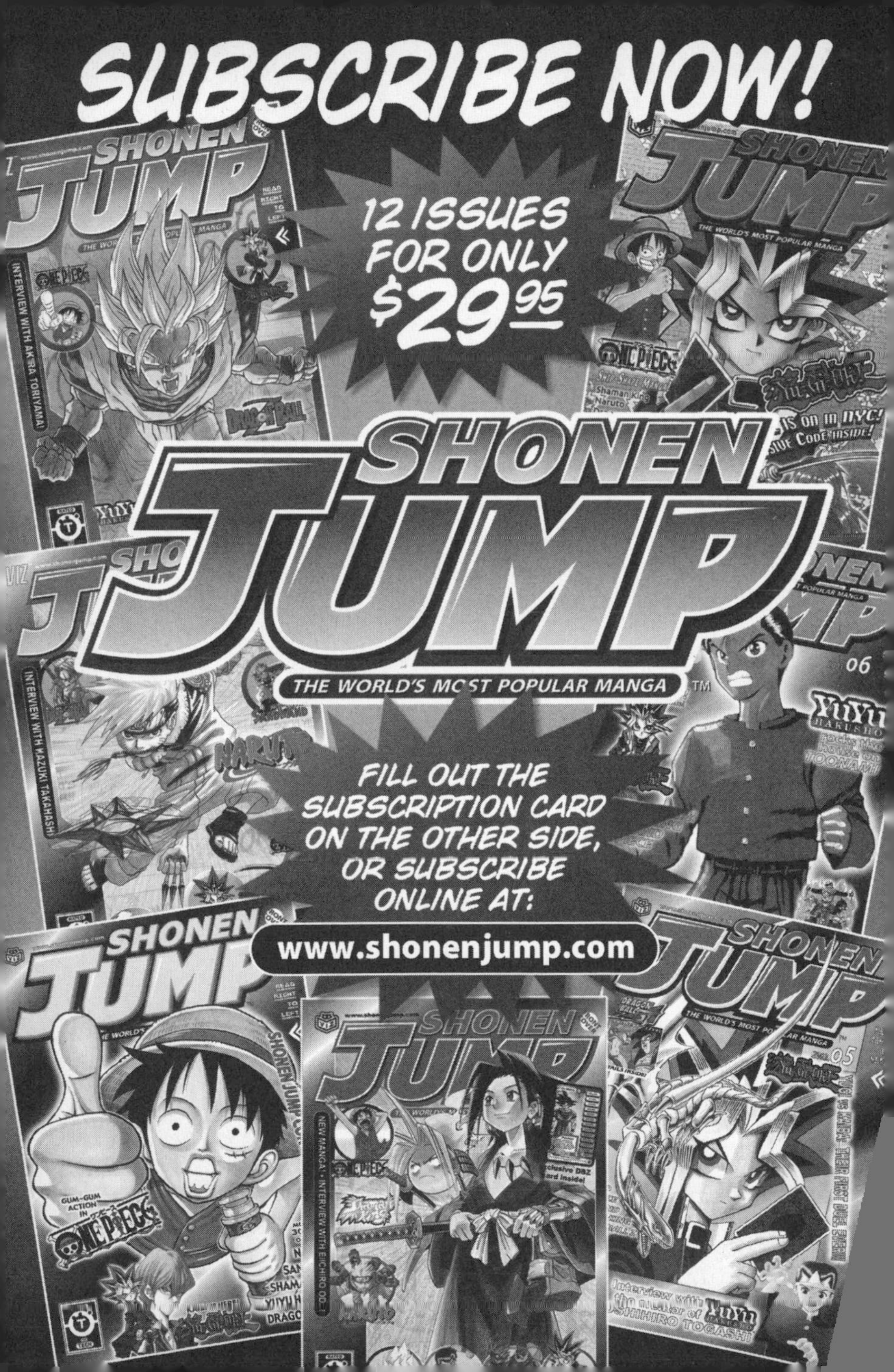
SUBSCRIBE NOW!
12 ISSUES FOR ONLY $29.95
SHONEN JUMP
THE WORLD'S MOST POPULAR MANGA ™
FILL OUT THE SUBSCRIPTION CARD ON THE OTHER SIDE, OR SUBSCRIBE ONLINE AT:
www.shonenjump.com

# COMPLETE OUR SURVEY AND LET
# US KNOW WHAT YOU THINK!

☐ Please check here if you DO NOT wish to receive information or future offers from VIZ

**Name:** _____

**Address:** _____

**City:** _____ **State:** _____ **Zip:** _____

**E-mail:** _____

☐ Male   ☐ Female   **Date of Birth** (mm/dd/yyyy): ___/___/_____   ( Under 13? Parental consent required )

## What race/ethnicity do you consider yourself? (please check one)

☐ Asian/Pacific Islander          ☐ Black/African American    ☐ Hispanic/Latino

☐ Native American/Alaskan Native  ☐ White/Caucasian           ☐ Other: _____

## What VIZ product did you purchase? (check all that apply and indicate title purchased)

☐ DVD/VHS _____

☐ Graphic Novel _____

☐ Magazines _____

☐ Merchandise _____

## Reason for purchase: (check all that apply)

☐ Special offer          ☐ Favorite title          ☐ Gift

☐ Recommendation         ☐ Other _____

## Where did you make your purchase? (please check one)

☐ Comic store            ☐ Bookstore               ☐ Mass/Grocery Store

☐ Newsstand              ☐ Video/Video Game Store  ☐ Other: _____

☐ Online (site: _____ )

## What other VIZ properties have you purchased/own? _____

_____

**How many anime and/or manga titles have you purchased in the last year? How many were VIZ titles?** (please check one from each column)

ANIME
- [ ] None
- [ ] 1-4
- [ ] 5-10
- [ ] 11+

MANGA
- [ ] None
- [ ] 1-4
- [ ] 5-10
- [ ] 11+

VIZ
- [ ] None
- [ ] 1-4
- [ ] 5-10
- [ ] 11+

**I find the pricing of VIZ products to be:** (please check one)
- [ ] Cheap
- [ ] Reasonable
- [ ] Expensive

**What genre of manga and anime would you like to see from VIZ?** (please check two)
- [ ] Adventure
- [ ] Comic Strip
- [ ] Science Fiction
- [ ] Fighting
- [ ] Horror
- [ ] Romance
- [ ] Fantasy
- [ ] Sports

**What do you think of VIZ's new look?**
- [ ] Love It
- [ ] It's OK
- [ ] Hate It
- [ ] Didn't Notice
- [ ] No Opinion

**Which do you prefer?** (please check one)
- [ ] Reading right-to-left
- [ ] Reading left-to-right

**Which do you prefer?** (please check one)
- [ ] Sound effects in English
- [ ] Sound effects in Japanese with English captions
- [ ] Sound effects in Japanese only with a glossary at the back

**THANK YOU! Please send the completed form to:**

NJW Research
42 Catharine St.
Poughkeepsie, NY 12601

**All information provided will be used for internal purposes only. We promise not to sell or otherwise divulge your information.**